I0888639

Evaluating Healthcare Leadership (HCL) Effectiveness: A Comprehensive Approach for Organizational Success

Hesham Almomani
Hashmite University, Jordan

Ahmad Al-Momani
Hashemite University, Jordan

Marya Al-Momani
The Jordanian Royal Medical Services, Jordan

IGI Global
Scientific Publishing
Publishing Tomorrow's Research Today

Vice President of Editorial	Melissa Wagner
Director of Acquisitions	Mikaela Felty
Director of Book Development	Jocelynn Hessler
Production Manager	Mike Brehm
Cover Design	Jose Rosado

Published in the United States of America by
IGI Global Scientific Publishing
701 East Chocolate Avenue
Hershey, PA, 17033, USA
Tel: 717-533-8845
Fax: 717-533-7115
Website: https://www.igi-global.com E-mail: cust@igi-global.com

Library of Congress Cataloging-in-Publication Data

Names: Almomani, Hesham, 1965- author
Title: Evaluating healthcare leadership effectiveness in hospitals / authored by Hesham Almomani.
Description: Hershey, PA : IGI Global Scientific Publishing, [2026] | Includes bibliographical references and index. | Summary: "This book aims to provide a comprehensive assessment of Healthcare Leadership (HCL) effectiveness in healthcare environments regarding its fundamental role for organizational success"-- Provided by publisher.
Identifiers: LCCN 2025022704 (print) | LCCN 2025022705 (ebook) | ISBN 9798337322254 h/c | ISBN 9798337322261 s/c | ISBN 9798337322278 ebook
Subjects: LCSH: Hospitals--Administration--Evaluation | Public health--Administration--Evaluation | Leadership--Psychological aspects
Classification: LCC RA971 .A46 2026 (print) | LCC RA971 (ebook)
LC record available at https://lccn.loc.gov/2025022704
LC ebook record available at https://lccn.loc.gov/2025022705

British Cataloguing in Publication Data
A Cataloguing in Publication record for this book is available from the British Library.

Evaluating Healthcare Leadership (HCL) Effectiveness: A Comprehensive Approach for Organizational Success

Hesham Almomani
Hashmite University, Jordan

Ahmad Al-Momani
Hashemite University, Jordan

Marya Al-Momani
The Jordanian Royal Medical Services, Jordan

IGI Global
Scientific Publishing
Publishing Tomorrow's Research Today

Vice President of Editorial Melissa Wagner
Director of Acquisitions Mikaela Felty
Director of Book Development Jocelynn Hessler
Production Manager Mike Brehm
Cover Design Jose Rosado

Published in the United States of America by
IGI Global Scientific Publishing
701 East Chocolate Avenue
Hershey, PA, 17033, USA
Tel: 717-533-8845
Fax: 717-533-7115
Website: https://www.igi-global.com E-mail: cust@igi-global.com

Library of Congress Cataloging-in-Publication Data

Names: Almomani, Hesham, 1965- author
Title: Evaluating healthcare leadership effectiveness in hospitals / authored by Hesham Almomani.
Description: Hershey, PA : IGI Global Scientific Publishing, [2026] | Includes bibliographical references and index. | Summary: "This book aims to provide a comprehensive assessment of Healthcare Leadership (HCL) effectiveness in healthcare environments regarding its fundamental role for organizational success"-- Provided by publisher.
Identifiers: LCCN 2025022704 (print) | LCCN 2025022705 (ebook) | ISBN 9798337322254 h/c | ISBN 9798337322261 s/c | ISBN 9798337322278 ebook
Subjects: LCSH: Hospitals--Administration--Evaluation | Public health--Administration--Evaluation | Leadership--Psychological aspects
Classification: LCC RA971 .A46 2026 (print) | LCC RA971 (ebook)
LC record available at https://lccn.loc.gov/2025022704
LC ebook record available at https://lccn.loc.gov/2025022705

British Cataloguing in Publication Data
A Cataloguing in Publication record for this book is available from the British Library.

Table of Contents

Preface v

Acknowledgment xiii

Introduction xiv

Chapter 1
Healthcare Leadership Within Organizational Systems 1

Chapter 2
Evolution and Fundamentals of Leadership 13

Chapter 3
A Comprehensive Synthesis of Healthcare Leadership and Continuous Improvement: Integrating Industrial Engineering Perspectives to Enhance Patient Outcomes 25

Chapter 4
Theoretical Foundations and Philosophies of Healthcare Leadership 39

Chapter 5
Exploration of Healthcare Leadership (HCL) 67

Chapter 6
Healthcare Leadership Competencies: Foundations, Applications, and Emerging Challenges 75

Chapter 7
Key Domains of Healthcare Leadership: Essential Attributes 87

Chapter 8
Technology's Transformation of Healthcare Leadership: A Comprehensive Synthesis 117

Chapter 9
Leadership Development and Training: Strategies to Enhance Healthcare Leadership Effectiveness 135

Chapter 10
Healthcare Leadership Under Pressure: Research Gaps and the Impact of Socioeconomic Policy and Cultural Dynamics 141

Chapter 11
Leadership in Practice: Concluding Insights and Perspectives From Healthcare Executives 151

Chapter 12
Distinctive Strengths and Research Excellence of Healthcare Leadership 161

Chapter 13
A Conceptual Model and Self-Assessment Framework for Healthcare Leadership 169

Chapter 14
Hospital Healthcare Leadership Assessment Personal Action Plan 233

Appendix 249

Compilation of References 259

About the Author 305

Index 309

Preface

OVERVIEW OF THE PUBLICATION

This book, Evaluating Healthcare Leadership (HCL) Effectiveness: A Comprehensive Approach for Organizational Success, adds significant value within healthcare settings is a complex, multifaceted, yet essential process that significantly impacts organizational performance and aims to evaluate the effectiveness of Healthcare Leadership (HCL) within healthcare settings, focusing on its pivotal role in organizational performance. It explores how leadership influences employees' attitudes, capabilities, and the achievement of organizational goals. The book investigates the competencies and factors that contribute to successful leadership in both public and private hospitals, offering a comprehensive approach to understanding leadership development. By employing a mixed-methods approach, combining qualitative and quantitative research, this book provides in-depth insights into the complexities of healthcare leadership. A systematic literature review identifies essential leadership competencies and enabling factors, while the development of a leadership competency framework offers a practical tool for healthcare leaders to refine their leadership capabilities. Additionally, an action plan based on SMART goal-setting methodology will guide healthcare sectors in applying effective leadership attributes to enhance healthcare delivery.

IMPACT ON THE RESEARCH COMMUNITY

This research will significantly impact the research community by synthesizing and expanding existing leadership competency models. It will offer valuable insights into the practical application of leadership development in healthcare systems, emphasizing the need for adaptability, continuous development, and long-term outcomes in leadership effectiveness. By introducing a framework that integrates global best practices and evidence from various health systems, the publication will contribute to advancing leadership development initiatives and policy-making in healthcare. Researchers in the field will benefit from a more comprehensive understanding of the dynamic factors that shape healthcare leadership effectiveness and the broader organizational impact.

INTENDED AUDIENCE

This publication is intended for healthcare policymakers, researchers, leadership development practitioners, and professionals within the healthcare industry. Policymakers will benefit from actionable insights into improving healthcare leadership at both the organizational and systemic levels. Researchers will find valuable resources for further exploring leadership development frameworks and assessing their effectiveness. Healthcare professionals, including managers and leaders in both public and private healthcare settings, will benefit from the practical tools and strategies presented in this publication to enhance their leadership capabilities. Finally, leadership development practitioners will use this research to guide the design of programs and initiatives aimed at fostering leadership excellence in the healthcare sector.

This systematic research synthesizes widely recognized leadership competencies and offers new insights for healthcare policymakers, researchers, and leadership development practitioners. By emphasizing professionalization and capacity building for healthcare leaders, this study supports the advancement of leadership excellence, enabling health systems to better navigate future challenges and deliver high-quality care.

ORGANIZATION OF THE BOOK

In Chapter 1, "Healthcare Leadership Within Organizational Systems", emphasizes the crucial role of healthcare leadership in building efficient and effective healthcare systems worldwide. Despite healthcare's importance for national development and individual well-being, challenges like infrastructure limitations, workforce shortages, and governance inefficiencies hinder progress toward improved patient outcomes. Strong leadership is essential to enhance service delivery and ensure sustainable improvements. This chapter addresses the gap in comprehensive research on healthcare leadership by identifying key competencies and proposing standardized assessment tools for accreditation councils and professionals. It highlights transformational leadership as a key approach to motivate teams, foster innovation, and improve care quality. Effective leaders combine adaptability, interprofessional collaboration, and data-driven decision-making to navigate complex environments. By integrating leadership theory with practical management tactics, such as planning and change management, healthcare leaders can drive equitable, high-quality care, ensuring resilience and continuous improvement in dynamic healthcare systems.

In Chapter 2: "Evolution and Fundamentals of Leadership", explores the evolution and fundamental principles of leadership, emphasizing its dynamic nature and essential role in organizational success. Leadership is no longer regarded as merely a hierarchical position but as a set of competencies that inspire teams, foster collaboration, and drive meaningful change. The chapter delves into various leadership theories, including creative leadership, which promotes innovation and strategic problem-solving. It traces the historical development of leadership thought, from early Great Man and Trait Theories to Behavioral, Situational, and contemporary leadership approaches. The modern leadership landscape integrates elements of transformational, servant, ethical, and adaptive leadership, emphasizing the necessity of flexibility in navigating complex organizational challenges. By understanding these diverse leadership paradigms, healthcare leaders can adopt effective strategies to enhance decision-making, strengthen management efficiency, and foster a culture of excellence within healthcare organizations. This foundational knowledge equips leaders to respond proactively to evolving industry demands, ensuring sustainable improvements in healthcare delivery.

In Chapter 3: "A Comprehensive Synthesis Of Healthcare Leadership And Continuous Improvement: Integrating Industrial Engineering Perspectives To Enhance Patient Outcomes", Healthcare systems are getting more complicated because of diverse teams, fast technological progress, and changing patient needs and and dynamic, active, self motivated and reciprocal process, best understood as a dynamic, ongoing process rather than a fixed personal trait or simple act of influence and leadership styles need to be flexible and based on evidence. It involves a series of actions aimed at achieving specific objectives, patient safety, care quality, and staff well-being shaped by interactions between leaders, followers, and the context in which they operate. In systems science and industrial engineering, the healthcare leadership parallels to all of the continuous improvement philosophy and methods like total quality management Lean and Six Sigma, emphasizing real time feedback, adaptation to change, and sustainable safe progress. The healthcare Leaders, much like processing engineers, alwyes foster a culture of ongoing learning and advances through iterative growth and reflection. And finally in order to build strong, high-performing, patient-centered healthcare systems, it's important to combine several leadership styles that are adapted to the needs of each situation.

In Chapter 4: "Theoretical Foundations And Philosophies Of Healthcare Leadership", various leadership styles and their impact on organizational performance, employee engagement, and overall productivity. in healthcare settings are examined. Transformational leadership inspires innovation and job satisfaction, motivating teams to enhance patient care quality. Transactional leadership ensures structure and compliance, effective in stable environments but less adaptable in dynamic ones. Servant leadership prioritizes employee well-being, fostering trust and loyalty, while charismatic leadership leverages personal vision but risks organizational instability upon leader departure. Strategic leadership aligns goals with long-term adaptability and sustainable growth. Multipliers amplify team potential, whereas diminishers stifle creativity. Toxic leadership, marked by unethical behavior, leads to low morale and high turnover. By integrating these styles with healthcare's complex, patient-centered challenges, this chapter proposes evidence-based strategies to enhance leadership effectiveness. Understanding these approaches equips healthcare leaders to navigate dynamic systems, drive collaboration, and deliver equitable, high-quality care.

In Chapter 5: "Exploration of Healthcare Leadership (HCL)",This chapter examines the dynamic role of Healthcare Leadership (HCL) in ensuring the efficiency and effectiveness of healthcare systems. While leadership and management are interconnected, HCL emphasizes shared leadership, where responsibilities are distributed to enhance performance. Over time, HCL has evolved alongside technological advancements and e-health, requiring leaders to drive sustainability and innovation. Effective HCL fosters collaboration, innovation, and positive organizational change while addressing the complexities of modern healthcare systems.The chapter also explores leadership assessment, which is crucial for evaluating strengths, improving healthcare outcomes, and aligning leadership with strategic goals. Continuous professional development is essential for cultivating skilled leaders. Additionally, healthcare governance plays a key role in maintaining service quality, accountability, and equitable care. According to the WHO, strong governance structures are essential for addressing policy changes and resource allocation. Ultimately, the chapter underscores the importance of leadership development, assessment frameworks, and governance in shaping resilient, patient-centered healthcare systems capable of meeting future challenges.

In Chapter 6: "Healthcare Leadership Competencies: Foundations, Applications, And Emerging Challenges", Healthcare leadership (HCL) is pivotal to organizational success and effective care delivery Effective leaders require a diverse skill set that goes beyond traditional management, including time and task management, multitasking, adaptability, emotional intelligence and strategic thinking.. A crucial aspect of HCL is the ability to manage crises effectively, demonstrate originality, and remain resilient under pressure. Additionally, leaders must excel in communication, motivation, and team guidance. At the same time the healthcare organizations and leaders face Potential Challenges To Proposed Healthcare Leadership Competencies, Main concerns include the cultural, ethical and social bias, overemphasis on leaders soft personal skills, and lack of proper change management and the adaptability to multi dimensional diverse settings Ultimately, healthcare leadership is an evolving field that requires balancing technical expertise, emotional intelligence, and the ability to inspire others, ensuring improved outcomes for both patients and healthcare professionals.

In Chapter 7: "Key Domains of Healthcare Leadership (Essential Attributes)",Healthcare leadership attributes are critical to the success and sustainability of healthcare organizations, enabling leaders to navigate complex and dynamic environments effectively. Strong healthcare leaders exhibit vision, strategic thinking, and a patient-centered focus, allowing them to set clear organizational goals, anticipate challenges, and drive innovation for improved health outcomes. Cultural competence and inclusivity enhance team collaboration, while effective communication fosters transparency and alignment with organizational values.Essential leadership qualities include integrity, credibility, humility, and resilience under pressure, which build trust and credibility. Emotional intelligence (EI) plays a key role in conflict resolution, team cohesion, and staff well-being. Leaders must also prioritize quality and patient safety, ensure evidence-based decision-making, and develop strategies for continuous improvement.As healthcare landscapes evolve, leaders must demonstrate resilience, adaptability, and strategic management to address workforce shortages, regulatory changes, and technological advancements. Through leadership development programs, they can refine change management, risk management, and innovation strategies, ensuring long-term success in delivering high-quality, patient-centered care.

In Chapter 8: "Technology's Transformation Of Healthcare Leadership: A Comprehensive Synthesis" The rapid integration of digital technologies—including electronic health records (EHRs), telemedicine, artificial intelligence (AI), and big data analytics—is fundamentally transforming healthcare leadership roles, competencies, and outcomes. Leaders must adopt new roles such as digital strategists, change agents, and stakeholder engagers, requiring digital literacy, strategic vision, ethical stewardship, and adaptive agility. Frameworks like the Technology-Organization-Environment (TOE) and Digital Transformational Leadership (DTL) elucidate how healthcare leaders navigate technological, organizational, and environmental factors to drive digital transformation. Effective leadership enhances patient-centered care, operational efficiency, workforce engagement, and data-driven decision-making, while addressing barriers including infrastructure limitations, user resistance, ethical concerns, and equity gaps—particularly in low-resource settings. Case studies from institutions such as Mayo Clinic, UCSF, and Cleveland Clinic demonstrate how strategic leadership in telemedicine, robotics, AI, and EHR implementation improves clinical outcomes and operational resilience. Despite advances, gaps remain in longitudinal research, AI integration, leadership training, and metrics for evaluating digital leadership effectiveness. Addressing these challenges through targeted leadership development and stakeholder engagement is critical for sustainable, equitable healthcare innovation in the digital era.

In Chapter 9: "Leadership Development and Training: Strategies to Enhance Healthcare Leadership Effectiveness", Healthcare leadership establishes and determines the strengths in collaborative, and adaptive practices between healthcare leaders and followers that enhance the patient-centered outcomes and drive inventions, innovation and modernization. Effective healthcare leaders integrate the new evolving technology—such as telemedicine, and predictive analytics—to enhance the healthcare domain interactions, efficiency, efficacy and improve the decision-making. Many success stories arise where at least in some cases include a 30% rise in prenatal care compliance through new technological advances and digital strategies. Nevertheless, challenges continue as happened in every new systems applications, including digital illiteracy, resistance to change management, new technology. The healthcare leadership models sometimes misaligned with followers and patients expectations. To address these gaps, opportunities lie in advancing digital transformational digital leadership, data-driven decision on making and equity strategies, and situational development programs. Comprehensive healthcare leadership training should include emotional intelligence, emphasizing strategic and systems thinking where it is essential to boost patient satisfaction, safety, raise staff morale, and improve healthcare system sustainability in a rapidly evolving digital technology environment.

In Chapter 10: Identified Challenges, Limitations, And Research Gaps In Healthcare Leadership Studies", Healthcare leadership significantly influences patient outcomes, staff satisfaction, and organizational resilience. Also The Impact Of Socioeconomic Conditions, Policy Changes And Cultural Competency On Healthcare Leadership Performance, External factors like socioeconomic conditions and changes in legislation have a big impact on how well healthcare leaders do their jobs and these dynamics fit with Contingency Leadership Theory. Leaders in places with few resources have to deal with problems like tight budgets, not enough workers, and infrastructural problems. This means they have to put operational demands ahead of new ideas. Policy changes and requirements that emerge from crises require flexible leaders who can quickly adjust to changing rules and make sure that clinical outcomes are in line with financial incentives. However, research gaps persist, including scarce quantitative and longitudinal studies, limited frameworks addressing adaptive, ethical, digital, and crisis leadership, and underrepresentation of gender, and diversity . Leadership development remains constrained by hierarchical cultures, digital skill deficits, and communication barriers, undermining strategic change and care equity.. Future research should priorities mixed-methods designs, validated measurement tools, and role-specific guidelines to enhance leadership practice and policy, ensuring high-quality, equitable, and patient-centred care across diverse healthcare settings.

In Chapter 11: "Leadership in Practice: Concluding Insights and Perspectives from Healthcare Executives", Explores and highlight the insights and provides a comprehensive evaluation of healthcare domain leadership effectiveness competencies, challenges, vision, mission and strategic priorities within hospital settings., emphasizing its critical role in improving healthcare systems. The study underscores the importance of staff feedback and continuous personal growth, from famous healthcare leaders and chief executives encouraging leaders to engage with their teams for enhanced performance. By offering valued guidance and strategies for creative leadership, competency development, and SMART-based action plans, the book provides practical tools for leadership improvement. With a structured framework and measurable goals, it equips current and aspiring leaders to navigate complexities, drive change, and enhance patient care, worldwide.

In Chapter 12: "The Distinctive Strengths And Research Excellence Of The Healthcare Leadership Book", It provides valued informationabout the new healthcare leadership studies and researches by pointing out the significant healthcare leadership skills needed to deal with these problems. The book manuscript might make its use in real-world healthcare settings even better by linking these skills to relevant case studies or well-known leadership theories. This would make the skills' real-world effects clearer. A big part of the book is how it combines theory and practice. It effectively connects basic leadership theories, such transformational, authentic, and servant leadership, with real-world examples that are specifically designed for healthcare settings. The book gives readers useful tactics that can be used in clinical, operational, and strategic settings by connecting these abstract concepts to real-life actions. This combination makes it easier for those who run complicated healthcare systems to understand and use leadership principles.

In Chapter 13: "A Conceptual Model And Self-Assessment Framework For Healthcare Leadership)", that introduces introduces a proposed Healthcare Leadership Competency Framework Self-Assessment Tool, designed to evaluate and enhance leadership capabilities across key domains such as strategic thinking, adaptability, communication, and collaboration. Complementing this tool is an Integrated Healthcare Leadership Framework that merges diverse leadership philosophies—transformational, authentic, servant, and distributed—into a cohesive model. It emphasizes leadership as a context-driven, relational process shaped by systemic dynamics, organizational culture, and external policies. This framework recognizes healthcare systems as complex adaptive environments that demand flexible, collaborative leadership strategies. It serves as a foundation for leadership development programs, empirical research, and organizational policy design. While the framework offers a structured and comprehensive approach, it also highlights the need for further theoretical refinement, empirical validation, and contextual customization. By addressing these limitations, the framework can support healthcare leaders in navigating complex challenges, fostering resilience, improving staff morale, and ultimately enhancing patient-centered care and organizational outcomes.

In Chapter 14: "Hospital Healthcare Leadership Assessment Personal Action Plan", focuses on the development of a comprehensive Hospital Healthcare Leadership Assessment Personal Action Plan. This chapter provides a structured approach for healthcare leaders to assess their leadership effectiveness, identify areas for improvement, and establish targeted goals for professional growth. Through self-reflection and feedback from peers, staff, and stakeholders, leaders can evaluate their leadership competencies across key domains, including communication, decision-making, team management, and patient-centered care. The chapter emphasizes the importance of continuous learning and the need for a personalized action plan that aligns with the individual's career aspirations and the hospital's strategic objectives. It also outlines methods for tracking progress, incorporating regular feedback, and adapting the plan to evolving challenges in the healthcare sector. Ultimately, this chapter serves as a guide for healthcare leaders to take actionable steps toward improving their leadership practices, fostering a culture of excellence, and driving sustainable improvements in healthcare delivery and patient outcomes.

Acknowledgment

I would like to express my deepest gratitude to all those who contributed to the successful completion of this book. This work would not have been possible without the unwavering support, encouragement, and collaboration of many individuals.

First and foremost, I am sincerely thankful to my wife and beloved family for their patience, understanding, and continuous inspiration throughout this journey. Special thanks to Dr. Ahmad H. Almomani and Dr. Marya H. Almomani, whose clinical expertise, thoughtful input, and active involvement greatly enriched the depth and relevance of this work. I am equally grateful to Marah, Solaf, Joanna, and Abdallah—each of whom played a unique and meaningful role in supporting me during the long hours of research, writing, and revision.

Their belief in the value of this project gave me the strength to persevere, and their contributions—whether academic, moral, or emotional—have left an indelible mark on this work.

Introduction

Evaluating healthcare leadership (HCL) development in healthcare contexts is a complex but crucial process that significantly impacts organizational performance. HCL influences employees' attitudes, beliefs, and capabilities in achieving organizational goals. Global health organizations emphasize the importance of leadership influence, recognizing its critical role in shaping the healthcare sector, affecting national economies, and presenting significant challenges to healthcare management systems. In the dynamic landscape of healthcare, traditional leadership paradigms are proving inadequate for the complexities of policy implementation. Healthcare leadership no longer operates within a conventional, definitive framework, as professional practices continually evolve. However, effective healthcare leaders (HCLs) exhibit specific shared characteristics, as not all competencies are mobilized simultaneously.

This book provides a comprehensive exploration of the multifaceted nature of healthcare leadership. It introduces a robust leadership competency framework and a self-assessment tool—customized through a structured survey questionnaire—designed based on insights from leading international healthcare systems experts. The book supports healthcare leaders in excelling by offering actionable strategies, including an initial series of "next steps." It presents a structured action plan that employs the Specific, Measurable, Achievable, Relevant, and Time-Bound (SMART) methodology to guide goal setting. Ultimately, this book aims to The ultimate aim is improving the healthcare Examining and highlighting the role of leadership by focusing on key competencies and styles, analyzing the factors that impact leadership effectiveness, and identifying strategies that drive successful leadership in healthcare organizations. This approach enhances leadership practices, particularly in evaluating leadership effectiveness and influencing factors among leaders in public health hospitals, ultimately fostering excellence and advancement in healthcare leadership.

The research methodology employed in this book integrates both qualitative and quantitative approaches, ensuring a comprehensive understanding of healthcare leadership. A systematic literature review was conducted to investigate the critical competencies and factors that enhance leadership practices and effectiveness in healthcare organizations. Additionally, a customized structured survey questionnaire was developed through a collaborative process, incorporating inputs from global healthcare systems experts. This book contributes to leadership excellence by introducing a robust leadership competency framework based on leading global assessment tools and expert insights. It serves as a valuable resource for healthcare organizations, aiding leaders in excelling in their roles. Furthermore, it outlines an actionable series of "next steps" for implementing best practices in healthcare leadership within local health industries.

As an educator in industrial engineering with a specialization in healthcare systems at both undergraduate and postgraduate levels, I recognize the increasing significance of integrating healthcare leadership into academic curricula. The future of healthcare leadership education demands a renewed emphasis on preparing future healthcare professionals, as leadership is a crucial component of care excellence. This book arrives at an opportune time, offering vital directions for the future of healthcare leadership. It recommends that healthcare organizations adopt a collaborative approach to uphold leadership needs, ethical best practices, and professional standards. It also highlights the importance of accreditation, educational services, certification courses, training programs, and workshops. By synthesizing widely recognized healthcare leadership competencies, this book provides novel insights for healthcare policymakers and researchers engaged in the professionalization of healthcare leadership.

The authors and contributors advocate for an assessment framework tailored to healthcare organizations, enabling effective monitoring and improvement of healthcare leadership. This perspective is crucial for enhancing the quadruple aim—improving patient care, reducing costs, enhancing the work-life of healthcare providers, and improving population health. Additionally, the book presents an international and global perspective on healthcare leadership, emphasizing the importance of considering social determinants of health and global disparities. Recognizing that healthcare leadership is an essential partner to other sectors, this text serves as a critical resource for healthcare leaders, providers, and students who aspire to drive transformative change in the healthcare industry.

Hesham Al-Momani
The Hashemite University, Jordan

Ahmad H. Almomani
Ministry of Health, Jordan

Marya H. Almomani
The Jordanian Royal Medical Services, Jordan

Chapter 1
Healthcare Leadership Within Organizational Systems

ABSTRACT

This chapter emphasizes the crucial role of healthcare leadership in building efficient and effective healthcare systems worldwide. Despite healthcare's importance for national development and individual well-being, challenges like infrastructure limitations, workforce shortages, and governance inefficiencies hinder progress toward improved patient outcomes. Strong leadership is essential to enhance service delivery and ensure sustainable improvements. This chapter addresses the gap in comprehensive research on healthcare leadership by identifying key competencies and proposing standardized assessment tools for accreditation councils and professionals. It highlights transformational leadership as a key approach to motivate teams, foster innovation, and improve care quality. Effective leaders combine adaptability, professional collaboration, and data-driven decision-making to navigate complex environments. By integrating leadership theory with practical management tactics.

HEALTH CARE MANAGEMENT SYSTEMS

The terms "health system" and "health sector" are often used interchangeably (Loureiro, Ferreira & Simoes, 2021; Theaker & Curran, 2025; Singh, Rai, & Singh, 2011; WHO, 2010; Raghupathi & Raghupathi, 2020). Healthcare is one of the most crucial and valuable services for both nations and individuals. It is a dynamic, complex, and ever-evolving field that plays a vital role in supporting a country's economy (Willie, 2023; Macintosh, Hernandez, Mehta, 2022; ACHEBAKER, 2015). Healthcare systems are composed of various components, including hospitals, primary care

DOI: 10.4018/979-8-3373-2225-4.ch001

facilities, and public health institutions, each playing a vital role in service delivery and patient care (Bodenheimer & Grumbach, 2020). The effectiveness of healthcare systems depends on governance, financing, human resources, and the adoption of innovative technologies (Frenk et al., 2010). The recent surge in pandemics and emerging diseases has driven rapid advancements in healthcare services, necessitating continuous improvement in leadership strategies (Sujith et al., 2022; Baker et al., 2021). The quality of healthcare is measured by the adequacy of the services provided, patient satisfaction, and overall health outcomes (Asif et al., 2019). High-reliability and well-qualified healthcare organizations can significantly improve the quality, efficiency, and effectiveness of healthcare delivery, ultimately enhancing patient outcomes (Marcelin et al., 2019). In contrast, poor healthcare management can have far-reaching consequences, leading to inefficiencies, increased medical errors, and poor patient care (Ferlie & Shortell, 2001; Economou et al., 2015).

HEALTHCARE IN DEVELOPING COUNTRIES

Delivering healthcare services in developing countries poses significant challenges. Low- and middle-income countries (LMICs) continue to strive toward achieving health-related Millennium Development Goals (MDGs) and Sustainable Development Goals (SDGs) (Sarihasan et al., 2022; Yamey, 2012). However, numerous challenges hinder these efforts. These challenges include inadequate healthcare infrastructure, high disease burdens, and unfavorable socioeconomic conditions, which affect access to essential healthcare services (Thomas et al., 2013; Iwuoha et al., 2021). Additionally, financial constraints, limited funding, and inefficient allocation of resources create further obstacles to achieving optimal healthcare service delivery (Iwuoha et al., 2021; Frumence, Nyamhanga, & Anaeli, 2017). Overcrowded healthcare facilities, long waiting times, and shortages of medical personnel exacerbate these issues, affecting the quality of care (Frumence, Nyamhanga, & Anaeli, 2017). A lack of governance and regulatory oversight also hinders the progress of healthcare systems in developing nations (Thomas et al., 2013; Yukl, 2020; Weberg, 2020; Weberg, 2010). Moreover, the shortage of a skilled healthcare workforce and insufficient health education remain critical issues (Leadership Competencies for Healthcare Services, 2015; Thomas et al., 2013; Yukl, 2020). Developing training programs and capacity-building initiatives is crucial for improving healthcare service delivery and achieving better health outcomes in developing countries (Kruk et al., 2018). Strengthening healthcare leadership and policy frameworks can help create sustainable healthcare models that address the diverse needs of populations in these regions (Kim et al., 2017).

LEADERSHIP AND MANAGEMENT IN HEALTHCARE

The healthcare leadership book synthesis looks at how to be a good leader and manager in healthcare. It focuses on transformational leadership as a key way to motivate teams, encourage new ideas, and improve the quality of patient care. Studies have demonstrated that leadership techniques that focus on giving employees control, clear communication, and supportive settings make employees happier, keep them longer, and make the organization run more smoothly. Combining the main management tasks of planning, allocating resources, and managing change makes operations and service delivery even better. Adaptability, imaginative decision-making, and a commitment to patient-centered care are other important traits of good healthcare executives. Leaders show their abilities by encouraging people from different fields to work together, getting everyone on the same page with their goals, and using data-driven solutions to make things better. New ideas say that we should look at different leadership styles to solve the problems that come up in today's healthcare systems. Overall, healthcare workers who learn both leadership theory and practical management tactics are better able to deal with changing situations, push for constant improvement, and provide safe, high-quality, and fair treatment in settings where both the organization and the patient care are becoming more complicated. Neil Gopee and Jo Galloway's book *Leadership and Management in Healthcare 3rd ed.* (2017) gives healthcare workers a thorough look into leadership theories and management concepts, especially in the context of the UK's NHS. They talk about many types of leadership, like transformational, transactional, and situational leadership. They stress that transformational leadership (TFL) is important for motivating teams, encouraging new ideas, and improving patient care results (Gopee & Galloway, 2017). The writers also talk about the main managerial tasks of planning, coordinating, and allocating resources, and how these tasks are related to service delivery, operational efficiency, and quality improvement. They also talk about team dynamics, working together across disciplines, resolving conflicts, and communication as the building blocks of strong healthcare teams. They give you useful skills like SWOT analysis and action planning, as well as ways to handle change, deal with opposition, and use technology to improve patient-centered care. These ideas are backed up and expanded on by recent research. Seljemo et al. (2020) found that TFL improves nurses' work environments by giving them more control and making them happier at work. This leads to fewer bad events and higher care quality. Asif et al. (2019) showed that TFL can also improve patient outcomes by making nurses happier and giving them more authority. Labrague (2024) validated similar results in emergency units, suggesting that TFL increases the quality of treatment and lowers bad occurrences by making people happy at work. Kakemam et al. (2024) looked at 26 research and found that good leadership and management techniques improve staff retention, care quality, and the efficiency of the company. This is similar to what Gopee and Galloway said about aligning management with leadership for the best results. Ree, Ellis, and Wiig (2021) further backed up the idea that TFL can help improve the culture of patient safety in nursing homes by balancing work demands and resources. Some fresh criticisms advise looking into newer models like authentic leadership, which is similar to TFL but may add something new to healthcare leadership (Siangchokyoo et al., 2020). Asif et al. (2019) also say that more research needs to be done on different groups of people and mediators like safety climate to make leadership frameworks stronger in practice. In general, Gopee and Galloway's work provides a solid basis for leadership and management in healthcare by combining theory with real-world techniques to improve patient outcomes, staff engagement, and team cohesiveness. Recent research back up TFL's good effects and suggest that we keep looking into leadership models and mediators to make healthcare leadership even more effective in changing, resource-limited settings.

Current healthcare leaders have a number of important skills that improve the functioning of their organizations and the health of their patients. During the COVID-19 pandemic, when quick decisions about telehealth integration, resource allocation, and infection control were necessary, many leaders showed visionary and adaptive leadership (Sfantou et al., 2017; Shingler-Nace, 2020). Leaders also strongly believe in putting patients first, making sure that the organization's goals are in line with what patients need and anticipate (Al-Abri & Al-Balushi, 2014). Effective healthcare leaders also encourage people from different fields to work together, such as doctors, nurses, IT workers, and policymakers, to provide care that is coordinated and integrated (West et al., 2015). In addition, more and more people are realizing how important it is to make decisions based on data. Leaders are using data analytics, electronic health records, and evidence-based practices to make their operations run more smoothly and enhance patient outcomes (Kellermann & Jones, 2013). Together, these abilities give healthcare executives the tools they need to deal with tough problems and keep making healthcare systems better.

EVALUATING HEALTHCARE LEADERSHIP EFFECTIVENESS IN HOSPITALS

Healthcare leadership is a critical determinant of organizational success, influencing healthcare delivery, patient outcomes, and workforce efficiency (Daly et al., 2014). As healthcare systems worldwide face increasing challenges, including financial constraints, workforce shortages, and evolving patient needs, effective leadership has never been more essential (West, Eckert, & Pasmore, 2014). Leaders in healthcare must navigate complex regulatory environments, drive innovation, and foster a culture of continuous improvement (Garman & Johnson, 2006). This book explores the multifaceted nature of healthcare leadership, highlighting key competencies, leadership styles, and strategies for enhancing effectiveness in diverse healthcare settings. The role of leadership in healthcare extends beyond traditional management functions; it involves strategic decision-making, ethical considerations, and the ability to inspire and engage multidisciplinary teams (Yukl, 2020). Research indicates that strong leadership directly correlates with improved patient care, staff satisfaction, and organizational resilience (McAlearney, 2006). This book introduces a robust leadership competency framework and a self-assessment tool developed in collaboration with international health systems experts. By incorporating best practices from global healthcare leadership models, the framework aims to support healthcare leaders in optimizing their impact and addressing contemporary challenges. To provide a comprehensive analysis, this book adopts a mixed-methods approach, combining qualitative and quantitative methodologies. A systematic literature review investigates the essential leadership competencies and the factors that enhance leadership effectiveness in healthcare organizations (Antonakis & House, 2014). Additionally, a structured survey questionnaire, designed with input from global healthcare experts, assesses leadership effectiveness in public health hospitals. The findings contribute to the ongoing discourse on healthcare leadership excellence and provide actionable insights for professionals seeking to improve their leadership capabilities. Furthermore, the book outlines practical steps for leadership development, offering an action plan based on the Specific, Measurable, Achievable, Relevant, and Time-Bound (SMART) methodology (Doran, 1981). By applying this structured approach, healthcare organizations can cultivate leadership excellence, ensuring sustainable improvements in healthcare management and service delivery. In an era of rapid change and uncertainty, the need for competent and adaptive healthcare leaders is more pressing than ever. This book serves as a valuable resource for healthcare professionals, educators, policymakers, and researchers striving to enhance leadership effectiveness. By synthesizing widely recognized leadership competencies and producing novel insights into healthcare leadership, this work aims to contribute to the ongoing professionalization of healthcare leaders and the advancement of healthcare management worldwide.

THE FOCUS ON LEADERSHIP EFFECTIVENESS

Healthcare management systems, delivery models, and professional practices are rapidly evolving, creating an urgent need for effective healthcare leadership. This shift has heightened concerns about the impact of healthcare leadership on the quality of healthcare services, patient outcomes, and organizational performance (King's Fund,

2021). As a result, healthcare policymakers are emphasizing the need to strengthen leadership capabilities at various levels within healthcare organizations. The need for effective healthcare leadership arises from a lack of comprehensive, internationally approved frameworks for evaluating and improving healthcare leadership. This issue is particularly pronounced in healthcare organizations, where limited research has focused on this critical area. The absence of structured healthcare leadership assessment tools highlights the need for deeper exploration and standardization of leadership competencies in the Jordanian context (Claramita & Susilo, 2024). This book case study aims to improve the quality of healthcare services provided by public hospitals in Jordan, aligning with the Health Care Accreditation Councils and healthcare professionals objectives for implementing evidence-based standards to drive quality improvement. Specifically, the book assesses healthcare leadership effectiveness at a case hospital, the largest hospital complex in healthcare organizations. By evaluating leadership competencies and identifying key challenges, this study provides insights that can inform policies and training programs aimed at enhancing healthcare leadership. The primary goal is to identify and strengthen key leadership competencies, understand the factors influencing leadership effectiveness, and determine the strategies that contribute to successful leadership in healthcare organizations. The study also seeks to develop customized, standardized leadership assessment tools tailored to the healthcare sector. These tools will be used by healthcare organizations and researchers to evaluate healthcare leadership performance in hospitals across healthcare organizations. To achieve these objectives, the study will gather insights from both medical staff and administrative personnel regarding the evaluation of healthcare leadership performance. Additionally, the book will propose recommendations for fostering leadership excellence, promoting sustainable healthcare development, and ensuring the delivery of high-quality healthcare services. That will help answer critical questions related to healthcare leadership domains (attributes) outlined in **Table 1** below. The book will also provide actionable recommendations and plans to enhance healthcare leadership excellence, thereby driving sustainable improvements in healthcare organizations healthcare sector.

Table 1. Healthcare leadership domains (attributes) leadership domains

1. General Parameters (Systems Perspective) 2. Professional, Ethical, and Social Responsibility 3. Commitment to Advancing People-Centered Services 4. Emotional Intelligence and Self-Awareness 5. Continuous Improvement 6. Translation and Implementation 7. Strategic Financial Management 8. Human Resource Management 9. Information Management 10. Administration and Business Development 11. Quality Improvement and Patient Safety 12. Monitoring and Evaluation 13. Visionary Leadership 14. Governance 15. Preparedness and Crisis Management 16. Digital Technologies in Healthcare 17. Executive Communication	18. Employee Support and Development 19. Compassionate Leadership 20. Interpersonal Relationships 21. Problem-Solving and Negotiation 22. Systems Thinking 23. Engaging Culture and Environment 24. Population Health Assessment and Promotion 25. Networks and Alliances 26. Advocacy 27. Public Relations and Marketing 28. Regulations and Health Systems 29. Strategic Planning 30. Sustainability Leadership 31. Organizational Resilience 32. Innovation and Entrepreneurship 33. Change Management 34. Ongoing Learning and Sharing

REFERENCES

ACHE. (2015). *Leadership competencies for health services managers leadership competencies for healthcare services managers*. https://www.ache.org/-/media/ache/about-ache/leadership_competencies_healthcare_services_managers.pdf

Al-Abri, R., & Al-Balushi, A. (2014). Patient satisfaction survey as a tool towards quality improvement. *Oman Medical Journal*, 29(1), 3–7. 22

Antonakis, J., & House, R. J. (2014). Instrumental leadership: Measurement and extension of transformational–transactiona31 leadership theory. *The Leadership Quarterly*, *25*(4), 746–771. https://www.sciencedirect.com/science/article/abs/pii/S1048984314000290

Asif, M., Jameel, A., Hussain, A., Hwang, J., & Sahito, N. (2019). Linking transformational leadership with nurse-assessed adverse patient outcomes and the quality of care: Assessing the role of job satisfaction and structural empowerment. *International Journal of Environmental Research and Public Health*, *16*(13), 1–15. https://pubmed.ncbi.nlm.nih.gov/31277478/ PMID: 31277478

Baker, M. A., Sands, K. E., Huang, S. S., Kleinman, K., Septimus, E. J., Varma, N., Blanchard, J., Poland, R. E., Coady, M. H., Yokoe, D. S., Fraker, S., Froman, A., Moody, J., Goldin, L., Isaacs, A., Kleja, K., Korwek, K. M., Stelling, J., Clark, A., & Platt, R. (2021). The Impact of COVID-19 on Healthcare-Associated Infections. *Clinical Infectious Diseases*, *74*(10). Advance online publication. DOI: 10.1093/cid/ciab688 PMID: 34370014

Bodenheimer, T., & Grumbach, K. (2020). *Understanding Health Policy: A Clinical Approach* (8th ed.). Mcgraw-Hill Education.

Claramita, M., & Susilo, A. P. (2024). *The Hierarchical Culture and Communication in Health Care*. 1–17. DOI: 10.1007/978-981-97-4320-9_1

Daly, J., Jackson, D., Mannix, J., Davidson, P. M., & Hutchinson, M. (2014). The importance of clinical leadership in the hospital setting. *Journal of Healthcare Leadership*, *6*, 75–83. DOI: 10.2147/jhl.s46161

Doran, G. T. (1981). There's a S.M.A.R.T. way to write management's goals and objectives. *Management Review*, *70*(11), 35–36. https://community.mis.temple.edu/mis0855002fall2015/files/2015/10/S.M.A.R.T-Way-Management-Review.pdf

Economou, C. Kaitelidou, D., Kentikelenis, A., Maresso, A., & Aris Sissouras. (2015). *The impact of the crisis on the health system and health in Greece*. Nih. gov; European Observatory on Health Systems and Policies. https://www.ncbi.nlm.nih.gov/books/NBK447857/

Ferlie, E., & Shortell, S. M. (2001). Improving the quality of healthcare in the United Kingdom and the United States: A framework for change. *The Milbank Quarterly*, *79*(2), 281–315. DOI: 10.1111/1468-0009.00206 PMID: 11439467

Frenk, J., Chen, L., & Bhutta, Z. A. (2010). Health Professionals for a New century: Transforming Education to Strengthen Health Systems in an Interdependent World. *Lancet*, *376*(9756), 1923–1958. PMID: 21112623

Frumence, G., Nyamhanga, T., & Anaeli, A. (2017). Facilitators and barriers to health care access among the elderly in Tanzania: A health system perspective from managers and service providers. *Journal of Ageing Research and Healthcare*, *2*(1), 20–31. DOI: 10.14302/issn.2474-7785.jarh-16-1354

Garman, A. N., & Johnson, M. P. (2006). Leadership Competencies: An Introduction. *Journal of Healthcare Management*, *51*(1), 13. https://journals.lww.com/jhmonline/Citation/2006/01000/Leadership_Competencies__An_Introduction.4.aspx PMID: 16479746

Gopee, N., & Galloway, J. (2017). *Leadership and Management in Healthcare* (3rd ed.). Sage. (Original work published 2008)

Iwuoha, V. C., Aniche, E. T., Obiora, C. A., & Umeifekwem, U. T. (2021). Citizens lack access to healthcare facilities: How COVID-19 lockdown and social distancing policies boost roadside chemist businesses in South-Eastern Nigeria. *The International Journal of Health Planning and Management*, *36*(6), 2411–2423. DOI: 10.1002/hpm.3316 PMID: 34476845

Kakemam, E., Albelbeisi, A. H., Rouzbahani, M., Gharakhani, M., Zahedi, H., & Taheri, R. (2024). Nurses' perceptions of patient safety competency: a cross-sectional study of relationships with occurrence and reporting of adverse events. Plos one, 19(1), e0297185.

Kellermann, A. L., & Jones, S. S. (2013). *What It Will Take to Achieve the As-Yet-Unfulfilled Promises of Health Information Technology*. Rand.org; Project HOPE. https://www.rand.org/pubs/external_publications/EP51265.html

Kim, J. Y., Farmer, P., & Porter, M. E. (2017). Redefining global healthcare delivery. *Lancet*, *382*(9897), 1060–1069. DOI: 10.1016/s0140-6736(13)61047-8 PMID: 23697823

King's Fund. (2021). "Developing leadership in healthcare: Evidence-based approaches." King's Fund Reports. https://www.kingsfund.org.uk/insight-and-analysis/reports/leadership-development-health-care

Kruk, M. E., Gage, A. D., Arsenault, C., Jordan, K., Leslie, H. H., Roder-DeWan, S., Adeyi, O., Barker, P., Daelmans, B., Doubova, S. V., English, M., Elorrio, E. G., Guanais, F., Gureje, O., Hirschhorn, L. R., Jiang, L., Kelley, E., Lemango, E. T., Liljestrand, J., & Malata, A. (2018). High-quality health systems in the Sustainable Development Goals era: Time for a revolution. *The Lancet. Global Health, 6*(11), e1196–e1252. https://www.thelancet.com/journals/langlo/article/PIIS2214-109X(18)30386-3/fulltext PMID: 30196093

Labrague, L. J. (2024). Relationship between transformational leadership, adverse patient events, and nurse-assessed quality of care in emergency units: The mediating role of work satisfaction. *Australasian Emergency Care (Online), 27*(1), 49–56. DOI: 10.1016/j.auec.2023.08.001 PMID: 37598031

Loureiro, R., Ferreira, J. J., & Simões, J. (2021). Understanding healthcare sector organizations from a dynamic capabilities perspective. *European Journal of Innovation Management, ahead-of-print*(ahead-of-print). DOI: 10.1108/ejim-02-2021-0085

Macintosh, T., Hernandez, M., & Mehta, A. S. (2022). Identifying, Addressing, and Eliminating Microaggressions in Healthcare. *HCA Healthcare Journal of Medicine, 3*(3). Advance online publication. DOI: 10.36518/2689-0216.1418 PMID: 37424615

Marcelin, J. R., Siraj, D. S., Victor, R., Kotadia, S., & Maldonado, Y. A. (2019). The Impact of Unconscious Bias in healthcare: How to Recognize and Mitigate It. *The Journal of Infectious Diseases, 220*(2), 62–73. DOI: 10.1093/infdis/jiz214 PMID: 31430386

McAlearney, A. S. (2006). Leadership development in healthcare: A qualitative study. *Journal of Organizational Behavior, 27*(7), 967–982. DOI: 10.1002/job.417

Raghupathi, V., & Raghupathi, W. (2020). Healthcare Expenditure and Economic Performance: Insights from the United States Data. *Frontiers in Public Health, 8*(156). NCBI. DOI: 10.3389/fpubh.2020.00156

Ree, E., Ellis, L. A., & Wiig, S. (2021). Managers' role in supporting resilience in healthcare: a proposed model of how managers contribute to a healthcare system's overall resilience. *International Journal of Health Governance, ahead-of-print*(ahead-of-print). DOI: 10.1108/ijhg-11-2020-0129

Sarihasan, I., Dajnoki, K., Oláh, J., & Al-Dalahmeh, M. (2022). The importance of the leadership functions of a high-reliability health care organization in managing the COVID-19 pandemic in Turkey. *Economia e Sociologia*, *15*(1), 78–93. DOI: 10.14254/2071-789x.2022/15-1/5

Seljemo, C., Viksveen, P., & Ree, E. (2020). The Role of Transformational leadership, Job Demands and Job Resources for Patient Safety Culture in Norwegian Nursing homes: A cross-sectional Study. *BMC Health Services Research*, *20*(1), 1–8. DOI: 10.1186/s12913-020-05671-y PMID: 32847598

Sfantou, D. F., Laliotis, A., Patelarou, A. E., Sifaki-Pistolla, D., Matalliotakis, M., & Patelarou, E. (2017). Importance of leadership style towards quality of care measures in healthcare settings: A systematic review. *Health Care*, *5*(4), 73. DOI: 10.3390/healthcare5040073 PMID: 29036901

Shingler-Nace, A. (2020). COVID-19: When Leadership Calls. *Nurse Leader*, *18*(4), 326–329. DOI: 10.1016/j.mnl.2020.03.017 PMID: 32346358

Siangchokyoo, N., Klinger, R. L., & Campion, E. D. (2020). Follower Transformation as the Linchpin of Transformational Leadership theory: A Systematic Review and Future Research Agenda. *The Leadership Quarterly*, *31*(1), 101341.

SINGH, L., RAI, R. K., & SINGH, P. K. (2011). Assessing the utilization of maternal and child health care among married adolescent women: evidence from India. *Journal of Biosocial Science*, *44*(1), 1–26. DOI: 10.1017/s0021932011000472 PMID: 21933465

Sujith, A. V. L. N., Sajja, G. S., Mahalakshmi, V., Nuhmani, S., & Prasanalakshmi, B. (2022). Systematic review of smart health monitoring using deep learning and Artificial intelligence. *Neuroscience Informatics*, *2*(3), 100028. DOI: 10.1016/j.neuri.2021.100028

Theaker, A., & Curran, J. (2025). The Public Relations Handbook. In *Routledge eBooks*. Informa., DOI: 10.4324/9781003517375

Thomas, S., Keegan, C., Barry, S., Layte, R., Jowett, M., & Normand, C. (2013). A framework for assessing health system resilience in an economic crisis: Ireland as a test case. *BMC Health Services Research*, *13*(1). Advance online publication. DOI: 10.1186/1472-6963-13-450 PMID: 24171814

Weberg, D. (2010). Transformational leadership and innovation in healthcare. *Journal of Healthcare Leadership*, *2*, 35–41. https://journals.lww.com/naqjournal/fulltext/2010/07000/Transformational_Leadership_and_Staff_Retention_.8.aspx

Weberg, D. (2020). Transformational Leadership and Staff Retention. *Nursing Administration Quarterly, 34*(3), 246–258. DOI: 10.1097/naq.0b013e3181e70298 PMID: 20562573

West, M., Armit, K., Loewenthal, L., Eckert, R., West, T., & Lee, A. (2015, February 25). *Leadership and Leadership Development in Health Care*. The Kings Fund; The King's Fund. https://www.kingsfund.org.uk/insight-and-analysis/reports/leadership-development-health-care

West, M., Eckert, R., & Pasmore, B. (2014, May 21). *Developing collective leadership for health care*. The King's Fund. https://www.kingsfund.org.uk/insight-and-analysis/reports/developing-collective-leadership-for-health-care

Willie, M. M. (2023). Defining the Population and Target Population in Clinical Studies: Clarifying Terminology and Enhancing Study Validity. *Journal of Medical and Clinical Nursing Studies, 1*(1), 1–3. DOI: 10.61440/jmcns.2023.v1.03

World Health Organization. (2010).. . *World Health Report, 2010*, •••. Www.who.int and https://www.who.int/publications/i/item/9789241564021

Yamey, G. (2012). What are the barriers to scaling up health interventions in low and middle income countries? A qualitative study of academic leaders in implementation science. *Globalization and Health, 8*(1), 11. DOI: 10.1186/1744-8603-8-11 PMID: 22643120

Yukl, G. A. (2020). *Leadership in organizations* (8th ed.). Pearson Education, Inc.

ADDITIONAL READING

Deng, C., Gulseren, D., Isola, C., Grocutt, K., & Turner, N. (2022). Transformational Leadership effectiveness: An evidence-based Primer. *Human Resource Development International, 26*(5), 627–641. DOI: 10.1080/13678868.2022.2135938

Tsapnidou, E., Kelesi, M., Rovithis, M., Katharakis, G., Gerogianni, G., Dafogianni, C., Toylia, G., Fasoi, G., & Stavropoulou, A. (2024). Transformational leadership—quality achievements and benefits for the healthcare organizations: A scoping review. *Hospitals, 1*(1), 87–103. DOI: 10.3390/hospitals1010008

Ystaas, L. M. K., Nikitara, M., Ghobrial, S., Latzourakis, E., Polychronis, G., & Constantinou, C. S. (2023). The impact of transformational leadership in the nursing work environment and patients' outcomes: A systematic review. *Nursing Reports, 13*(3), 1271–1290. DOI: 10.3390/nursrep13030108 PMID: 37755351

Chapter 2
Evolution and Fundamentals of Leadership

ABSTRACT

This chapter explores the evolution and fundamental principles of leadership, emphasizing its dynamic nature and essential role in organizational success. Leadership is no longer regarded as merely a hierarchical position but as a set of competencies that inspire teams, foster collaboration, and drive meaningful change. The chapter delves into various leadership theories, including creative leadership, which promotes innovation and strategic problem-solving. It traces the historical development of leadership thought, from early Great Man and Trait Theories to Behavioral, Situational, and contemporary leadership approaches. The modern leadership landscape integrates elements of transformational, servant, ethical, and adaptive leadership, emphasizing the necessity of flexibility in navigating complex organizational challenges. By understanding these diverse leadership paradigms, healthcare leaders can adopt effective strategies to enhance decision-making, strengthen management efficiency, and foster a culture of excellence within healthcare organizations.

LEADERSHIP (GENERAL)

In modern science, leadership is regarded as a role rather than a position, requiring a dynamic combination of skills, knowledge, and attributes to drive success (White, 2019). Leadership theory is an evolving discipline, continually reshaped by historical events, socio-economic changes, and advancements in organizational science (Keshtiban, Callahan, & Harris, 2023; Al Masaeid & Upadhyay, 2023;

DOI: 10.4018/979-8-3373-2225-4.ch002

Stone & Patterson, 2005). Effective leadership plays a pivotal role in determining the success of organizations across various sectors, including healthcare, by empowering diverse teams and fostering an inclusive culture (Bourbonnais, Brisson, & Vezina, 2010; White, Mische, & Winn, 2019). Leadership significantly impacts the performance of individuals within an organization, enabling them to achieve their full potential and contribute to positive organizational change (Hashimy et al., 2023; Karmysov, 2023; Hoffmeister et al., 2015). It involves guiding, motivating, and supporting teams to meet organizational goals while fostering innovation and adaptability. Although leadership is widely studied, scholars and practitioners continue to debate its definition and scope (Gini, 2020; Silva, 2016; Bennis, 1974; Batliwala, 2011). The concept of leadership remains fluid, adapting to changing organizational needs and societal expectations (Silva, 2016; Zuber-Skerritt, 2011). Administrative leadership, in particular, is a fundamental aspect of governance and organizational processes. It involves strategic decision-making, policy implementation, and the effective management of resources to achieve institutional objectives (Al-Maliki, 2020). Administrative leaders play a crucial role in shaping organizational culture, ensuring compliance with regulations, and fostering a collaborative work environment (Beauvais, 2019; Van Wart & Suino, 2017).

CREATIVE LEADERSHIP

Traditional leadership models, which emphasize hierarchical authority and rigid structures, are becoming increasingly insufficient in today's rapidly evolving business and healthcare environments. In response, organizations are embracing Creative Leadership (CL) as a necessary approach to navigate complex challenges and foster innovation (Khaled, 2020; Vaccaro et al. (2010). Creative Leadership is particularly essential in healthcare, where leaders must continually develop new strategies to enhance patient care, optimize resource allocation, and improve service delivery. Creative Leadership has been defined in multiple ways. Khaled (2020) and Vaccaro et al. (2010) describe it as "the ability of a manager to influence others and bring about change." Other researchers emphasize its role in generating innovative ideas and problem-solving strategies to address organizational challenges (Al-Zahrani et al., 2016; Alqahtani & Al-Enezi, 2025; Issa et al., 2024). Al-Maliki (2020) highlights Creative Leadership as a key driver of organizational transformation, enabling leaders to "design for innovation" and cultivate a culture of continuous improvement. Amabile & Khaire (2008) and Khalifa (2023) further stress the importance of stimulating creativity within teams, encouraging employees to think outside the box and contribute to the organization's long-term success. Several studies link Creative Leadership with enhanced employee motivation, engagement, and productivity (Alqahtani & Al-Enezi, 2025; Dakhilallah & Jahdali, 2021; Khalifa, 2023; Abdulaziz-al-Humaidan, 2025; Layne et al., 2019; Hsieh et al., 2019; Ng'ambi & Bozalek, 2013; Ved, Gupta, & Singh, 2019). Leaders who embrace creativity empower individuals, turning employees into a strategic asset for the organization (Abdulaziz-al-Humaidan, 2025; Kotter, 1996). The defining characteristic of Creative Leadership is the ability to translate innovative ideas into actionable solutions. Leaders who excel in this domain foster an organizational culture that encourages experimentation, calculated risk-taking, and continuous learning (Al-Zahrani et al., 2016; Kuwait Times, 2024; Alqahtani & Al-Enezi, 2025; Ved, Gupta, & Singh, 2019). This competency is particularly critical in healthcare leadership, where the demand for creative solutions to improve patient outcomes, enhance operational efficiency, and ensure financial sustainability is constantly growing.

LEADERSHIP HISTORY

The study of leadership has a well-documented history, evolving over centuries as societies recognized the importance of effective governance, decision-making, and organizational management. Leadership theories have been influenced by philosophical, political, and scientific advancements, leading to the emergence of various leadership paradigms (Chemers, 2000; Bowman, 2025). Scholars generally categorize the evolution of leadership into five main eras:

The Trait Era (1840s–1940s)

- o The Great Man Theory emerged, proposing that leaders possess inherent qualities that make them naturally suited for leadership (Benmira & Agboola, 2021).
- o Research focused on identifying personality traits, such as charisma, intelligence, and wisdom, believed to distinguish effective leaders (Cawthorn, 2017; Dziak, 2019).
- o Trait Theory evolved, emphasizing the identification of key leadership attributes like integrity, self-confidence, and emotional intelligence (Anderson, 2024).

The Behavioral Era (1940S–1950S)

- o This era shifted the focus from inherited traits to learned behaviors, suggesting that leadership effectiveness is determined by actions rather than inherent qualities.

- Leadership behaviors were categorized into task-oriented and people-oriented dimensions (Anderson, 2024; Denison & Mishra, 1995).
- Organizations developed leadership training programs based on behavioral theories, reinforcing the idea that leadership can be taught.

The Situational Era (1960S)

- The Situational Leadership Theory introduced the concept that leadership effectiveness depends on contextual factors and the specific needs of followers (Safaonov, Maslennikov, & Lenska, 2018).
- Contingency Theory further emphasized the need for leaders to adapt their styles based on environmental conditions and organizational demands.

The Modern Era (1990S)

- The rise of Transactional and Transformational Leadership theories marked this era (Van Seters & Field, 1990).
- Transactional Leadership focused on reward-based leadership, while Transformational Leadership emphasized motivation, vision-setting, and organizational change.

The New Leadership Era (2000S–PRESENT)

- The modern leadership landscape incorporates Adaptive Leadership, Servant Leadership, Ethical Leadership, and Authentic Leadership.
- Leadership theories now recognize the importance of emotional intelligence, moral values, and ethical decision-making (Soriano & Lagman, 2011).
- Recent studies emphasize the role of leadership in fostering resilience, collaboration, and innovation in the face of uncertainty and rapid change.

Throughout history, leadership has evolved in response to societal and organizational challenges, continuously shaping the way institutions function. In the healthcare sector, leadership plays a critical role in ensuring high-quality patient care, improving healthcare delivery systems, and responding effectively to emerging health crises. As leadership continues to evolve, it remains a cornerstone of organizational success, requiring continuous development and adaptation to meet the demands of an ever-changing world.

Table 1. Summary of the central leadership theories

Era	Period	Theory	Description
Trait	1840s	Great Man	Focus on natural-born leaders
	1930s–1940s	Trait	Focus on identifying traits and characteristics of effective leaders
Behavioral	1940s–1950s	Behavioral	Focus on the actions and skills of leaders
Situational	1960s	Contingent and	Focus on leaders adapting their style, taking into account the environment
		Situational	
New Leadership	1990s	Transactional	Focus on Leadership as a cost-benefit exchange
	1990s	Transformational	Focus on an inspirational style, pushing followers to higher and higher levels of achievement.
	2000s	Shared	Focus on followers leading each other
	2000s	Collaborative	Focus on engaging followers. Person-centered style
	2000s	Collective	Focus on the whole system of an organization
		Servant	
		Inclusive	
		Complexity	

(Benmira & Agboola, 2021)

LEADERSHIP BENEFITS

Leadership plays a central role in guiding organizations toward their goals, whether it is imposed through authority or voluntarily accepted by members as a means to achieve shared objectives (Volckmann, 2012; Raelin, 2005). In any organizational context, leadership is vital for steering efforts, aligning resources, and motivating individuals and teams to work toward a common vision. Effective leadership enhances organizational efficiency and plays a critical role in shaping employee behaviors, attitudes, and overall job satisfaction (Guglielmin et al., 2022). One significant benefit of leadership is its influence on employee attitudes. Leaders set the tone for the organizational culture, impacting how employees perceive their work environment and their relationship with the organization. Leadership styles and behaviors directly influence trust, loyalty, and commitment, which in turn affect employee retention and engagement (Skar et al., 2022). Positive leadership practices that foster an open, transparent, and supportive environment tend to result in more motivated and satisfied employees, leading to higher productivity and better organizational outcomes.

In the healthcare sector, leadership is particularly critical as it directly influences both patient outcomes and overall healthcare system effectiveness (Allen, 2022). Effective leadership in healthcare organizations helps improve communication, reduces errors, and enhances patient care. Leaders in healthcare settings are tasked with guiding teams of diverse professionals, balancing complex needs, and managing change in a dynamic environment. Strong leadership helps ensure that these organizations remain responsive to patient needs, adopt evidence-based practices, and engage in continuous quality improvement. Moreover, leadership drives motivation, collaboration, and innovation, which are essential for organizational adaptability and success in changing environments. Leaders who encourage open communication and foster a culture of collaboration help organizations stay agile and responsive. By supporting the development of innovative ideas and solutions, leaders enable organizations to remain competitive and effectively navigate external challenges (Guglielmin et al., 2022). Leaders who invest in fostering creativity and innovation within teams contribute to sustainable growth and improvement, particularly in industries where continuous advancement is necessary.

Leadership also plays a key role in managing change and uncertainty. Effective leaders help organizations not only adapt to change but also anticipate and plan for future challenges. This includes guiding teams through periods of transformation, fostering resilience, and ensuring that organizational objectives are met despite changing circumstances. Leaders who excel in strategic thinking and change management create a sense of stability and purpose during times of upheaval, ultimately improving organizational sustainability (Kotter, 1996). Overall, the benefits of leadership are multifaceted and critical to an organization's ability to achieve long-term success. Whether in terms of employee satisfaction, innovation, organizational performance, or healthcare outcomes, leadership is a fundamental driver of positive organizational dynamics.

REFERENCES

Abdulaziz-al-Humaidan, A. (2025). The effect of innovation and sustainability ethics on reputation: A moderating role of social media. *Social Responsibility Journal, 21*(6), 1205–1223. https://www.emerald.com/insight/content/doi/10.1108/srj-09-2024-0634/full/html

Al Masaeid, T. & Upadhyay, D. (2023). *Shared Leadership Practices on the Role of the Employees' Effectiveness*. DOI: 10.1109/icbats57792.2023.10111379

Al-Zahrani, E. (2024). The Role of Healthcare Leaders in Promoting Vaccine Acceptance in Saudi Arabia. *Journal of Healthcare Leadership, 16*, 279–286. DOI: 10.2147/jhl.s470522 PMID: 39072262

Al-Zahrani, J. M., Aldossari, K. K., Abdulmajeed, I., Al-Ghamdi, S. H., Al-Shamrani, A. M., & Al-Qahtani, N. S. (2016). Daytime sleepiness and academic performance among Arab medical students. *Journal of Thoracic Disease, 8*(2). Advance online publication. DOI: 10.3978/j.issn.2072-1439.2016.AB006

Allen, J. (2022). *The Effects of a Formal Organizational Program on Nursing Supervisor Self-Perception of Leadership*. UNM Digital Repository. https://digitalrepository.unm.edu/dnp/24/

Alqahtani, A. A., & Al-Enezi, Mutlaq M. (2025). Mastering Leadership Concepts through Utilizing Critical Thinking Strategies within Educational Administration Courses at Kuwait University. *College Student Journal, 46*(3), 508–525. https://eric.ed.gov/?id=EJ996950

Amabile, T. M., & Khaire, M. (2008). Creativity and the role of the leader. *Harvard Business Review, 86*(10), 100–109, 142. https://pubmed.ncbi.nlm.nih.gov/18822674/ PMID: 18822674

Anderson, D. (2024). *FROM TRAIT TO TRANSFORMATION- THE EVOLUTION OF LEADERSHIP THEORIES*. Scribd. https://www.scribd.com/document/687075302/FROM-TRAIT-TO-TRANSFORMATION-THE-EVOLUTION-OF-LEADERSHIP-THEORIES

Batliwala, S. (2011). *Feminist Leadership for Social Transformation*. CREA India.

Beauvais, A. M. (2019). *Leadership and management competence in nursing practice: competencies, skills, decision making*. Springer Publishing Company.

Benmira, S., & Agboola, M. (2021). Evolution of Leadership Theory. *BMJ Leader, 5*(1), 3–5. DOI: 10.1136/leader-2020-000296

Bennis, W. G. (1974). Learning to lead: A workbook on becoming a leader. Addison Wesley. Retrieved from https://archive.org/details/learningtoleadwo0000benn

Bourbonnais, R., Brisson, C., & Vezina, M. (2010). Long-term effects of an intervention on psychosocial work factors among healthcare professionals in a hospital setting. *Occupational and Environmental Medicine*, *68*(7), 479–486. DOI: 10.1136/oem.2010.055202 PMID: 21098832

Bowman, R. F. (2025). Examining Six Different Leadership Styles in Relation to Constrained Change at Winona State University. *Education*, •••, 3–13. https://www.semanticscholar.org/paper/Examining-Six-Different-Leadership-Styles-in-to-at-Bowman/2699050d89d20dece685325b98e67feb6d4d146d

Cawthorn, D. (2017). *Philosophical foundations of leadership*. Routledge.

Chemers, M. M. (2000). Leadership research and theory: A functional integration. *Group Dynamics*, *4*(1), 27–43. DOI: 10.1037/1089-2699.4.1.27

Dakhilallah, K., & Jahdali Bsc, A. (2021). *Towards an Intelligent Holy City: Assessing the Current Training Needs for the Ministry of Hajj and Umrah*. https://irep.ntu.ac.uk/id/eprint/46404/1/Khalid%20Aljahdali%202022.pdf

Denison, D. R., & Mishra, A. K. (1995). Toward a Theory of Organizational Culture and Effectiveness. *Organization Science*, *6*(2), 204–223. https://www.jstor.org/stable/2635122

Dziak, M. (2019). *Great man theory*. Salem Press Encyclopedia, 2024.

Gini, A. (2020). Moral Leadership and Business Ethics. *Journal of Leadership Studies*, *4*(4), 64–81. DOI: 10.1177/107179199700400406

Guglielmin, M., Shankardass, K., Bayoumi, A., O'Campo, P., Kokkinen, L., & Muntaner, C. (2022). A Realist Explanatory Case Study Investigating How Common Goals, Leadership, and Committed Staff Facilitate Health in All Policies Implementation in the Municipality of Kuopio, Finland. *International Journal of Health Policy and Management*. Advance online publication. DOI: 10.34172/ijhpm.2022.6355 PMID: 35247936

Hashimy, S., Jahromi, A., Hamza, M., Naaz, I., & Nyamwero, N., Sayed, & Hashimy, Q. (2023). Nurturing Leadership and Capacity Building for Success: Empowering Growth International Journal of Rehabilitation and Special Education. *International Journal of Rehabilitation and Special Education*, *3*(3). Advance online publication. DOI: 10.48165/ijrse.2023.3.2.5

Hoffmeister, K., Gibbons, A., Schwatka, N., & Rosecrance, J. (2015). Ergonomics Climate Assessment: A measure of operational performance and employee well-being. *Applied Ergonomics, 50*(1), 160–169. DOI: 10.1016/j.apergo.2015.03.011 PMID: 25959331

Hsieh, C.-C., Huang, H.-P., & Tung, T.-H., Chen, I-Chien., Beaton, R. D., & Jane, S.-W. (2019). The exploration of the knowledge, attitudes and practice behaviors of advanced care planning and its related predictors among Taiwanese nurses. *BMC Palliative Care, 18*(1). Advance online publication. DOI: 10.1186/s12904-019-0483-9 PMID: 31711482

Issa, W. B., & Shorbagi, A., Alham Al-Sharman, Rababa, M., Khalid Al-Majeed, Radwan, H., Ahmed, F. R., Nabeel Al-Yateem, Mottershead, R., Abdelrahim, D. N., Hijazi, H., Wafa Khasawneh, Ali, I., Abbas, N., & Fakhry, R. (2024). Shaping the future: perspectives on the Integration of Artificial Intelligence in health profession education: a multi-country survey. *BMC Medical Education, 24*(1). Advance online publication. DOI: 10.1186/s12909-024-06076-9 PMID: 39425151

Karmysov, S. (2023). LEADERSHIP FOR EVERYONE: EMPOWERING LEADING FEMALES. In *EDULEARN23 Proceedings* (pp. 6593-6599). IATED.

Keshtiban, A. E., Callahan, J. L., & Harris, M. (2023). Leaderlessness in social movements: Advancing space, symbols, and spectacle as modes of "Leadership". *Human Resource Development Quarterly, 34*(1), 19–43.

Khaled, S. M. (2020). STRATEGIC LEADERSHIP THROUGH CRISIS. *Ndc E-Journal, 1*(1), 1–16.

Khalifa, D. (2023). *AN EXAMINATION OF THE INTEGRATION OF SUSTAINABLE DEVELOPMENT PRINCIPLES IN GOVERNMENTAL PROJECT MANAGEMENT IN THE GOVERNMENT OF THE KINGDOM OF BAHRAIN*. PEARL. https://pearl.plymouth.ac.uk/pbs-theses/2/

Kotter, J. P. (1996). *Leading Change*. Harvard Business School Press.

Kuwait Times. (2024). *Concrete action needed to prevent mental health risks at work: Doctor | Kuwait Times Newspaper*. Kuwait Times. https://kuwaittimes.com/article/19929/kuwait/other-news/concrete-action-needed-to-prevent-mental-health-risks-at-work-doctor/

Layne, D., Nemeth, L., Mueller, M., & Martin, M. (2019). Negative Behaviors among Healthcare Professionals: Relationship with Patient Safety Culture. *Health Care, 7*(1), 23. DOI: 10.3390/healthcare7010023 PMID: 30717313

Ng'ambi, D., & Bozalek, V. (2013). Editorial: Emerging technologies and changing learning/teaching practices. *British Journal of Educational Technology*, *44*(4), 531–535. DOI: 10.1111/bjet.12061

Raelin, J. A. (2005). We the Leaders: In Order to Form a Leaderful Organization. *Journal of Leadership & Organizational Studies*, *12*(2), 18–30. DOI: 10.1177/107179190501200202

Safonov, Y., Maslennikov, Y., & Lenska, N. (2018). EVOLUTION AND MODERN TENDENCIES IN THE THEORY OF LEADERSHIP. *Baltic Journal of Economic Studies*, *4*(1), 304–310.

Safonov, Y., Maslennikov, Y., & Lenska, N. (2018). EVOLUTION AND MODERN TENDENCIES IN THE THEORY OF LEADERSHIP. *Baltic Journal of Economic Studies*, *4*(1), 304–310.

Silva, A. (2016). What is Leadership? *ProQuest, 8*(1), 1–5. https://www.proquest.com/docview/1831706711?fromopenview=true&pq-origsite=gscholar

Skar, A.-M. S., Braathu, N., Peters, N., Bækkelund, H., Endsjø, M., Babaii, A., Borge, R. H., Wentzel-Larsen, T., Ehrhart, M. G., Sklar, M., Brown, C. H., Aarons, G. A., & Egeland, K. M. (2022). A stepped-wedge randomized trial investigating the effect of the Leadership and Organizational Change for Implementation (LOCI) intervention on implementation and transformational leadership, and implementation climate. *BMC Health Services Research*, *22*(1). Advance online publication. DOI: 10.1186/s12913-022-07539 PMID: 35246135

Soriano, M. A., & Lagman, R. (2011). When the Patient Says No. *The American Journal of Hospice & Palliative Care*, *29*(5), 401–404. DOI: 10.1177/1049909111421163 PMID: 21998441

Stone, G. & Patterson, K. (2005). *The History of Leadership Focus Servant Leadership Research Roundtable – August 2005*. https://www.regent.edu/acad/global/publications/sl_proceedings/2005/stone_history.pdf

Vaccaro, I. G., Jansen, J. J. P., Van Den Bosch, F. A. J., & Volberda, H. W. (2010). Management Innovation and Leadership: The Moderating Role of Organizational Size. *Journal of Management Studies*, *49*(1), 28–51. DOI: 10.1111/j.1467-6486.2010.00976.x

Van Seters, D., & Field, R. (1990). The Evolution of Leadership Theory. *Journal of Organizational Change Management*, *3*, 29–45. DOI: 10.1108/09534819010142139

Van Wart, M. & Suino, P. (2017). *Leadership in Public Organizations*. Taylor & Francis Group. DOI: 10.4324/9781315268699

Ved, R., Gupta, G., & Singh, S. (2019). India's health and wellness centres: Realizing universal health coverage through comprehensive primary health care. *WHO South-East Asia Journal of Public Health, 8*(1), 18. DOI: 10.4103/2224-3151.255344 PMID: 30950425

Volckmann, R. (2012). Leadership in the Modern Organization: A Framework for the 21st Century. *Journal of Business Leadership, 17*(2), 35–45.

White, A. N., Mische, S., & Winn, M. (2019). Leadership in Science. *Journal of Biomolecular Techniques : JBT, 30*(Suppl), S54. https://pmc.ncbi.nlm.nih.gov/articles/PMC6938080/

Zuber-Skerritt, O. (2011). *Action Leadership*. Springer Netherlands., DOI: 10.1007/978-90-481-3935-4

ADDITIONAL READING

BAnotes.org (2023). Evolution of Leadership Theories: From Trait to Transformational Models. Springer. https://banotes.org/organisational-behaviour/evolution-leadership-theories-trait-transformational/

Harati, L. W. (2025). Relationship between Emotional Intelligence and Ethical Decision Making in Educational Leaders. In *ProQuest LLC*. ProQuest LLC. 789 East Eisenhower Parkway, P.O. Box 1346, Ann Arbor, MI 48106. Tel: 800-521-0600; Web site: https://www.proquest.com/en-US/products/dissertations/individuals.shtml. https://eric.ed.gov/?id=ED558431

Northouse, P. G. (2021). *Leadership: Theory and practice* (9th ed.). Sage Publishing.

Riza, M. F., Nimran, U., Musadieq, M. A., & Utami, H. N. (2020). The Effect of Innovative Leadership and Creative Leadership to Organizational Learning, Organizational Adaptation and Adaptive Performance. *Journal of Public Administration Studies, 005*(02), 51–55. DOI: 10.21776/ub.jpas.2020.005.02.2

Chapter 3

A Comprehensive Synthesis of Healthcare Leadership and Continuous Improvement:

Integrating Industrial Engineering Perspectives to Enhance Patient Outcomes

ABSTRACT

Healthcare systems are getting more complicated because of diverse teams, fast technological progress, and changing patient needs and dynamic, active, self-motivated and reciprocal process, best understood as a dynamic, ongoing process rather than a fixed personal trait or simple act of influence and leadership styles need to be flexible and based on evidence. It involves a series of actions aimed at achieving specific objectives, patient safety, care quality, and staff well-being shaped by interactions between leaders, followers, and the context in which they operate. In systems science and industrial engineering, the healthcare leadership parallels to all of the continuous improvement philosophy and methods like total quality management Lean and Six Sigma, emphasizing real time feedback, adaptation to change, and sustainable safe progress. The healthcare Leaders, much like processing engineers, always foster a culture of ongoing learning and advances through iterative growth and reflection.

DOI: 10.4018/979-8-3373-2225-4.ch003

LEADERSHIP AS A CONTINUOUS PROCESS: INTEGRATING INDUSTRIAL ENGINEERING PERSPECTIVES ON CONTINUOUS IMPROVEMENT

Since Leadership can be devilishly hard to define. (Gini, 1997; Silva, 2016; Bennis, 1974; Batliwala, 2011). Researchers satisfactorily considered it a "process," a series of actions that produce something or lead to a particular result." (Burns, 2017) and not just a personal quality or the leader's Influence upon followers to accomplish shared goals between leader and followers (Sukha, 2019; Stogdill, 1950; Tannenbaum, Weschler, & Massarik, 2015; Rost, 1991), stated that leadership it is the process of "influence behavior to achieve the objectives (Mohammed, 2014; Stogdill, 1950) and (Kotter, 1988; Bass & Avolio, 1990). Key scholars highlight that leadership is not a one-way interaction but an "interactive influence" (Silva, 2016; Stogdill, 1950; Kotter, 1988; Bass & Avolio, 1990), that evolves with time, place, and circumstances (Burns, 2017; Kotter, 1988). The active role of followers is critical, as their trust and commitment are necessary for the success of the leadership process (Silva, 2016; Shamir & Eilam, 2005). In the context of industrial engineering, leadership aligns with the principles of continuous improvement, such as Lean and Six Sigma. These approaches emphasize iterative cycles of feedback, adaptation, and long-term sustainability, mirroring the ongoing nature of leadership. Leaders, like process engineers, guide their teams through cycles of challenge, reflection, and progress to foster a culture of continuous learning and improvement (Deming, 1986; Womack & Jones, 2003). The leadership process may end if the followers decide not to continue following their leader (Silva, 2016; Shamir & Eilam, 2005; DeRue, 2011). Besides "influencing a group in a particular situation, time, and circumstances); (Vroom & Yetton, 1973; Avolio, 2007; Javidan et al., 2010); and (Kellerman, 2012), (Mohammed, 2014; Stogdill, 1950) and (Kotter, 1988; Bass & Avolio, 1990), and " interactive influence that occurs when between the leader and the followers in a given context." (Silva, 2016; Stogdill, 1950; Kotter, 1988; Bass & Avolio, 1990), the leadership process may be pretentious if healthcare followers notice that the healthcare leader needs to act on their behalf. (Den, 2012; Yorges, Weiss, & Strickland, 1999). Besides "influencing a group in a particular situation, time, and circumstances); (Vroom & Yetton, 1973; Avolio, 2007; Javidan et al.,2010); and (Kellerman, 2012), the leadership process may be affected if followers perceive that the leader needs to act on their behalf. (Sørensen et al., 2012; Yorges, Weiss, & Strickland, 1999). The leadership process may end if the followers decide not to continue following their leader (Silva, 2016; Shamir & Eilam, 2005; DeRue, 2011). Leadership remains a complex and multifaceted concept, challenging to define with precision (Gini, 1997; Silva, 2016; Bennis & Goldsmith, 2010; Batliwala, 2011). Despite the difficulty in reaching a single definition, many scholars agree that leadership should be viewed as a "process" rather than an innate quality or a simple act of influence. As Burns (2017) emphasizes, leadership can be understood as a "series of actions that produce something or lead to a particular result." This process-oriented view shifts the focus from static traits to the dynamic interactions between leaders, followers, and the context in which they operate.

This perspective positions leadership as the ability to influence behaviors in order to achieve objectives (Mohammed, 2014; Stogdill, 1950; Kotter, 1988; Bass & Avolio, 1990). It highlights that leadership is not a one-way interaction but rather an "interactive influence" between leaders and followers, shaped by contextual factors (Silva, 2016; Stogdill, 1950; Kotter, 1988; Bass & Avolio, 1990). This context includes not only the time, place, and circumstances in which the leadership process occurs but also the evolving dynamics of the organizational environment, including changes in technology, strategy, and stakeholder expectations (Vroom & Yetton, 1973; Avolio, 2007; Javidan et al., 2010; Kellerman, 2012). A key insight of the process-oriented view is the active role that followers play in leadership. Their participation is not passive but integral to the leadership process. If followers perceive that the leader is not serving their best interests, the leadership process may be disrupted or even cease entirely if followers choose to withdraw their support (Den, 2012; Yorges, Weiss, & Strickland, 1999). Trust and commitment from followers, therefore, are foundational to the success of the leadership process (Silva, 2016; Shamir & Eilam, 2005; DeRue, 2011). In the context of industrial engineering, leadership as a continuous process aligns closely with the principles of continuous improvement. Just as leadership requires ongoing interaction and adjustment, industrial engineering emphasizes continuous refinement in processes, systems, and performance. The theory of continuous improvement, central to industrial engineering practices like Lean and Six Sigma, mirrors the dynamic and iterative nature of leadership. Both leadership and continuous improvement rely on feedback loops, adaptation, and the sustained involvement of all stakeholders (Deming, 1986; Womack & Jones, 2003). Leaders in industrial environments must continually assess and respond to changes, ensuring that their influence fosters a culture of learning and progress. Leadership and continuous improvement share a commitment to evolving over time. In industrial engineering, this is reflected in the emphasis on data-driven decision-making, iterative cycles of improvement (Plan-Do-Check-Act), and a focus on long-term sustainability (Imai, 1986; Liker, 2004). These principles can be seamlessly integrated into leadership practices, reinforcing the notion that leadership is not static but requires continuous adjustment and growth. Leaders, much like process engineers, must guide their teams through iterative cycles of challenge, reflection, and progress, ensuring that the process itself evolves in alignment with organizational goals.

In this expanded view, the leadership process becomes not only about achieving immediate objectives but also about fostering an environment conducive to continuous learning, adaptation, and improvement. By examining leadership through the lens of continuous improvement, we gain a deeper understanding of its ongoing, evolving nature and its critical role in driving organizational success. This approach encourages scholars and practitioners alike to move beyond traditional notions of leadership as a singular, heroic act, and instead embrace its dynamic, process-oriented character, central to both leadership theory and industrial engineering practice.

COMPREHENSIVE SYNTHESIS: HEALTHCARE LEADERSHIP AND ITS IMPACT ON PATIENT OUTCOMES

Healthcare Leadership in Complex Systems

Healthcare organizations have inherent complexity and uncertainty since they depend upon multiple determinants -technical, social, organizational, and cultural industry's unique challenges (Mutonyi et al., 2024; Durrah, 2023; Yousef & Zubi, 2023). The Leadership of health systems is arguably the most complex block of any health system (Bjegovic-Mikanovic, 2016). that requires effective Leadership for high-quality care (Thomas et al., 2013) and superior ability to manage multifaceted systems and navigate through a myriad of complexities while inspiring change within H.C. organizations to effectively address the challenges and opportunities in the dynamic healthcare landscape (Zaccaro, LaPort, & Jose, 2013; Achua & Lussier, 2010; Carragher & Gormley, 2017), Besides, I deeply understand political and technical action to protect the public interest. (Mutale et al., 2013; Price et al., 2018; Bruce et al., 2022; Ranmuthugala et al., 2011; Berkes, Colding, & Folke, 2008).

Modern healthcare systems are complicated because they have diverse teams, technology that changes quickly, and patients whose requirements change over time. This means that leaders need to be flexible and effective. Healthcare systems around the world are under more and more pressure to keep costs down, enhance quality, and keep patients safe. This shows how important leadership is in dealing with these problems. More and more people are realizing that good healthcare leadership is important for making sure patients get good care, making organizations run better, and creating supportive work environments for healthcare workers. The Institute of Medicine's groundbreaking report "To Err is Human" pointed out that leadership is a major difference between organizations that do well and those that have problems with safety and efficiency. It stressed that leadership affects both the culture of the organization and the safety of patients. This synthesis looks at how well different leadership styles work in healthcare, such as transformational, transactional, servant, collaborative, and complexity leadership. It also gives evidence-based information about how these styles affect patient care. As healthcare systems get more complicated because of things like new technologies, an aging population, a lack of workers, and global health problems like COVID-19, the responsibility of leadership in making sure that care is safe, effective, and fair has become even more important.

Recent systematic reviews and meta-analyses show that there is a lot of research that links different styles and behaviors of leaders to measurable results for patients. Leadership styles that make people feel safe psychologically allow staff to voice their concerns, which encourages proactive problem-solving and risk reduction. For instance, Almalki, Fitzgerald, and Clark (2012) looked at what affects nurses' motivation and well-being and found that leadership behaviors like giving nurses more control and communicating in a supportive way were important for lowering prescription errors and making patients happier.

Empirical studies have further shown that hospitals with strong nurse-reported leadership have significantly lower patient mortality and failure-to-rescue rates (Kutney-Lee, Lake, & Aiken, 2009). Wong, Cummings, & Ducharme (2013) reported that effective nursing leadership is associated with decreased hospital-acquired infections, pressure ulcers, and falls. Similarly, O'Connor (2014) found that patients treated in units with supportive and communicative leadership report higher satisfaction, improved pain management, and better discharge readiness. Moreover, effective leadership shapes positive organizational cultures and safety climates. Shipton et al. (2008) found that top management team leadership predicted lower patient complaints and higher hospital performance ratings within the NHS. Foronda, MacWilliams, & McArthur (2016) demonstrated that effective clinical leadership within interprofessional teams improved patient outcomes, particularly by enhancing handover practices and discharge processes. Additionally, Smith, Prom, and Ng (2024) noted that patient-centered leadership approaches reduce disparities in care access, especially within the context of telehealth implementation.

Healthcare Leadership Significance and Impacts

Healthcare leadership (HCL) is of paramount significance and is considered an essential and prominent topic (Asmri et al., 2020). HCL includes administrators, clinicians, researchers, policymakers, and other professionals with the skills, knowledge, and vision to drive positive transformation (Avolio, Walumbwa, & Weber, 2009; Carter et al., 2013). HCL is becoming more critical to the success of healthcare organizations (Chen, 2025), significantly impacts various aspects of healthcare organizations and patient outcomes (Avolio, Walumbwa, & Weber, 2009), and is considered one of the main factors that help organizations achieve excellent success (Carter et al., 2013). Investing in organizational professional healthcare leaders' Leadership is critical for improving health status. It can inspire and empower those around them to achieve their full potential and drive positive change (Carter et al., 2013), driving innovation and change (Avolio et al., 2005; Day et al., 2014) increase staff satisfaction, improve retention rates, and enhance patient experiences (Avolio, Walumbwa, & Weber, 2009). This can be achieved by HCL, which possesses the qualities necessary to achieve the desired goals (Carragher & Gormley, 2017), depending on their role, qualities included administrative and technical expertise that applies, facilitates, achieves, or sustains the actions delivering preventive, promotive, curative, and rehabilitative interventions through a combination of public health actions (WHO, 2010). HCL effectively and ethically influences others (nurses and hospital crew) to achieve patient satisfaction (Hargett et al., 2017; De Brún, O'Donovan, & McAuliffe, 2019; Specchia et al., 2021). In addition, HCL directly affects (patient care and outcomes), shapes (organizational Culture and employee satisfaction), and (drives innovation and change) (de la Cruz et al., 2015) by articulating a compelling vision providing a sense of purpose and direction, with considerable empathy, Compassion, adaptability, and excellent delegation skills (Turner, 2018; Clark et al., 2021; West, Eckert, & Pasmore, 2014; Lantz, 2008), with good attention to system design (WHO, 2010) and handling information quickly (Bensimon, 1989) that ultimately leads to improved healthcare delivery and outcomes (Carragher & Gormley, 2017) actively pursue organizational resilience. Motivates employees (Hirst et al., 2018) and improves performance and productivity (Tierney, Farmer, & Graen, 2019; Mumford & Licuanan, 2004). Challenge the process (Strack & Fottler, 2002) and the status quo (Lobdell, 2019). Moreover, HCL impact can vary based on each healthcare organization's context and challenges (Avolio, Walumbwa, & Weber, 2009; Day et al., 2014), and the HCL patient care actions are evaluated based on the patient's view as a crucial indicator of healthcare quality (Oti-Boadi, Asante, & Malm, 2019; Leonard & Masatu, 2005).

Overall, leadership styles that promote autonomy, provide support, and encourage professional development enhance nurse performance, interprofessional collaboration, and patient-centered care, ultimately translating into safer and higher-quality patient outcomes.

REFERENCES

Achua, C. F., & Lussier, R. N. (2010). *Effective Leadership* (4th ed.). South-Western.

Almalki, M. J., Fitzgerald, G., & Clark, M. (2012). Quality of work life and turnover intention of primary health care nurses in Saudi Arabia: A cross-sectional study. *BMC Health Services Research, 12*, 314. Advance online publication. DOI: 10.1186/1472-6963-12-314 PMID: 22970764

Asmri, M. A., Almalki, M. J., Fitzgerald, G., & Clark, M. (2020). The public health care system and primary care services in Saudi Arabia: A system in transition. *Eastern Mediterranean Health Journal, 26*(4), 468–476. PMID: 32338366

Avolio, B. J. (2007). Promoting more integrative strategies for leadership theory-building. *The American Psychologist, 62*(1), 25–33. DOI: 10.1037/0003-066x.62.1.25 PMID: 17209677

Avolio, B. J., Walumbwa, F. O., & Weber, T. J. (2009). Leadership: Current theories, research, and future directions. *Annual Review of Psychology, 60*(1), 421–449. DOI: 10.1146/annurev.psych.60.110707.163621 PMID: 18651820

Bass, B. M., & Avolio, B. J. (1990). *Transformational leadership development: manual for the multifactor leadership questionnaire*. Consulting Psychologists Press.

Batliwala, S. (2011). Feminist leadership for social transformation: Clearing the conceptual cloud. CREA. https://creaworld.org/resource/feminist-leadership-for-social-transformation/

Bennis, W. G. (1974). Learning to lead: A workbook on becoming a leader. Addison Wesley. Retrieved from https://archive.org/details/learningtoleadwo0000benn

Bennis, W. G., & Goldsmith, J. (2010). *Learning to lead: a workbook on becoming a leader*. Basic Books.

Bensimon, E. M. (1989). The Meaning of "Good Presidential Leadership": A Frame Analysis. *Review of Higher Education, 12*(2), 107–123. DOI: 10.1353/rhe.1989.0024

Berkes, F. Colding, J., & Folke, C. (2008). *Navigating social-ecological systems: building resilience for complexity and change*. Cambridge University Press.

Bjegovic-Mikanovic, V. (2016). Governance and management of health care institutions in Serbia: An overview of recent developments. *South Eastern European Journal of Public Health, 5*(1). Advance online publication. DOI: 10.4119/UNIBI/SEEJPH-2016-94

Bruce, I. N., Golam, S., Steenkamp, J., Wang, P., Worthington, E., Desta, B., Psachoulia, K., Erhardt, W., & Tummala, R. (2022). Indirect treatment comparison of anifrolumab efficacy versus belimumab in adults with systemic lupus erythematosus. *Journal of Comparative Effectiveness Research, 11*(10), 765–777. DOI: 10.2217/cer-2022-0040 PMID: 35546484

Burns, J. M. (2017). Leadership: A higher view. HarperCollins Publishers. https://www.harpercollins.com/products/leadership-james-m-burns

Carragher, J., & Gormley, K. (2017). Leadership and Emotional Intelligence in Nursing and Midwifery Education and Practice: A Discussion Paper. *Journal of Advanced Nursing, 73*(1), 85–96.

Carter, M. Z., Armenakis, A. A., Feild, H. S., & Mossholder, K. W. (2013). Transformational leadership, relationship quality, and employee performance during continuous incremental organizational change. *Journal of Organizational Behavior, 34*(7), 942–958. DOI: 10.1002/job.1824

Chen, L. J. (2025). Health Policy Challenges for 2025 and Beyond. *JAMA Health Forum, 6*(1), e250184. DOI: 10.1001/jamahealthforum.2025.0184 PMID: 39883473

Clark, C. R., Wilkins, C. H., Rodriguez, J. A., Preininger, A. M., Harris, J., DesAutels, S., Karunakaram, H., Rhee, K., Bates, D. W., & Dankwa-Mullan, I. (2021). Health Care Equity in the Use of Advanced Analytics and Artificial Intelligence Technologies in Primary Care. *Journal of General Internal Medicine, 36*(10), 3188–3193. DOI: 10.1007/s11606-021-06846-x PMID: 34027610

Day, D. V., Fleenor, J. W., Atwater, L. E., Sturm, R. E., & McKee, R. A. (2014). Advances in Leader and Leadership development: A Review of 25 Years of Research and Theory. *The Leadership Quarterly, 25*(1), 63–82.

De Brún, A., O'Donovan, R., & McAuliffe, E. (2019). Interventions to Develop Collectivistic Leadership in Healthcare settings: A Systematic Review. *BMC Health Services Research, 19*(1), 1–22. DOI: 10.1186/s12913-019-3883-x PMID: 30683089

de la Cruz, L. F., Llorens, M., Jassi, A., Krebs, G., Vidal-Ribas, P., Radua, J., Hatch, S. L., Bhugra, D., Heyman, I., Clark, B., & Mataix-Cols, D. (2015). Ethnic inequalities in the use of secondary and tertiary mental health services among patients with obsessive–compulsive disorder. *The British Journal of Psychiatry, 207*(6), 530–535. DOI: 10.1192/bjp.bp.114.154062 PMID: 26206866

Deming, W. E. (1986). *Out of the crisis*. The Mit Press.

DeRue, D. S. (2011). Adaptive leadership theory: Leading and following as a complex adaptive process. *Research in Organizational Behavior, 31*, 125–150.

Durrah, S. K. (2023). *Strategies for Improving Performance Through Diversity and Inclusion in the Workplace.* Walden University ScholarWorks. https://scholarworks.waldenu.edu/cgi/viewcontent.cgi?article=15955&context=dissertations

Foronda, C., MacWilliams, B., & McArthur, E. (2016). Interprofessional communication in healthcare: An integrative review. *Nurse Education in Practice, 19*(1), 36–40. DOI: 10.1016/j.nepr.2016.04.005 PMID: 27428690

Gini, A. (1997). Moral leadership and business ethics. *The Journal of Leadership Studies, 4*(4), 64–81.

Hargett, C., Doty, J., Hauck, J., Webb, A., Cook, S., Tsipis, N., Neumann, J., Andolsek, K., & Taylor, D. (2017). Developing a Model for Effective Leadership in healthcare: A Concept Mapping Approach. *Journal of Healthcare Leadership, 9*(9), 69–78. DOI: 10.2147/JHL.S141664 PMID: 29355249

Hirst, G., Van Knippenberg, D., Chen, C. H., & Sacramento, C. A. (2018). How does bureaucracy impact individual creativity? A cross-level investigation of team contextual influences on goal orientation–creativity relationships. *Academy of Management Journal, 54*(3), 624–641. https://www.jstor.org/stable/23045099

Javidan, M. Dorfman, P. W., Howell, J. P., & Hanges, P. (2010). Leadership and cultural context: A theoretical and empirical examination based on Project GLOBE. *ResearchGate*, 335–376. https://www.researchgate.net/publication/288927197_Leadership_and_cultural_context_A_theoretical_and_empirical_examination_ba

Kellerman, B. (2012). *The end of leadership.* Harper Business.

Kotter, J. P. (1988). *The leadership factor*. Free Press.

Kutney-Lee, A., Lake, E. T., & Aiken, L. H. (2009). Development of the hospital nurse surveillance capacity profile. *Research in Nursing & Health, 32*(2), 217–228. DOI: 10.1002/nur.20316 PMID: 19161172

Lantz, P. M. (2008). Gender and leadership in healthcare administration: 21st century progress and challenges. *Journal of Healthcare Management, 53*(5). PMID: 18856135

Leonard, K. L., & Masatu, M. C. (2005). The use of direct clinician observation and vignettes for health services quality evaluation in developing countries. *Social Science & Medicine, 61*(9), 1944–1951. DOI: 10.1016/j.socscimed.2005.03.043 PMID: 15936863

Liker, J. K. (2004). *The Toyota Way: 14 Management Principles from the World's Greatest Manufacturer*. McGraw-Hill.

Lobdell, J. (2019) Leadership—A new view. *The Actuary Magazine*. https://www.theactuarymagazine.org/wp-content/uploads/2019/09/act-2019-vol16-iss5.pdf#page=34

Mohammed, N. (2014). Theories of Leadership: A Comprehensive Review. *Journal of Management, 28*(2), 57–78.

Mumford, M. D., & Licuanan, B. (2004). Leading for innovation: Conclusions, issues, and directions. *The Leadership Quarterly, 15*(1), 163–171. DOI: 10.1016/j.leaqua.2003.12.010

Mutale, W., Mwanamwenge, M. T., Balabanova, D., Spicer, N., & Ayles, H. (2013). Measuring governance at health facility level: Developing and validation of simple governance tool in Zambia. *BMC International Health and Human Rights, 13*(1). Advance online publication. DOI: 10.1186/1472-698x-13-34 PMID: 23927531

Mutonyi, B. R., González-Piñero, M., Slåtten, T., & Lien, G. (2024). Driving innovation in health care: Exploring the impact of ambidextrous leadership on creative performance among frontline health professionals in Norway. *BMC Health Services Research, 24*(1), 268. DOI: 10.1186/s12913-024-10641-9 PMID: 38431584

O'Connor, S. (2014). Leadership for future libraries. *Library Management, 35*(1/2), 78–87. https://www.emerald.com/lm/article/35/1-2/78/267697/Leadership-for-future-libraries

Oti-Boadi, M., Oppong Asante, K., & Malm, E. K. (2019). The Experiences of Ageing Parents of Young Adults with Autism Spectrum Disorders (ASD). *Journal of Adult Development*. Advance online publication. DOI: 10.1007/s10804-018-09325-6

Price, L., MacDonald, J., Gozdzielewska, L., Howe, T., Flowers, P., Shepherd, L., Watt, Y., & Reilly, J. (2018). Interventions to improve healthcare workers' hand hygiene compliance: A systematic review of systematic reviews. *Infection Control and Hospital Epidemiology, 39*(12), 1449–1456. DOI: 10.1017/ice.2018.262 PMID: 30526716

Ranmuthugala, G., Plumb, J. J., Cunningham, F. C., Georgiou, A., Westbrook, J. I., & Braithwaite, J. (2011). How and Why Are Communities of Practice Established in the Healthcare sector? a Systematic Review of the Literature. *BMC Health Services Research, 11*(1). Advance online publication. DOI: 10.1186/1472-6963-11-273 PMID: 21999305

Rost, J. C. (1991). *Leadership for the twenty-first century*. Praeger.

Shamir, B., & Eilam, G. (2005). "What's Your Story?" A Life-stories Approach to Authentic Leadership Development. *The Leadership Quarterly*, *16*(3), 395–417. DOI: 10.1016/j.leaqua.2005.03.005

Shipton, H., Armstrong, C., West, M., & Dawson, J. (2008). The impact of leadership and quality climate on hospital performance. *International Journal for Quality in Health Care : Journal of the International Society for Quality in Health Care*, *20*(6), 439–445. DOI: 10.1093/intqhc/mzn037 PMID: 18786932

Silva, A. (2016). What is leadership?. *Journal of business studies quarterly, 8*(1), 1.

Smith, A. M., Prom, M. C., & Ng, L. C. (2024). A Qualitative Investigation of Characteristics Impacting Clinical Decision Making in Integrated Behavioral Health Care. *The Journal of Behavioral Health Services & Research*, *51*(4), 561–587. DOI: 10.1007/s11414-024-09891-6 PMID: 38982024

Sørensen, K., Van den Broucke, S., Fullam, J., Doyle, G., Pelikan, J., Slonska, Z., & Brand, H. (2012). Health Literacy and Public health: A Systematic Review and Integration of Definitions and Models. *BMC Public Health*, *12*(1). Advance online publication. DOI: 10.1186/1471-2458-12-80 PMID: 22276600

Specchia, M. L., Cozzolino, M. R., Carini, E., Di Pilla, A., Galletti, C., Ricciardi, W., & Damiani, G. (2021). Leadership styles and nurses' job satisfaction. Results of a systematic review. *International Journal of Environmental Research and Public Health*, *18*(4), 1552. PMID: 33562016

Stogdill, R. M. (1950). Leadership, membership and organization. *Psychological Bulletin*, *47*(1), 1–14. DOI: 10.1037/h0053857

Strack, G., & Fottler, M. D. (2002). Spirituality and effective leadership in healthcare: Is there a connection? *Frontiers of Health Services Management*, *18*(4), 3–18. PMID: 12087690

Sukha, N. (2019). *Influence of leadership style on organisational citizenship behaviours (OCB's) in achieving innovation*. University of Pretoria. https://core.ac.uk/download/528258795.pdf

Tannenbaum, R., Weschler, I. R., & Massarik, F. (2015). *Leadership and organization: a behavioural science approach*. Routledge.

Thomas, S., Keegan, C., Barry, S., Layte, R., Jowett, M., & Normand, C. (2013). A framework for assessing health system resilience in an economic crisis: Ireland as a test case. *BMC Health Services Research*, *13*(1). Advance online publication. DOI: 10.1186/1472-6963-13-450 PMID: 24171814

Tierney, P., Farmer, S. M., & Graen, G. B. (2019). An examination of leadership and employee creativity: The relevance of traits and relationships. *Personnel Psychology, 52*(3), 591–620. DOI: 10.1111/j.1744-6570.1999.tb00173.x

Turner, P. (2018). *Leadership in healthcare: delivering organizational transformation and operational excellence.* Springer.

Vroom, V. H., & Yetton, P. W. (1973). *Leadership and decision-making.* University of Pittsburgh Press.

West, M., Eckert, R., & Pasmore, B. (2014, May 21). *Developing collective leadership for health care.* The King's Fund. https://www.kingsfund.org.uk/insight-and-analysis/reports/developing-collective-leadership-for-health-care

Womack, J. P., & Jones, D. T. (2003). *Lean Thinking: Banish Waste and Create Wealth in Your Corporation.* Free Press.

Wong, C. A., Cummings, G. G., & Ducharme, L. (2013). The Relationship between Nursing Leadership and Patient outcomes: A Systematic Review Update. *Journal of Nursing Management, 21*(5), 709–724. https://pubmed.ncbi.nlm.nih.gov/23865924/ PMID: 23865924

World Health Organization. (2010). *Framework for action on interprofessional education & collaborative practice.* World Health Organization. https://www.who.int/publications/i/item/framework-for-action-on-interprofessional-education-collaborative-practice

Yorges, S. L., Weiss, H. M., & Strickland, O. J. (1999). The effect of leader outcomes on influence, attributions, and perceptions of charisma. *The Journal of Applied Psychology, 84*(3), 428. PMID: 10380422

Yousef, R., & Zubi, K. A. (2023). Providing Home Healthcare Services for Patients during Pandemics: Applicability in Developing Countries. *Journal of Health Management, 25*(4), 772–778. DOI: 10.1177/09720634231215162

Zaccaro, S. J., LaPort, K., & Jose, I. (2013, January 1). *Attributes of successful leaders: A performance requirements approach.* https://www.researchgate.net/publication/287105619_Attributes_of_successful_leaders_A_performance_requirements_approach

ADDITIONAL READING

Bigland, C., Evans, D., Bolden, R., & Rae, M. (2020). Systems leadership in practice: Thematic insights from three public health case studies. *BMC Public Health*, *20*(1). Advance online publication. DOI: 10.1186/s12889-020-09641-1 PMID: 33203397

Bjegović Mikanović, V. (2016). Governance and management of health care institutions in Serbia: An overview of recent developments. *South Eastern European Journal of Public Health*, *5*(1), 81. https://www.seejph.com/index.php/seejph/article/view/81

Boamah, S. A., Laschinger, H. K. S., Wong, C., & Clarke, S. (2018). Effect of transformational leadership on job satisfaction and patient safety outcomes. *Nursing Outlook*, *66*(2), 180–189. DOI: 10.1016/j.outlook.2017.10.004 PMID: 29174629

Cummings, G. G., Tate, K., Lee, S., Wong, C. A., Paananen, T., Micaroni, S. P. M., & Chatterjee, G. E. (2018). Leadership Styles and Outcome Patterns for the Nursing Workforce and Work environment: A Systematic Review. *International Journal of Nursing Studies*, *85*(1), 19–60. DOI: 10.1016/j.ijnurstu.2018.04.016 PMID: 29807190

Imai, M. (1986). *Kaizen (Ky'zen): the key to Japan's competitive success*. Mcgraw-Hill.

Kohn, L. T., Corrigan, J., & Donaldson, M. S. (2000). *To err is human: Building a safer health system*. National Academy Press.

MANGANO. A. (2024). *Leadership across cultures: A global perspective*. Linkedin.com. https://www.linkedin.com/pulse/leadership-across-cultures-global-perspective-aurelien-mangano-nlidde/

Mattioli, M. (2018). *The Role of Followers in Leadership*. St. Bonaventure University Online. https://online.sbu.edu/blog/role-of-followers-in-leadership

Weil, T. P. (2013). Health management education in Europe and in the United States: A comparative review and analysis. *Health Services Management Research*, *26*(2-3), 76–85. DOI: 10.1177/0951484813512288 PMID: 25595004

Chapter 4
Theoretical Foundations and Philosophies of Healthcare Leadership

ABSTRACT

This chapter examines various leadership styles and their impact on organizational performance, employee engagement, and overall productivity. in healthcare settings. Transformational leadership inspires innovation and job satisfaction, motivating teams to enhance patient care quality. Transactional leadership ensures structure and compliance, effective in stable environments but less adaptable in dynamic ones. Servant leadership prioritizes employee well-being, fostering trust and loyalty, while charismatic leadership leverages personal vision but risks organizational instability upon leader departure. Strategic leadership aligns goals with long-term adaptability and sustainable growth. Multipliers amplify team potential, whereas diminishers stifle creativity. Toxic leadership, marked by unethical behavior, leads to low morale and high turnover. By integrating these styles with healthcare's complex, patient-centered challenges, this chapter proposes evidence-based strategies to enhance leadership effectiveness.

CONCEPTUALIZING HEALTHCARE LEADERSHIP

Healthcare leadership research has evolved significantly over recent decades, transitioning from traditional business-oriented theories—such as transactional and transformational leadership models—to frameworks specifically tailored to address the complex, interdisciplinary, and patient-centered challenges unique to healthcare settings. Healthcare leadership encompasses the ability to influence and mobilize individuals and teams toward achieving shared goals (Sfantou et al., 2017; West

DOI: 10.4018/979-8-3373-2225-4.ch004

et al., 2015). Unlike general leadership, healthcare leadership requires managing complex organizations where errors can have life-threatening consequences (West et al., 2015). Leadership philosophies in healthcare have traditionally ranged from hierarchical, command-and-control models that emphasize authority and structured decision-making, to contemporary relational and transformational approaches that prioritize collaboration, empowerment, and shared vision (Gilmartin & D'Aunno, 2007; Sfantou et al., 2017). Effective healthcare leadership is a multidimensional paradigm influenced by various factors, including individual behaviors of staff and patients, organizational hierarchical structures, and dynamics throughout the system. To systematically understand effective healthcare leadership, it is essential to integrate theories from leadership science, organizational theory, and holistic systems thinking.

EXPLORING LEADERSHIP STYLES

Researchers study leadership styles to address what underpins successful leaders. Leadership styles can affect the quality of wok life (Nanjundeswaraswamy & Swamy, 2014). Leadership has different styles (Charismatic, Servant Leadership, and Strategic Leadership; (Denmark, 1977). Transformational, transactional, and servant Leadership carry distinct implications for organizational Culture, team dynamics, and patient outcomes. According to Weberg (2010), the pioneering leadership style is Servanrt Leadership (S.L.), where the leader (prefers his followers and their desires and is eager to put followers' needs) over his interests and priorities (Barbuto & Wheeler, 2006). Furthermore, some researchers stated that there are two types of leaders: Diminishers, who operate in a way that shuts down the Intelligence of others. Multipliers: Leaders amplify Intelligence, produce better outcomes, and grow talent (Wiseman, Mckeown, & Covey, 2017). The Diminishers considered "Toxic Leadership (toxic silent killing) of the ambition of the workers, the organization and the deadly poisonous medicine to see their followers," (Kim, 2008).

Research into leadership styles seeks to understand the underlying principles that contribute to successful leadership. Different leadership styles influence organizational culture, team performance, and employee well-being in diverse ways. They also impact the quality of work life, which in turn affects employee engagement, job satisfaction, and overall organizational productivity (Nanjundeswaraswamy & Swamy, 2014). Leadership styles play a crucial role in shaping the way organizations adapt to challenges, foster innovation, and ensure sustainable growth.

Transformational Leadership in Healthcare: Theoretical Foundations, Efficacy, and Implications

Transformational leadership (TFL), rooted in Burns' (1978) foundational theory and expanded by Bass and Avolio (1994), emphasizes idealized influence, inspirational motivation, intellectual stimulation, and individualized consideration. This leadership style inspires and motivates followers through a shared vision, relationship-building, and empowerment (Bass & Riggio, 2006). In healthcare, transformational leaders foster psychological safety, enabling staff to report errors and suggest improvements without fear of punishment, thus enhancing problem identification and continuous quality improvement (Edmondson, 1999; Cummings et al., 2018). Transformational leadership is one of the most studied and widely recognized leadership styles. It emphasizes the ability to inspire and motivate employees to achieve their full potential, fostering a culture of innovation and change (Weberg, 2010). Transformational leaders are often characterized by their vision, charisma, intellectual stimulation, and individualized consideration, which empowers their teams. This leadership style has been linked to numerous positive organizational outcomes, including improved performance, higher employee satisfaction, and greater employee commitment (Bass & Avolio, 1994). Transformational leaders encourage creativity and adaptability, which is particularly important in fast-changing environments.

TFL motivates followers by articulating a compelling vision and encouraging intellectual stimulation to exceed expectations, appealing to higher-order needs and fostering commitment to shared goals (Bass & Riggio, 2006; Burns, 1978; Bass & Avolio, 1994). It comprises four core components: idealized influence (leaders as ethical role models earning respect and trust), inspirational motivation (clear vision energizing staff), intellectual stimulation (encouraging innovation and critical thinking), and individualized consideration (mentorship addressing unique developmental needs) (Bass & Riggio, 2006; Northouse, 2022). Together, these components foster motivation, empowerment, and high performance, making TFL particularly effective in complex healthcare settings (Hutchinson & Jackson, 2013). In healthcare, TFL encourages innovation, empowers professionals, and advances patient-centered goals. Green (2020) define TFL as fostering employee empowerment through initiative, autonomy, and engagement, correlating with higher job satisfaction, lower turnover, and improved patient outcomes including reduced adverse events and enhanced care quality. They highlight TFL's role in driving cultural change, continuous learning, and innovation while promoting trust, psychological safety, and open communication—factors crucial for organizational resilience amid complexity, technological change, and resource constraints. They also underscore challenges in developing TFL competencies, recommending targeted training incorporating emotional intelligence, experiential learning, coaching, and reflective practice to meet evolving healthcare demands.

Recent empirical studies support and extend these findings. Gabel et al. (2022) and Cummings et al. (2018) reinforce TFL's positive influence on outcomes, while Seljemo, Viksveen, & Ree (2020) identify mediators such as structural empowerment, organizational commitment, and job satisfaction. Asif et al. (2019) found TFL indirectly improves care quality and reduces adverse outcomes via job satisfaction and empowerment. Ree, Ellis, and Wiig (2021) demonstrated TFL's role in enhancing patient safety culture in nursing homes, and Labrague (2023) reported improved nurse-assessed care quality and reduced adverse events in emergency units through increased work satisfaction. Kakemam et al.'s (2024) scoping review confirmed TFL's benefits in staff retention, quality of care, and resource management, while Siangchokyoo and Klinger (2021) suggest exploring additional mediators and integrating newer leadership models.

Overall, transformational leadership fosters a patient-centered approach and nurse empowerment, enabling continuous learning and quality improvement (Boamah et al., 2018; Cummings et al., 2018). Empirical evidence consistently demonstrates its positive impact on patient outcomes. For example, Kutney-Lee et al. (2009) found hospitals with better nurse-reported leadership had significantly lower patient mortality and failure-to-rescue rates. Wong, Cummings, and Ducharme (2013) reported that effective nursing leadership correlated with decreased hospital-acquired infections, pressure ulcers, and falls. O'Connor (2014) showed supportive, communicative leadership improved patient satisfaction, pain management, and discharge readiness. Additionally, Shipton et al. (2008) found top management leadership predicted fewer patient complaints and higher hospital performance ratings in the NHS. Al-Thawabiya et al. (2023) demonstrated that transformational leadership improved patient care quality by increasing staff compliance and fostering a culture of accountability, with structural empowerment and job satisfaction mediating these effects. Lappalainen (2020) confirmed transformational leadership by nurse managers enhanced medication safety by reducing errors in acute care.

Case studies, such as Magnet Recognition Program hospitals in the United States, exemplify TFL's effectiveness, showing improved nurse satisfaction and retention, better patient outcomes (lower mortality, fewer complications), and increased organizational innovation. In summary, transformational leadership's emphasis on inspiring and motivating staff, fostering autonomy, collaboration, and innovation makes it highly effective in dynamic healthcare environments, contributing to improved clinical outcomes, workforce morale, and organizational performance.

Transactional Leadership in Healthcare: Theoretical Foundations, Efficacy, and Limitations

Transactional leadership, rooted in contingency theories, assumes followers are motivated primarily by rewards and punishments, emphasizing compliance with established rules and protocols to achieve organizational goals (Bass, 1985; Northouse, 2018). This leadership style is characterized by clear structures, supervision, and systems of rewards and penalties designed to ensure task completion and adherence to standards (Bass, 1990). Spinelli (2006) noted that transactional leadership remains prevalent in healthcare due to its focus on standardization, protocol adherence, and operational efficiency, especially in surgical and acute care settings. In contrast to transformational leadership, transactional leadership focuses on maintaining order, achieving established goals, and ensuring compliance with policies and procedures. It is often referred to as "management by exception," where leaders only intervene when deviations from standards occur (Weberg, 2010). Transactional leadership relies heavily on rewards and punishments as motivators to achieve desired outcomes. While this style is effective for managing short-term tasks and stable environments, it may be less suitable for organizations that require adaptability and innovation (Bass, 1990). In contexts where routine and efficiency are paramount, transactional leadership can be highly effective, but it lacks the ability to inspire and transform.

Transactional leadership works well to get people to follow the rules and keep things running smoothly, especially in high-risk situations when rigorous adherence to guidelines and consistent procedures are needed (Sfantou et al., 2017; Bender, 2016). For example, Shipton et al. (2008) found that transactional leadership in top management was linked to better hospital performance metrics. Poels et al. (2020) found that transactional leadership in homecare settings where clear task expectations are important led to higher patient satisfaction.

But everyone knows that transactional leadership has its problems. Its strict focus on defined duties and accountability may make it harder for healthcare organizations to be flexible and come up with new ideas in complex, changing situations (Poels et al., 2020; Sfantou et al., 2017). Boamah et al. (2018) discovered that transactional leadership was less linked to healthcare outcomes than transformational leadership, especially when it came to long-term innovation, staff motivation, and a culture of collaboration. Most scholars agree that while transactional leadership effectively manages routine tasks and short-term goals, it is less suitable for complex adaptive challenges requiring creativity, flexibility, and interdisciplinary problem-solving (Bass & Riggio, 2006; Yukl, 2020). Spinelli (2006) cautioned that over-reliance on transactional leadership limits adaptability in dynamic clinical contexts, potentially compromising patient-centered care. Consequently, an integrative leadership approach that blends transactional leadership's emphasis on structure and accountability with transformational leadership's focus on innovation, empowerment, and shared vision may optimize healthcare outcomes, balancing operational stability with adaptive capacity to address evolving patient and system needs.

Servant Leadership Theoretical Foundations, Efficacy, and Implications

Servant leadership, first introduced by Greenleaf (1970), centers on serving others to promote individual and organizational growth. In healthcare, this approach prioritizes the needs, development, and well-being of staff, fostering ethical behavior, empathy, humility, and empowerment (Greenleaf, 1977). Servant leaders cultivate trust and promote team cohesion through active listening, empathy, and stewardship—qualities essential for effective patient management (Spears, 2010; van Diggele et al., 2020). This philosophy builds high-trust environments that strengthen internal relationships among healthcare workers, which in turn improves teamwork, communication, and ultimately patient outcomes (Eva et al., 2019). Servant leadership is a style that prioritizes the leader's role as a servant to their followers. In this model, the leader focuses on the needs and well-being of their employees, fostering a supportive and nurturing environment (Barbuto & Wheeler, 2006). Servant leaders engage in behaviors such as listening, empathy, healing, awareness, persuasion, and stewardship. This approach aims to develop and grow followers while cultivating a community-oriented culture. Servant leadership has been shown to improve employee morale, loyalty, and trust, ultimately leading to higher levels of employee engagement and organizational performance (Greenleaf, 1977). Leaders who embrace this style often inspire commitment and foster a sense of belonging within their teams.

Recent reviews corroborate servant leadership's positive effects on staff trust, job satisfaction, and organizational social responsibility, which have downstream benefits for patient care quality (Wahlstrom, 2024). However, further longitudinal research is needed to assess its long-term impacts on staff retention and patient safety. By aligning leadership with patient-centered values, servant leadership fosters collaboration, ethical practice, and staff well-being—factors critical to enhancing care quality and safety in complex healthcare settings (Eva et al., 2019; Greenleaf, 1970, 1977).

Charismatic Leadership Theoretical Foundations, Efficacy, and Implications

Charismatic leadership relies on the personal charm, vision, and emotional appeal of the leader to inspire and motivate followers. Charismatic leaders possess the ability to articulate a compelling vision for the future, instilling a sense of purpose and direction in their teams (Conger & Kanungo, 1987). The strong personal connection charismatic leaders form with their followers often results in high levels of motivation, enthusiasm, and organizational commitment. However, this leadership style can also have drawbacks. Over-reliance on a single, charismatic leader may leave the organization vulnerable to disruption if that leader departs (House, 1977). Charismatic leaders can drive significant change, but their impact may be dependent on their personal presence.

Strategic Leadership Theoretical Foundations, Efficacy, and Implications

Strategic leadership is centered on aligning an organization's goals with its mission, vision, and values. Strategic leaders operate at the intersection of leadership and strategic management, making decisions that have long-term implications for the organization's success. They are responsible for forecasting challenges, analyzing trends, and creating strategies that drive sustainable growth (Boal & Hooijberg, 2000). This style emphasizes adaptability, forward-thinking, and effective change management. Strategic leaders play a key role in guiding organizational transformation, fostering innovation, and promoting learning throughout the organization (Ireland & Hitt, 1999). The strategic leadership approach is particularly essential in environments that require vision and adaptability to navigate uncertainty.

Diminishers and Multipliers Theoretical Foundations, Efficacy, and Implications

Wiseman, Mckeown, and Covey (2017) categorize leaders into two distinct types: Diminishers and multipliers.

Diminishers

These leaders suppress the intelligence, creativity, and potential of their followers. By dominating conversations, making all decisions unilaterally, and failing to acknowledge the capabilities of team members, diminishers stifle innovation and growth. Kim (2008) refers to diminishers as engaging in "toxic leadership," as their behavior undermines employee morale and inhibits organizational potential.

Multipliers

In contrast, multipliers amplify the intelligence, creativity, and potential of their teams. They encourage independent thinking, empower employees to take initiative, and promote higher levels of performance. Multipliers create a culture of continuous improvement, learning, and growth, leading to higher innovation, employee development, and organizational success (Wiseman, Mckeown, & Covey, 2017).

The distinction between diminishers and multipliers offers valuable insight into how leaders can shape organizational culture and drive outcomes, with multipliers fostering an environment where employees feel empowered and valued.

Toxic Leadership Theoretical Foundations, Efficacy, and Implications

Toxic leadership refers to leadership behaviors that are destructive and counterproductive to organizational health. These behaviors can include narcissism, authoritarianism, bullying, and unethical decision-making. Toxic leaders use their position of power to manipulate, intimidate, and control their followers, often undermining their well-being and morale (Kim, 2008). Toxic leadership is often subtle and difficult to detect, but over time, it leads to high levels of stress, burnout, low employee morale, and high turnover rates. Organizations under toxic leadership may suffer from reduced productivity, damaged reputations, and eroded employee trust (Padilla, Hogan, & Kaiser, 2007). Preventing toxic leadership requires awareness and active efforts to cultivate a supportive and ethical work environment.

Authentic Leadership Theoretical Foundations, Efficacy, and Implications

Authentic leadership is defined by self-awareness, relational transparency, balanced processing of information, and an internalized moral perspective (Walumbwa et al., 2008). This leadership style emphasizes genuineness and ethical behavior, which fosters trust and psychological safety among healthcare professionals—key elements for effective interprofessional collaboration and patient-centered care. Research demonstrates that authentic leadership enhances staff empowerment, job satisfaction, and work engagement, particularly among new graduate nurses, which indirectly leads to improved patient outcomes (Giallonardo, Wong, & Iwasiw, 2010; Wong & Laschinger, 2013). By promoting open communication and ethical decision-making, authentic leaders create supportive environments where healthcare teams can thrive amidst complexity and dynamic clinical challenges. These qualities underscore authentic leadership's relevance and positive impact within healthcare settings striving to improve workforce morale and patient care quality.

Clinical Leadership Theoretical Foundations, Efficacy, and Implications

Clinical leadership is commonly exercised by frontline healthcare professionals, such as nurses and physicians, who focus on direct patient care, fostering teamwork, and implementing evidence-based practices. Effective clinical leaders demonstrate approachability, strong communication skills, and visibility, all of which contribute to reducing patient complaints and enhancing overall patient satisfaction (Khrais & Nashwan, 2023). For instance, during the COVID-19 pandemic, clinical leaders at Singapore General Hospital played a pivotal role in rapidly implementing protocols, minimizing healthcare worker infections, and maintaining essential non-COVID services, illustrating how operational decision-making authority improves system responsiveness during crises (Tan et al., 2020). Similarly, clinical leaders within England's Clinical Commissioning Groups (CCGs) have been instrumental in service redesign by advocating for tailored interventions addressing complex patient needs, promoting collaboration between commissioners and providers, and improving service delivery outcomes.

Distributed, Collaborative, and Shared Leadership Theoretical Foundations, Efficacy, and Implications

In healthcare settings, dispersed, collaborative, and shared leadership styles are becoming more and more important, in addition to individual leadership styles. These models break down hierarchical barriers by giving team members leadership roles based on their skills and the needs of the situation, rather than their formal position. This encourages shared decision-making, collective sense-making, and team cohesion (Spillane, 2006; Uhl-Bien, 2006; Denis, Langley, & Sergi, 2012). In healthcare, which is a complex adaptive system, distributed leadership is especially important since it allows for quick decision-making, makes use of expertise from many fields, and encourages adaptability (West, Armit, Loewenthal, Eckert, West, & Lee, 2015). Studies that use real data show that these methods work. Distributed leadership makes organizations learn, adapt, and coordinate better, which lowers mistakes and improves patient outcomes, especially in high-stress situations like trauma centers and intensive care units (Martin, Currie, & Finn, 2009; West et al., 2015). Collaborative leadership makes it easier for professionals to work together, reduces conflict, and reinforces shared team goals. This leads to better service delivery through co-designed experimentation and adaptive problem-solving (Belrhiti,

Giralt, & Marchal, 2018; Lowe, 2025). Bolton, Brunnermeier, and Veldkamp (2013) found that shared leadership encourages professionals from different fields to work together, which improves patient care on multidisciplinary teams. West et al. (2015) say that leadership should be spread out among multidisciplinary teams because healthcare organizations are so complicated. This will give frontline practitioners more influence, stimulate collaborative problem-solving, and drive patient-centered innovation. Using these leadership approaches together makes organizations more resilient, flexible, and able to provide better care.

Complexity Leadership Theoretical Foundations, Efficacy, and Implications

Complexity leadership theory is based on complexity science and combines administrative, enabling, and adaptive leadership to deal with the nonlinear and changing nature of complex adaptive systems like healthcare (Uhl-Bien, Marion, & McKelvey, 2007). This method works well for dealing with the unforeseen and linked problems that come up in modern healthcare settings, especially during times of crisis. The COVID-19 pandemic showed how important complexity leadership is because healthcare organizations had to deal with quick changes and unpredictability that needed flexible responses (Wu et al., 2022).

Instead of depending only on traditional hierarchical management, complexity leadership focuses on enabling adaptive behaviors, encouraging innovation, and making relationships within organizations more dynamic (Uhl-Bien et al., 2007). It focuses on making it possible for frontline personnel and teams to organize themselves and work together to address problems as they come up. This is very important in healthcare systems as things are always changing and people are dependent on each other. Complexity leadership improves an organization's ability to adapt and respond to changing patient and system needs by balancing administrative tasks with adaptive leadership.

Systems Theory Leadership Theoretical Foundations, Efficacy, and Implications

Systems theory conceptualizes organizations as open systems comprised of interrelated and interdependent components that interact dynamically with each other and the external environment (von Bertalanffy, 1968). Leadership within this framework is understood as both influencing and being influenced by these broader systemic factors, necessitating a holistic perspective on organizational functioning. This theory is especially relevant to healthcare, where the effective management of interactions among clinical teams, administrative units, and external regulatory bodies is critical for delivering high-quality patient care (Begun, Zimmerman, & Dooley, 2003).

In healthcare organizations, systems theory encourages leaders to consider not only individual components but also the relationships and feedback loops that impact system behavior. By adopting a systems thinking approach, healthcare leaders can better address complexity, improve coordination across disciplines, and anticipate the consequences of decisions within a broader organizational and environmental context. This holistic viewpoint supports continuous learning and adaptation in response to evolving healthcare demands and regulatory pressures.

HEALTHCARE LEADERSHIP COMPARATIVE ANALYSIS OF EFFICACY

The following tables present a structured comparative analysis of leadership styles in healthcare, synthesizing evidence from recent systematic reviews and theoretical frameworks. Table 1 examines the relative efficacy of transformational, servant, transactional, collaborative, and complexity leadership across patient outcomes, workforce morale, and organizational performance, while acknowledging methodological limitations in existing research. Table 2 outlines practical implications derived from these findings, offering actionable recommendations for leadership development and contextual adaptation in healthcare settings. Finally, Table 3 highlights current gaps in the literature and directions for future research to strengthen the evidence base and inform leadership practice across diverse healthcare contexts.

Table 1. Comparative analysis of healthcare leadership styles in healthcare

Leadership Style	Theoretical Foundations	Core Characteristics	Efficacy in Healthcare Settings	Limitations / Considerations	Key References
Transformational	Burns (1978); Bass & Avolio (1994)	Idealized influence, inspirational motivation, intellectual stimulation, individualized consideration	Enhances staff morale, patient satisfaction, innovation, and system improvement	Risk of burnout if overused; requires high emotional intelligence and trust	Bass & Avolio (1994); Spinelli (2006)
Transactional	Bass (1990); Burns (1978)	Contingent rewards, structured goals, passive/ active management by exception	Effective for short-term outcomes, crisis management, and performance incentives	May suppress creativity and long-term innovation	Bass (1990); Podsakoff et al. (1984)
Servant	Greenleaf (1970, 1977)	Empathy, listening, stewardship, community building	Promotes team cohesion, ethical behavior, and trust; improves patient-centered care	May be less effective in fast-paced or hierarchical systems	Spears (1995); Eva et al. (2019)
Charismatic	House (1977); Conger & Kanungo (1987)	Visionary influence, emotional connection, personal charm	Inspires motivation and loyalty, particularly in change efforts	Risk of overdependence on leader; unsustainable if personality-driven	Conger & Kanungo (1987); Shamir, House, & Arthur (1993)
Strategic	Boal & Hooijberg (2000); Ireland & Hitt (1999)	Vision alignment, long-term planning, environmental scanning	Supports sustainable reform and system-wide transformation	Requires systems thinking and strategic planning capacity; slow impact	Boal & Hooijberg (2000); Wolfson & Rowe (2001)
Multipliers	Wiseman, Mckeown, & Covey, (2017)	Amplifies team intelligence and autonomy	Enhances team creativity, learning, and problem-solving	Ineffective if leader fails to recognize individual strengths	Wiseman, Mckeown, & Covey, (2017)
Toxic	Padilla, Hogan, & Kaiser (2007); Kim (2008)	Narcissism, micromanagement, unethical control	May deliver short-term performance gains under pressure	Leads to burnout, staff turnover, and poor culture	Padilla, Hogan, & Kaiser (2007); Lipman-Blumen (2005)

continued on following page

Table 1. Continued

Leadership Style	Theoretical Foundations	Core Characteristics	Efficacy in Healthcare Settings	Limitations / Considerations	Key References
Authentic	Walumbwa et al. (2008); Avolio & Gardner (2005)	Self-awareness, transparency, moral perspective	Builds ethical cultures, improves staff engagement and patient satisfaction	May be perceived as slow or soft in urgent scenarios	Walumbwa et al. (2008); Wong & Laschinger (2019)
Clinical	Tan (2023); Awadat et al. (2023)	Frontline decision-making, patient focus, clinical insight	Directly improves patient outcomes and rapid responses to care needs	Needs strong clinical credibility; may lack broader strategic impact	Awadat et al. (2023); Stanley (2017)
Distributed / Collaborative	Spillane (2006); West et al. (2015)	Shared leadership, collective accountability	Enhances team decision-making, engagement, and interprofessional collaboration	May cause confusion without clear boundaries; slower decision-making	Spillane (2006); West et al. (2015)
Complexity	Uhl-Bien et al. (2007); Plowman et al. (2007)	Adaptive, systems-based, enabling leadership	Ideal for dynamic healthcare environments, fosters resilience and innovation	Requires high tolerance for ambiguity and change	Uhl-Bien et al. (2007); Marion & Gonzales (2013)
Systems Theory	von Bertalanffy (1968); Begun, Zimmerman, & Dooley (2003)	Holistic thinking, interconnectivity, feedback loops	Facilitates integrated decision-making, long-term sustainability	May require cultural shift and long-term investment	Begun, Zimmerman, & Dooley (2003); Senge (2006); von Bertalanffy (1968)

SUMMARY OF LEADERSHIP STYLES

The wide range of leadership styles discussed in this chapter highlights the complexity and diversity of modern leadership practices. Effective leadership in healthcare is vital for navigating the intricate challenges of modern systems, where leaders must foster innovation, collaboration, and patient-centered care amidst workforce shortages, technological advancements, and governance complexities. This chapter explores a spectrum of leadership styles—transformational, transactional, servant, charismatic, strategic, authentic, clinical, distributed, collaborative, shared, complexity, and systems theory leadership—alongside the contrasting dynamics of diminishers, multipliers, and toxic leadership. Each style shapes organizational culture, team dynamics, and patient outcomes differently, offering unique strengths and limitations for addressing the demands of dynamic healthcare environments. By understanding these approaches, healthcare leaders can adopt strategies that enhance employee engagement, improve care quality, and ensure systemic resilience.

Transformational leadership inspires healthcare teams by articulating a compelling vision, encouraging innovation, and empowering individuals to exceed expectations. This approach fosters a culture of psychological safety, where staff feel confident reporting errors or suggesting improvements, leading to enhanced patient safety and care quality. For example, hospitals adopting this style often see reduced errors, such as infections or patient falls, alongside higher staff satisfaction and retention. Transformational leaders prioritize mentorship and individualized support, creating environments that drive continuous learning and adaptability, though developing these skills requires dedicated training in emotional intelligence and reflective practice. Transactional leadership, in contrast, emphasizes structure, clear expectations, and rewards or corrective actions to ensure compliance with protocols. This style excels in high-stakes settings like surgical units, where adherence to standards is critical for patient safety and operational efficiency. However, its focus on routine tasks can limit flexibility in rapidly changing environments, making it less effective for fostering innovation or addressing complex challenges. Servant leadership centers on prioritizing the well-being and development of staff, cultivating trust, empathy, and team cohesion. By creating supportive workplaces, servant leaders enhance employee morale and patient care quality, aligning with healthcare's patient-centered ethos, though its long-term impacts require further exploration. Charismatic leadership relies on a leader's personal vision and charm to inspire teams, driving motivation and commitment but risking instability if the leader leaves. Strategic leadership aligns organizational goals with long-term adaptability, fostering sustainable growth and innovation in response to technological and regulatory shifts. Authentic leadership, grounded in self-awareness and ethical decision-making, builds trust and psychological safety, particularly among new healthcare professionals, enhancing teamwork and patient outcomes. Clinical leadership, led by frontline providers like nurses and physicians, focuses on direct care and evidence-based practices, improving patient satisfaction and system responsiveness, as seen in rapid protocol implementation during health crises. Distributed, collaborative, and shared leadership models empower frontline staff by breaking down hierarchical barriers, leveraging diverse expertise to enhance adaptability and reduce errors in high-pressure settings like intensive care units. These approaches promote collective decision-making and co-designed solutions, improving service delivery and patient outcomes. Complexity leadership addresses healthcare's unpredictable challenges by balancing administrative oversight with adaptive, innovative behaviors, proving essential during crises like pandemics. Systems theory leadership views healthcare organizations as interconnected systems, encouraging leaders to manage relationships and feedback loops holistically to improve coordination and adaptability across clinical and administrative units.

In contrast, diminishers suppress team creativity and morale, stifling innovation, while multipliers amplify staff potential, fostering environments of growth and high performance. Toxic leadership, marked by unethical or authoritarian behaviors, undermines morale, increases turnover, and compromises care quality, necessitating proactive efforts to cultivate supportive cultures. No single leadership style is universally effective in healthcare. Integrating transformational and servant leadership's emphasis on empowerment with transactional leadership's structure, alongside distributed, collaborative, and complexity approaches for adaptability, equips leaders to address multifaceted challenges. This blended approach fosters equitable, high-quality care, enhances workforce engagement, and ensures organizational resilience in the face of evolving healthcare demands. A summary of the key characteristics of these leadership styles is provided in **Table 2**. This summary highlights the core differences between styles and offers insights into their implications for organizations and employees. Table 2 below summarizes the leadership styles. Leadership styles and components on which leadership styles affect (Nanjundeswaraswamy & Swamy, 2014).

Table 2. The leadership styles

Author(s)	Dimensions of Leadership Styles	Components	Type of Industry	Outcomes
Burns (1978), Bass & Avolio (1994)	Transformational Leadership	Idealized influence, inspirational motivation, intellectual stimulation, individualized consideration	Healthcare	Improved job satisfaction, reduced turnover, enhanced patient outcomes, higher innovation and empowerment
Bass (1990), Spinelli (2006)	Transactional Leadership	Contingent reward, management by exception (active/ passive), structured goals, reward/ punishment	Acute care, surgery	Operational efficiency, task completion, short-term goals met, limited adaptability
Greenleaf (1970, 1977)	Servant Leadership	Empathy, stewardship, listening, commitment to growth of others, community building	Healthcare	Increased trust, job satisfaction, team cohesion, ethical practice, enhanced care quality
Conger & Kanungo (1987), House (1976)	Charismatic Leadership	Vision articulation, personal charm, emotional appeal	General (various)	High motivation and loyalty, risk of dependence on leader
Boal & Hooijberg (2000), Ireland & Hitt (1999)	Strategic Leadership	Vision alignment, adaptability, long-term planning, strategic foresight	Healthcare & Corporate	Sustained growth, organizational transformation, innovation
Wiseman, Mckeown, & Covey, (2017); Kim (2008)	Multipliers vs. Diminishers	Amplifying intelligence vs. suppressing creativity	General	Multipliers: talent development & innovation; Diminishers: toxic culture, reduced morale
Kim (2008), Padilla, Hogan, & Kaiser (2007)	Toxic Leadership	Narcissism, authoritarianism, unethical control, suppression	General	High burnout, low morale, high turnover, reduced productivity
Walumbwa et al. (2008), Wong & Laschinger (2019)	Authentic Leadership	Self-awareness, relational transparency, balanced processing, internalized moral perspective	Healthcare	Staff empowerment, ethical climate, improved engagement and patient care

continued on following page

Table 2. Continued

Author(s)	Dimensions of Leadership Styles	Components	Type of Industry	Outcomes
Tan (2023)	Clinical Leadership	Direct patient care, communication, visibility, responsiveness	Healthcare	Better patient satisfaction, rapid crisis response, improved frontline coordination
Spillane (2006), West et al. (2015)	Distributed / Shared / Collaborative Leadership	Shared decision-making, collective leadership, teamwork	Multidisciplinary Healthcare	Improved adaptability, better team cohesion, higher-quality service delivery
Uhl-Bien et al. (2007), Wu et al. (2022)	Complexity Leadership	Adaptive, enabling, administrative leadership	Complex systems (healthcare)	Enhanced resilience, system responsiveness, innovation during crisis
von Bertalanffy (1968), Begun, Zimmerman, & Dooley (2003)	Systems Theory Leadership	Systems thinking, feedback loops, holistic perspective	Healthcare Systems	Better coordination, systemic problem-solving, continuous learning and adaptability
Nanjundeswaraswamy & Swamy (2014)	Quality of Work Life and Leadership Impact	Work-life balance, job satisfaction, engagement	General	Enhanced morale, organizational productivity

LEADERSHIP GENDER EFFECT

Research into gender effects on leadership has consistently highlighted distinct differences in the approaches men and women take when leading teams or organizations. These differences are not merely anecdotal but are supported by a growing body of empirical studies that analyze leadership behaviors across various contexts and cultures. Below, I'll elaborate on the initial findings, extend the discussion with additional insights, and integrate citations to provide a robust foundation for the analysis. One seminal study by Eagly and Johannesen-Schmidt (2001) conducted a meta-analysis of leadership styles and gender, synthesizing data from multiple research efforts spanning decades. Their findings underscored that while men and women are equally capable of effective leadership, their styles tend to diverge in meaningful ways. Women, for instance, are often associated with transformational leadership—a style characterized by inspiring and motivating followers, fostering innovation, and emphasizing personal development. This aligns with broader social expectations of women as nurturers, which may translate into leadership behaviors that prioritize collaboration and empathy. Building on this, more recent work by Eagly and Johannesen-Schmidt delves deeper into the nuances of transformational leadership, particularly the dimension of individualized consideration. This facet involves leaders paying close attention to the needs of individual followers, offering tailored support, and acting as mentors or coaches. Eagly and Johannesen-Schmidt's 2023 study, published in Leadership Quarterly, found that female leaders consistently outperformed their male counterparts in this area. The research attributes this partly to socialization processes that encourage women to develop strong interpersonal skills and emotional intelligence—qualities that enhance their ability to connect with and uplift their teams. For example, in organizational settings ranging from corporate boardrooms to nonprofit sectors, women leaders were rated higher by subordinates for fostering a supportive environment.

In contrast, men are more frequently observed employing transactional leadership styles, such as active management-by-exception and passive management-by-exception. Mekonnin (2014), in a study of Ethiopian business leaders, described active management-by-exception as a style where leaders intervene only when standards are not met, focusing on correcting deviations rather than proactively inspiring change. Passive management-by-exception, meanwhile, involves even less engagement, with leaders stepping in only after problems escalate significantly. Asegu and Gedifew (2022), in a comparative analysis of leadership in East African public sectors, corroborated these findings, noting that male leaders leaned toward these structured, reactive approaches more often than their female counterparts. This may reflect societal norms that emphasize authority and control in male leadership roles, as opposed to the relational focus often seen in women. Beyond these core distinctions, additional research provides a broader perspective. For instance, a study by Bass and Riggio (2006) on transformational and transactional leadership frameworks suggests that while gender influences style, context also plays a critical role. In high-stakes, competitive environments—like finance or military settings—men's transactional tendencies may be more pronounced, whereas women's transformational strengths shine in collaborative or creative industries, such as education or healthcare. Furthermore, a cross-cultural analysis by Hofstede (2001) indicates that cultural masculinity or femininity can amplify or mitigate these gender-based differences, adding another layer of complexity. To extend this discussion, it's worth considering how these leadership styles impact organizational outcomes. A 2018 study by Zenger and Folkman, published in the Harvard Business Review, found that women scored higher overall in leadership effectiveness, particularly in competencies like collaboration, resilience, and adaptability—all hallmarks of transformational leadership. Meanwhile, men's strengths in decisiveness and strategic planning, often linked to transactional styles, were notable but less consistently tied to long-term team satisfaction or innovation.

REFERENCES

Al-Thawabiya, A., Singh, K., Al-Lenjawi, B. A., & Alomari, A. (2023). Leadership styles and transformational leadership skills among nurse leaders in Qatar, a cross-sectional study. *Nursing Open*, *10*(6), 3440–3446. PMID: 36760040

Asegu, D. A., & Gedifew, M. T. (2022). Lived experiences of secondary school principals in practicing teacher leadership. *Global Journal of Education and Training*, *5*(8), 1–12.

Asif, M., Jameel, A., Hussain, A., Hwang, J., & Sahito, N. (2019). Linking Transformational Leadership with Nurse-Assessed Adverse Patient Outcomes and the Quality of Care: Assessing the Role of Job Satisfaction and Structural Empowerment. *International Journal of Environmental Research and Public Health*, *16*(13), 2381. DOI: 10.3390/ijerph16132381 PMID: 31277478

Barbuto, J. E.Jr, & Wheeler, D. W. (2006). Scale development and construct clarification of servant leadership. *Group & Organization Management*, *31*(3), 300–326.

Bass, B. M. (1985). *Leadership and Performance beyond Expectations*. Free Press.

Bass, B. M. (1990). *Bass & Stogdill's Handbook of Leadership: theory, research, and Managerial Applications* (3rd ed.). Free Press.

Bass, B. M., & Avolio, B. J. (1994). *Improving Organizational Effectiveness Through Transformational leadership*. Sage Publications.

Bass, B. M., & Riggio, R. E. (2006). *Transformational Leadership* (2nd ed.). Routledge.

Begun, J. W., Zimmerman, B., & Dooley, K. (2003). *Health care organizations as complex adaptive systems. 253*, 253–288. https://www.researchgate.net/publication/228384399_Health_care_organizations_as_complex_adaptive_systems

Belrhiti, Z., Giralt, A. N., & Marchal, B. (2018). Complex leadership in healthcare: A scoping review. *International Journal of Health Policy and Management*, *7*(12), 1073. PMID: 30709082

Bender, M. (2016). Conceptualizing clinical nurse leader practice: An interpretive synthesis. *Journal of Nursing Management*, *24*(1), E23–E31. PMID: 25655928

Boal, K. B., & Hooijberg, R. (2000). Strategic leadership research: Moving on. *The Leadership Quarterly*, *11*(4), 515–549. DOI: 10.1016/s1048-9843(00)00057-6

Boamah, S. A., Laschinger, H. K. S., Wong, C., & Clarke, S. (2018). Effect of transformational leadership on job satisfaction and patient safety outcomes. *Nursing Outlook*, *66*(2), 180–189. DOI: 10.1016/j.outlook.2017.10.004 PMID: 29174629

Bolton, P., Brunnermeier, M. K., & Veldkamp, L. (2013). Leadership, coordination, and corporate culture. *The Review of Economic Studies*, *80*(2), 512–537.

Burns, J. M. (1978). *Leadership*. Harper & Row.

Conger, J. A., & Kanungo, R. N. (1987). Toward a behavioral theory of charismatic leadership in organizational settings. *Academy of Management Review*, *12*(4), 637–647. DOI: 10.2307/258069

Cummings, G. G., Tate, K., Lee, S., Wong, C. A., Paananen, T., Micaroni, S. P. M., & Chatterjee, G. E. (2018). Leadership Styles and Outcome Patterns for the Nursing Workforce and Work environment: A Systematic Review. *International Journal of Nursing Studies*, *85*(1), 19–60. DOI: 10.1016/j.ijnurstu.2018.04.016 PMID: 29807190

Denis, J.-L., Langley, A., & Sergi, V. (2012). Leadership in the Plural. *The Academy of Management Annals*, *6*(1), 211–283.

Eagly, A. H., & Johannesen-Schmidt, M. C. (2001). The Leadership Styles of Women and Men. *The Journal of Social Issues*, *57*(4), 781–797. DOI: 10.1111/0022-4537.00241

Edmondson, A. (1999). Psychological Safety and Learning Behavior in Work Teams. *Administrative Science Quarterly*, *44*(2), 350–383. DOI: 10.2307/2666999

Eva, N., Robin, M., Sendjaya, S., van Dierendonck, D., & Liden, R. C. (2019). Servant leadership: A systematic review and call for future research. *The Leadership Quarterly*, *30*(1), 111–132. DOI: 10.1016/j.leaqua.2018.07.004

Gabel Shemueli, R., Tzafrir, S., Rodriguez Perez, B., Bahamonde, D., & Enosh, G. (2022). Collective compass to unit performance: Linking transformational leadership climate, trust and engagement. *Leadership and Organization Development Journal*, *43*(5), 802–813.

Giallonardo, L. M., Wong, C. A., & Iwasiw, C. L. (2010). Authentic leadership of preceptors: Predictor of new graduate nurses' work engagement and job satisfaction. *Journal of Nursing Management*, *18*(8), 993–1003. DOI: 10.1111/j.1365-2834.2010.01126.x PMID: 21073571

Gilmartin, M. J., & D'Aunno, T. A. (2007). Leadership Research in Healthcare. *The Academy of Management Annals*, *1*(1), 387–438. DOI: 10.5465/078559813

Green, J. P. (2020). *A taxonomy of leadership situations: Development, validation, and implications for the science and practice of leadership* (Doctoral dissertation, George Mason University).

Greenleaf, R. K. (1970). *The Servant as Leader.* Greenleaf Center for Servant Leadership.

Greenleaf, R. K. (1977). *Servant leadership: A Journey into the Nature of Legitimate Power and Greatness.* Paulist Press.

Hofstede, G. (2001). *Culture's Consequences: Comparing values, behaviors, institutions, and Organizations across Nations* (2nd ed.). Sage.

House, R. J. (1976, October). *A 1976 Theory of Charismatic Leadership. Working Paper Series 76-06.* Ed.gov. https://eric.ed.gov/?id=ED133827

Hutchinson, M., & Jackson, D. (2013). Transformational Leadership in nursing: Towards a More Critical Interpretation. *Nursing Inquiry*, *20*(1), 11–22. PMID: 23033817

Ireland, R. D., & Hitt, M. A. (1999). Achieving and Maintaining Strategic Competitiveness in the 21st Century: The Role of Strategic Leadership. *The Academy of Management Perspectives*, *13*(1), 43–57.

Kakemam, E., Ahmed Hassan Albelbeisi, Mahtab Rouzbahani, Mehdi Gharakhani, Zahedi, H., & Taheri, R. (2024). Nurses' perceptions of patient safety competency: A cross-sectional study of relationships with occurrence and reporting of adverse events. *PLoS One*, *19*(1), e0297185–e0297185. DOI: 10.1371/journal.pone.0297185 PMID: 38271447

Khrais, H., & Nashwan, A. J. (2023). Leadership practices as perceived by emergency nurses during the COVID-19 pandemic: The role of structural and psychological empowerment. *Journal of Emergency Nursing: JEN*, *49*(1), 140–147. PMID: 36369071

Kim, J. S. (2008). Examining the effectiveness of solution-focused brief therapy: A meta-analysis. *Research on Social Work Practice*, *18*(2), 107–116. DOI: 10.1177/1049731507307807

Kutney-Lee, A., McHugh, M. D., Sloane, D. M., Cimiotti, J. P., Flynn, L., Neff, D. F., & Aiken, L. H. (2009). Nursing: A Key To Patient Satisfaction. *Health Affairs*, *28*(Supplement 3), w669–w677. DOI: 10.1377/hlthaff.28.4.w669 PMID: 19525287

Labrague, L. J. (2023). Relationship between Transformational leadership, Adverse Patient events, and nurse-assessed Quality of Care in Emergency units: The Mediating Role of Work Satisfaction. *Australasian Emergency Care (Online)*, *27*(1), 49–56. DOI: 10.1016/j.auec.2023.08.001 PMID: 37598031

Lappalainen, P. (2020). Walking and talking sensors: Conceptualising restorative leadership to enhance people management education in engineering. *European Journal of Engineering Education*, *45*(3), 473–490.

Lipman-Blumen, J. (2005). Toxic leadership: When grand illusions masquerade as noble visions. *Leader to Leader*, *2005*(36), 29–36. DOI: 10.1002/ltl.125

Lowe, M. E. (2025). *Breaking the Stained Glass Ceiling: Collaborative Leadership Theory as a Model for Women in Theological Higher Education*. DigitalCommons@ University of Nebraska - Lincoln. https://digitalcommons.unl.edu/jwel/12/

Martin, G. P., Currie, G., & Finn, R. (2009). Leadership, service reform, and public-service networks: The case of cancer-genetics pilots in the English NHS. *Journal of Public Administration: Research and Theory*, *19*(4), 769–794.

Mekonnin, L. (2014). *Females Participation in Educational Leadership in Secondary Schools of Ilu Aba Bora Zone* (Doctoral dissertation, The Institute of Development Studies and Partner Organisations).

Nanjundeswaraswamy, T. S., & Swamy, D. R. (2014). Leadership styles. *Advances in management,* 7(2), 57.

Northouse, P. G. (2018). *Leadership: Theory and Practice* (8th ed.). Sage Publications.

Northouse, P. G. (2022). *Leadership: Theory and Practice* (9th ed.). Sage Publications.

O'Connor, S. (2014). Leadership for future libraries. *Library Management*, *35*(1/2), 78–87. https://www.emerald.com/lm/article/35/1-2/78/267697/Leadership-for-future-libraries

Padilla, A., Hogan, R., & Kaiser, R. B. (2007). The Toxic triangle: Destructive leaders, Susceptible followers, and Conducive Environments. *The Leadership Quarterly*, *18*(3), 176–194. DOI: 10.1016/j.leaqua.2007.03.001

Plowman, D. A., Baker, L. T., Beck, T. E., Kulkarni, M., Solansky, S. T., & Travis, D. V. (2007). Radical Change Accidentally: The Emergence and Amplification of Small Change. *Academy of Management Journal*, *50*(3), 515–543. DOI: 10.5465/amj.2007.25525647

Poels, J., Verschueren, M., Milisen, K., & Vlaeyen, E. (2020). Leadership styles and leadership outcomes in nursing homes: A cross-sectional analysis. *BMC Health Services Research, 20*(1), 1009. PMID: 33148249

Ree, E., Ellis, L. A., & Wiig, S. (2021). Managers' role in supporting resilience in healthcare: a proposed model of how managers contribute to a healthcare system's overall resilience. *International Journal of Health Governance, ahead-of-print*(ahead-of-print). DOI: 10.1108/ijhg-11-2020-0129

Seljemo, C., Viksveen, P., & Ree, E. (2020). The Role of Transformational leadership, Job Demands and Job Resources for Patient Safety Culture in Norwegian Nursing homes: A cross-sectional Study. *BMC Health Services Research, 20*(1), 1–8. DOI: 10.1186/s12913-020-05671-y PMID: 32847598

Senge, P. (2006). *The Fifth Discipline: The Art and Practice of the Learning Organization* (2nd ed.). Doubleday/Currency.

Sfantou, D., Laliotis, A., Patelarou, A., Sifaki-Pistolla, D., Matalliotakis, M., & Patelarou, E. (2017). Importance of leadership style towards quality of care measures in healthcare settings: A systematic review. *Healthcare, 5*(4), 73. NCBI. DOI: 10.3390/healthcare5040073

Shamir, B., House, R. J., & Arthur, M. B. (1993). The motivational effects of charismatic leadership: A self-concept based theory. *Organization Science, 4*(4), 577–594. DOI: 10.1287/orsc.4.4.577

Shipton, H., Armstrong, C., West, M., & Dawson, J. (2008). The impact of leadership and quality climate on hospital performance. *International Journal for Quality in Health Care : Journal of the International Society for Quality in Health Care, 20*(6), 439–445. DOI: 10.1093/intqhc/mzn037 PMID: 18786932

Siangchokyoo, N., & Klinger, R. L. (2021). Shared Leadership and Team Performance: The Joint Effect of Team Dispositional Composition and Collective Identification. *Group & Organization Management, 47*(1), 105960112110199. DOI: 10.1177/10596011211019928

Spears, L. (2010). *Character and servant leadership: Ten characteristics of effective, caring leaders* (pp. 25–30). https://www.regent.edu/wp-content/uploads/2020/12/Spears_Final.pdf

Spillane, J. P. (2006). *Distributed Leadership*. ResearchGate. https://www.researchgate.net/publication/233061505_Distributed_Leadership

Spinelli, R. J. (2006). The Applicability of Bass's Model of Transformational, Transactional, and Laissez-Faire Leadership in the Hospital Administrative Environment. *Hospital Topics*, *84*(2), 11–19. DOI: 10.3200/htps.84.2.11-19 PMID: 16708688

Stanley, D. (2017). *Clinical leadership in nursing and healthcare: Values into action* (2nd ed.). John Wiley & Sons.

Tan, K. L. (2023). Responsible leadership-a brief review of literature. *Journal of Responsible Tourism Management*, *3*, 44–55.

Uhl-Bien, M. (2006). Relational Leadership Theory: Exploring the Social Processes of Leadership and Organizing. *The Leadership Quarterly*, *17*(6), 654–676. DOI: 10.1016/j.leaqua.2006.10.007

Uhl-Bien, M., Marion, R., & McKelvey, B. (2007). Complexity leadership theory: Shifting leadership from the industrial age to the knowledge era. *The Leadership Quarterly*, *18*(4), 298–318. DOI: 10.1016/j.leaqua.2007.04.002

van Diggele, C., Burgess, A., Roberts, C., & Mellis, C. (2020). Leadership in healthcare education. *BMC Medical Education*, *20*, 1–6. PMID: 33272264

Von Bertalanffy, L. (1968). *General system theory*. New York, 41973(1968), 40.

Wahlstrom, G. (2024, December). *Healthcare Leadership 2024: A Year in Review*. The Healthcare Executive. https://www.thehealthcareexecutive.net/newsletter/healthcare-leadership-2024/

Walumbwa, F. O., Avolio, B. J., Gardner, W. L., Wernsing, T. S., & Peterson, S. J. (2008). Authentic leadership: Development and validation of a theory-based measure. *Journal of Management*, *34*(1), 89–126. DOI: 10.1177/0149206307308913

Weberg, D. (2010). Transformational leadership and innovation in healthcare. *Journal of Healthcare Leadership*, *2*, 35.

West, M., Armit, K., Loewenthal, L., Eckert, R., West, T., & Lee, A. (2015, February 25). *Leadership and Leadership Development in Health Care*. https://www.kingsfund.org.uk/insight-and-analysis/reports/leadership-development-health-care

Wiseman, L., Mckeown, G., & Covey, S. R. (2017). *Multipliers: how the best leaders make everyone smarter*. Harper Business.

Wolfson, M., & Rowe, G. (2001) . On measuring inequalities in health. Bulletin of the World Health Organization, *79* (6) , 553 - 560. World Health Organization. https://iris.who.int/handle/10665/268350

Wong, C. A., Cummings, G. G., & Ducharme, L. (2013). The Relationship between Nursing Leadership and Patient outcomes: A Systematic Review Update. *Journal of Nursing Management, 21*(5), 709–724. PMID: 23865924

Wong, C. A., & Laschinger, H. K. S. (2019). Authentic leadership, performance, and job satisfaction: The mediating role of empowerment. *Journal of Advanced Nursing, 69*(4), 947–959. DOI: 10.1111/j.1365-2648.2012.06089.x PMID: 22764828

Wu, C. H., Weisman, H., Sung, L. K., Erdogan, B., & Bauer, T. N. (2022). Perceived overqualification, felt organizational obligation, and extra-role behavior during the COVID-19 crisis: The moderating role of self-sacrificial leadership. *Applied Psychology, 71*(3), 983–1013. PMID: 36433921

Yukl, G. A. (2020). *Leadership in organizations* (8th ed.). Pearson Education, Inc.

Zenger, J., & Folkman, J. (2018). Women score higher than men in most leadership skills. *Leadership & Leaders*. https://leadershipandleaders.com/knowledge-skills-attributes-behaviours/women-score-higher-than-men-in-most-leadership-skills-jack-zenger-joseph-folkman-harvard-business-review/

ADDITIONAL READING

Byq, T., Nws, C., & Gkh, L. M, J., Y, G., Lll, Y., K, Z., Hk, C., A, A., Fa, K., Gn, S., Bpl, C., S, S., B, C., Jjy, O., Pr, P., Lyh, W., R, S., Jt, C., & Ay, Y. N. (2020, April 6). *Psychological Impact of the COVID-19 Pandemic on Health Care Workers in Singapore*. Annals of Internal Medicine. https://pubmed.ncbi.nlm.nih.gov/32251513/

Çoban, C. (2022). The dark side of leadership: A conceptual assessment of toxic leadership. *Business Economics and Management Research Journal, 5*(1), 50–61.

Deng, C., Gulseren, D., Isola, C., Grocutt, K., & Turner, N. (2022). Transformational Leadership effectiveness: An evidence-based Primer. *Human Resource Development International, 26*(5), 627–641. DOI: 10.1080/13678868.2022.2135938

Eagly, A. H., Johannesen-Schmidt, M. C., & van Engen, M. L. (2003). Transformational, transactional, and laissez-faire leadership styles: A meta-analysis comparing women and men. *Psychological Bulletin, 129*(4), 569–591. DOI: 10.1037/0033-2909.129.4.569 PMID: 12848221

Liden, R. C., Wang, X., & Wang, Y. (2025). The evolution of leadership: Past insights, present trends, and future directions. *Journal of Business Research, 186*, 115036.

Ratnapalan, S., & Lang, D. (2019). Health Care Organizations as Complex Adaptive Systems. *The Health Care Manager*, *39*(1), 1. DOI: 10.1097/hcm.0000000000000284 PMID: 31876589

Tsapnidou, E., Kelesi, M., Rovithis, M., Katharakis, G., Gerogianni, G., Dafogianni, C., Toylia, G., Fasoi, G., & Stavropoulou, A. (2024). Transformational leadership—quality achievements and benefits for the healthcare organizations: A scoping review. *Hospitals*, *1*(1), 87–103. DOI: 10.3390/hospitals1010008

Ystaas, L. M. K., Nikitara, M., Ghobrial, S., Latzourakis, E., Polychronis, G., & Constantinou, C. S. (2023). The impact of transformational leadership in the nursing work environment and patients' outcomes: A systematic review. *Nursing Reports*, *13*(3), 1271–1290. DOI: 10.3390/nursrep13030108 PMID: 37755351

Chapter 5
Exploration of Healthcare Leadership (HCL)

ABSTRACT

This chapter examines the dynamic role of Healthcare Leadership (HCL) in ensuring the efficiency and effectiveness of healthcare systems. While leadership and management are interconnected, HCL emphasizes shared leadership, where responsibilities are distributed to enhance performance. Over time, HCL has evolved alongside technological advancements and e-health, requiring leaders to drive sustainability and innovation. Effective HCL fosters collaboration, innovation, and positive organizational change while addressing the complexities of modern healthcare systems. The chapter also explores leadership assessment, which is crucial for evaluating strengths, improving healthcare outcomes, and aligning leadership with strategic goals. Continuous professional development is essential for cultivating skilled leaders. Additionally, healthcare governance plays a key role in maintaining service quality, accountability, and equitable care. According to the WHO, strong governance structures are essential for addressing policy changes and resource allocation.

HEALTHCARE LEADERSHIP OVERVIEW

Healthcare leadership (HCL) and management are closely intertwined, yet distinct, as both play pivotal roles in achieving organizational success in healthcare settings. They are not mutually exclusive but rather complement each other, working together to ensure efficient and effective delivery of services. Healthcare administrators, in particular, are tasked with high-level responsibilities that include navigating complex systems and making decisions that shape the trajectory of healthcare delivery (Lee et al., 2021). Leadership in healthcare is rooted in the concept of shared leadership, where leadership responsibilities are distributed across individuals and teams to maximize effectiveness in achieving organizational goals (Algahtani, 2014). Research

DOI: 10.4018/979-8-3373-2225-4.ch005

consistently emphasizes that engaged, accessible, and dynamic healthcare leadership is a fundamental component of healthcare excellence (Adair et al., 2022). HCL is no longer confined to the traditional hierarchical structures of healthcare organizations (McAlearney, 2006) and is instead evolving due to technological advancements and the rise of e-health transformations (Hartley & Benington, 2010). These changes underscore the critical role of leadership in shaping the future of healthcare systems (Chatterjee et al., 2018). The increasing complexity and demands placed on healthcare systems necessitate an adaptable and proactive leadership approach (Kumar & Khiljee, 2016), which is defined by an ability to manage organizational pressures and rapid advancements (Sahertian & Graha, 2016; Weberg, 2020).

Healthcare leadership extends beyond mere management; it involves guiding healthcare systems toward future sustainability and innovation (Robbins & Davidhizar, 2020). The definition of healthcare leadership varies across contexts, but it is commonly described as the ability to inspire, guide, and influence individuals and groups toward a shared vision, fostering collaboration, innovation, and positive change (Avolio & Yammarino, 2013; Weberg, 2020). It also entails understanding oneself, clearly communicating a vision, building trust among colleagues, and taking strategic actions to realize leadership potential (Kumar & Khiljee, 2016). Leadership in healthcare is therefore a dynamic process that requires both personal and organizational vision, adaptability, and the capacity to inspire others.

HEALTHCARE LEADERSHIP ASSESSMENT

Researchers agree that the strengthening of Health Systems is absolute. Strengthening must start with a broad-based assessment of the system's environment, allow objective baseline and follow-up evaluations, inform stakeholders of aspects of the Leadership in healthcare, build consensus around the priority needs, and mobilize joint technical and financial support for improving Leadership in healthcare, and this can be achieved by overcoming weak areas by development and training courses, attracting qualified and creative talents (Tierney, Farmer, & Graen, 1999). Leadership assessment in healthcare is paramount for complete organizational success. It can identify areas of strength that may need professional skill development, leading to more robust health system performance and improved public health. Assessment should be comprehensive and cover the many aspects and planning for its strengthening, involves implementing robust management systems (erban & Herciu, 2019). Through this research, Enhanced by different global assessment tools (American College of Healthcare Executives, National Health Service Leadership Academy Global Healthcare Leadership Competency Model).

HEALTHCARE LEADERSHIP GOVERNANCE

Healthcare leadership and governance are critical elements of any effective health system, ensuring that services are delivered efficiently and in alignment with organizational objectives. Healthcare leadership assessment is a cornerstone of improving health systems and ensuring quality care delivery. Strengthening health systems requires a comprehensive approach that begins with assessing the current environment, identifying gaps, and aligning leadership with the system's strategic goals. Researchers agree that strengthening health systems is essential and must start with a broad-based assessment that allows for objective baseline evaluations, follow-up assessments, and the identification of leadership strengths and weaknesses (Shoukat, Shah, & Muneeb, 2023; de Kok et al., 2023). The World Health Organization (WHO) has emphasized that leadership and governance are integral to the health system's overall performance. In fact, leadership and governance are considered one of the six core building blocks of health systems, alongside service delivery, health workforce, information, medical products, and financing as shown in Figure 1, The WHO Health Systems Framework (2010) (WHO, 2010). Effective leadership assessment in healthcare is critical for developing a high-functioning and responsive health system. It not only informs stakeholders of leadership performance but also builds consensus on priority areas that need improvement and mobilizes both technical and financial resources. Leadership evaluation must go beyond measuring technical skills; it must also assess the alignment of leaders' decisions with organizational goals, patient outcomes, and the overall quality of care.

One of the key steps in healthcare leadership assessment is addressing weak areas through targeted development and training programs, as well as attracting creative and qualified talents (Tierney, Farmer, & Graen, 1999). By focusing on continuous professional development and leadership capacity-building, healthcare systems can ensure they are adaptive to challenges and ready to implement effective solutions (Hipp, 2023). Leadership assessment also supports organizational success by identifying areas where professional skills need enhancement, which in turn strengthens health system performance and improves public health outcomes. Healthcare leadership assessment must be comprehensive, examining all facets of leadership, from governance to clinical care, and creating strategies for strengthening leadership within the healthcare system (Mutonyi et al., 2024; Durrah & Kahwaji, 2023; Yousef, 2023). This includes implementing robust management systems and using strategic assessments to evaluate both strengths and weaknesses, which serve as the baseline for future improvements (erban & Herciu, 2019; ACHE 2024). For example, the author has developed a specialized leadership assessment tool through a collaborative process, allowing for continuous monitoring and improvement with the support of experts from both local and international health systems. This tool is further enhanced by globally recognized frameworks, such as those from the American College of Healthcare Executives and the National Health Service Leadership Academy, which support the development of leadership competencies in healthcare systems worldwide.

The role of leadership in healthcare governance is multifaceted. It involves setting strategic directions, making key decisions, and ensuring accountability to stakeholders. Effective governance in healthcare not only ensures the quality of care but also fosters a culture of transparency, collaboration, and ethical decision-making (Dwyer et al., 2006; Khudyakov et al., 2014). Leadership in this context goes beyond administrative functions; it is about creating an environment where innovation can thrive, patient care is prioritized, and the workforce is motivated and engaged. The WHO's framework underscores the importance of governance structures that are both responsive and accountable to the needs of the population, with a focus on equity and accessibility in healthcare delivery. As healthcare systems become more complex, the role of leadership in governance must evolve to address emerging challenges, including policy changes, resource allocation, and evolving public health needs (Khudyakov et al., 2014). Furthermore, effective healthcare leadership and governance are essential for navigating the increasing complexity of healthcare systems, which require leaders to balance strategic planning with day-to-day operational demands.

Figure 1. The WHO health systems framework (2010)

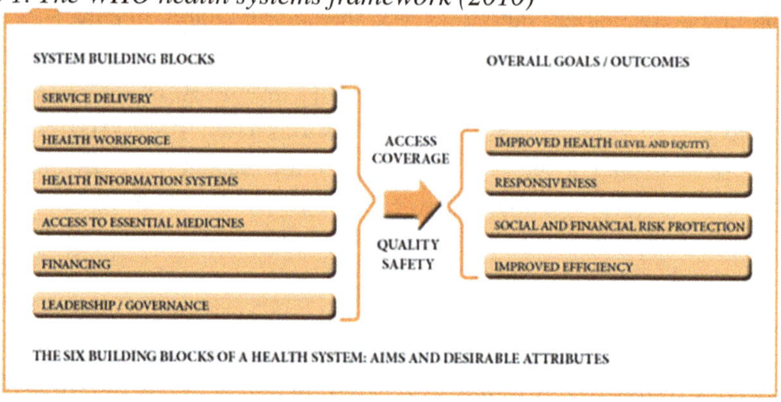

REFERENCES

ACHE. (2024). ACHE [*Competencies Assessment Tool.* https://www.ache.org/-/media/ache/career-resource-center/cat-competencies-assessment-tool.pdf]. *Healthcare Executive, 2024.*

Adair, K. C., Levoy, E., Tawfik, D. S., Palassof, S., Profit, J., Frankel, A., Leonard, M., & Sexton, J. B. (2022). Assessing leadership behavior in health care: Introducing the Local Leadership Scale of the SCORE Survey. [PMC]. *Joint Commission Journal on Quality and Patient Safety*, *49*(3), 166–173. DOI: 10.1016/j.jcjq.2022.12.007 PMID: 36717344

Algahtani, A. (2014). Are leadership and management different? A review. *Journal of management policies and practices*, 2(3), 71-82.

Avolio, B. J., & Yammarino, F. J. (2013). *Transformational And Charismatic Leadership: The Road Ahead.* Emerald Group Publishing.

Chatterjee, R., Suy, R., Yen, Y., & Chhay, L. (2018). Literature review on leadership in healthcare management. *J Soc Sci Stud*, *5*(1), 38–47.

Durrah, O., & Kahwaji, A. (2023). Chameleon leadership and innovative behavior in the health sector: The mediation role of job security. *Employee Responsibilities and Rights Journal*, *35*(2), 247–265. PMID: 40477989

Dwyer, J., Paskavitz, M., Vriesendorp, S., & Johnson, S. (2006). *An urgent call to professionalize leadership and management in health care worldwide.* Management Sciences for Health.

de Kok, E. Schoonhoven, L., Pieterbas Lalleman, & Anne Marie Weggelaar-Jansen. (2023). Understanding rebel nurse leadership-as-practice: Challenging and changing the status quo in hospitals. *Nursing Inquiry*, *30*(4). Advance online publication. DOI: 10.1111/nin.12577 PMID: 37408336

Hartley, J., & Benington, J. (2010). *Leadership for healthcare*. Policy Press.

Hipp, F. (2023). *The Effect of a Leadership Development Program on Healthcare Leaders* (Doctoral dissertation, The University of North Carolina at Charlotte).

Khudyakov, A., Jean, C., Jankovic, M., Cardinal, J. S. L., & Bocquet, J. C. (2014). Simulation methods in the healthcare systems. In *Complex Systems Design & Management: Proceedings of the Fourth International Conference on Complex Systems Design & Management CSD&M 2013* (pp. 141-149). Cham: Springer International Publishing.

Kumar, R. D., & Khiljee, N. (2016). Leadership in healthcare. *Anaesthesia and Intensive Care Medicine*, *17*(1), 63–65.

Lee, T. H., Volpp, K. G., Cheung, V. G., & Dzau, V. J. (2021). Diversity and inclusiveness in health care leadership: Three key steps. *NEJM Catalyst Innovations in Care Delivery*, *2*(3).

McAlearney, A. S. (2006). Leadership development in healthcare: A qualitative study. *Journal of Organizational Behavior*, *27*(7), 967–982. DOI: 10.1002/job.417

Mutonyi, B. R., González-Piñero, M., Slåtten, T., & Lien, G. (2024). Driving innovation in health care: Exploring the impact of ambidextrous leadership on creative performance among frontline health professionals in Norway. *BMC Health Services Research*, *24*(1), 268. PMID: 38431584

Robbins, B., & Davidhizar, R. (2020). Transformational leadership in health care today. *The Health Care Manager*, *39*(3), 117–121. PMID: 32701607

. Sahertian, P., & Graha, A. N. (2016). Exploring leadership dimension among organizations (the analysis against leadership excellence based on cultural and ethnical backgrounds in Indonesia). *Indian Journal of Commerce and Management Studies,* *7*(1), 01-07

erban, R.-A., & Herciu, M. (2019). Performance Management Systems – Proposing and Testing a Conceptual Model. *Studies in Business and Economics*, *14*(1), 231–244. DOI: 10.2478/sbe-2019-0018

Shoukat, M. H., Shah, S. A., & Muneeb, D. (2023). Shared leadership and team performance in health care: How intellectual capital and team learning intervene in this relationship. *The Learning Organization*L: *An International Journal*. https://www.emerald.com/tlo/article/30/4/426/456261/Shared-leadership-and-team-performance-in-health

Tierney, P., Farmer, S. M., & Graen, G. B. (1999). An examination of leadership and employee creativity: The relevance of traits and relationships. *Personnel Psychology*, *52*(3), 591–620. DOI: 10.1111/j.1744-6570.1999.tb00173.x

Weberg, D. (2020). Transformational Leadership and Staff Retention. *Nursing Administration Quarterly*, *34*(3), 246–258. DOI: 10.1097/naq.0b013e3181e70298 PMID: 20562573

WHO. 2010 - World Health Organization (WHO). (2010). *Leadership and Governance 85*. Geneva: WHO Press. https://cdn.who.int/media/docs/default-source/service-availability-and-readinessassessment(sara)/related-links-(sara)/who_mbhss_2010_section6_web.pdf?sfvrsn=71928980_3

Yousef, H. (2023). Strategic Healthcare Leadership Assessment for Global Health Systems. *Global Health Journal (Amsterdam, Netherlands)*, *28*(1), 77–92.

Chapter 6
Healthcare Leadership Competencies:
Foundations, Applications, and Emerging Challenges

ABSTRACT

Healthcare leadership (HCL) is pivotal to organizational success and effective care delivery. Effective leaders require a diverse skill set that goes beyond traditional management, including time and task management, multitasking, adaptability, emotional intelligence and strategic thinking. A crucial aspect of HCL is the ability to manage crises effectively, demonstrate originality, and remain resilient under pressure. Additionally, leaders must excel in communication, motivation, and team guidance. At the same time the healthcare organizations and leaders face Potential Challenges To Proposed Healthcare Leadership Competencies, Main concerns include the cultural, ethical and social bias, overemphasis on leaders soft personal skills, and lack of proper change management and the adaptability to multi-dimensional diverse settings Ultimately, healthcare leadership is an evolving field that requires balancing technical expertise, emotional intelligence, and the ability to inspire others, ensuring improved outcomes for both patients and healthcare professionals.

BACKGROUND

Healthcare leadership (HCL) is a central aspect of the administrative process and is key to an organization's overall competency and success (Al-Maliki, 2020; Kalaitzi et al., 2019). Effective healthcare leaders are distinguished by a combination of competencies and behaviors that enhance their effectiveness in the workplace and are essential for the sustained success of healthcare organizations (Behrens, 2014;

DOI: 10.4018/979-8-3373-2225-4.ch006

Ashade, 2020). These competencies go beyond traditional management roles and encompass a diverse set of skills necessary to navigate the complex healthcare environment (Dwyer et al., 2006; Wiley, 2013). A blend of time management, effective oversight, multitasking, and prioritization is essential, along with the ability to adapt to rapidly changing healthcare environments (Al-Ghamdi et al., 2024; Culp, 1992; Goleman, Boyatzis, & McKee, 2013). Furthermore, these leaders must demonstrate a commitment to continuous improvement, resilience, and the capacity to manage the challenges inherent in healthcare systems (Bass, 1985; Lasrado & Kassem, 2021). HCL is not limited to typical managerial behaviors but extends to strategic leadership, emphasizing the ability to inspire, guide, and engage others in the pursuit of common goals (Sahertian & Jawas, 2021; Sahertian & Graha, 2016; Beauvais, 2018; Terry, 1998. A key framework for understanding these competencies is the Leadership Efficacy Model, which identifies three essential components: philosophy, practice, and criteria (Lisá et al., 2023). The model suggests that effective healthcare leaders not only excel in operational competencies but also possess a deep understanding of their leadership approach and the ability to enact positive changes within their organizations.

Healthcare leadership is considered a basic concept for the administrative process (Al-Maliki, 2020), and leadership actions reflect an organization's competency (Kalaitzi et al., 2019). HCL requires a high competency, hold a set of observable behaviors that, with deliberate practice, enable them to be more effective in the workplace" (Behrens, 2014; Ashade, 2020) Moreover, (Wiley, 2013; Dwyer et al., 2006) goes beyond traditional managerial roles or managerial behavior, (Sahertian & Jawas, 2021; Sahertian & Graha, 2016; Beauvais, 2018; Terry, 1998) have good time management, (Al-Haddad & Psych, 2003; Finzel, 2007; Goleman, Boyatzis, & McKee, 2013; Alghamdi et al., 2024; Culp, 1992; Finzel, 2007; Goleman, Boyatzis, & McKee, 2013) boosts productivity and health services improvement (Ellis, 2025; De Brún, O'Donovan, & McAuliffe, 2019), focus on tasks carried out (Spreier, Fontaine, & Malloy, 2006), educate others (Lobdell et al., 2020), have effective oversight (WHO, 2008), can multitask, (Al-Ghamdi, 2020; Culp, 1992; Finzel, 2007; Goleman, Boyatzis, & McKee, 2013); ability to prioritize (Al-Ghamdi et al., 2024; Culp, 1992; Finzel, 2007; Goleman, Boyatzis, & McKee, 2013), boost productivity and health services improvement (Ellis, 2021; De Brún, O'Donovan, & McAuliffe, 2019), have the inherent elements of the Leadership Efficacy Model, Philosophy, Practice, and Criteria, (Lisá et al., 2023) have good crisis management with its dimensions (problem sensitivity, originality, initiative, and perseverance). Others stated that excellence in Leadership refers to the highest level of leadership performance characterized by exceptional skills, qualities, outcomes, and experiences (Bass, 1985; Ni ă, 2015; Lasrado & Kassem, 2021) that work in rapidly changing regulations environment and increasing demands for quality patient care (Siraj-Blatchford, Siraj, & Manni, 2007).

HEALTHCARE LEADERSHIP CORE COMPETENCIES

Several core competencies are crucial to effective healthcare leadership like "TIME MANAGEMENT" he should hold Strong time management skills, and Efficient task prioritization, where Healthcare leaders must efficiently allocate their time to balance multiple responsibilities, set priorities, and meet deadlines. Effective time management leads to enhanced productivity and improved patient care outcomes (Al-Haddad & Psych, 2003; Finzel, 2007; Goleman, Boyatzis, & McKee, 2013; Alghamdi et al., 2024; Culp, 1992)." TASK MANAGEMENT AND OVERSIGHT" where healthcare leadership have s and Proficient in organizing tasks and ensuring accountability strong capability in managing and overseeing assignments where Healthcare leaders are responsible for ensuring that key tasks are completed efficiently and that operational workflows are optimized. The ability to prioritize and manage various tasks simultaneously improves service delivery and overall healthcare outcomes (Spreier, Fontaine, & Malloy, 2006; WHO, 2008; Ellis, 2025; De Brún, O'Donovan, & McAuliffe, 2019).also hold "EDUCATIONAL AND DEVELOPMENTAL ROLE," he should have the cabability of instructional and capacity-building role beside teaching and professional development function and role in learning facilitation and skill enhancement, where As mentors, health-care leaders play a critical role in educating and guiding their teams, fostering a culture of continuous learning and professional development. This competency is vital for maintaining high standards of care and ensuring patient safety (Lobdell et al., 2020). Also, experts in "HEALTHCARE LEADERSHIP RISK AND CRISIS MANAGEMENT" where effective leaders in healthcare are expected to manage crises with problem sensitivity, originality, initiative, and perseverance. Their ability to act decisively during emergencies strengthens the organization's resilience and ensures that patient care continues during challenging times (Lisá et al., 2023). Demonstrates and provs strong leadership efficacy by consistently guiding teams toward achieving strategic goals "LEADERSHIP EFFICACY" where healthcare The Leadership Efficacy Model highlights the importance of philosophical alignment, practical application of leadership principles, and clear criteria for assessing leadership performance. Leaders who excel in these areas are better equipped to guide organizations toward achieving strategic goals (Lisá et al., 2023). Exhibits robust leadership" ADAPTABILITY AND FLEXIBILITY" by adapting speedily to change and remaining flexible in managing diverse operational demands where hHealthcare leaders must be highly adaptable, given the constantly evolving healthcare regulations and patient care demands. Their ability to navigate regulatory changes while maintaining the quality of care is essential for organizational success (Siraj-Blatchford, Siraj, & Manni, 2007). And finally, "EXCELLENCE IN LEADERSHIP" beside showing a high level of leadership competence, fostering trust, motivation, and collaboration he must be characterized by exceptional decision-making, emotional intelligence, and the capacity to inspire others. Leaders who exhibit these qualities are considered to have mastered their craft, leading their teams with vision, integrity, and effectiveness (Bass, 1985; Ni ă, 2015; Lasrado & Kassem, 2021).

HEALTHCARE LEADERSHIP CONTINUOUS LEARNING AND SELF-IMPROVEMENT

Excellency in Leadership refers to the highest level of leadership performance (Bass, 1985; Ni ă, 2015), continuous learning and self-improvement are among the tools and fundamental strategies for developing effective HCL and achieving sustainable success (Al-Issa & Omar, 2024) and achieve changeability (Turyadi et al., 2023; Piotrowski, 2020), the continuous learning can be achieved through ongoing education and commitment to assessing and improving healthcare leadership and processes (Carayon et al., 2006; Hargett et al., 2017), adopting new ideas, (Quinn & Spreitzer, 1997; Alolab, Ayupp, & Dwaikat, 2021); Advance HCL skills in technical, cognitive, and emotional competencies (Richards, 2020), encourages attention to detail (Shalley & Lemoine, 2018) staying abreast of the latest trends, engaging in self-directed learning, and looking for best healthcare practices. (Al-Issa & Omar, 2024; Turyadi et al., 2023; Piotrowski, 2020), and stay updated on medical advancements (Hargett et al., 2017). These competencies collectively ensure that healthcare leaders are equipped to address the unique challenges of the healthcare sector. By fostering an environment where strategic thinking, innovation, and collaboration are prioritized, healthcare leaders can improve both organizational performance and patient outcomes (Beauvais, 2018). Effective healthcare leadership, therefore, is integral to the ongoing evolution of healthcare systems and the delivery of high-quality care. **Table 1** below shows the healthcare competencies.

Table 1. Summary table of healthcare leadership competencies

Competency	Description	Related References
Time Management	Efficient use of time, prioritizing tasks, and managing multiple responsibilities to enhance productivity and health outcomes.	Al-Ghamdi et al. (2024), Goleman, Boyatzis, & McKee (2013), Culp (1992)
Task Management and Oversight	Overseeing operational workflows and ensuring tasks are executed effectively and on time.	Spreier, Fontaine, & Malloy (2006), WHO (2008), Ellis (2025)
Educational and Developmental Role	Promoting knowledge-sharing, mentoring, and continuous professional development to improve service quality and patient safety.	Lobdell et al. (2020)
Crisis Management	Leading decisively and effectively during crises, demonstrating problem sensitivity, initiative, and perseverance.	Lisá et al. (2023), Al-Sarhan & Al-Oyouni (2018)
Leadership Efficacy	A holistic approach to leadership involving philosophy, practice, and measurable outcomes to achieve organizational goals.	Lisá et al. (2023), Al-Sarhan & Al-Oyouni (2018)
Adaptability and Flexibility	Adapting to changing healthcare demands, regulations, and evolving patient care needs.	Siraj-Blatchford, Siraj, & Manni (2007)
Excellence in Leadership	Exceptional leadership skills, including emotional intelligence, strategic thinking, and the ability to inspire and guide others.	Bass (1985), Ni ă (2015), Lasrado & Kassem (2021)

POTENTIAL CHALLENGES TO PROPOSED HEALTHCARE LEADERSHIP COMPETENCIES

The suggested healthcare leadership skills are meant to help executives deal with difficult problems, but there have been a number of complaints about how they are designed and put into action. One big problem is that skills sometimes presume that they can be used in any situation and that they are too broad or Western-focused, not taking into consideration the fact that people come from different cultures, work in different organizations, and have different resources (Hofstede, 1984). For instance, competencies that stress shared governance or distributed leadership may not work well in hierarchical or collectivist cultures where authority is usually centralized. On the other hand, competencies that focus on advanced data analytics may not be useful in places that don't have enough resources or systems that can work together. Another complaint is that frameworks put too much focus on soft skills like communication, emotional intelligence, and transformational behaviors while not enough on clinical credibility and operational skills that are necessary for good leadership (Garman & Johnson, 2006; Geerts, 2018). This imbalance may make it hard for leaders to deal with real-world problems like budget cuts or following the rules.

Also, nurse leaders who don't have the most up-to-date clinical expertise may have trouble gaining trust on the front lines, even if they are good at working with people.

Another worry is that competency frameworks often show idealized leader profiles that no one person can fully embody, which can lead to burnout, imposter syndrome, or not prioritizing competencies that are relevant to the situation (Shanafelt & Noseworthy, 2019). Critics also say that competency inflation is bad since it doesn't have measurable effects. They say that competencies could become buzzwords that don't have clear behavioral indicators or show how they affect patient care and organizational performance (Yukl, 2012). Competency-based approaches may also not take into account structural and systemic barriers, which means that improving leadership is only an individual effort and ignores systemic problems like chronic staff shortages or lack of funding, which can make competencies impractical for smaller facilities (Denis & Van Gestel, 2016).

Another problem is that models tend to focus on individual leaders, even though modern healthcare systems need team-based leadership across specialties and levels (West et al., 2015). Also, many frameworks don't have enough empirical validation and evaluation, and they often rely on expert consensus instead of thorough empirical testing. This makes it hard to know if they are useful in all situations and how they relate to clinical and organizational outcomes (Calhoun et al., 2008; Golinelli et al., 2020). Resistance from current leaders is also common, especially when new skills threaten established hierarchies or call for major changes in behavior. For example, older leaders have pushed back against digital literacy requirements or transformational approaches that they think are less important than traditional management skills (Kotter, 1995; Saifman, Patel, & Williams, 2023).

A major problem is that leaders aren't getting enough training on health equity and cultural competence. This means they aren't prepared to deal with differences in care delivery, language challenges, or community mistrust, which makes them less useful in diverse or underserved areas (Brown, 2021). Also, competency overload is a practical problem since suggesting too many skills can make leaders who are already under a lot of stress from their work feel overwhelmed, which can make it harder for them to focus and make things happen, especially for those who have to do both clinical and administrative work. Finally, there isn't much evidence of impact because there isn't enough empirical data connecting competences to real-world results like better patient care, lower costs, or happier staff. This makes organizations doubt their worth and return on investment (Geerts, 2018).

To deal with these concerns, people who design healthcare leadership competencies should make sure that the frameworks are useful in real-world situations and test them out using pilot programs. They need to give clear guidelines on how to prioritize soft skills, technical skills, and skills that focus on fairness. Training that is easy to get, such online classes and peer mentorship, can help with little resources. Competencies should be linked to measurable, evidence-based results utilizing strong assessment techniques. It's important to teach people how to deal with socioeconomic and policy problems, and to get input from all stakeholders, including leaders, clinicians, and patients, to make sure the plan is relevant, doable, and supported. In the end, healthcare leadership development can better prepare leaders to make real changes in complicated healthcare settings by adapting frameworks, balancing skill types, and focusing on a small number of key skills.

Current healthcare management organizations is a complex arena that requires a subtle balance between delivering high-quality patient care, ensuring financial availability and sustainability, complying with countries regulations, and strengthening rapidly advancing technologies. Healthcare managers face increasing challenges amid these transformations. One of the greatest prominent is balancing healthcare quality of care with affordable financial management, as the rising expenditure on medical technologies creates pressure to adopt innovative models that improve efficiency. Speedy technological advances change—from artificial intelligence to telemedicine and electronic health records, etc. also demand advanced change management skills and up-to-date techniques to ensure performance and information security (FasterCapital, 2025). Moreover, the challenges related to staff well-being require special attention from leadership. Reports by the Institute for Healthcare Improvement (IHI) emphasize the critical role of leaders in promoting the psychological and physical healthcare of their teams to ensure optimal performance. Evidence suggests that effective leaders provide guidance, mentoring, and education to others; break the status quo; and establish empathy, good communication, and strategic, quick decision-making skills (Al-Saheb, 2022). In response to these challenges, continuous training is one of the most important tools for leadership development. For this reason, the British Academy for Training in London offers specialized programs focusing on financial management, human resources, technological integration, and legal compliance to equip qualified individuals to lead healthcare systems effectively amid rapid change.

REFERENCES

Al-Ghamdi, H. S. H., & Alshammari, S. W., sultan Alowayqil, A., Alawthah, S. H., Alyami, F. M., Almansour, M. M., ... & Alneami, S. Y. (2024). Assessment of Determinants of Managerial Competencies among Healthcare Managers in Healthcare Hospitals from their Perspectives at KSA. *Journal of International Crisis and Risk Communication Research*, *7*(S5), 819.

Al-Haddad, M., & Psych, F. R. C. (2003). Leadership in healthcare management. *Bahrain Medical Bulletin*, *25*(1), 1.

Al Issa, H. E., & Omar, M. M. S. (2024). Digital innovation drivers in retail banking: The role of leadership, culture, and technostress inhibitors. *The International Journal of Organizational Analysis*, *32*(11), 19–43.

Al-Saheb, A. (2022). Effective leadership in healthcare: Essential traits for every leader. *Health Quality Magazine.* https://m-quality.net/?p=45447&utm_source=chatgpt.com

Alghamdi, S., Tajaldeen, A., Alghamdi, A., Aljondi, R., Alghamdi, A., Alqahtani, M., Habbosh, T., & Alzahrani, W. (2024). *Investigation of utilising electronic medical records on the quality of healthcare services at hospitals in Saudi Arabia*. https://isisn.org/BR-21-4-2024/750-759-21(4)2024BR24-93.pdf

Ashade, O. A. (2020). *Community Involvement in the Implementation of the National Policy on Public-private Partnership: A Study of Infrastructural Development in Lagos State, Nigeria* (Doctoral dissertation, University of KwaZulu-Natal, Howard College).

Bass, B. M. (1985). *Leadership and Performance beyond Expectations*. Free Press.

Beauvais, A. M. (Ed.). (2018). *Leadership and management competence in nursing practice: Competencies, skills, decision-making*. Springer Publishing Company.

Behrens, J. E. (2014). *Leadership in collaborative governance: Understanding the relationship of leadership and collaborative performance of Local Departments of Social Services executives*. Virginia Commonwealth University.

Brown, N. O. (2021). *The Lived and Perceived Experiences of Healthcare Leaders Deploying Lean Six Sigma Methods: A Phenomenological Study*. Baker College.

Calhoun, J. G., Ramiah, K., Weist, E. M., & Shortell, S. M. (2008). Development of a Core Competency Model for the Master of Public Health Degree. *American Journal of Public Health, 98*(9), 1598–1607. DOI: 10.2105/ajph.2007.117978 PMID: 18633093

Carayon, P., Schoofs Hundt, A., Karsh, B.-T., Gurses, A. P., Alvarado, C. J., Smith, M., & Flatley Brennan, P. (2006). Work system design for patient safety: The SEIPS model. *Quality & Safety in Health Care, 15*(suppl_1), i50–i58. https://www.ncbi.nlm.nih.gov/pmc/articles/PMC2464868/ PMID: 17142610

Culp, C. A. (1992). *Leadership styles in organizations committed to continuous quality improvement and those not committed to continuous improvement.* United States International University.

De Brún, A., O'Donovan, R., & McAuliffe, E. (2019). Interventions to Develop Collectivistic Leadership in Healthcare settings: A Systematic Review. *BMC Health Services Research, 19*(1), 1–22. DOI: 10.1186/s12913-019-3883-x PMID: 30683089

Denis, J. L., & Van Gestel, N. (2016). Medical doctors in healthcare leadership: Theoretical and practical challenges. *BMC Health Services Research, 16*(Suppl 2), 158. PMID: 27230551

Dwyer, J., Paskavitz, M., Vriesendorp, S., & Johnson, S. (2006). *An urgent call to professionalize leadership and management in health care worldwide.* Management Sciences for Health.

Ellis, P. (2025). *Leadership, management and team working in nursing.* Learning Matters Limited.

FasterCapital. (2025). *Healthcare leadership: The power of leadership in transforming healthcare organizations.* Retrieved from https://www.fastercapital.com/content/Healthcare-leadership--The-Power-of-Leadership-in-Transforming-Healthcare-Organizations.html fastercapital.co.

. Finzel, H. (2007). *The top ten mistakes leaders make.* Colorado Springs, Col. Cook.

Garman, A. N., & Johnson, M. P. (2006). Leadership competencies: An introduction. *Journal of Healthcare Management, 51*(1), 13–17. PMID: 16479746

Geerts, J. M. (2018). *Optimal leadership development for professionals* (Doctoral dissertation).

Goleman, D., Boyatzis, R., & McKee, A. (2013). *Primal Leadership: Unleashing the Power of Emotional Intelligence.* Harvard Business Press.

Golinelli, D., Boetto, E., Carullo, G., Nuzzolese, A. G., Landini, M. P., & Fantini, M. P. (2020). How the COVID-19 pandemic favored the adoption of digital technologies in healthcare: A systematic review of early scientific literature (Preprint). *Journal of Medical Internet Research*, *22*(11). https://www.ncbi.nlm.nih.gov/pmc/articles/PMC7652596/ PMID: 33079693

Hargett, C., Doty, J., Hauck, J., Webb, A., Cook, S., Tsipis, N., Neumann, J., Andolsek, K., & Taylor, D. (2017). Developing a Model for Effective Leadership in healthcare: A Concept Mapping Approach. *Journal of Healthcare Leadership*, *9*(9), 69–78. DOI: 10.2147/JHL.S141664 PMID: 29355249

Hofstede, G. (1984). *Culture's consequences: International Differences in Work-related Values*. Sage Publications.

Kalaitzi, S., Czabanowska, K., Azzopardi-Muscat, N., Cuschieri, L., Petelos, E., Papadakaki, M., & Babich, S. (2019). Women, healthcare leadership and societal culture: A qualitative study. *Journal of Healthcare Leadership*, *11*, 43–59. DOI: 10.2147/jhl.s194733 PMID: 31043802

Kotter, J. (1995). *Leading change: Why transformation efforts fail*. Harvard Business Review. https://hbr.org/1995/05/leading-change-why-transformation-efforts-fail-2

Lasrado, F., & Kassem, R. (2021). Let's get everyone involved! The effects of transformational leadership and organizational culture on organizational excellence. *International Journal of Quality & Reliability Management*, *38*(1), 169–194.

Lisá, E., Sousa, J., Morais, C., & Gomes, A. R. (2023). Leadership cycles, styles, and antecedent factors: The perspective of coaches and young soccer athletes from national Slovak leagues. *Frontiers in Psychology*, *14*, 1218290. PMID: 37609500

Lobdell, K. W., Hariharan, S., Smith, W., Rose, G. A., Ferguson, B., & Fussell, C. (2020). Improving health care leadership in the COVID-19 era. *NEJM Catalyst Innovations in Care Delivery*, *1*(3).

Muhammad Ahmed Al-Maliki, Y. (2020). The reality of activating work teams in public schools within the Al-Dayer Education Office from the perspective of school leadership. *Journal of Faculty of Education-Assiut University*, *36*(4), 465–495.

Ni ă, M. A. (2015). The new intelligence, the new leader and the organizational stress. *Revista de Management Comparat Interna ional*, *16*(3), 335–342.

Piotrowski, C. C. (2020, January 1). *Chapter 15 - ACEs and trauma-informed care* (G. J. G. Asmundson & T. O. Afifi, Eds.). ScienceDirect; Academic Press. https://www.sciencedirect.com/science/article/abs/pii/B978012816065700015X

. Quinn, R. E., & Spreitzer, G. M. (1997). Empowering middle managers to be transformational leaders. *Journal of Management Development, 16*(2), 90–102. This expands on continuous learning and self-improvement in leadership development. PMC+3PMC+3PMC+3ResearchGate+2SAGE Journals+2ResearchGate+2

Richards, A. (2020). Exploring the Benefits and Limitations of Transactional Leadership in Healthcare. *Nursing Standard, 35*(12), 46–50. https://insight.cumbria.ac.uk/id/eprint/5755/ PMID: 33089675

. Sahertian, P., & Graha, A. N. (2016). Exploring leadership dimension among organizations (the analysis against leadership excellence based on cultural and ethnical backgrounds in Indonesia). *Indian Journal of Commerce and Management Studies, 7*(1), 01-07.

Sahertian, P., & Jawas, U. (2021). Cultural Values and Leadership Excellence. In *2nd Annual Conference on Social Science and Humanities (ANCOSH 2020)* (pp. 310-313). Atlantis Press.

Saifman, R., Patel, S., & Williams, K. (2023). Resistance to competency-based leadership development in healthcare. *Journal of Organizational Change Management, 36*(1), 55–72.

. Shalley, C. E., & Lemoine, G. J. (2018). Leader behaviors and employee creativity: Taking stock of the current state of research. *Creative leadership*, 79-94

Shanafelt, T. D., & Noseworthy, J. H. (2019). Executive Leadership and Physician Well-being. *Mayo Clinic Proceedings, 92*(1), 129–146. https://pubmed.ncbi.nlm.nih.gov/27871627/ PMID: 27871627

Siraj-Blatchford, I., Siraj, I., & Manni, L. (2007). *Effective leadership in the early years sector: The ELEYS study*. Institute of Education Press.

Spreier, S. W., Fontaine, M. H., & Malloy, R. L. (2006). Leadership run amok. *Harvard Business Review, 84*(6), 72–82. PMID: 16770895

Terry, L. D. (1998). Administrative leadership, neo-managerialism, and the public management movement. *Public Administration Review*, 194–200.

Turyadi, I., Zulkifli, Z., Tawil, M. R., Ali, H., & Sadikin, A. (2023). The role of digital leadership in organizations to improve employee performance and business success. *Jurnal Ekonomi, 12*(02), 1671–1677.

West, M., Armit, K., Loewenthal, L., Eckert, R., West, T., & Lee, A. (2015). *Leadership and Leadership Development in Health Care*. https://www.kingsfund.org.uk/insight-and-analysis/reports/leadership-development-health-care

WHO. (2008). *Assessing the national health information system: An assessment tool* (Version 4.00) [PDF]. Health Metrics Network. https://www.afro.who.int/sites/default/files/2017-06/AHO_HealthMetricsNetwork_Assessment_Tool_version4.00.pdf

Wiley (2013). *Wiley Pfeiffer learning and development resources*. Wiley Workplace Learning Solutions.http://www.pfeiffer.com/WileyCDA/Section/id-811878.html

Yukl, G. (2012). Effective Leadership Behavior: What We Know and What Questions Need More Attention. *The Academy of Management Perspectives*, *26*(4), 66–85. https://www.jstor.org/stable/23412661

Chapter 7
Key Domains of Healthcare Leadership:
Essential Attributes

ABSTRACT

Healthcare leadership attributes are critical to the success and sustainability of healthcare organizations, enabling leaders to navigate complex and dynamic environments effectively. Strong healthcare leaders exhibit vision, strategic thinking, and a patient-centered focus, allowing them to set clear organizational goals, anticipate challenges, and drive innovation for improved health outcomes. Cultural competence and inclusivity enhance team collaboration, while effective communication fosters transparency and alignment with organizational values. Essential leadership qualities include integrity, credibility, humility, and resilience under pressure, which build trust and credibility. Emotional intelligence (EI) plays a key role in conflict resolution, team cohesion, and staff well-being. Leaders must also prioritize quality and patient safety, ensure evidence-based decision-making, and develop strategies for continuous improvement.

HEALTHCARE LEADERSHIP DOMAINS (ATTRIBUTES)

Healthcare leadership attributes encompass a range of characteristics, skills, and capabilities that define the effectiveness of a healthcare leader. These attributes play a crucial role in shaping the leadership effectiveness and the success of healthcare organizations. Various scholars have identified essential leadership qualities and behavioral competencies, which can be categorized into core leadership qualities and behavioral competencies. Below is a comprehensive exploration of these critical attributes:

DOI: 10.4018/979-8-3373-2225-4.ch007

Vision and Strategic Thinking

Leadership is defined as a function of having a vision (Al-Sawai, 2013) and being responsible for the realization of institutional vision (Osmani, 2013); updating the vision is considered an essential stimulus for improving national Leadership in healthcare reform (Health Metric Network, 2023). HCL, in particular, needs leaders looking at the future of healthcare and how to improve it, (Ellis, 2021), articulate a clear future vision, and inspire a shared vision of strategic visionary thinking to explore the leadership potential, (Kumar & Khiljee, 2016; Al-Haddad & Psych, 2003; Strack & Fottler, 2002; Van, 2020; West, Eckert, & Pasmore, 2014; Bass, 1985; Burns, 1978; Kouzes & Posner, 2023; Advisory Cloud, 2023; Fernandez et al., 2016; Brazier, 2005). Effective healthcare leaders are visionaries who guide their organizations toward long-term success. They develop, communicate, and update organizational vision, inspiring collective commitment and innovative approaches to strategic planning (Al-Sawai, 2013; Osmani, 2013). Strategic thinking involves the ability to identify opportunities for reform and foster a culture of adaptability and foresight (Kumar & Khiljee, 2016). A visionary leader in healthcare is capable of shaping the future of an organization through strategic thinking, maintaining a clear vision for the future, and fostering innovation. Through strategic management, healthcare leaders define organizational priorities, drive change, and navigate external pressures to ensure that healthcare organizations remain agile and adaptable to shifts in policy, technology, and patient needs. By embedding patient welfare at the core of every decision, leaders enhance both care quality and patient safety, which are the foundations of a successful healthcare system.

Patient-Centered Focus

The evaluation of service quality and best healthcare practices based on what the patient anticipates (West, Eckert, & Pasmore, 2014; Asif et al., 2019), excellent healthcare leadership holds the significance of patient-centered Care (Weberg, 2012), Patient-centered care focuses on meeting the unique needs and preferences of individual patients. Thus HCL decisions always prioritize patient welfare (Bruning & Baghurst, 2013), they enhance EBP (evidence-based practice) (Heinen et al., 2019; Perez, 2021), optimize operational efficiency, improve care quality, attain effectiveness of the care provision, and deliver excellent patient care (Nzinga, McGivern, & English, 2018; Al-Touby, 2012; Heinen et al., 2019; Barbuto & Wheeler, 2006; Sendjaya, Sarros, & Santora, 2008; Ellis, 2021; Lantz, 2008; Weberg, 2012; Carayon et al, 2013; St. Pierre, Hofinger, & Buerschaper, 2008) without compromising quality and safety (Bauer et al., 2023; Guo, 2023; Junaid et al., 2023). The primary focus of healthcare leadership is on patient welfare. Effective leaders ensure that organizational strategies align with the goal of providing high-quality, patient-centered care. They prioritize safety, minimize errors, and seek to improve patient experiences and health outcomes (Nzinga, McGivern, & English, 2018; Al-Touby, 2012). Utilizing evidence-based practices (EBP) further supports the delivery of safe, effective care (Heinen et al., 2019; Perez, 2021).

Cultural Compatibility

Leaders in healthcare operate in diverse environments and must demonstrate cultural competence and inclusivity. This requires sensitivity to different cultures, fostering harmonious work environments, and integrating cultural considerations into leadership practices (Warrick, 2017; Javidan et al., 2010). Cultural compatibility enhances collaboration and strengthens the team's performance in delivering healthcare services. Leaders work in a cross-cultural organizational environment to foster inclusivity and capitalize on the strengths of multi-generational and culturally varied teams (Perez, 2021). HCL leaders should be culturally compatible, and cultural values are inherent in their personalities that contribute to their excellence; furthermore, because of the ultimate importance of culturally–compatible attributes, the human factors engineers cogitate the cultural context when designing healthcare systems and interventions. (Warrick, 2017; Sahertian & Jawas, 2021; Beauvais, 2019; Terry, 1998; Javidan et al., 2010; Zayas-Cabán & Valdez, 2012).

Quality and Safety

In current days, the improvements in quality and patient safety have received much attention (Almomani et al., 2020) because it is so directly tied to human health and survival rate (Izadi et al., 2017), the diverse health systems and the range of healthcare professionals with various expertise develop various approaches to encourage quality enhancement (El-Jardali & Fadlallah, 2017). HCL should hold the significance of safety quality Improvement (Weberg, 2012), make sure the organization has a solid error reporting and analysis system to identify systemic issues and prevent future mistakes, (Weinger, 2012), maintain organizational efficiency, safety climate, and providing high-quality care, in turn, impacted on medication errors (Sfantou et al., 2017; Al Kuwaiti & Al Muhanna, 2019) enhance the service quality (De Brún, O'Donovan, & McAuliffe, 2019), increase the quality of everything (Cleary et al., 2018). Healthcare leadership is fundamentally concerned with maintaining quality and ensuring patient safety. Leaders develop systems that enhance error reporting, promote learning, and support continuous improvement efforts (Sfantou et al., 2017). By focusing on quality and safety, leaders can reduce the risk of harm, improve patient outcomes, and strengthen the organizational culture around healthcare excellence.

Communication

Healthcare leaders should facilitate effective communication and Interpersonal skills among healthcare professionals and other stakeholders (Al-Haddad & Psych, 2003; Sarihasan et al., 2022; Ellis, 2021; West, Eckert, & Pasmore, 2014; Turner, 2018; Lantz, 2008; Al-Ghamdi et al., 2022; Culp, 1992; Finzel, 2007; Goleman, Boyatzis, & McKee, 2013; Bensimon, 1989; Sfantou, 2017; Kumar & Khiljee, 2016; Strack & Fottler, 2002), Leaders who excel in communication create an environment of trust and collaboration and achieve more success in business, enhancing interaction and collaboration among employees (Mahsud, Yukl, & Prussia, 2010; Sias & Cahill, 1998; Wang & Wang, 2022). HCL should deliver clear and concise communication of their vision, goals, and expectations to enhance his ability to listen (as it enhances trust and engagement, ensuring messages are understood and delivered correctly), help to prevent misunderstandings, and ensure that critical information is accurately conveyed (Karsh et al., 2012; Bass, 1985; Burns, 1978; Kouzes & Posner, 2023; Denis & Van Gestel, 2016; Mahsud, Yukl, & Prussia, 2010) build an environment of trust and safety and maintain the credibility of their organizations through excellent communication and organizational context, treating employees as trusted and honest people, (Al-Sawai, 2013; Sarihasan et al., 2022; Spreier, Fontaine, & Malloy, 2006; Chen & Sriphon, 2022; Ismayilova, & Bolander, 2023; Miller, et al., 2023; Fullan, 2016; Polden, 2019; Kumar & Khiljee, 2016; Salman & Auso, 2022).

Clear, concise, and timely communication is integral to successful healthcare leadership. Effective leaders must be able to communicate with various stakeholders, including healthcare professionals and patients, to ensure coordinated, efficient care delivery (Sarihasan et al., 2022; Turner, 2018). Strong communication skills foster trust, collaboration, and a culture of openness within healthcare teams (Mahsud, Yukl, & Prussia, 2010; Wang & Wang, 2022).

Personal Qualities

Healthcare leadership (HCL) has high personal qualities (Sahertian & Graha, 2016), responsible and admit their mistakes (Lobdell et al., 2020) committed (Ismayilova & Bolander, 2023; Miller et al., 2023), credible, humility (Lobdell et al., 2020) calm and relaxed under pressure (Al-Ghamdi et al., 2022; Culp, 1992; Finzel, 2007; Goleman, Boyatzis, & McKee, 2013; Al-Ghamdi et al., 2022; Culp, 1992; Finzel, 2007; Goleman, Boyatzis, & McKee, 2013), has excellent delegation skills (Al-Ghamdi et al., 2022; Culp, 1992; Finzel, 2013; Goleman, Boyatzis, & McKee, 2013) optimistic, (Beauvais, 2019; Terry, 1998), Persistence (Beauvais, 2019; Terry, 1998) full of wisdom, knowledge and skill (International Hospital Federation, 2023; Al-Ghamdi et al., 2022; Culp, 1992; Finzel, 2007; Goleman, Boyatzis, & McKee,

2013), have high morale and be selfless. (Beauvais, 2019; Terry, 1998). Courage (Al-Ghamdi et al., 2022; Culp, 1992; Finzel, 2007; Goleman, Boyatzis, & McKee, 2013), excellent aptitudes (International Hospital Federation, 2023), excellent medical knowledge (Lantz, 2008), Self-awareness, and excellent situational awareness (Al-Haddad & Psych, 2003; Sarihasan et al., 2022), fairness, excellent negotiation skills, operating with integrity and upholding professional standards (Bruning & Baghurst, 2013), agile and adaptive (Perez, 2021), can identify obvious and obscure vulnerabilities of the organization, (Fullan, 2016; Polden, 2019) can model the way, (Strack & Fottler, 2002) Self-awareness (Al-Ghamdi et al., 2022; Culp, 1992; Finzel, 2007; Goleman, Boyatzis, & McKee, 2013) has a sense of mission (Anderson, 2024) and deep understanding of the healthcare industry, (Bass, 1985; Burns, 1978; Kouzes & Posner, 2023). Personal attributes such as responsibility, credibility, and calm under pressure are critical for healthcare leaders. These qualities influence their decision-making and how they engage with others, particularly under stressful circumstances. Other important personal qualities include commitment, humility, delegation, and integrity (Lobdell et al., 2020; Ismayilova & Bolander, 2023). These qualities help leaders inspire confidence, navigate challenges, and maintain a positive work environment.

Emotional Intelligence

One important thing about healthcare leadership is that emotional intelligence is becoming more and more important. Emotional intelligence includes empathy, social skills, self-awareness, self-regulation, and motivation (Al-Zu'bi, 2021; Ahsan, 2023). Research has focused on the traits of emotional intelligence (Hargett et al., 2017) and the importance of empathy. (Strack & Fottler, 2002). In environments where empathy and compassion are essential, leaders with emotional intelligence can better connect with patients, families, and medical staff, as these qualities are vital for successful healthcare leadership (Palmer et al., 2001; Batool, 2025; Mittal & Sindhu, 2012; Bass, 1985; Burns, 1978; Kouzes & Posner, 2023). This emotional intelligence is crucial for managing complex organizational crises (Zaccaro, LaPort, & Jose, 2013; Achua & Lussier, 2010; Turner, 2018), as it enables leaders to build meaningful connections, motivate their teams, and navigate conflicts and challenges effectively (Palmer et al., 2001). Successful HCLs are the highest-performing managers with greater "emotional competence" than other managers, impacting their decisions on numerous stakeholders (Abdullah & Aziz, 2021; Batool, 2025; Mittal & Sindhu, 2012; Bass, 1985; Burns, 1978; Kouzes & Posner, 2023; Al-Hashemi & Mosaab, 2021). Empathy as a part of Emotional Intelligence management can be imposed on patients and providers. (Strack, 2002; Palmer et al., 2001; Batool, 2025; Mittal & Sindhu, 2012; Bass, 1985; Burns, 1978; Kouzes & Posner, 2023;

Al-Hashemi & Mosaab, 2021). Moreover, by demonstrating empathy, leaders create a compassionate and supportive culture that enhances patient experiences and employee satisfaction. (Palmer, et al., 2001; Batool, 2025; Mittal & Sindhu, 2012; Bass, 1985; Burns, 1978; Kouzes & Posner, 2023; Al-Hashemi & Mosaab, 2021). An effective HCL also motivates employees to think creatively and provide creative solutions. Basadur, 2004; Zhou & George, 2003; Mahsud, Yukl, & Prussia, 2010; Basadur, 2004; Zhou & George, 2003; Connor & Pokora, 2017; Lobdell et al., 2020; Al-Haddad & Psych, 2003) and provide valuable insights to motivate people to achieve common goals innovatively and effectively (Amabile & Khaire, 2008).

Emotional intelligence (EI) is very important for leaders in healthcare. Leaders with high emotional intelligence (EI) are empathic, self-aware, and good at handling their own and others' emotions. This makes the workplace more supportive and caring (Al-Zu'bi, 2021; Ahsan, 2023). Empathy-driven leadership improves team morale, employee engagement, and patient satisfaction. It also encourages creative problem-solving and conflict resolution (Bass, 1985; Kouzes & Posner, 2023).

Also, emotional intelligence is also important for creating a supportive and cooperative work atmosphere. Healthcare executives who are self-aware and have empathy may get along with their staff and patients, which boosts morale and engagement. These emotional intelligence skills also help people solve problems, settle disagreements, and come up with creative ways to deal with difficult healthcare issues. Healthcare executives also need to be very good at managing risks and crises. They need to be able to handle emergencies and unknowns with strength and good decision-making skills.

Healthcare Leadership and Innovation

Innovation is a cornerstone of effective healthcare leadership. Leaders who embrace innovation drive the development of new solutions to complex healthcare challenges (Carvajal & Sanchez, 2023; Zank, Araujo, & Hanazaki, 2019). Creative leadership fosters a culture of continuous improvement and encourages teams to explore innovative approaches to enhance healthcare outcomes (Khalili, 2017; Heinen et al., 2019).

Healthcare Leadership and Transparent Decision-Making

Decision-making in creative Leadership requires unique skills that differ from those used in traditional Leadership, like Critical thinking and multiple options to make optimal decisions (Hantula, 2018). Transparent Decision-Making is a fundamental attribute of successful healthcare leaders (Fullan, 2016; Polden, 2019; Bruning & Baghurst, 2013); they should have full engagement and facilitate transparent, adequate, and rapid ethical in the organizational decision-making, (De Brún, O'Donovan, & McAuliffe, 2019; Al-Ghamdi et al., 2022; Culp, 1992; Finzel, 2007; Goleman, Boyatzis, & McKee, 2013), as well as audacity and taking risks and courageous action in order to achieve the set goals. (Turner, 2018; Lantz, 2008; Mahsud, Yukl, & Prussia, 2010; Fullan, 2016; Polden, 2019; Bruning & Baghurst, 2013). The decisions should be evidence-based (Salman & Auso, 2022), and involving stakeholders in the decision-making process, especially the rationale behind their choices, is necessary (Salman & Auso, 2022).To excel in HCL and make more accurate and effective decision-making by using artificial Intelligence it can lead (Raza et al., 2023), encourage design thinking that can help leaders reach creative solutions and make optimal decisions (Brown, 2021), learn to think creatively, improve the quality of team relationships can most effectively resolve it increases the quality of thinking and anticipate future trends and challenges, (Upshaw et al., 2023; Cleary et al., 2018). Since the making of bold and innovative decisions requires relying on creative thinking (Rizzo & Bouchard, 2019; Noor et al., 2024).

Transparent decision-making is a hallmark of effective healthcare leadership. Leaders must utilize critical thinking to make well-informed decisions, incorporating stakeholder input and evidence-based insights (Fullan, 2016; Polden, 2019). Transparency fosters accountability, ethical decision-making, and a culture of trust, which ultimately supports organizational success (Bruning & Baghurst, 2013; Culp, 1992).

Healthcare Leadership and Problem-Solving

Problem-solving means "the ability of the individual leadership to deal with problems and choose the appropriate alternative that suits each case." (Dogan & Schroevers, 2018) and is considered one of the essential creative leadership skills. HCL should be able to deal with the organization's complex problems, challenges, and complications to achieve goals. (Turner, 2018; Wang & Wang, 2022) by improving creative thinking and adopting a set of steps, such as (understanding the problem well and analyzing it accurately, gathering information and available sources. Searching for innovative and fresh solutions, and choosing the best solution and implementing, beside the susceptibility to change and improve the ability and flexibility to accept change. Problem-solving is a key competency for healthcare leaders. Leaders must address complex issues with creativity and adaptability, exploring innovative solutions and guiding their organizations toward optimal outcomes (Dogan, 2019). Systematic problem-solving strategies, such as information gathering and solution evaluation, are essential for tackling the challenges of healthcare management (Turner, 2018).

Healthcare Leadership in Complexity and Uncertainty

The healthcare sector is characterized by complexity and uncertainty (Khan et al., 2018), and healthcare organizations can cultivate a pipeline of influential leaders who can navigate complexity. (Frich, et al., 2015). Influential HCL is paramount to addressing healthcare organizations' complexities and challenges. (Kalaitzi et al., 2019), They navigate intricate systems, diverse stakeholders, rapidly evolving technologies, treatments, complex healthcare regulations, and quality standards. (Khan et al., 2018; Al Kuwaiti & Al Muhanna, 2019), make critical decisions in the face of uncertainty (Newman & Newman, 2021), analyze complex situations, think critically, and make informed decisions in dynamic and uncertain environments (Newman & Newman, 2021). Healthcare leaders must navigate an environment characterized by complexity and uncertainty. They are tasked with leading organizations through dynamic changes, regulatory shifts, and evolving technological landscapes (Frich et al., 2015; Kalaitzi et al., 2019). Leaders must demonstrate resilience, creativity, and adaptability to manage these complexities and make informed decisions (Newman & Newman, 2021). Healthcare leadership is an essential force in steering the complex and evolving healthcare landscape. As healthcare organizations face increasing challenges—ranging from regulatory changes and technological advancements to workforce shortages—leaders must possess a diverse set of attributes and competencies to ensure long-term sustainability and high-quality patient care. The multifaceted nature of healthcare leadership is reflected in the array of critical skills, including strategic thinking, patient-centered care, cultural competence, quality and safety, and effective communication.

Healthcare Leadership Development Programs

Healthcare organizations need help to realize the benefits of professional management, considering that the role of the healthcare manager is only recognized as a profession in some countries. (ACHE, 2015), Healthcare leaders should have a minimum level of education and training courses (Bensimon, 1989). Leadership development programs play a vital role in building and enhancing leadership skills in healthcare to navigate complex medical situations effectively (Carayon et al., 2013; Sonnino, 2016).To excel in leadership roles, leaders need to run robust leadership development programs that contain proper training and ongoing education Since improving leadership competency through training is practical in healthcare organizations (Al-Issa & Omar, 2024; Turyadi et al., 2023; Sfantou, 2017); besides the need to collaborate with higher educational institutions to promote and facilitate the training and development of the healthcare workforce. (Professional Leadership Coaching, 2023; Qureshi et al., 2013; Lobdell et al., 2020) recommended training, including (specialized training courses, workshops, seminars, and formal education on creative Leadership, enhancement of strategic thinking, communication skills, emotional Intelligence, and change management (Al-Mutawa & Al-Otaibi, 2021; Frich, et al., 2015). Leadership development programs are essential for preparing healthcare leaders to address industry challenges. These programs should focus on developing skills such as communication, emotional intelligence, and strategic thinking (Al-Mutawa & Al-Otaibi, 2021; Frich et al., 2015). Partnerships with educational institutions enhance continuous learning, contributing to improved leadership performance and organizational effectiveness (Qureshi et al., 2013).

Healthcare Leadership and Human Resources

Adequate human resources (Al-Fadhalah & Elamir, 2021), availability of effective teamwork among healthcare professionals (Gosbee, 2002), building interdisciplinary teams (Griffith, 2023), work environmental influence (Sahertian & Jawas, 2021; Sahertian & Graha, 2016), are vital in reforming the organization's mindset, build organizational capabilities, crucial organizational goal and vigorous for delivering high-quality care since HCL need help to do the job professionally. A lack of workforce poses a significant challenge for healthcare leaders like the shortages of healthcare professionals and availability of medical cadres in the event of crises and emergencies (Professional Leadership Coaching, 2023; Qureshi et al., 2013). HCL should focus on supervision and group performance (Anderson, 2024; Fullan, 2016; Polden, 2019), develop comprehensive plans to drive team organizational success. Inspire, enhance, and motivate effective teamwork and collaboration with professionals (Gosbee, 2002; Hasan, Ahmad, & Osman, 2023), encourage shared decision-making, enable healthcare staff to make their best effort in any situation, inspire multidisciplinary teams, social exchange dynamic relationships with employees, and other health agencies (Heinen et al., 2019; Lantz, 2008; De Brún, O'Donovan, & McAuliffe, 2019; Nzinga, McGivern, & English, 2018; Strack & Fottler, 2002; Van, 2020; Chen & Sriphon, 2022; Mahsud, Yukl, & Prussia, 2010; Al-Sawai, 2013; Kelly, 2023) addresses this challenge by implementing strategies to attract and retain talented healthcare professionals (Professional Leadership Coaching, 2023; Qureshi et al., 2013) by creating opportunities for others (Lobdell et al., 2020), improve coalition-building, with adequate accountability (WHO, 2020) to achieve healthcare organization goals. Human resources and teamwork are foundational to healthcare leadership. Leaders must build cohesive teams and encourage interdisciplinary collaboration to enhance healthcare delivery (Al-Fadhalah & Elamir, 2021; Gosbee, 2002). Effective healthcare leaders address workforce challenges, attract and retain talent, and foster strong relationships within their teams.

Healthcare Leadership and Embracing Diversity

Diversity and inclusion are integral to effective healthcare leadership. Leaders must foster a culture that celebrates diversity and supports inclusive practices to enhance decision-making and patient outcomes (Simonsen & Shim, 2019). An inclusive culture strengthens organizational performance by incorporating diverse perspectives and approaches (Lee et al., 2021). Every leader is at risk for blind spots, and leadership concepts may limit efforts for cultural inclusiveness and operational success (Lee et al., 2021); noble HCL embraces diversity and Inclusion (Simonsen & Shim, 2019) by attracting diverse people engaging in the pluralism of ideas and perspectives (Bradley, 2020) and this can lead to better decision-making, patient outcomes, and commitment at all levels, (Simonsen & Shim, 2019). Besides that, HCL should know diversity is necessary but will not, alone, create a just and inclusive culture," (Lee et al., 2021). Strategic management is the set of decisions and actions used to formulate and implement specific strategies that will achieve a competitively superior fit to achieve organizational goals (Yuguda et al., 2023; Budak et al., 2014) and foster a culture of excellence, (Moradi-Moghadam et al., 2023). HCL is responsible for the company's success and failure," (Pyzdek & Keller, 2018; Karneli, 2023; Omar, 2018; Davies & Davies, 2004). Strategic HCLs should have the ability to identify strategic priorities (Spreier, Fontaine, & Malloy, 2006), conceptualize and formulate the organization's vision, mission, and objectives, facilitate organizational learning, and act as role models for others) (Alsharari, Salihu, & Alshammari, 2025; Omar, 2018; Choucair, 2023), anticipate, envision, think strategically, to create a viable future for the organization," (Pyzdek & Keller, 2018; Karneli, 2023; Omar, 2018; Davies & Davies, 2004) and leading by example in embracing new systems and processes (Sfantou, 2017).

Healthcare Leadership and Strategic Management

Strategic management is a critical responsibility for healthcare leaders. They must define organizational priorities, shape mission-driven strategies, and lead by example in embracing innovation (Yuguda et al., 2023; Moradi-Moghadam et al., 2023). Effective strategic management ensures long-term organizational sustainability and growth (Sfantou, 2017; Choucair, 2023).

Healthcare Leadership Challenges

Healthcare leaders face numerous challenges, including technological advancements, workforce shortages, and evolving patient needs (Hargett, 2017; Richards, 2020). Effective leadership requires adaptability, resilience, and the ability to inspire a shared vision to overcome challenges (Kouzes & Posner, 2023; Strack & Fottler, 2002). Leaders must anticipate challenges and create innovative solutions that align with sustainable healthcare practices. HCL faces many challenges because of the industry's rapid evolution and emerging technologies (Perez, 2021), more complexity in the system (Hargett, 2017), emerging workplace Design (Leonard, Graham, & Bonacum, 2004), professional human resources availability conflicts and empowerments (Richards, 2020; Hargett, 2017), Cultivating cultural differences (Zayas-Cabán & Valdez, 2012), HCL is more than maintaining the status quo and identifying challenges and solutions in the system. According to Robbins and Judge (2023), the primary challenge of Leadership is to help individuals develop their capacity to inspire a shared vision and inspire others to greatness. (Kouzes & Posner, 2023; Strack & Fottler, 2002). Moreover, they should be adaptable and resilient in rapidly changing healthcare environments (Zank, de Araujo, & Hanazaki, 2019). HCL must respond proactively to new challenges (Zank, de Araujo, & Hanazaki, 2019) through improved benchmarking performance and sound measurement systems and look for solutions agreeable to most stakeholders. (Richards, 2020) and concurrent with the sustainability of health and social care systems (WHO, 2020).

Healthcare Leadership Navigating Policy and Regulatory Changes

This in-depth look at healthcare leadership highlights a number of important talents and abilities that leaders need to have in order to deal with the healthcare environment, which is becoming more complex and changing all the time. One of the most important abilities is being able to deal with changes in rules and policies. To stay in compliance and stay ahead of the competition, healthcare leaders (HCLs) need to know about new rules, laws, and industry standards. Good leaders work with lawmakers, advocacy organizations, and regulatory authorities to stay ahead of changes and change their plans as needed (Zayas-Cabán & Valdez, 2012). Strong relationships with important stakeholders help CEOs make sure that their organizations are successful even when healthcare legislation change (Anderson, 2015; Al Kuwaiti & Al Muhanna, 2019). Health care organizations must keep up with changes in regulations, and HCL must do the same. Another aspect of healthcare leadership is being able to handle changes in policies and regulations (Zayas-Cabán & Valdez, 2012), which means building strong relationships with policymakers, advocacy groups, and regulatory bodies to make sure their organizations do well in the changing healthcare landscape. (Anderson, 2015; Al Kuwaiti & Al Muhanna, 2019).

Healthcare Leadership Financial Management

Another important job for HCLs is managing money. They have to make sure that resources are used wisely while still providing high-quality, patient-centered care. To stay profitable without sacrificing treatment quality or patient safety, you need to use creative financial tactics like cost analysis, budgeting, and investment planning. Leaders must also make operations as efficient as possible and cut down on waste (Gifford et al., 2023; Helbling, 2023; Bauer et al., 2023; Guo, 2023; Junaid et al., 2023). These financial plans make sure that healthcare businesses will develop and stay in business for a long time. Balancing financial constraints is an essential aspect of healthcare leadership (Gifford et al., 2023; Helbling, 2023); healthcare leaders must navigate difficult decisions regarding financial resource allocation and devise innovative strategies to enhance operational efficiency while preserving patient-centered care without sacrificing quality and safety (Bauer et al., 2023; Guo, 2023; Junaid et al., 2023).

Healthcare Leadership Continuous Learning and Self-Improvement

Continuous learning and self-improvement are pivotal in fostering leadership excellence. HCLs must engage in ongoing education and skill development, adopting new leadership models and enhancing technical, cognitive, and emotional intelligence skills. Staying updated on technological advancements and industry trends ensures that healthcare leaders remain adaptable and innovative in dynamic environments (Bass, 1985; Ni ă, 2015; Lasrado & Kassem, 2021; van, 2020; Al-Issa & Omar, 2024; Carayon et al., 2013; Hargett et al., 2017; Richards, 2020; Shalley & Lemoine, 2018; Al-Zoubi et al., 2023; Turyadi et al., 2023; Piotrowski, 2020).

Healthcare Leadership Risk and Crisis Management

Healthcare leadership also involves effective risk and crisis management. Leaders who embrace risk-taking and develop proactive strategies and emergency response plans contribute to the organization's resilience and overall performance. Risk management frameworks and decision support systems play an essential role in ensuring informed decision-making during crises (Simsek, 2007; Mumford & Todd, 2019; Al-Issa & Abdelsalam, 2021; Wetterneck et al., 2012). High-level companies adopt creative leadership practices to enhance their risk and crisis management capabilities. Leaders who make risky decisions are more likely to succeed in managing crises, and achieving achievement can help them succeed more in business (Simsek, 2007; Mumford et al., 2019; Al-Issa & Abdelsalam, 2021) and considered the heartbeat of innovation since risk-taking requires daring, courage, and readiness for challenges and risks (Al-Issa & Abdelsalam, 2021). HCL should have the needed competencies to manage crisis events (Beauvais, 2019; Terry, 1998; Bensimon, 1989) through good preparation for the crisis and planning for it before it occurs, enhance suitable risk-taking initiative helps achieve success and excellence in changing work environments (Martinez, 2018; Quinn & Spreitzer, 1997), drive change and improvement in organizations, improve overall performance, (Simsek, 2007), enhances creativity, development, and performance improvement (Mumford & Todd, 2019) and make sure the availability of and Decision Support Systems assist healthcare professionals in making informed decisions. (Wetterneck et al., 2012). Moreover, finally enhances the organization's crisis management capabilities (Ismayilova & Bolander, 2023; Miller et al., 2023).

Healthcare Leadership Change Management

Change management is another crucial leadership competency, as healthcare environments are constantly evolving. Effective HCLs must articulate and manage change through adaptability, creative problem-solving, and strategic leadership. By promoting a culture of innovation and fostering flexibility, leaders can drive continuous improvement and maintain a competitive edge (West, Eckert, & Pasmore, 2014; Fullan, 2016; Polden, 2019; Strong et al., 2013; Al-Zahrani & Brek, 2024; Kilic, 2023; Mainemelis, Kark, & Epitropaki, 2015; Hargadon & Bechky, 2006; Kotter, 1996; Frich et al., 2015; Piotrowski, 2020; Murray et al., 2023). The rapidly changing healthcare landscape requires effective Leadership to articulate and manage change effectively. Change management is defined as learning from others to effect change (West, Eckert, & Pasmore, 2014; Fullan, 2016; Polden, 2019). Changeability is undeniably a pivotal component of creative Leadership; managing change and the ability to change are crucial components of the leadership job (Strong et al., 2013; Quinn & Spreitzer, 1997), moreover, organizations can cultivate a pipeline of influential leaders who can drive positive change. (Frich, et al., 2015). HCL should have the susceptibility to change as an essential component of creative Leadership (Al-Zahrani & Brek, 2024; Kilic, 2023; Mainemelis, Kark, & Epitropaki, 2015; Hargadon & Bechky, 2006; Khalili, 2017), embrace change is a hallmark of creative leaders, (Kotter, 1996), foster a culture of Stimulating (innovation) and renewal as a vital policy change to be the best in the industry (Kotter, 1996), inspire positive organizational change (Piotrowski, 2020), adapt to new challenges, improve performance, and achieve sustainable success. (Hargadon & Bechky, 2006; Halili, 2022; Carmeli et al., 2010; Al-Zahrani & Brek, 2024; Kilic, 2023; Mainemelis, Kark, & Epitropaki, 2015). Finally, the change can be mobilized by leadership for inclusive excellence, student service delivery and engagement, recruitment retention and advancement, community engagement, and research and scholarship in health equity, (Murray et al., 2023).

Healthcare Leadership Stimulating Creativity

Leaders must also stimulate creativity within healthcare organizations. Innovation and creative thinking are key to achieving competitive advantages, improving patient satisfaction, and enhancing revenue. By encouraging creative leadership practices and rewarding creative contributions, HCLs foster a culture of continuous technological transformation and innovation (Carvajal & Sanchez, 2023; Zank, Araujo, & Hanazaki, 2019; Amabile & Khaire, 2008; Weinger, 2012; Simonsen & Shim, 2019).

High-reliability organization's Leadership fosters and embraces innovation and creativity (Carvajal & Sanchez, 2023; Zank, Araujo, & Hanazaki, 2019) since the encouragement of innovation is an essential component of creative Leadership (Hargadon & Bechky, 2006; Khalili, 2017; Heinen et al., 2019; Van, 2020; Simonsen & Shim, 2019), and stimulating creativity is a vital policy change to be the best in the industry (BXL622 Organizations as Complex Environments and Change Assignment Sample SUSS Singapore. 20232) achieve more customers and improve revenues (Amabile & Khaire, 2008). HCL encourages creativity and creative methods and promotes creative leadership practices to become the catalyst that transforms doubts into possibilities. (Weinger, 2012; Simonsen & Shim, 2019; Amabile & Khaire, 2008), adapt to continuous technological transformations, and enhance creative thinking (Amabile & Khaire, 2008). Finally, Successful healthcare leaders reward employees for creative ideas. (Amabile & Khaire, 2008).

Healthcare Leadership Embracing Diversity and Inclusion

Diversity, equality, and inclusion (DEI) are important parts of being a leader in healthcare today. HCLs need to think about DEI not just when they hire people, but also when they create a culture where different points of view are respected. This diversity leads to better decision-making, better patient outcomes, and more dedicated employees. An inclusive workplace fosters equitable opportunity and guarantees that varied perspectives enhance the organization's success (Lee et al., 2021; Simonsen & Shim, 2019).

Healthcare Leadership Strategic Management

Strategic management is an essential component of HCL's jobs since they have to come up with and carry out plans that fit with the organization's goals and promote a culture of excellence. Long-term growth requires leaders to be able to think strategically and see the big picture. They need to be able to deal with outside pressures, find new opportunities, and help the organization learn (Moradi-Moghadam et al., 2023; Pyzdek & Keller, 2018; Karneli, 2023; Omar, 2018; Davies & Davies, 2004).

Healthcare Leadership Challenges: Adaptability And Resilience

Lastly, healthcare executives today need to be flexible and strong in the face of adversities. HCLs need to come up with proactive plans, accept that things can always get better, and be resilient leaders to make sure their organizations stay strong and successful (Perez, 2021; Hargett, 2017; Zank, Araujo, & Hanazaki, 2019; Richards, 2020; WHO, 2020).

These talents and competences highlight how diverse and complex healthcare leadership is. They also show how important resilience, creativity, adaptation, and innovation are for modern healthcare organizations to be successful. This in-depth look of healthcare leadership shows the important skills, abilities, and plans needed to deal with the problems of modern healthcare. Each subdomain shows how complex healthcare leadership is and how important it is to be flexible, creative, and strong in order to make an organization successful. These attributes collectively define the effectiveness of healthcare leadership, which is essential for navigating the complexities of the modern healthcare landscape and achieving high-quality patient outcomes. The summary of definitions attributes for healthcare leadership excellence shown below in **Tables 1 and 2.**

Table 1. Key attributes for healthcare leadership excellence

Attribute	Definition	Key References
Visionary Thinking	The ability to anticipate future challenges and opportunities, craft a compelling vision, and inspire others to achieve it.	(Bass, 1985; Lasrado & Kassem, 2021; Avolio, 2007)
Strategic Decision-Making	The capacity to analyze complex information, weigh alternatives, and make informed decisions that benefit the organization.	(Beauvais, 2019; Terry, 1998; Van, 2020)
Emotional Intelligence (EI)	Self-awareness, empathy, and the ability to manage relationships effectively. Leaders with high EI foster positive team dynamics.	(Goleman, Boyatzis, & McKee, 2013; Finzel, 2007; Al-Ghamdi et al. (2022)
Change Management	The ability to lead and support change within the organization, often in response to shifting regulatory or market demands.	(Thomas & Suresh, 2023; Siraj-Blatchford et al., 2007)
Resilience	The ability to recover from setbacks and maintain focus and determination during adversity. Resilience is essential for navigating complex healthcare systems.	(Sahertian & Jawas, 2021; Sahertian & Graha, 2016)
Effective Communication	The capacity to clearly articulate ideas, listen actively, and engage in meaningful dialogue with stakeholders.	(Spreier, Fontaine, & Malloy, 2006; Ellis, 2021; De Brún, O'Donovan, & McAuliffe, 2019)

continued on following page

Table 1. Continued

Attribute	Definition	Key References
Ethical Decision-Making	Upholding integrity and transparency in all decisions, guided by ethical principles and the well-being of patients and staff.	(WHO, 2020; Bass, 1985)
Empathy and Compassion	Demonstrating concern for others, especially patients and team members, which fosters trust and strengthens relationships.	(Van, 2020; De Brún, O'Donovan, & McAuliffe, 2019; Turner, 2018)
Delegation Skills	Knowing how to delegate tasks effectively to improve efficiency and empower team members.	Goleman, Boyatzis, & McKee, 2013; Culp, 1992; Al-Ghamdi et al. (2022)
Innovation and Creativity	The ability to drive innovation and develop creative solutions to complex challenges within healthcare systems.	(Avolio, 2007; Day et al., 2014; Lobdell et al., 2020)
Accountability and Responsibility	Taking ownership of decisions and ensuring accountability for the outcomes of leadership actions.	(Oti-Boadi, Asante, & Malm, 2019; Leanord & Masatu, 2005)
Team Building and Collaboration	Building cohesive teams, promoting collaboration, and fostering a supportive organizational culture.	(Lantz, 2008; Turner, 2018)
Adaptability	The ability to adjust strategies and leadership approaches in response to change or uncertainty.	(Siraj-Blatchford et al., 2007)
Self-Reflection and Self-Awareness	Reflecting on one's actions, assessing strengths and weaknesses, and engaging in continuous self-improvement.	(Culp, 1992; Finzel, 2007; Goleman, Boyatzis, & McKee, 2013)
Technical Expertise	Possessing deep knowledge of healthcare systems, operations, and emerging trends.	(Sahertian & Graha, 2016; Beauvais, 2019)
Operational Efficiency	Streamlining processes and ensuring efficient use of resources to improve healthcare service delivery.	(WHO, 2020; Spreier, Fontaine, & Malloy, 2006)
Crisis Leadership	Leading organizations during emergencies or crises with courage, clarity, and decisiveness.	(Lisá et al., 2023)

These domains are interrelated and collectively form the foundation for effective healthcare leadership. Mastery of these attributes enables healthcare leaders to navigate the complexities of healthcare systems, drive innovation, and ensure the well-being of patients and staff alike.

Table 2. Healthcare leadership domains (attributes)

1. General Parameters (Systems Perspective)	18. Employee Support and Development
2. Professional, Ethical, and Social Responsibility	19. Compassionate Leadership
3. Commitment to Advancing People-Centered Services	20. Interpersonal Relationships
4. Emotional Intelligence and Self-Awareness	21. Problem-Solving and Negotiation
5. Continuous Improvement	22. Systems Thinking
6. Translation and Implementation	23. Engaging Culture and Environment
7. Strategic Financial Management	24. Population Health Assessment and Promotion
8. Human Resource Management	25. Networks and Alliances
9. Information Management	26. Advocacy
10. Administration and Business Development	27. Public Relations and Marketing
11. Quality Improvement and Patient Safety	28. Regulations and Health Systems
12. Monitoring and Evaluation	29. Strategic Planning
13. Visionary Leadership	30. Sustainability Leadership
14. Governance	31. Organizational Resilience
15. Preparedness and Crisis Management	32. Innovation and Entrepreneurship
16. Digital Technologies in Healthcare	33. Change Management
17. Executive Communication	34. Ongoing Learning and Sharing

Leadership in healthcare also requires an unwavering commitment to continuous learning and self-improvement. As healthcare practices and technologies rapidly evolve, so too must the leaders who guide these changes. By engaging in leadership development programs and remaining informed about industry advancements, leaders can stay ahead of trends, maintaining flexibility and creative solutions to new problems. A strong focus on diversity, equity, and inclusion ensures that healthcare leaders foster environments where all voices are valued and contribute to enhanced decision-making and improved patient outcomes. Furthermore, effective leaders recognize the importance of collaboration and teamwork, ensuring that interdisciplinary cooperation is central to organizational success. Leaders must also navigate financial management to strike the delicate balance between fiscal responsibility and delivering high-quality patient care.

In conclusion, the traits talked about in this chapter show how complicated and linked healthcare leadership is. Healthcare leaders need to be able to handle the problems of the current healthcare system. They need to have vision, strategic thinking, emotional intelligence, cultural compatibility, and resilience. Healthcare companies will be able to succeed in a world that is always changing if these skills keep getting better. Leadership in healthcare isn't just about making decisions. It's also about motivating and driving teams toward a future of quality, safety, and innovation, which will lead to the best health outcomes for both patients and communities.

REFERENCES

Abdullah, K. H., & Abd Aziz, F. S. (2021). Mapping of laboratory safety research: A bibliometric review. *Malaysian Journal of Public Health Medicine, 21*(1), 303–310. DOI: 10.37268/mjphm/vol.21/no.1/art.864

ACHE. (2015). *Leadership competencies for health services managers leadership competencies for healthcare services managers*. https://www.ache.org/-/media/ache/about-ache/leadership_competencies_healthcare_services_managers.pdf

Achua, C. F., & Lussier, R. N. (2010). *Effective Leadership* (4th ed.). South-Western.

Ahsan, M. J. (2023). The role of emotional intelligence in effective corporate social responsibility leadership. *The International Journal of Organizational Analysis, 31*(8), 75–91.

Al-Fadhalah, T., & Elamir, H. (2021). Organizational culture, quality of care and leadership style in government general hospitals in Kuwait: A multimethod study. *Journal of Healthcare Leadership*, 243–254. PMID: 34703349

Al-Ghamdi, A. O., Al-Mtairi, K. Q., Bin Gadeeb, F. A., Ali, I., Al-Mutairi, A. O., & Al-Resheedi, F. S. (2022). Evaluating the Performance of the Health Staff and its Role in Improving the Efficiency of Services. *International Journal (Toronto, Ont.), 10*(6).

Al-Haddad, M., & Psych, F. R. C. (2003). Leadership in healthcare management. *Bahrain Medical Bulletin, 25*(1), 1.

Al-Issa, H. E., & Abdelsalam, M. K. (2021). Antecedents to Leadership: A CB-SEM and PLS-SEM Validation. *International Journal of Sustainable Development and Planning, 16*(8).

Al-Issa, H. E., & Omar, M. M. S. (2024). Digital innovation drivers in retail banking: The role of leadership, culture, and technostress inhibitors. *The International Journal of Organizational Analysis, 32*(11), 19–43.

Al Kuwaiti, A., & Al Muhanna, F. A. (2019). Challenges facing healthcare leadership in attaining accreditation of teaching hospitals. *Leadership in Health Services, 32*(2), 170–181. PMID: 30945601

Al-Sawai, A. (2013). Leadership of Healthcare Professionals: Where Do We Stand? *Oman Medical Journal, 28*, 285. DOI: 10.5001/omj.2013.79 PMID: 23904925

Al-Touby, S. S. (2012). Functional results-oriented healthcare leadership: A novel leadership model. *Oman Medical Journal, 27*(2), 104. PMID: 22496933

Al-Zahrani, I. A., & Brek, T. M. (2024). Comprehensive Genome Analysis of Colistin-Only–Sensitive KPC-2 and NDM1-1-Coproducing *Klebsiella pneumoniae* ST11 and *Acinetobacter baumannii* ST2 From a Critically Ill Patient With COVID-19 in Saudi Arabia. *International Journal of Microbiology, 2024*(1). DOI: 10.1155/2024/9233075

Al-Zu'Bi. Ahmad (2021). *Asymmetric information, fraud, and switching costs in healthcare insurance markets.* PhD Thesis, UQ Business School, The University of Queensland. DOI: 10.14264/653d111

Al Zoubi, F., Khalaf, G., Beaulé, P. E., & Fallavollita, P. (2023). Leveraging machine learning and prescriptive analytics to improve operating room throughput. *Frontiers in Digital Health, 5*. Advance online publication. DOI: 10.3389/fdgth.2023.1242214 PMID: 37808917

Almomani, E., Sullivan, J., Hajjieh, M., & Leighton, K. (2020). Simulation-based education programme for upskilling non-critical care nurses for COVID-19 deployment. *BMJ Simulation and Technology Enhanced Learning, 7*(5), bmjstel-2020-000711. DOI: 10.1136/bmjstel-2020-000711

Alsharari, A. F., Salihu, D., & Alshammari, F. F. (2025). Effectiveness of virtual clinical learning in nursing education: A systematic review. *BMC Nursing*, *24*(1). Advance online publication. DOI: 10.1186/s12912-025-03076- PMID: 40241119

Amabile, T. M., & Khaire, M. (2008). Creativity and the role of the leader. *Journal of the Management Training Institute. SAIL, Ranchi*, *36*(3), 48–51.

Anderson, D. (2024). *From trait to transformation- The evolution of leadership theories.* Scribd. https://www.scribd.com/document/687075302/from-trait-to transformation-the-evolution-of-leadership-theories

Asif, M., Jameel, A., Sahito, N., Hwang, J., Hussain, A., & Manzoor, F. (2019). Can leadership enhance patient satisfaction? Assessing the role of administrative and medical quality. *International Journal of Environmental Research and Public Health*, *16*(17), 3212. PMID: 31484308

Avolio, B. J. (2007). Promoting more integrative strategies for leadership theory-building. *The American Psychologist*, *62*(1), 25–33. DOI: 10.1037/0003-066x.62.1.25 PMID: 17209677

Barbuto, J. E.Jr, & Wheeler, D. W. (2006). Scale development and construct clarification of servant leadership. *Group & Organization Management*, *31*(3), 300–326.

Basadur, M. (2004). Leading others to think innovatively together: Creative leadership. *The Leadership Quarterly*, *15*(1), 103–121. DOI: 10.1016/j.leaqua.2003.12.007

Bass, B. M. (1985). *Leadership and Performance beyond Expectations*. Free Press.

Batool, I. (2025). *RealTime Health Monitoring Using 5G Networks: A Deep Learning-Based Architecture for Remote Patient Care*. ArXiv.org. https://arxiv.org/abs/2501.01027

Bauer, T., Erdogan, B., Caughlin, D., & Truxillo, D. (2023). *Human resource management: People, data, and analytics*. Sage Publications.

Beauvais, A. M. (2019). *Leadership and management competence in nursing practice: competencies, skills, decision making*. Springer Publishing Company.

Bensimon, E. M. (1989). The Meaning of "Good Presidential Leadership": A Frame Analysis. *Review of Higher Education, 12*(2), 107–123. DOI: 10.1353/rhe.1989.0024

Brazier, D. K. (2005). Influence of contextual factors on health-care leadership. *Leadership and Organization Development Journal, 26*(2), 128–140. DOI: 10.1108/01437730510582563

Brown, N. O. (2021). *The Lived and Perceived Experiences of Healthcare Leaders Deploying Lean Six Sigma Methods: A Phenomenological Study*. Baker College.

Bruning, P., & Baghurst, T. (2013). Improving ethical decision making in health care leadership. *Business and Economics Journal, 4*(2), 1–5.

Budak, N. H., Aykin, E., Seydim, A. C., Greene, A. K., & Guzel-Seydim, Z. B. (2014). Functional Properties of Vinegar. *Journal of Food Science, 79*(5), R757–R764. DOI: 10.1111/1750-3841.12434 PMID: 24811350

Burns, J. M. (1978). *Leadership*. Harper & Row.

Carayon, P., Karsh, B.-T., Gurses, A. P., Holden, R. J., Hoonakker, P., Schoofs Hundt, A., Montague, E., Rodriguez, A. J., & Wetterneck, T. B. (2013). Macroergonomics in Health Care Quality and Patient Safety. *Review of Human Factors and Ergonomics, 8*(1), 4–54. DOI: 10.1177/1557234x13492976 PMID: 24729777

Carmeli, A., Gelbard, R., & Gefen, D. (2010). The importance of innovation leadership in cultivating strategic fit and enhancing firm performance. *The Leadership Quarterly, 21*(3), 339–349.

Carvajal, A. L. P., & Sanchez, R. D. (2023). Strategic considerations, challenges, and opportunities in establishing the International Journal of Open-access, Interdisciplinary, and New Educational Discoveries (iJOINED). *International Journal of Open-access* [iJOINED ETCOR]. *Interdisciplinary and New Educational Discoveries of ETCOR Educational Research Center, 2*(2), 539–546.

Chen, J. K., & Sriphon, T. (2022). Authentic leadership, trust, and social exchange relationships under the influence of leader behavior. *Sustainability*, *14*(10), 5883.

Choucair, I. (2023). *Perceptions of Business Leaders on Achieving Organizational Alignment: A Qualitative Exploratory Case Study* (Doctoral dissertation, University of Phoenix).

Cleary, S., Toit, A. D., Scott, V., & Gilson, L. (2018). Enabling relational leadership in primary healthcare settings: Lessons from the DIALHS collaboration. *Health Policy and Planning*, *33*(suppl_2), ii65–ii74. PMID: 30053037

Cloud, A. (2023). *Understanding the Role of an Advisory Board at a Privately Held Professional Company*. Advisorycloud.com. https://advisorycloud.com/blog/understanding-the-role-of-an-advisory-board-at-a-privately-held-professional-company

Connor, M., & Pokora, J. (2017). *Coaching and mentoring at work: Developing effective practice* (3rd ed.). Open University Press.

Culp, C. A. (1992). *Leadership styles in organizations committed to continuous quality improvement and those not committed to continuous improvement*. United States International University.

Davies, B. J., & Davies, B. (2004). Strategic leadership. *School Leadership & Management*, *24*(1), 29–38.

Day, D. V., Fleenor, J. W., Atwater, L. E., Sturm, R. E., & McKee, R. A. (2014). Advances in Leader and Leadership development: A Review of 25 Years of Research and Theory. *The Leadership Quarterly*, *25*(1), 63–82.

De Brún, A., O'Donovan, R., & McAuliffe, E. (2019). Interventions to develop collectivistic leadership in healthcare settings: A systematic review. *BMC Health Services Research*, *19*(1), 72. PMID: 30683089

Denis, J. L., & Van Gestel, N. (2016). Medical doctors in healthcare leadership: Theoretical and practical challenges. *BMC Health Services Research*, *16*(Suppl 2), 158. PMID: 27230551

Dogan, A., & Schroevers, S. (2018). *Linking leadership: to cross-cultural expectations across nations*. Amsterdam University Of Applied Sciences.

El-Jardali, F., & Fadlallah, R. (2017). Approaches to quality improvement in healthcare. *International Journal for Quality in Health Care : Journal of the International Society for Quality in Health Care*, *29*(7), 882–887.

Ellis, P. (2021). Leadership Approaches for Modern Nursing Practice. *British Journal of Cardiac Nursing*, *16*(2), 1–5. DOI: 10.12968/bjca.2020.0091

Fernandez, C. S. P., Noble, C. C., Jensen, E. T., & Chapin, J. (2016). Improving Leadership Skills in Physicians: A 6-Month Retrospective Study. *Journal of Leadership Studies*, *9*(4), 6–19. DOI: 10.1002/jls.21420

Finzel, H. (2007). *The top ten mistakes leaders make*. Colorado Springs, Col. Cook.

Frich, J. C., Brewster, A. L., Cherlin, E. J., & Bradley, E. H. (2015). Leadership development programs for physicians: A systematic review. *Journal of General Internal Medicine*, *30*(5), 656–674. PMID: 25527339

Fullan, M. (2016). *The New Meaning of Educational Change* (4th ed.). Teachers College Press.

Gifford, R., van de Baan, F., Westra, D., Ruwaard, D., & Fleuren, B. (2023). Through the looking glass: Confronting health care management's biggest challenges in the wake of a crisis. *Health Care Management Review*, *48*(2), 185–196. PMID: 36792956

Goleman, D., Boyatzis, R., & McKee, A. (2013). *Primal Leadership: Unleashing the Power of Emotional Intelligence*. Harvard Business Press.

Gosbee, J. (2002). Human factors engineering and patient safety. *Quality & Safety in Health Care*, *11*(4), 352–354. PMID: 12468696

Griffith, A. (2023). The creativity lab: Interdisciplinary creativity in higher education. *Journal of Interdisciplinary Studies in Education*, *12*(1), 85–108.

Guo, W. (2023). Exploring the value of AI technology in optimizing and implementing supply chain data for pharmaceutical companies. *Innovation in Science and Technology*, *2*(3), 1–6.

Halili, E. (2022). *The gender gap in technical maritime industry leadership in Lithuania: why women are not progressing as fast in leadership positions as men in this industry* (Doctoral dissertation, LCC tarptautinis universitetas).

Hantula, D. A. (2018). Job satisfaction: The management tool and leadership responsibility. In *Leadership and Cultural Change* (pp. 123–136). Routledge.

Hargadon, A. B., & Bechky, B. A. (2006). When collections of creatives become creative collectives: A field study of problem solving at work. *Organization Science*, *17*(4), 484–500.

Hargett, C., Doty, J., Hauck, J., Webb, A., Cook, S., Tsipis, N., Neumann, J., Andolsek, K., & Taylor, D. (2017). Developing a Model for Effective Leadership in healthcare: A Concept Mapping Approach. *Journal of Healthcare Leadership*, *9*(9), 69–78. DOI: 10.2147/JHL.S141664 PMID: 29355249

Hasan, A. A., Ahmad, S. Z., & Osman, A. (2023). Transformational leadership and work engagement as mediators on nurses' job performance in healthcare clinics: Work environment as a moderator. *Leadership in Health Services*, *36*(4), 537–561. PMID: 37093237

Health Metric Network. (2023) *Assessing the National Health Information System An Assessment Tool*. Iris.who.int. Retrieved May 13, 2025, from https://iris.who.int/bitstream/handle/10665/43932/9789241547512_eng.pdf?sequence=1

Heinen, M., van Oostveen, C., Peters, J., Vermeulen, H., & Huis, A. (2019). An integrative review of leadership competencies and attributes in advanced nursing practice. *Journal of Advanced Nursing*, *75*(11), 2378–2392. PMID: 31162695

Helbling, N. (2023). *Rural Healthcare Finance: An Examination of Challenges and Opportunities* (Master's thesis, The College of St. Scholastica).

International Hospital Federation. (2023). *Competencies for future-focused leadership Global Healthcare Leadership Competency Model 2023*. https://ihf-fih.org/wp-content/uploads/2023/06/IHF-Global-Healthcare-Leadership-Competency-Model-2023.pdf

Ismayilova, K., & Bolander Laksov, K. (2023). Teaching creatively in higher education: The roles of personal attributes and environment. *Scandinavian Journal of Educational Research*, *67*(4), 536–548.

Izadi, A., Jahani, Y., Rafiei, S., Masoud, A., & Vali, L. (2017). Evaluating health service quality: Using importance performance analysis. *International Journal of Health Care Quality Assurance*, *30*(7), 656–663. DOI: 10.1108/ijhcqa-02-2017-0030 PMID: 28809594

Javidan, M., Dorfman, P. W., Howell, J. P., & Hanges, P. J. (2010). Leadership and cultural context. *Handbook of leadership theory and practice*, 346-372.

Junaid, M., Zhang, Q., Cao, M., & Luqman, A. (2023). Nexus between technology enabled supply chain dynamic capabilities, integration, resilience, and sustainable performance: An empirical examination of healthcare organizations. *Technological Forecasting and Social Change*, *196*, 122828.

Kalaitzi, S., Cheung, K. L., Hiligsmann, M., Babich, S., & Czabanowska, K. (2019). Exploring women healthcare leaders' perceptions on barriers to leadership in Greek context. *Frontiers in Public Health*, *7*, 68. PMID: 31024874

Karneli, O. (2023). The role of adhocratic leadership in facing the changing business environment. [ADMAN]. *Journal of Contemporary Administration and Management*, *1*(2), 77–83.

Karsh, W. T. B., Lapin, J. A., Karsh, B. T., & Beasley, J. W. (2012). Human factors and ergonomics in primary care. *Handbook of Human Factors and Ergonomics in Health Care and Patient Safety. Boca Raton, FL: Taylor and& Francis Group*, 763-74.

Kelly, L. (2023). The contextual dynamics of mindfulness for authentic leadership: industry and work influences. In *Mindfulness for Authentic Leadership: Theory and Cases* (pp. 193–214). Springer International Publishing.

Khalili, A. (2017). Creative and innovative leadership: Measurement development and validation. *Management Research Review*, *40*(10), 1117–1138.

Khan, S., Vandermorris, A., Shepherd, J., Begun, J. W., Lanham, H. J., Uhl-Bien, M., & Berta, W. (2018). Embracing uncertainty, managing complexity: Applying complexity thinking principles to transformation efforts in healthcare systems. *BMC Health Services Research*, *18*(1). Advance online publication. DOI: 10.1186/s12913-018-2994-0 PMID: 29562898

Kilic, B. E. (2023). Program development for leaders in the post-truth era: Arts-based creative leadership communication program. *Evaluation and Program Planning*, *98*, 102295. PMID: 37148650

Kotter, J. P. (1996). Leading change. In *Internet Archive*. Harvard Business School Press., https://archive.org/details/leadingchange0000kott

Kouzes, J. M., & Posner, B. Z. (2023). *The Leadership Challenge* (4th ed.). Jossey-Bass.

Kumar, R. D., & Khiljee, N. (2016). Leadership in healthcare. *Anaesthesia and Intensive Care Medicine*, *17*(1), 63–65.

Lantz, P. M. (2008). Gender and leadership in healthcare administration: 21st century progress and challenges. *Journal of Healthcare Management*, *53*(5). PMID: 18856135

Lasrado, F., & Kassem, R. (2021). Let's get everyone involved! The effects of transformational leadership and organizational culture on organizational excellence. *International Journal of Quality & Reliability Management*, *38*(1), 169–194.

Lee, T. H., Volpp, K. G., Cheung, V. G., & Dzau, V. J. (2021). Diversity and inclusiveness in health care leadership: Three key steps. *NEJM Catalyst Innovations in Care Delivery*, *2*(3).

Leonard, M., Graham, S., & Bonacum, D. (2004). The human factor: The critical importance of effective teamwork and communication in providing safe care. *BMJ Quality & Safety*, *13*(suppl 1), i85–i90. PMID: 15465961

Lisá, E., Sousa, J., Morais, C., & Gomes, A. R. (2023). Leadership cycles, styles, and antecedent factors: The perspective of coaches and young soccer athletes from national Slovak leagues. *Frontiers in Psychology*, *14*, 1218290. PMID: 37609500

Lobdell, K. W., Hariharan, S., Smith, W., Rose, G. A., Ferguson, B., & Fussell, C. (2020). Improving health care leadership in the COVID-19 era. *NEJM Catalyst Innovations in Care Delivery*, *1*(3).

Mahsud, R., Yukl, G., & Prussia, G. (2010). Leader empathy, ethical leadership, and relations-oriented behaviors as antecedents of leader-member exchange quality. *Journal of Managerial Psychology*, *25*(6), 561–577.

Mainemelis, C., Kark, R., & Epitropaki, O. (2015). Creative leadership: A multi-context conceptualization. *The Academy of Management Annals*, *9*(1), 393–482.

Martinez, F. J., Han, M. K., Allinson, J. P., Barr, R. G., Boucher, R. C., Calverley, P. M. A., Celli, B. R., Christenson, S. A., Crystal, R. G., Fagerås, M., Freeman, C. M., Groenke, L., Hoffman, E. A., Kesimer, M., Kostikas, K., Paine, R., Rafii, S., Rennard, S. I., Segal, L. N., & Shaykhiev, R. (2018). At the Root: Defining and Halting Progression of Early Chronic Obstructive Pulmonary Disease. *American Journal of Respiratory and Critical Care Medicine*, *197*(12), 1540–1551. DOI: 10.1164/rccm.201710-2028pp PMID: 29406779

Miller, K. A., Nagler, J., Wolff, M., Schumacher, D. J., & Pusic, M. V. (2023). It takes a village: Optimal graduate medical education requires a deliberately developmental organization. *Perspectives on Medical Education*, *12*(1), 282. PMID: 37520509

Mittal, E. V., & Sindhu, E. (2012). Emotional intelligence and leadership. *Global Journal of Management and Business Research*, *12*(16), 35–37.

Moradi-Moghadam, M., Safari, H., Moghadam, M. R. S., & Fathi, M. R. (2023). Re-creation fundamental concepts on the culture of excellence to achieve maturity of organisational excellence. *International Journal of Business Excellence*, *30*(2), 234–256.

Mumford, M. D., & Todd, E. M. (2019). Creativity and innovation at work. In *Creativity and innovation in organizations* (pp. 1–16). Routledge.

Murray, T. A., Benz, M. R., Cole, B., Jackson, J., Llamas, D., Marquard, S., & Taylor, C. L. (2023). The journey toward inclusive excellence. *The Journal of Nursing Education*, *62*(4), 225–232. PMID: 37021946

Newman, N., & Newman, D. (2021). Leadership behind masked faces: From uncertainty to resilience at a Jamaican academic library. *Journal of Academic Librarianship*, *47*(5), 102377.

Ni ă, M. A. (2015). The new intelligence, the new leader and the organizational stress. *Revista de Management Comparat Interna ional*, *16*(3), 335–342.

Nzinga, J., McGivern, G., & English, M. (2018). Examining clinical leadership in Kenyan public hospitals through the distributed leadership lens. *Health Policy and Planning*, *33*(suppl_2), ii27–ii34. PMID: 30053035

Omar, N. (2018). Influence of strategic leadership on performance of manufacturing companies in Kenya: A case study of Zenko Kenya Limited. *Core.ac.uk*. oai:repository.mua.ac.ke:2631

Osmani, S. S. N. (2013). Effective leadership – The way to excellence in health professions education. *Medical Teacher*, *35*(11), 956–958. DOI: 10.3109/0142159x.2013.818629 PMID: 23924363

Oti-Boadi, M., Oppong Asante, K., & Malm, E. K. (2019). The Experiences of Ageing Parents of Young Adults with Autism Spectrum Disorders (ASD). *Journal of Adult Development*. Advance online publication. DOI: 10.1007/s10804-018-09325-6

Palmer, B., Walls, M., Burgess, Z., & Stough, C. (2001). Emotional intelligence and effective leadership. *Leadership and Organization Development Journal*, *22*(1), 5–10.

Perez, J. (2021). Leadership in healthcare: Transitioning from clinical professional to healthcare leader. *Journal of Healthcare Management*, *66*(4), 280–302. PMID: 33929398

Piotrowski, M. (2020). Relationship of self-directed learning and resilience in healthcare middle managers. *International Journal of Self-Directed Learning*, *17*(1), 19–38.

Polden, D. J. (2019). Army leadership and the profession. *ADP*, *6*(22), i.

Professional Leadership Coaching | Coaching with CT. (2023). *Healthcare leadership development programs*. https://www.coachingwithct.com

Pyzdek, T., & Keller, P. A. (2018). *The Six Sigma Handbook* (5th ed.). Mcgraw-Hill Education.

Quinn, R. E., & Spreitzer, G. M. (1997). The road to empowerment: Seven questions every leader should consider. *Organizational Dynamics*, *26*(2), 37–49. DOI: 10.1016/s0090-2616(97)90004-8

Qureshi, J. S., Young, S., Muyco, A. P., Borgstein, E., Charles, A. G., Mulwafu, W., & Mkandawire, N. (2013). Addressing Malawi's surgical workforce crisis: A sustainable paradigm for training and collaboration in Africa. *Surgery*, *153*(2), 272–281. PMID: 23063312

Raza, M. H., Rind, Y. M., Javed, I., Zubair, M., Mehmood, M. Q., & Massoud, Y. (2023). Smart meters for smart energy: A review of business intelligence applications. *IEEE Access : Practical Innovations, Open Solutions*, *11*, 120001–120022.

Richards, A. (2020). Exploring the benefits and limitations of transactional leadership in healthcare. *Nursing Standard*, *35*(12), 46–50. PMID: 33089675

Rizzo, A., & Bouchard, S. (2019). *Virtual reality for psychological and neurocognitive interventions*. Springer.

Robbins, S. P. Judge, Timothy, A. (2023). *Organizational Behavior* (19th ed.). Pearson.

Sahertian, P., & Graha, A. N. (2016). Exploring leadership dimension among organizations (the analysis against leadership excellence based on cultural and ethnical backgrounds in Indonesia). *Indian Journal of Commerce and Management Studies*, *7*(1), 01-07.

Sahertian, P., & Jawas, U. (2021, April). Cultural Values and Leadership Excellence. In *2nd Annual Conference on Social Science and Humanities (ANCOSH 2020)* (pp. 310-313). Atlantis Press.

Salman, D. A., & Auso, K. A. (2022). [Retracted] The Sequential Influence of Creative Leadership and Organizational Environment on Strategic Performance. *Journal of Environmental and Public Health*, *2022*(1), 5948806. PMID: 38288294

Sarihasan, I., Dajnoki, K., Oláh, J., & Al-Dalahmeh, M. (2022). The importance of the leadership functions of a high-reliability health care organization in managing the COVID-19 pandemic in Turkey. *Economia e Sociologia*, *15*(1), 78–93. DOI: 10.14254/2071-789x.2022/15-1/5

Sendjaya, S., Sarros, J. C., & Santora, J. C. (2008). Defining and measuring servant leadership behaviour in organizations. *Journal of Management Studies*, *45*(2), 402–424. DOI: 10.1111/j.1467-6486.2007.00761.x

Sfantou, D. F., Laliotis, A., Patelarou, A. E., Sifaki-Pistolla, D., Matalliotakis, M., & Patelarou, E. (2017, October). Importance of leadership style towards quality of care measures in healthcare settings: A systematic review. [). MDPI.]. *Health Care*, *5*(4), 73. PMID: 29036901

Shalley, C. E., & Lemoine, G. J. (2018). Leader behaviors and employee creativity: Taking stock of the current state of research. *Creative leadership*, 79-94.

Sias, P. M., & Cahill, D. J. (1998). From coworkers to friends: The development of peer friendships in the workplace. *Western Journal of Communication*, *62*(3), 273–299. DOI: 10.1080/10570319809374611

Simonsen, K. A., & Shim, R. S. (2019). Embracing diversity and inclusion in psychiatry leadership. *The Psychiatric Clinics of North America*, *42*(3), 463–471. PMID: 31358125

Simsek, Z. (2007). CEO tenure and organizational performance: An intervening model. *Strategic Management Journal*, *28*(6), 653–662.

Sonnino, R. E. (2016). Health care leadership development and training: Progress and pitfalls. *Journal of Healthcare Leadership*, 19–29. PMID: 29355187

Spreier, S. W., Fontaine, M. H., & Malloy, R. L. (2006). Leadership run amok. *Harvard Business Review*, *84*(6), 72–82. PMID: 16770895

St. Pierre, M., Hofinger, G., & Buerschaper, C. (Eds.). (2008). *Crisis Management in Acute Care Settings*. Springer Berlin Heidelberg., DOI: 10.1007/978-3-540-71062-2

Strack, G., & Fottler, M. D. (2002). Spirituality and effective leadership in healthcare: Is there a connection? *Frontiers of Health Services Management*, *18*(4), 3–18. PMID: 12087690

Strong, E. A., De Castro, R., Sambuco, D., Stewart, A., Ubel, P. A., Griffith, K. A., & Jagsi, R. (2013). Work–life balance in academic medicine: Narratives of physician-researchers and their mentors. *Journal of General Internal Medicine*, *28*(12), 1596–1603. PMID: 23765289

Terry, L. D. (1998). Administrative leadership, neo-managerialism, and the public management movement. *Public Administration Review*, 194–200.

Thomas, A., & Suresh, M. (2023). Readiness for agility adaptability and alignment in healthcare organizations. *IISE Transactions on Healthcare Systems Engineering*, *13*(2), 161–174.

Turner, P. (2018). *Leadership in healthcare: delivering organisational transformation and operational excellence*. Springer.

Turyadi, I., Zulkifli, Z., Tawil, M. R., Ali, H., & Sadikin, A. (2023). The role of digital leadership in organizations to improve employee performance and business success. *Jurnal Ekonomi, 12*(02), 1671–1677.

Upshaw, T. L., Craig-Neil, A., Macklin, J., Gray, C. S., Chan, T. C., Gibson, J., & Pinto, A. D. (2023). Priorities for artificial intelligence applications in primary care: A Canadian deliberative dialogue with patients, providers, and health system leaders. *Journal of the American Board of Family Medicine : JABFM, 36*(2), 210–220. PMID: 36948537

Van, D. (2020). Creativity stimulation in healthcare leadership. *Journal of Healthcare Innovation, 7*(3), 26–37.

Wang, Y., & Wang, Y. (2022). Developing creative leadership in the use of digital communication tools: A psychological perspective. *Sustainability, 14*(19), 11796.

Warrick, D. D. (2017). What leaders need to know about organizational culture. *Business Horizons, 60*(3), 395–404.

Weberg, D. (2012, October). Complexity leadership: A healthcare imperative. *Nursing Forum, 47*(4), •••. PMID: 23127241

Weinger, M. B. (2012). *Human factors in anesthesiology. Handbook of Human Factors and Ergonomics in Health Care and Patient Safety* (2nd ed.). Taylor & Francis.

West, M., Eckert, R., & Pasmore, B. (2014). *Developing collective leadership for health care*. The King's Fund. https://www.kingsfund.org.uk/insight-and-analysis/reports/developing-collective-leadership-for-health-care

Wetterneck, T. B., Lapin, J. A., Karsh, B. T., & Beasley, J. W. (2012). *Human factors and ergonomics in primary care. Handbook of Human Factors and Ergonomics in Health Care and Patient Safety*. Taylor and& Francis Group.

World Health Organization. (2020). Global strategy on human resources for health: Workforce 2030 (ISBN 978-92-4-151113-1). https://apps.who.int/iris/bitstream/handle/10665/250368/9789241511131-eng.pdf?sequence=1 frontlinehealthworkers.org+8apps.who.int+8iris.who.int

Yuguda, A. Abdulrazak Yuguda MADU, Abbo, U., & Shehu Jafaru Salisu. (2023, October 20). *Strategic leadership: A key to organisational effectiveness and improvement*. ResearchGate; unknown. https://www.researchgate.net/publication/374867917_strategic_leadership_a_key_t

Zaccaro, S. J., LaPort, K., & Jose, I. (2013, January 1). *Attributes of successful leaders: A performance requirements approach.* https://www.researchgate.net/publication/287105619_Attributes_of_successful_leaders_

Zank, S., de Araujo, L. G., & Hanazaki, N. (2019). Resilience and adaptability of traditional healthcare systems. *Ecology and Society*, *24*(1).

Zayas-Cabán, T., & Valdez, R. S. (2012). Human factors and ergonomics in home care. *Handbook of human factors and ergonomics in health care and patient safety*, 2, 743-762.

Zhou, J., & George, J. M. (2003). Awakening employee creativity: The role of leader emotional intelligence. *The Leadership Quarterly*, *14*(4-5), 545–568. DOI: 10.1016/S1048-9843(03)00051-1

Chapter 8
Technology's Transformation of Healthcare Leadership:
A Comprehensive Synthesis

ABSTRACT

The rapid integration of digital technologies—including electronic health records (EHRs), telemedicine, artificial intelligence (AI), and big data analytics—is fundamentally transforming healthcare leadership roles, competencies, and outcomes. Leaders must adopt new roles such as digital strategists, change agents, and stakeholder engagers, requiring digital literacy, strategic vision, ethical stewardship, and adaptive agility. Frameworks like the Technology-Organization-Environment (TOE) and Digital Transformational Leadership (DTL) elucidate how healthcare leaders navigate technological, organizational, and environmental factors to drive digital transformation. Effective leadership enhances patient-centered care, operational efficiency, workforce engagement, and data-driven decision-making, while addressing barriers including infrastructure limitations, user resistance, ethical concerns, and equity gaps—particularly in low-resource settings.

TECHNOLOGY-DRIVEN HEALTHCARE LEADERSHIP

The quick adoption of digital technologies like electronic health records (EHRs), telemedicine, artificial intelligence (AI), and big data analytics is changing the responsibilities and skills needed for healthcare professionals. To make sure that care is centered on the patient, operations are efficient, and the staff is engaged, leaders must now operate in complicated, technology-driven settings (Avolio et al., 2014). This synthesis looks at how technology is changing healthcare leadership by looking

DOI: 10.4018/979-8-3373-2225-4.ch008

at new positions, necessary skills, and effects on outcomes. It also talks about how previous frameworks didn't focus enough on digital leadership.

THEORETICAL FRAMEWORKS FOR TECHNOLOGY-DRIVEN LEADERSHIP

Healthcare leadership in the digital age builds on transformational, servant, and complexity leadership ideas, but it needs to be adapted to deal with the unique problems that technology brings. The Technology-Organization-Environment (TOE) framework. The adoption of healthcare technology depends on elements related to technology (like how easy it is to use), the organization (like how ready the leaders are), and the environment (like the rules). To accelerate digital transformation, improve organizational agility, and get more people involved, leaders need to align these dimensions. Studies have shown that digital health technology make healthcare professionals far more productive.

Digital Transformational Leadership (DTL) builds on transformational leadership by focusing on digital literacy, having a strategic plan for how to use technology, and being able to adapt to digital settings (Berniak-Woźny & Rataj, 2023). DTL leaders encourage teams to use digital technologies, deal with change, and encourage new ideas, which makes primary care more digitally intense and flexible (Berniak-Woźny & Rataj, 2023). El Sawy et al. (2020) came up with the idea of Digital Leadership Theory, which is about leadership techniques that help businesses use digital technologies to make big changes. It takes leaders who are good at both traditional skills and new ones like digital literacy, change management, and encouraging innovation. In general, these frameworks stress that good digital leadership includes having a vision, being digitally literate, and being able to adapt to new technologies and healthcare systems that change quickly.

TECHNOLOGICAL INFLUENCES ON DIGITAL HEALTHCARE LEADERSHIP: THE ROLES OF TELEMEDICINE, EHRS, AND DATA ANALYTICS

The new t has been integrated with the Healthcare Leadership, Telemedicine, electronic health records (EHRs), artificial intelligence (AI), and data analytics have all changed the way healthcare is delivered. This means that leaders need to come up with new ways to deal with digital transformation (Avolio et al., 2014; Kruse et al., 2018). These technologies make it easier to get to things, work more efficiently, and make decisions, but they also create problems including data security, user resistance, and infrastructure limits (Boonstra & Broekhuis, 2010; Tabibzadeh & Tran, 2022). To get better results for patients, better performance from workers, and more resilient organizations, healthcare executives need to be digital strategists, change agents, and ethical stewards (El Sawy et al., 2020). Leadership has changed from making decisions based on gut feelings to using data to make decisions, which has led to cultures of measurement, accountability, and real-time analytics for being ready for a crisis. To strike a balance between the benefits of AI and the hazards to patient safety, ethical leadership and critical evaluation are also needed. This will encourage curiosity about technology while protecting clinical judgment and patient confidence (Kruse et al., 2018). Change management leadership is very important for using robotics while keeping staff morale high and putting patients first (Catinella & Esparza, 2021). As EHR transition requires compassionate leadership to deal with change fatigue and workflow integration (Boonstra & Broekhuis, 2010), leaders must make sure that technological investments are in line with proven benefits and long-term operational strategy. So, technology is changing the way healthcare leaders work from hierarchical, protocol-based models to digital, adaptive, and transformational leadership styles that combine technical skills with traditional skills to promote innovation and keep patient-centered care (El Sawy et al., 2020; Berniak-Woźny & Rataj, 2023).

TELEMEDICINE AND VIRTUAL LEADERSHIP

Telemedicine has changed the way healthcare professionals work by letting them reinvent how care is delivered, make it easier for people to get care, and use resources more effectively (Contreras et al., 2020; Kruse et al., 2018). To be able to implement something well, leaders need to be able to adapt, which means they need to be able to use technology, manage change, and make sure that virtual care fits with the goals of the business (Avolio et al., 2014; Tabibzadeh & Tran, 2022). Leaders need to coordinate virtual teams, oversee remote care delivery, make sure patient safety requirements are met, and deal with problems like clinician resistance, digital inequities, and getting patients involved (Wosik et al., 2020). Strategic leadership is also very important for making telemedicine rules, keeping data private, and encouraging professionals to work together on virtual platforms (Shigekawa et al., 2018). For example, the Cleveland Clinic Tele-ICU program connected intensivists with remote ICUs, redefining workflows through virtual rounding and remote staff training. This resulted in a 20% reduction in ICU mortality and a 25% reduction in ICU length of stay (Cleveland Clinic, 2018). Telemedicine enables remote care delivery, requiring leaders to develop strategies for virtual integration, patient engagement, and regulatory compliance. It improves access, reduces costs, and enhances patient satisfaction when supported by effective leadership (Talias & Pikoulis, 2024).

CASE STUDIES

Telemedicine In Rural Maternity Care (New Mexico, (USA)

The New Mexico Rural Maternity and Obstetrics Management Strategies (RMOMS) network expanded access to obstetrics care across five rural counties through telemedicine, resulting in a 30% increase in timely prenatal visits and reduced travel costs for patients. Leaders addressed digital literacy gaps through community education campaigns.

Telemedicine for Autism Spectrum Disorder (ASD) Assessment (USA)

A telemedicine-based ASD assessment tool, developed with machine learning and stakeholder input, improved diagnostic access for rural and low-income communities by reducing wait times by 25%, accurately classifying ASD in 63% of cases (Paulson et al., 2022).

Telemedicine During COVID-19 (Italy)

Italian healthcare organizations rapidly scaled telemedicine to minimize physical contact and optimize system capacity, resulting in a 15% reduction in hospital admissions and improved patient safety by minimizing infection exposure. However, uneven regional adoption highlighted the need for infrastructure investment (Cannavacciuolo, Capaldo, & Ponsiglione, 2023). Overall, telemedicine reshapes leadership roles by demanding proactive vision, technological integration capabilities, and a commitment to equitable, patient-centered virtual care.

Data-Driven Decision-Making and Big Data Analytics

Transformational leadership integrated with digital competencies enables healthcare leaders to inspire innovation while effectively managing technological change (El Sawy et al., 2020). Leaders require e-leadership skills, change management expertise, and strategic vision to scale up digital solutions that bridge care access gaps (Avolio et al., 2014). Effective leadership of geographically dispersed or technology-mediated teams necessitates strong virtual communication skills, the ability to build trust remotely, and robust performance monitoring (Avolio et al., 2014). Additionally, navigating complex technological changes demands leadership approaches grounded in continuous learning, experimentation, and frontline empowerment (Heifetz & Linsky, 2002). The growing role of data-driven decision-making and big data analytics is transforming healthcare leadership. Leaders must now demonstrate data literacy skills to interpret analytics for strategic decisions and foster data-driven cultures within clinical teams. Leadership decisions are increasingly guided by predictive analytics, real-time monitoring, and population health data (Garrido et al., 2005). For example, Kaiser Permanente's HealthConnect system integrated electronic health records with analytics to monitor outcomes and identify care gaps. Leaders championed data transparency initiatives and trained clinical managers to use dashboards for decision-making, leading to improved preventive care compliance and a 26% reduction in hospital admissions for chronic disease patients (Garrido et al., 2005).

CASE STUDIES

Cleveland Clinic Tele-ICU (USA)

The Cleveland Clinic implemented a Tele-ICU program connecting intensivists at a central command center with remote ICU sites. Leadership actions included re-engineering ICU workflows to integrate virtual rounds and training nurses and respiratory therapists on telecommunication protocols. Outcomes included a 20% reduction in ICU mortality and a 25% decrease in average ICU length of stay (Cleveland Clinic, 2018).

India's eSanjeevani Telemedicine Platform

The Government of India launched the eSanjeevani telemedicine platform during COVID-19, training over 100,000 doctors in virtual consultation. Outcomes included over 200 million consultations within two years, significantly improving rural access to specialist care (Ministry of Health, 2022).

Overall, transformational digital leadership enables leaders to integrate technology with human-centered critical care, fostering innovation, operational efficiency, and equitable patient outcomes in the digital era.

ARTIFICIAL INTELLIGENCE (AI) AND CLINICAL DECISION SUPPORT IN HEALTHCARE LEADERSHIP

Artificial intelligence (AI) tools are increasingly used for diagnostic support, patient triage, and administrative optimization, creating new challenges and opportunities for healthcare leadership. Leaders must develop technological curiosity balanced with critical evaluation of AI limitations, alongside ethical leadership to address issues such as patient data privacy and algorithmic bias. Leadership Competencies Required included (Critical appraisal of AI capabilities and limitations, Ethical stewardship of patient data and algorithm transparency and Change management to integrate AI within clinical workflows while maintaining staff morale and clinical judgment)

CASE STUDIES

Babylon Health AI Symptom Checker (UK NHS)

Babylon Health deployed AI symptom checkers within the NHS to enhance triage services. Leadership challenges included ensuring clinical safety, integrating AI recommendations into care pathways, and managing staff fears of deskilling. The outcome was improved access to triage services, but risks of over-reliance without human validation were highlighted.

Kaiser Permanente Health Connect

Kaiser Permanente integrated electronic health records (EHR) with big data analytics to improve preventive care and manage chronic diseases. Leadership actions focused on training clinical managers to interpret data dashboards, resulting in a 26% improvement in preventive care compliance rates and a significant reduction in hospital admissions for chronic diseases (Garrido et al., 2005).

Mount Sinai Predictive Analytics for COVID-19

During COVID-19, Mount Sinai Health System (2020) used predictive analytics to forecast ICU bed demand. Leadership actions included collaborations between data science teams and operational leaders to develop surge prediction models, resulting in avoided ICU overcapacity through dynamic resource reallocation.

Mayo Clinic AI in Radiology

Mayo Clinic implemented AI algorithms for radiology image analysis, particularly in cardiac MRI assessments, to detect anomalies more efficiently. Outcomes included improved diagnostic speed and accuracy for targeted conditions (Mayo Clinic, n.d.).

AI integration in healthcare leadership requires adaptive, ethical, and technologically literate leadership approaches to ensure tools enhance rather than undermine patient-centered care. Leaders must foster innovation while safeguarding clinical oversight, workforce confidence, and patient trust in AI-enabled health systems.

ROBOTICS AND AUTOMATION WHERE (LEADERSHIP COMPETENCIES)

The integration of robotics and automation in healthcare necessitates strong leadership in change management and strategic vision to ensure these technologies enhance patient care rather than disrupt workforce morale. Change management involves transitioning staff to new roles, redesigning workflows, and upskilling personnel to maximize the value of automation. Strategic leadership is required to align technology investments with long-term operational goals and patient-centered outcomes (Intuitive Surgical, 2020). The University of California San Francisco (UCSF) Medical Center set up a robotic pharmacy system that took care of getting and preparing medications. Leadership was very important because they changed the duties of pharmacists to focus on direct patient care and drug therapy management. They also managed the redeployment of workers to ease worries about job security. This strategic integration almost completely got rid of pharmaceutical errors and made pharmacists more available for clinical consultation, which made patient safety and care quality better overall.

The use of Da Vinci robotic surgical systems in many institutions is another example of good leadership in adopting robotics. Leaders paid for training programs for surgeons to help them learn how to use robotic systems and set up new schedules and sterilization processes to make room for more complicated surgeries. These actions made patients heal faster and made surgeries more accurate, showing that "proactive leadership in robotics integration leads to measurable improvements in care delivery" (Intuitive Surgical, 2020). Overall, robotics and automation are changing how healthcare works. To drive innovations that improve safety, efficiency, and staff satisfaction, executives need to combine technological curiosity with change management competence and strategic foresight.

ELECTRONIC HEALTH RECORDS (EHR) IMPLEMENTATION

Electronic health records (EHRs) are changing the way healthcare leaders make decisions by making data administration easier, improving care coordination, and allowing them to make decisions based on facts. When leaders put policies in place to protect patient data and follow rules like the General Data Protection Regulation (GDPR) and the Health Insurance Portability and Accountability Act (HIPAA), they are responsible for making sure that systems can work together, are safe, and are used by everyone. Effective EHR integration can lower medical errors, make care coordination better, and make it easier for organizations to make decisions. For instance, the Mayo Clinic's switch to Epic Systems EHR showed how hard it is for leaders to deal with doctors who don't want to change, train personnel, and make sure patient safety during the switch. Even though there were problems, the result was better data integration, better care coordination, and more research opportunities (Mayo Clinic, n.d.). Similarly, Partners HealthCare (Mass General Brigham, 2019) conducted the largest Epic rollout in New England. Leadership established interdisciplinary task forces to incorporate frontline design input and maintained strong leadership visibility to address concerns and resistance. This approach improved clinical documentation accuracy and billing processes, although it also led to initial clinician burnout, highlighting the need for sustained leadership engagement and support throughout digital transitions. Another example is UCSF Health's collaboration with GE Healthcare, where leaders integrated EHR systems with predictive analytics to identify patients at risk of deterioration. This initiative reduced ICU mortality rates by 15% and decreased the length of stay by 12% through early interventions. Leadership was critical in ensuring data-driven alerts were adopted by clinicians to improve patient response times and outcomes. Overall, EHR advancements require leaders to combine technical, strategic, and change management competencies to navigate implementation barriers and maximize benefits for both care delivery and organizational performance the summary Synthesis of Leadership Challenges and Opportunities in digital healthcare leadership era shown in **Table 1** below.

Table 1. Synthesis of leadership challenges and opportunities in digital healthcare leadership era

Technological Area	Leadership Challenges	Opportunities
Telemedicine	Virtual team management, regulatory compliance	Expanded access, operational efficiency
Big Data Analytics	Data literacy gaps, change resistance	Evidence-based decisions, predictive care
AI Tools	Ethical concerns, workforce displacement fears	Diagnostic accuracy, triage optimization
Robotics	Role redefinition, cost justification	Zero errors, efficiency gains
EHR Systems	Implementation fatigue, interoperability issues	Integrated care, research facilitation

KEY IMPACTS OF TECHNOLOGY ON HEALTHCARE LEADERSHIP

Technology is transforming healthcare leadership across multiple dimensions, reshaping leadership roles, required competencies, and healthcare outcomes. The evolving leadership roles in this digital era include:

Digital Strategist

Leaders must strategically align technology adoption, such as electronic health records (EHRs) and telemedicine, with organizational goals. Kraus et al. (2018) identified five clusters of digital transformation in healthcare—operational efficiency, patient-centered approaches, organizational factors, workforce practices, and socio-economic aspects—that leaders need to integrate holistically.

Change Agent

Healthcare leaders facilitate the adoption of disruptive technologies like artificial intelligence (AI) and robotic surgery by managing resistance, reducing technological anxiety, and fostering a culture of innovation and continuous learning. Talwar et al. (2020) emphasize that overcoming barriers such as user resistance requires leaders to engage and train staff effectively.

Stakeholder Engager

Technology enables expanded collaboration across stakeholders, including patients, providers, and policymakers, through digital platforms such as social media. Massaro (2023) notes that digital tools improve public health communication, making it imperative for leaders to effectively engage diverse audiences.

In the digital age, healthcare leaders need to know how to use technologies like AI, big data, and the Internet of Things (IoT) to help them make decisions. Wosny, Strasser, and Hastings (2023) talk on the paradox that leaders face when they use digital technology: they have to weigh the benefits of greater efficiency against the fact that users will have to think more. Adaptive leadership is very important in healthcare since it is always changing and getting more complicated. Ethics also come into play when data privacy and AI bias make it harder to provide fair treatment. Berniak-Woźny and Rataj (2023) stress how important it is for digital leaders to put ethical technology use and sustainability first. Also, encouraging collaboration between professionals is important for bringing together technologies across teams with different areas of expertise. This is because transformational leadership and digital tools improve teamwork and patient outcomes, especially in nursing settings (Al-Thawabiya et al., 2023). Digital healthcare executives who are good at their jobs have a big effect on healthcare outcomes. According to Morrison, Hughes, and Doi (2022), telemonitoring and teleconsultation lead by digital champions made physiotherapy work better for cystic fibrosis patients. Using digital health technology (DHT) in hospitals in Somalia made healthcare personnel work better and less. Digital transformation makes things like implementing electronic health records (EHRs) easier, but leaders have to deal with problems like data security and getting users to use the new system (Talias & Pikoulis, 2024). Digital leadership also helps the environment by adding eco-friendly technologies to healthcare systems (Berniak-Woźny & Rataj, 2023). **Table 2** shows the Leadership Competencies needed for Technology Integration case studies The presented case studies demonstrate that technology is not merely a tool but a catalyst for leadership transformation in healthcare. Effective leaders integrate technological knowledge with strategic vision, ethical judgment, and change management to drive patient-centered innovation

Table 2. Leadership competencies for technology integration: case studies and synthesized insights

Competency	Description	Illustrative Case Study	Leadership Actions	Outcomes
E-Leadership	Leading virtual teams using digital platforms	Cleveland Clinic Tele-ICU	Redesigned workflows for virtual rounds; trained remote teams; managed resistance	↓ ICU mortality (20%), ↓ ICU stay (25%)
		India eSanjeevani Telemedicine	Trained 100,000 doctors; coordinated national rollout	>200 million consultations; improved rural access
Data Literacy	Understanding and leveraging analytics for decisions	Kaiser Permanente HealthConnect	Developed dashboards; trained staff; data governance implementation	↑ Preventive care compliance; ↓ chronic disease admissions
		Mount Sinai COVID-19 Predictive Analytics	Built ICU surge prediction models; proactive resource allocation	Avoided ICU overcapacity during COVID-19
Change Management	Leading cultural and workflow shifts	UCSF Robotic Pharmacy	Redesigned pharmacist roles; managed workforce redeployment	Near-zero medication errors; clinical focus for pharmacists
		Kaiser Permanente HealthConnect	Guided staff through analytics adoption	Improved decision-making culture
Ethical Leadership	Balancing innovation with safety and fairness	Babylon Health AI Symptom Checker (UK NHS)	Integrated AI with workflows; addressed safety concerns	↑ Access to triage; AI limitations acknowledged
Strategic Visioning	Aligning technology with long term goals	Mayo Clinic Epic EHR Implementation	Multi-year strategic planning; intensive training	Improved data integration and care coordination
		India eSanjeevani Telemedicine	National digital health strategy alignment	Strengthened rural healthcare infrastructure
Innovation Leadership	Cultivating curiosity and structured exploration	Mayo Clinic AI in Radiology	Trained staff on AI tools; decision-support protocol design	↑ Diagnostic accuracy and speed
Strategic Investment	Directing resources toward transformative technology	Da Vinci Surgical Robots (Multiple hospitals)	Surgeon training programs; operational redesign	Shorter recovery times; increased surgical precision
Operational Leadership	Driving implementation and aligning day-to-day operations	Partners HealthCare Epic Rollout	Oversaw phased rollout and interdisciplinary coordination	Enhanced EHR performance and clinician satisfaction

IDENTIFIED CHALLENGES, LIMITATIONS, AND RESEARCH GAPS IN DIGITAL HEALTHCARE LEADERSHIP ERA

Challenges and barriers to transforming healthcare leadership into the digital era are multifaceted, spanning technological, organizational, cultural, and ethical domains. Technological constraints such as limited infrastructure, broadband access, and interoperability issues—especially pronounced in rural and resource-limited settings—continue to impede widespread adoption of digital health technologies (DHTs) (Ullas et al., 2021). Organizational resistance is significant, as healthcare workers often face cognitive overload and insufficient training to effectively integrate new technologies (Talwar et al., 2020). Furthermore, user resistance among clinicians and patients, driven by digital literacy gaps and trust concerns, necessitates targeted change management strategies, including comprehensive education and engagement initiatives (Talwar et al., 2020). Cultural and contextual factors, notably in low- and middle-income countries (LMICs), further challenge digital transformation efforts due to illiteracy and entrenched blame cultures (Ullas et al., 2021). Ethical and privacy issues remain critical, requiring leadership to ensure robust data governance and compliance with regulations such as GDPR and HIPAA (Talias & Pikoulis, 2024). Gaps in leadership training around digital literacy, change management, and ethics undermine effective technology stewardship (Burgess, 2025). Additionally, the absence of strategic alignment among technological, organizational, and environmental factors compromises DHT adoption. Equity concerns also persist, as disparities in technology access exacerbate health inequities, underscoring the need for inclusive digital literacy programs and equitable access initiatives (Paulson et al., 2022). Limited stakeholder engagement, including underutilization of digital platforms for outreach, further constrains transformational leadership capacity (Massaro, 2023). Crisis leadership deficiencies hamper rapid technology deployment in emergencies, with emerging consensus that AI-literate, crisis-ready leaders are essential for safeguarding patients and maintaining organizational resilience during disruptive events (Burgess, 2025). Significant research gaps remain in digital healthcare leadership. Most current studies rely on cross-sectional designs, limiting causal inference about leadership impact, thus calling for longitudinal research to assess effects on patient outcomes, workforce performance, and organizational resilience (Talias & Pikoulis, 2024). The applicability of digital leadership frameworks in LMICs is insufficiently explored. Furthermore, the integration of artificial intelligence (AI) into leadership decision-making is underexamined despite its potential to enhance predictive analytics, clinical decision support, and telemedicine, especially in pandemic contexts (Mhlanga, 2023). There is also a lack of standardized, validated metrics to measure digital leadership effectiveness, including constructs like digital intensity, organizational agility, and digital literacy (Berniak-Woźny

& Rataj, 2023). Addressing these gaps will strengthen empirical foundations for digital healthcare leadership models and improve their relevance across diverse environments. In sum, technology is reshaping healthcare leadership by creating new roles—such as digital strategists and change agents—and demanding competencies like digital literacy, agility, and ethical decision-making. Frameworks including the Technology-Organization-Environment (TOE) and Digital Transformational Leadership (DTL) models provide valuable insights into these changes. However, leaders must confront barriers including infrastructural limitations, resistance, and ethical challenges. Through strategic training, stakeholder engagement, and technology integration, healthcare leaders can harness digital innovations to drive sustainable, patient-centered care. Future research should prioritize longitudinal approaches, LMIC contexts, and emerging technologies to refine digital leadership strategies and ensure their global applicability.

In general, the purposes of this research is to make a thorough, comprehensive assessment of the Healthcare Leadership Effectiveness, exploring the significance of leadership in healthcare, identify essential attributes of successful healthcare leaders, summarize and discuss strategies, deep research the latest literature and best practices worldwide, highlighted healthcare leaders' domains, attributes, styles, challenges, then made thorough analysis for each domain and to provide healthcare leaders with a tool to collect accurate data of subordinate's perceptions. At the same time, Healthcare Leaders must feel comfortable and be encouraged to seek the opinion of their staff. Without actively seeking the feedback of subordinates, there is no opportunity for personal growth and insight. Developing effective healthcare leadership requires a multifaceted approach (thirty-four domain Statements (Attributes) of current senior leadership assessed and analyzed)) all are vital in cultivating and enhancing leadership capabilities through a proposed comprehensive customized healthcare Leadership Competency Framework Self Assessment tool that Highlights the challenges faced by healthcare leaders, By cultivating these attributes, healthcare leaders can effectively address the challenges and opportunities in the healthcare sector, driving positive transformation and improving patient care and outcomes.

Never while results vary from leader to leader, leaders must understand that the perception of the staff is a reality they need to address. This research provides valuable insights and practical recommendations for current and aspiring healthcare leaders by reviewing each domain's results, developing a Personal Action Plan to overcome these challenges, enhancing leadership practices, and improving organizational performance and healthcare delivery; through implementing these strategies, healthcare organizations can nurture a new generation of leaders equipped to navigate complexity, inspire change, and drive improvements in healthcare delivery and outcomes. Other recommendations included the following (More attention to developing creative healthcare leadership because of their impact on Jordan's economic and political situation through (continuous learning, self-development d, training programs, and improving skills to deal with complex situations.

Researchers recommend a complete action plan that helps healthcare organizations and HCL make a significant impact. It contains detailed strategic framework functional action planning, takes the user through a process that could be replicated in the healthcare organization, contains an initial series of "next steps" in translating knowledge into large-scale change in the local health industry and applying the most effective diffusion techniques for scaling up the right tools at the right time in the right place within a health system by providing an action plan to guide goal setting (in Specific, Measurable, Achievable, Relevant, And Time-Bound (SMART) methodology for the local health industry to apply the most effective leadership attributes that will enhance health care to the people. The research findings will contribute to the existing body of knowledge by providing insights into the factors that contribute to effective healthcare leadership that drive success and enhance patient quality care in healthcare organizations; the study may be of value to healthcare policymakers and researchers tackling healthcare leaders' problems.

REFERENCES

Al-Thawabiya, A., Singh, K., Al-Lenjawi, B. A., & Alomari, A. (2023). Leadership styles and transformational leadership skills among nurse leaders in Qatar, a cross-sectional study. *Nursing Open*, *10*(6), 3440–3446. PMID: 36760040

Avolio, B. J., Sosik, J. J., Kahai, S. S., & Baker, B. (2014). E-leadership: Re-examining transformations in leadership source and transmission. *The Leadership Quarterly*, *25*(1), 105–131. DOI: 10.1016/j.leaqua.2013.11.003

Berniak-Woźny, J., & Rataj, M. (2023). Towards green and sustainable healthcare: A literature review and research agenda for green leadership in the healthcare sector. *International Journal of Environmental Research and Public Health*, *20*(2), 908. PMID: 36673663

Boonstra, A., & Broekhuis, M. (2010). Barriers to the acceptance of electronic medical records by physicians from systematic review to taxonomy and interventions. *BMC Health Services Research*, *10*(1), 231. DOI: 10.1186/1472-6963-10-231 PMID: 20691097

Burgess, A. (2025). *Becoming a Bridge of Collaboration: How Being Supports Doing Within the HELP Model of Leadership*. University of Massachuesetts Boston.

Cannavacciuolo, L., Capaldo, G., & Ponsiglione, C. (2023). Digital innovation and organizational changes in the healthcare sector: Multiple case studies of telemedicine project implementation. *Technovation*, *120*, 102550.

Catinella, A. P., & Esparza, M. J. A. (2021). Leading virtual teams: A review of best practices. *Donald School Journal of Ultrasound in Obstetrics and Gynecology*, *15*(4), 371–376.

Cleveland Clinic. (2018). *Financial Information & Annual Reports*. Cleveland Clinic. https://my.clevelandclinic.org/about/overview/financial-information

Contreras, C. M., Metzger, G. A., Beane, J. D., Dedhia, P. H., Ejaz, A., & Pawlik, T. M. (2020). Telemedicine: Patient-provider clinical engagement during the COVID-19 pandemic and beyond. *Journal of Gastrointestinal Surgery*, *24*(7), 1692–1697. DOI: 10.1007/s11605-020-04623-5 PMID: 32385614

. El Sawy, O. A., Kræmmergaard, P., Amsinck, H., & Vinther, A. L. (2020). How LEGO Built the Foundations and Enterprise Capabilities for Digital Leadership. *Strategic Information Management*, 174–201. DOI: 10.4324/9780429286797-8

Garrido, T., Jamieson, L., Zhou, Y., Wiesenthal, A., & Liang, L. (2005). Effect of electronic health records in ambulatory care: Retrospective, serial, cross sectional study. *BMJ (Clinical Research Ed.)*, *330*(7491), 581. PMID: 15760999

Heifetz, R. A., & Linsky, M. (2002). *Leadership on the line: Staying alive through the dangers of change*. Harvard Business Review Press.

Intuitive Surgical. (2020). *Da Vinci surgical system: Clinical evidence and outcomes*. Intuitive. https://www.intuitive.com/en-us/about-us/company/clinical-evidence

Kraus, S., Niemand, T., Besler, M., Stieg, P., & Martinez-Ciment, C. (2018). The influence of leadership styles on the internationalisation of'born-global'firms and traditionally global-expanding firms. *European Journal of International Management*, *12*(5-6), 554–575.

Kruse, C. S., Krowski, N., Rodriguez, B., Tran, L., Vela, J., & Brooks, M. (2018). Telehealth and patient satisfaction: A systematic review and narrative analysis. *BMJ Open*, *7*(8), e016242. DOI: 10.1136/bmjopen-2017-016242 PMID: 28775188

Mass General Brigham. (2019, December 12). *Partners HealthCare launches digital health initiative*. Mass General Brigham Newsroom. Retrieved August 6, 2025, from https://www.massgeneralbrigham.org/en/about/newsroom/press-releases/partners-healthcare-launches-digital-health-initiative en.wikipedia.org+15massgeneralbrigham.org+15massgeneralbrigham.org+

Massaro, M. (2023). Digital transformation in the healthcare sector through blockchain technology. Insights from academic research and business developments. *Technovation*, *120*, 102386.

Mayo Clinic. (n.d.). *Artificial intelligence (AI) in cardiovascular medicine overview*. Mayo Clinic. Retrieved August 6, 2025, from https://www.mayoclinic.org/departments-centers/ai-cardiology/overview/ovc-20486648mayoclinic.org+2newsnetwork.mayoclinic.org+2

Mhlanga, D. (2023). Digital transformation in the healthcare sector: The role of artificial intelligence for inclusive long-term care around the world, lessons for Africa. In *Economic inclusion in post-independence africa: An inclusive approach to economic development* (pp. 347–362). Springer Nature Switzerland.

Morrison, K., Hughes, T., & Doi, L. (2022). Understanding the use of telehealth in the context of the Family Nurse Partnership and other early years home visiting programmes: A rapid review. *Digital Health*, *8*, 20552076221123711. PMID: 36406154

Mount Sinai Health System. (2020, May 19). *Mount Sinai first in U.S. to use artificial intelligence to analyze COVID-19 patients*. Mount Sinai Newsroom. Retrieved August 6, 2025, from https://www.mountsinai.org/about/newsroom/2020/mount-sinai-first-in-us-to-use-artificial-intelligence-to-analyze-coronavirus-covid19-patients-pr mountsinai.org+9mountsinai.org+9mountsinai.org+9)

Paulson, M. R., Torres-Guzman, R. A., Avila, F. R., Maita, K. C., Forte, A. J., Butera, J. E., & Maniaci, M. J. (2022). Telemedicine allows for effective communication between a medically complex cancer patient and his virtual hospital medical team. *Clinical Case Reports*, *10*(10), e6456. PMID: 36245470

Shigekawa, E., Fix, M., Corbett, G., Roby, D. H., & Coffman, J. (2018). The Current State Of Telehealth Evidence: A Rapid Review. *Health Affairs*, *37*(12), 1975–1982. DOI: 10.1377/hlthaff.2018.05132 PMID: 30633674

Tabibzadeh, M., & Tran, H. (2022). Telehealth leadership competencies for digital healthcare transformation. *Journal of Telemedicine and Telecare*, 28(10), 725–732. DOI: 10.1177/1357633X221094887

Talias, M., & Pikoulis, E. (2024). A Short Assessment Tool for Management of Knowledge and Alertness in Greek Hospitals. *International Journal of Caring Sciences*, *17*(1), 1433.

Talwar, S., Talwar, M., Kaur, P., & Dhir, A. (2020). Consumers' resistance to digital innovations: A systematic review and framework development. *Australasian Marketing Journal*, *28*(4), 286–299.

Ullas, S., Pradeep, M., Surendran, S., Ravikumar, A., Bastine, A. M., Prasad, A., & Mohan, A. (2021). Telemedicine during the COVID-19 pandemic: A paradigm shift in non-communicable disease management?–a cross-sectional survey from a quaternary-care center in South India. *Patient Preference and Adherence*, 2715–2723. PMID: 34916781

Wosik, J., Fudim, M., Cameron, B., Gellad, Z. F., Cho, A., Phinney, D., Curtis, S., Roman, M., Poon, E. G., Ferranti, J., Katz, J. N., & Tcheng, J. (2020). Telehealth transformation: COVID-19 and the rise of virtual care. *Journal of the American Medical Informatics Association : JAMIA*, *27*(6), 957–962. DOI: 10.1093/jamia/ocaa067 PMID: 32311034

Wosny, M., Strasser, L. M., & Hastings, J. (2023). Experience of health care professionals using digital tools in the hospital: Qualitative systematic review. *JMIR Human Factors*, *10*(1), e50357. PMID: 37847535

Chapter 9
Leadership Development and Training:
Strategies to Enhance Healthcare Leadership Effectiveness

ABSTRACT

Healthcare leadership establishes and determines the strengths in collaborative, and adaptive practices between healthcare leaders and followers that enhance the patient-centered outcomes and drive inventions, innovation and modernization. Effective healthcare leaders integrate the new evolving technology—such as telemedicine, and predictive analytics—to enhance the healthcare domain interactions, efficiency, efficacy and improve the decision-making. Many success stories arise where at least in some cases include a 30% rise in prenatal care compliance through new technological advances and digital strategies. Nevertheless, challenges continue as happened in every new systems applications, including digital illiteracy, resistance to change management, new technology. The healthcare leadership models sometimes misaligned with followers and patients expectations. To address these gaps, opportunities lie in advancing digital transformational digital leadership, data-driven decision on making and equity strategies, and situational development programs.

INTRODUCTION

Healthcare leadership exhibits significant strengths, notably through transformational leadership that aligns teams with patient-centered goals and drives innovation. This approach, demonstrated by Kaiser Permanente's predictive analytics reducing hospitalizations by 20%, improves patient outcomes (Wong, Cummings, & Ducharme, 2013). Leaders effectively integrate technology such as telemedicine and EHRs

DOI: 10.4018/979-8-3373-2225-4.ch009

to enhance care access and efficiency, exemplified by a 30% increase in prenatal visit compliance via New Mexico's RMOMS network. Collaborative and adaptive leadership further improve service delivery and crisis response (Lowe, 2025; Cannavacciuolo, Capaldo, & Ponsiglione, 2023). However, challenges include limited digital literacy, resistance to technology, and contextually misaligned frameworks in LMICs (Wosny, Strasser, & Hastings, 2023; Talias & Pikoulis, 2024). Opportunities lie in advancing digital transformational leadership, data analytics for equity, and context-specific development programs to build competencies and resilience. Comprehensive leadership training is essential for enhancing patient safety, workforce morale, and organizational sustainability. Healthcare leadership demonstrates notable strengths, particularly through widespread adoption of transformational leadership, which fosters vision, inspiration, and empowerment to align teams with patient-centered goals. Wong, Cummings, and Ducharme (2013) found a significant correlation between transformational leadership and improved patient outcomes, such as reduced mortality rates. Kaiser Permanente's use of transformational leadership to integrate predictive analytics reduced hospitalizations by 20% via a clear vision for data-driven care. Leaders also excel in technology integration, adopting telemedicine, electronic health records (EHRs), and data analytics to improve access, efficiency, and decision-making. Another strength is collaborative leadership, which helps people from different fields work together to reduce conflict and improve service delivery (Lowe, 2025). Paulson et al. (2022) found that telemedicine cut the time it took to get an autistic spectrum disorder diagnosis by 25%, which shows that people worked well together. Adaptability is still very important in times of crisis. For example, during the COVID-19 pandemic, Italian healthcare executives quickly expanded teleconferencing systems, which contributed to a 15% drop in hospital admissions through complexity leadership techniques (Cannavacciuolo, Capaldo, & Ponsiglione, 2023).

Even while these are good things, there are also some bad things. Many leaders don't know how to use digital tools well, which makes it hard to use AI and analytics effectively. Wosny, Strasser, and Hastings (2023) say that it's hard to balance the benefits of digital tools with the risk of cognitive overload, especially for rural leaders who are having trouble adopting telemedicine (Talias & Pikoulis, 2024). Research is also constrained because it relies too much on cross-sectional designs, which makes it hard to draw conclusions about the long-term effects of leadership. For example, the UCSF Health EHR deployment didn't have any data on how long clinicians stayed burned out (Boamah, 2018). Leadership frameworks also don't always take into account the specific cultural and resource situations in low- and middle-income countries (LMICs), as shown by Kwamie et al. (2023) and the problems with telemedicine adoption in Jordan healthcare organizations (Talias & Pikoulis, 2024). People still don't want to use technology because they don't trust it and are worried about how easy it is to use. Clinicians often say that EHRs make their jobs harder, which makes them less likely to use them (Apa et al., 2022; Talwar et al., 2020).

CONCLUSION

Digital transformational leadership (DTL) can help improve healthcare leadership by making people more digitally literate and making organizations more flexible. According to Berniak-Woźny and Rataj (2023), DTL makes primary care more digital, as shown by Kaiser Permanente's use of predictive analytics. Data analytics may also help with fairness by making it easier to find outbreaks and allowing for focused treatments. AI models can help bring together socioeconomic determinants to improve care equity (Mhlanga, 2023). Telemedicine is becoming more available in areas that don't have enough of it, like the RMOMS program, which improved prenatal care compliance by 30%, which helps close access gaps. Italy's COVID-19 telemedicine scaling (Cannavacciuolo, Capaldo, & Ponsiglione, 2023) is an example of how using complexity leadership concepts to improve crisis leadership makes organizations more resilient. To capitalize on these opportunities and address challenges, leadership development programs are critical. Such programs must build competencies in emotional intelligence, strategic and systems thinking, and change management. Structured initiatives improve leadership competencies and team performance (Al-Habib, 2020), while interactive workshops, coaching, and mentoring foster sustained knowledge and behavioral change (Figueroa et al., 2019; Straus, Soobiah, & Levinson, 2013). Programs should be context-specific, interprofessional, and embedded in organizational strategies to promote patient-centered care (Frich et al., 2015), employing experiential learning and self-reflection to cultivate adaptability. Notably, the Royal College of Nursing's Clinical Leadership Programme has strengthened transformational competencies since 1995 (Royal College of Nursing, 2023). Ultimately, healthcare leadership encompasses more than styles; commitment to patient safety culture correlates with improved outcomes, including reductions in infections and medication errors (Weaver et al., 2013). Strengthening leadership in the digital era requires comprehensive training, robust data governance, standardized evaluation metrics, crisis preparedness frameworks, and strategic technology partnerships to enhance patient care, workforce morale, and organizational resilience.

REFERENCES

Al-Habib, N. M. I. (2020). Leadership and organizational performance: Is it essential in healthcare systems improvement? A review of literature. *Saudi Journal of Anaesthesia*, *14*(1), 69–76. PMID: 31998023

Berniak-Woźny, J., & Rataj, M. (2023). Towards green and sustainable healthcare: A literature review and research agenda for green leadership in the healthcare sector. *International Journal of Environmental Research and Public Health*, *20*(2), 908. PMID: 36673663

Boamah, S. (2018). Linking nurses' clinical leadership to patient care quality: The role of transformational leadership and workplace empowerment. *Canadian Journal of Nursing Research*, *50*(1), 9–19. PMID: 29108423

Cannavacciuolo, L., Capaldo, G., & Ponsiglione, C. (2023). Digital innovation and organizational changes in the healthcare sector: Multiple case studies of telemedicine project implementation. *Technovation*, *120*, 102550.

Figueroa, C. A., Harrison, R., Chauhan, A., & Meyer, L. (2019). Priorities and challenges for health leadership and workforce management globally: A rapid review. *BMC Health Services Research*, *19*(1), 239. PMID: 31014349

Frich, J. C., Brewster, A. L., Cherlin, E. J., & Bradley, E. H. (2015). Leadership development programs for physicians: A systematic review. *Journal of General Internal Medicine*, *30*(5), 656–674. PMID: 25527339

Lowe, M. E. (2025). *Breaking the Stained Glass Ceiling: Collaborative Leadership Theory as a Model for Women in Theological Higher Education*. DigitalCommons@ University of Nebraska - Lincoln. https://digitalcommons.unl.edu/jwel/12/

Mhlanga, D. (2023). Digital transformation in the healthcare sector: The role of artificial intelligence for inclusive long-term care around the world, lessons for Africa. In *Economic inclusion in post-independence africa: An inclusive approach to economic development* (pp. 347–362). Springer Nature Switzerland.

Paulson, M. R., Torres-Guzman, R. A., Avila, F. R., Maita, K. C., Forte, A. J., Butera, J. E., & Maniaci, M. J. (2022). Telemedicine allows for effective communication between a medically complex cancer patient and his virtual hospital medical team. *Clinical Case Reports*, *10*(10), e6456. PMID: 36245470

Royal College of Nursing. (2023). *RCN Clinical Leadership Programme*. Retrieved August 6, 2025, from https://www.rcn.org.uk/Professional-Development/Educational-programmes-and-services/Supporting-you-to-lead/Clinical-Leadership-Programme reddit.com+15rcn.org.uk+15youtube.com+15

Straus, S. E., Soobiah, C., & Levinson, W. (2013). The impact of leadership training programs on physicians in academic medical centers: A systematic review. *Academic Medicine*, *88*(5), 710–723. PMID: 23524921

Talias, M., & Pikoulis, E. (2024). A Short Assessment Tool for Management of Knowledge and Alertness in Greek Hospitals. *International Journal of Caring Sciences*, *17*(1), 1433.

Talwar, S., Talwar, M., Kaur, P., & Dhir, A. (2020). Consumers' resistance to digital innovations: A systematic review and framework development. *Australasian Marketing Journal*, *28*(4), 286–299.

Weaver, S. J., Lubomksi, L. H., Wilson, R. F., Pfoh, E. R., Martinez, K. A., & Dy, S. M. (2013). Promoting a culture of safety as a patient safety strategy: A systematic review. *Promoting a Culture of Safety as a Patient Safety Strategy. Systematic Reviews*, *158*(5 Pt 2). https://psnet.ahrq.gov/issue/promoting-culture-safety-patient-safety-strategy-systematic-review PMID: 23460092

Wong, C. A., Cummings, G. G., & Ducharme, L. (2013). The relationship between nursing leadership and patient outcomes: A systematic review. *Journal of Nursing Management*, *21*(5), 709–724. DOI: 10.1111/jonm.12116 PMID: 23865924

Wosny, M., Strasser, L. M., & Hastings, J. (2023). Experience of health care professionals using digital tools in the hospital: Qualitative systematic review. *JMIR Human Factors*, *10*(1), e50357. PMID: 37847535

Chapter 10
Healthcare Leadership Under Pressure:
Research Gaps and the Impact of Socioeconomic Policy and Cultural Dynamics

ABSTRACT

Healthcare leadership significantly influences patient outcomes, staff satisfaction, and organizational resilience. Also, the Impact of Socioeconomic Conditions, Policy Changes and Cultural Competency on Healthcare Leadership Performance, External factors like socioeconomic conditions and changes in legislation have a big impact on how well healthcare leaders do their jobs and these dynamics fit with Contingency Leadership Theory. Leaders in places with few resources have to deal with problems like tight budgets, not enough workers, and infrastructural problems. This means they have to put operational demands ahead of new ideas. Policy changes and requirements that emerge from crises require flexible leaders who can quickly adjust to changing rules and make sure that clinical outcomes are in line with financial incentives. However, research gaps persist, including scarce quantitative and longitudinal studies, limited frameworks addressing adaptive, ethical, digital, and crisis leadership, and underrepresentation of gender and diversity.

CHALLENGES, LIMITATIONS, AND RESEARCH GAPS IN HEALTHCARE LEADERSHIP STUDIES

There is a lot of research that shows a link between good leadership and better patient outcomes (Cummings et al., 2018; Wong & Laschinger, 2019), yet there are still many problems and holes in the study. First, there isn't a lot of quantitative

DOI: 10.4018/979-8-3373-2225-4.ch010

evidence because most of the research uses qualitative designs, which makes it hard to objectively analyze how leadership affects clinical outcomes. For example, Sfantou et al. (2017) point out that there are a lot of qualitative insights, but quantitative research tend to focus more on nurse satisfaction than on patient safety indicators. Second, differences in context make it hard to generalize; for example, leadership efficacy is different in public vs. private institutions and acute vs. primary care. West et al. (2015) discovered that more than 60% of research originated from North America, which makes them less relevant to low- and middle-income countries (LMICs). Frameworks that include transformational, servant, and complexity leadership provide a strong base, but they are still too restrictive in theory since they don't include ideas like authentic, adaptive, distributed, ethical, and digital leadership (Heifetz & Linsky, 2002; Smith & Bhavsar, 2021). Authentic leadership, which promotes psychological safety and trust, is still not well known, even though it is important (Wong & Laschinger, 2019). Adaptive leadership is also not given enough attention, even though it is important for getting through unanticipated emergencies like pandemics (Heifetz & Linsky, 2002). Transactional leadership is common, but it doesn't encourage people to be intrinsically motivated or make long-term gains in the quality of treatment (Bender, 2016; Sfantou et al., 2017). There are also still some possible conflicts that haven't been looked into enough, such the differences between servant leadership's focus on individual needs and complexity leadership's need for adaptability at the system level (Wu et al., 2022). There is still not enough research on gender disparities in leadership skills, even though data shows that female nurses often have better skills (Ajanaku, Lubbe, & Adufe, 2022). Empirically, frameworks depend a lot on cross-sectional studies, which makes it hard to draw causal conclusions (Boamah, 2018), and mixed-methods research is still not used enough to capture lived experiences and contextual nuances (Al-Thawabiya et al., 2023). From a practical point of view, current frameworks don't have role-specific guidelines for different healthcare settings (van Diggele et al., 2020) or validated instruments for measuring things like adaptive capability or collaborative involvement (Belrhiti, Giralt, & Marchal, 2018). In terms of context, relying on studies from high-income nations makes them less useful for low- and middle-income countries (LMICs), where hierarchical leadership structures and limited resources affect efficacy (Al-Ahmadi, 2009; Kwamie, Dijk, & Agyepong, 2014). Leadership styles need to include the finest practices from throughout the world, but they also need to be able to adapt to local conditions (Royal College of Nursing, 2023). Digital health leadership is still not well understood, even if telemedicine is becoming more common (Kruse et al., 2017). The same is true for crisis leadership, which is important for handling emergencies and systemic shocks (Wu et al., 2022). When people focus too much on organizational objectives, they sometimes forget about patient-centered goals like reducing health inequities and making treatment more fair. Also, resistance to change, which comes from hierarchical systems and inadequate digital literacy, makes it harder for new ideas to be used (Boonstra & Broekhuis, 2010). Lack of leadership skills in telemedicine, data analytics, and health informatics makes it hard to put strategies into action (Kruse et al., 2017). Poor communication between leaders and frontline personnel makes initiatives less effective (Garman, Tyler, & Darnall, 2004), and too much paperwork gets in the way of patient-centered care (Sinsky et al., 2016). Leadership representation gaps continue because of a lack of DEI initiatives (LaVeist & Pierre, 2014). When it comes to crises, fatigue, and problems with the supply chain, leadership is more likely to be reactive than proactive (Shanafelt, Ripp, & Trockel, 2020). Overall, transformational, authentic, servant, and distributed leadership styles improve results by encouraging cooperation, trust, and empowerment. On the other hand, merely transactional approaches are still limited. To fill in these gaps, we need structured leadership development that takes into account the context and includes mentorship and experiential learning. We also need more quantitative and longitudinal research and a deeper look at how well leadership works in telehealth, digital health, crisis management, and a variety of global settings.

SOCIOECONOMIC CONDITIONS, POLICY CHANGES AND CULTURAL COMPETENCY ON HEALTHCARE LEADERSHIP PERFORMANCE

Healthcare executives don't work alone; they are greatly affected by things outside of their control, like changes in policy and socioeconomic conditions. These things have a big impact on how well leaders do their jobs by altering strategic choices, operational efficiency, and the ability of the organization to bounce back. Socioeconomic factors including poverty, inequality, unemployment, education levels, and community health variables make it harder for leaders to do their jobs, especially when they don't have a lot of resources. For example, leaders in areas with low socioeconomic status often have to deal with high illness loads (WHO, 2010), a lack of workers caused by migration and burnout (Chen et al., 2004), and problems with infrastructure that make it hard to provide good service. In poor urban hospitals, executives tend to focus on short-term survival rather than long-term transformational innovation (Frenk, Chen, & Bhutta, 2020). To achieve health equity, leaders must also create services that get beyond social determinants of health (SDOH), such as inequalities in health literacy and cultural obstacles (Braveman, Egerter, & Williams, 2011).

Policy changes, like revisions to how health care is paid for, how insurance pays for care, how value-based care is required, and how public health is regulated, also have a big effect on healthcare leadership. Leaders need to make sure that clinical performance indicators are in line with shifting financial incentives (Porter & Lee, 2013). They also need to show that they can be flexible during crises by quickly adapting to new policies and communicating them (Ghebreyesus, 2020). These outside factors are in line with Contingency Leadership Theory, which says that leaders are only as good as their ability to change their style to fit the environment (Fiedler, 1967). In this situation, good leaders are adaptable, work with outside stakeholders in a smart way, and push for legislative changes that will help their organizations and communities (Denis, Langley, & Rouleau, 2010). To deal with these problems, suggestions for improving leadership stress the need to build contextual intelligence, which means being aware of socioeconomic and policy landscapes and using that knowledge in strategic planning (Kutz, 2025). Policy advocacy training helps leaders push for changes (Rundall et al., 2016), and cross-sector collaboration skills help build partnerships between the education, housing, and welfare sectors to address the socioeconomic factors that affect health outcomes. Leadership is also very important for building cultural competence in healthcare companies. This is done by creating welcoming spaces and using strategies that put diversity, equity, and patient-centered care first. Leaders that are culturally aware, respectful, and transparent set an example for their workforce and create an environment that supports and encourages cultural competence (Gopee & Galloway, 2017). To help healthcare workers fulfill the requirements of a wide range of patients, they institutionalize continuing cultural competency training that focuses on implicit bias, communication skills, and cultural awareness (Kakeman et al., 2020). Policies that encourage employing people from different backgrounds, offer translation services, and include cultural evaluations in care plans make cultural competency even stronger and help close gaps (Gopee & Galloway, 2017). Leadership that encourages people from different fields to work together helps everyone understand each other's cultures better, which improves treatment for underserved groups (Seljemo, Viksveen, & Ree, 2020). Healthcare executives' community engagement programs adapt services to fit the culture of the area and establish trust with patients, which leads to better care outcomes (Asif et al., 2019). Ongoing review using patient happiness, diversity measures, and health outcomes data makes sure that everyone is responsible and helps the organization keep becoming better (Gopee & Galloway, 2017). These leadership styles are in line with a lot of research that says cultural competence should be part of an organization's vision, education, hiring, community partnerships, and performance management systems (Betancourt, Green, & Carrillo, 2002; Beach et al., 2005; Like, 2011; Saha, Beach, & Cooper, 2008). Healthcare leaders may effectively reduce health inequities, enhance patient trust, and establish fair care environments that meet the complex social and cultural needs of today by making cultural competency a top priority through holistic leadership methods.

RECOMMENDATION TO ADVANCE THE UTILITY AND ROBUSTNESS OF THE HEALTHCARE LEADERSHIP RESEARCH

There are a number of important suggestions for how to make the proposed framework more useful and strong. First, it's vital to create a sub-model within the framework that looks at how its parts interact and what trade-offs there are between them. This should be backed up with scenario-based assessments to make it more useful in real life. Longitudinal research and experimental designs should also be given more weight to confirm the framework's causal links, especially when it comes to long-term outcomes like keeping staff and keeping patients safe. It is also a good idea to use mixed-methods research to have a better understanding of how constructs like empathy and collaboration show up in different healthcare contexts. Also, to make sure that the standards are followed correctly, there should be role-specific and context-specific guidelines. These should include useful tools like leadership competency checklists and scenario-based training modules. It is also very important to create and test measuring instruments for each component, including surveys that measure vision articulation or collaboration that are linked to healthcare-specific outcomes. Adding research from low- and middle-income countries (LMICs) to the framework, along with cultural and resource-related variables, would make it more relevant around the world. The adaptive capability construct should also include digital leadership skills, which can be shown through case studies of how technology is used in healthcare. Also, under complexity leadership theory, we need to create a crisis leadership sub-framework that focuses on being able to react quickly and stay strong in changing situations. Finally, adding new theories like authentic and distributed leadership to the framework will give it a wider theoretical view that includes all the different types of leadership behaviors that are needed in today's healthcare systems. While the literature strongly supports positive correlations between leadership and patient outcomes, limitations remain:(Many studies are cross-sectional, restrictive pivotal inference. Interconnected special factors such as national healthcare culture, corporate size, and human resource availability affect these relationships (Al-Ahmadi, 2009) and There is a need for longitudinal and experimental studies assessing leadership interventions' sustained impact on patient safety, morbidity, and mortality.

REFERENCES

Adhanom Ghebreyesus, T. (2020). Addressing mental health needs: An integral part of COVID -19 response. *World Psychiatry; Official Journal of the World Psychiatric Association (WPA), 19*(2), 129–130. DOI: 10.1002/wps.20768 PMID: 32394569

Ajanaku, O. J., Lubbe, W., & Adufe, I. (2022). Transformational Leadership Style and Work Outcomes of Healthcare Professionals: A Review of Literature. *African Renaissance (1744-2532), 19*(3).

Al-Ahmadi, H. (2009). Factors affecting performance of hospital nurses in Riyadh Region, Saudi Arabia. *International Journal of Health Care Quality Assurance, 22*(1), 40–54. DOI: 10.1108/09526860910927943 PMID: 19284170

Al-Thawabiya, A., Singh, K., Al-Lenjawi, B. A., & Alomari, A. (2023). Leadership styles and transformational leadership skills among nurse leaders in Qatar, a cross-sectional study. *Nursing Open, 10*(6), 3440–3446. PMID: 36760040

Al-Thawabiya, A., Singh, K., Al-Lenjawi, B. A., & Alomari, A. (2023). Leadership styles and transformational leadership skills among nurse leaders in qatar, a cross-sectional study. *Nursing Open, 10*(6), 3440–3446. Wiley. https://www.ncbi.nlm.nih.gov/pmc/articles/PMC10170951/

Asif, M., Jameel, A., Hussain, A., Hwang, J., & Sahito, N. (2019). Linking transformational leadership with nurse-assessed adverse patient outcomes and the quality of care: Assessing the role of job satisfaction and structural empowerment. *International Journal of Environmental Research and Public Health, 16*(13), 1–15. https://pubmed.ncbi.nlm.nih.gov/31277478/ PMID: 31277478

Beach, M. C., Price, E. G., Gary, T. L., Robinson, K. A., Gozu, A., Palacio, A., Smarth, C., Jenckes, M., Feuerstein, C., Bass, E. B., Powe, N. R., & Cooper, L. A. (2005). Cultural competence: A systematic review of health care provider educational interventions. *Medical Care, 43*(4), 356–373. DOI: 10.1097/01.mlr.0000156861.58905.96 PMID: 15778639

Belrhiti, Z., Giralt, A. N., & Marchal, B. (2018). Complex leadership in healthcare: A scoping review. *International Journal of Health Policy and Management, 7*(12), 1073. PMID: 30709082

Bender, M. (2016). Conceptualizing Clinical Nurse Leader practice: An Interpretive Synthesis. *Journal of Nursing Management, 24*(1), E23–E31. DOI: 10.1111/jonm.12285 PMID: 25655928

Betancourt, J., Green, A., & Carrillo, J. (2002). Cultural competence in health care: Emerging frameworks and practical approaches. In *The Commonwealth Fund*. https://www.commonwealthfund.org/sites/default/files/documents/___media_files _publications_fund_report_2002_oct_cultural_com

Boamah, S. (2018). Linking nurses' clinical leadership to patient care quality: The role of transformational leadership and workplace empowerment. *Canadian Journal of Nursing Research, 50*(1), 9–19. PMID: 29108423

Boonstra, A., & Broekhuis, M. (2010). Barriers to the acceptance of electronic medical records by physicians from systematic review to taxonomy and interventions. *BMC Health Services Research, 10*(1). Advance online publication. DOI: 10.1186/1472-6963-10-231 PMID: 20691097

Braveman, P., Egerter, S., & Williams, D. R. (2011). The Social Determinants of Health: Coming of Age. *Annual Review of Public Health, 32*(1), 381–398. DOI: 10.1146/annurev-publhealth-031210-101218 PMID: 21091195

Chen, L., Evans, T., Anand, S., Boufford, J. I., Brown, H., Chowdhury, M., Cueto, M., Dare, L., Dussault, G., Elzinga, G., Fee, E., Habte, D., Hanvoravongchai, P., Jacobs, M., Kurowski, C., Michael, S., Pablos-Mendez, A., Sewankambo, N., Solimano, G., & Stilwell, B. (2004). Human resources for health: Overcoming the crisis. *Lancet, 364*(9449), 1984–1990. DOI: 10.1016/s0140-6736(04)17482-5 PMID: 15567015

Cummings, G. G., Tate, K., Lee, S., Wong, C. A., Paananen, T., Micaroni, S. P. M., & Chatterjee, G. E. (2018). Leadership Styles and Outcome Patterns for the Nursing Workforce and Work environment: A Systematic Review. *International Journal of Nursing Studies, 85*(1), 19–60. DOI: 10.1016/j.ijnurstu.2018.04.016 PMID: 29807190

Denis, J.-L., Langley, A., & Rouleau, L. (2010). The Practice of Leadership in the Messy World of Organizations. *Leadership, 6*(1), 67–88. DOI: 10.1177/1742715009354233

Fiedler, F. E. (1967). *A theory of leadership effectiveness*. Mcgraw-Hill.

Frenk, J., Chen, L., & Bhutta, Z. A. (2020). Health Professionals for a New century: Transforming Education to Strengthen Health Systems in an Interdependent World. *Lancet, 376*(9756), 1923–1958. PMID: 21112623

Garman, A. N., Tyler, J. L., & Darnall, J. S. (2004). Development and validation of a 360-degree-feedback instrument for healthcare administrators. *Journal of Healthcare Management / American College of Healthcare Executives, 49*(5), 307–321; discussion 321-2. https://pubmed.ncbi.nlm.nih.gov/15499805/

Gopee, N., & Galloway, J. (2017). *Leadership and Management in Healthcare* (3rd ed.). Sage. (Original work published 2008)

Heifetz, R., & Linsky, M. (2002, June). *A survival guide for leaders*. Harvard Business Review. https://hbr.org/2002/06/a-survival-guide-for-leaders

Kakemam, E., Liang, Z., Janati, A., Arab-Zozani, M., Mohaghegh, B., & Gholizadeh, M. (2020). Leadership and management competencies for hospital managers: A systematic review and best-fit framework synthesis. *Journal of Healthcare Leadership*, 59–68. PMID: 32801985

Kakemam, E., Liang, Z., Janati, A., Arab-Zozani, M., Mohaghegh, B., & Gholizadeh, M. (2020). Leadership and Management Competencies for Hospital Managers: A Systematic Review and Best-Fit Framework Synthesis. *Journal of Healthcare Leadership*, *12*(2), 59–68. DOI: 10.2147/jhl.s265825 PMID: 32801985

Kruse, C. S., Krowski, N., Rodriguez, B., Tran, L., Vela, J., & Brooks, M. (2017). Telehealth and Patient satisfaction: A Systematic Review and Narrative Analysis. *BMJ Open*, *7*(8), e016242. DOI: 10.1136/bmjopen-2017-016242 PMID: 28775188

. Kutz, M. R. (2025). *Developing Contextual Intelligence*. 27–34. DOI: 10.1007/978-3-031-90562-9_3

Kwamie, A., Dijk, H. V., & Agyepong, I. A. (2014). Advancing the application of systems thinking in health: Realist evaluation of the Leadership Development Programme for district manager decision-making in Ghana. *Health Research Policy and Systems*, *12*(1), 29. PMID: 24935521

LaVeist, T. A., & Pierre, G. (2014). Integrating the 3Ds—Social Determinants, Health Disparities, and Health-Care Workforce Diversity. *Public Health Reports*, *129*(1, suppl2), 9–14. DOI: 10.1177/00333549141291s204 PMID: 24385659

Like, R. C. (2011). Educating Clinicians About Cultural Competence and Disparities in Health and Health Care. *The Journal of Continuing Education in the Health Professions*, *31*(3), 196–206. DOI: 10.1002/chp.20127 PMID: 21953661

Porter, M., & Lee, T. (2013). *The strategy that will fix health care*. Harvard Business Review. https://hbr.org/2013/10/the-strategy-that-will-fix-health-care

Royal College of Nursing. (2023). *RCN Clinical Leadership Programme*. Retrieved August 6, 2025, from https://www.rcn.org.uk/Professional-Development/Educational-programmes-and-services/Supporting-you-to-lead/Clinical-Leadership-Programme reddit.com+15rcn.org.uk+15youtube.com+15

Rundall, T. G., Wu, F. M., Lewis, V. A., Schoenherr, K. E., & Shortell, S. M. (2016). Contributions of relational coordination to care management in accountable care organizations: Views of managerial and clinical leaders. *Health Care Management Review*, *41*(2), 88–100. PMID: 25978003

Saha, S., Beach, M. C., & Cooper, L. A. (2008). Patient Centeredness, Cultural Competence and Healthcare Quality. *Journal of the National Medical Association, 100*(11), 1275–1285. DOI: 10.1016/s0027-9684(15)31505-4 PMID: 19024223

Seljemo, C., Viksveen, P., & Ree, E. (2020). The Role of Transformational leadership, Job Demands and Job Resources for Patient Safety Culture in Norwegian Nursing homes: A cross-sectional Study. *BMC Health Services Research, 20*(1), 1–8. DOI: 10.1186/s12913-020-05671-y PMID: 32847598

. Sfantou, D., Laliotis, A., Patelarou, A., Sifaki-Pistolla, D., Matalliotakis, M., & Patelarou, E. (2017). Importance of leadership style towards quality of care measures in healthcare settings: A systematic review. *Healthcare, 5*(4), 73. NCBI. DOI: 10.3390/healthcare5040073

Shanafelt, T., Ripp, J., & Trockel, M. (2020). Understanding and Addressing Sources of Anxiety Among Health Care Professionals During the COVID-19 Pandemic. *Journal of the American Medical Association, 323*(21). PMID: 32259193

Sinsky, C., Colligan, L., Li, L., Prgomet, M., Reynolds, S., Goeders, L., Westbrook, J., Tutty, M., & Blike, G. (2016). Allocation of Physician Time in Ambulatory Practice: A Time and Motion Study in 4 Specialties. *Annals of Internal Medicine, 165*(11), 753. DOI: 10.7326/m16-0961 PMID: 27595430

Smith, K., & Bhavsar, M. (2021, November). A new era of health leadership. []. Sage CA: Los Angeles, CA: SAGE Publications]. *Healthcare Management Forum, 34*(6), 332–335. PMID: 34592860

van Diggele, C., Burgess, A., Roberts, C., & Mellis, C. (2020). Leadership in healthcare education. *BMC Medical Education, 20*(Suppl 2), 456. PMID. 33272264

West, M., Armit, K., Loewenthal, L., Eckert, R., West, T., & Lee, A. (2015, February 25). *Leadership and Leadership Development in Health Care*. The King's Fund. https://www.kingsfund.org.uk/insight-and-analysis/reports/leadership-development-health-care

Wong, C. A., & Laschinger, H. K. S. (2019). Authentic leadership, performance, and job satisfaction: The mediating role of empowerment. *Journal of Advanced Nursing, 69*(4), 947–959. DOI: 10.1111/j.1365-2648.2012.06089.x PMID: 22764828

World Health Organization. (2010). *Monitoring the building blocks of health systems: A handbook of indicators and their measurement strategies*. https://iris.who.int/bitstream/handle/10665/258734/9789241564052-eng.pdf

Wu, C. H., Weisman, H., Sung, L. K., Erdogan, B., & Bauer, T. N. (2022). Perceived overqualification, felt organizational obligation, and extra-role behavior during the COVID-19 crisis: The moderating role of self-sacrificial leadership. *Applied Psychology*, *71*(3), 983–1013. PMID: 36433921

Chapter 11
Leadership in Practice:
Concluding Insights and Perspectives From Healthcare Executives

ABSTRACT

This chapter explores and highlight the insights and provides a comprehensive evaluation of healthcare domain leadership effectiveness competencies, challenges, vision, mission and strategic priorities within hospital settings., emphasizing its critical role in improving healthcare systems. The study underscores the importance of staff feedback and continuous personal growth, from famous healthcare leaders and chief executives encouraging leaders to engage with their teams for enhanced performance. By offering valued guidance and strategies for creative leadership, competency development, and SMART-based action plans, the book provides practical tools for leadership improvement. With a structured framework and measurable goals, it equips current and aspiring leaders to navigate complexities, drive change, and enhance patient care, worldwide

CONCLUDING INSIGHTS ON HEALTHCARE LEADERSHIP

This book serves as a comprehensive assessment of Healthcare Leadership Effectiveness in Hospitals, exploring the significance of leadership within the healthcare sector, identifying essential attributes of successful healthcare leaders, and synthesizing the latest research and best practices globally. Through deep research and analysis, the book has highlighted key healthcare leadership domains, attributes, styles, and challenges. The study provides healthcare leaders with a tool to collect accurate data regarding the perceptions of their subordinates, promoting the importance of feedback for continuous personal growth and insight. Effective

DOI: 10.4018/979-8-3373-2225-4.ch011

leadership in healthcare requires a multifaceted approach. The thirty-four domain statements (attributes) assessed and analyzed in this study are integral to developing and enhancing leadership capabilities. By cultivating these attributes, healthcare leaders can successfully address the evolving challenges within the sector, drive positive transformation, and ultimately improve patient care and outcomes. A key takeaway from this study is the understanding that the perception of staff is a reality that healthcare leaders must actively address. Feedback from subordinates serves as a crucial aspect of leadership growth, offering leaders the insights needed to refine their approach and improve organizational performance. Without engaging in consistent feedback loops with their teams, leaders miss opportunities for improvement and development.

This research offers valuable insights and practical recommendations for both current and aspiring healthcare leaders. By reviewing the results from each of the leadership domains, this work empowers healthcare leaders to develop Personal Action Plans to overcome challenges, enhance leadership practices, and improve organizational performance. These strategies can lead to improved healthcare delivery and outcomes in healthcare hospitals and similar healthcare environments. By implementing these practices, healthcare organizations can foster a new generation of leaders capable of navigating complexity, inspiring change, and improving healthcare delivery systems. Given the increasingly complex and dynamic nature of today's healthcare environment, the need for creative, adaptable, and forward-thinking leadership within hospitals and healthcare organizations has become more urgent than ever. Key recommendation start with healthcare Leaders where they must be equipped to navigate continuous change, operational pressures, and evolving patient expectations. To address these demands, leadership development must prioritize continuous learning, self-directed growth, and access to specialized training programs that enhance decision-making and crisis management capabilities. This book presents a comprehensive action plan designed to catalyze transformative leadership practices across hospital systems. Central to this plan is a strategic framework based on the SMART (Specific, Measurable, Achievable, Relevant, and Time-bound) methodology, guiding healthcare leaders in applying the most appropriate leadership behaviors at pivotal moments. To facilitate targeted development, the book introduces a Healthcare Leadership Competency Framework and a Self-Assessment Tool tailored to the specific demands of healthcare institutions. These tools enable leaders to evaluate their competencies, identify performance gaps, and cultivate both individual and organizational excellence. Furthermore, the strategic diffusion of these tools across various hospital settings supports the consistent application of effective leadership practices, driving improvements in care quality, operational efficiency, and patient outcomes. The insights and findings presented throughout this book contribute to the broader discourse on healthcare leadership and provide hospital administrators, policymakers, and researchers with evidence-based strategies for fostering resilient, high-performing leadership systems in healthcare organizations.

In light of healthcare orgnizations evolving economic and political landscape, developing creative and adaptable healthcare leadership has become imperative. Effective leaders in the healthcare sector must be empowered through continuous learning, self-development, and specialized training programs that enhance their capacity to manage complex, dynamic challenges. This book proposes a comprehensive action plan designed to generate meaningful impact within healthcare organizations. Centered around a replicable strategic framework, the plan leverages the SMART (Specific, Measurable, Achievable, Relevant, and Time-bound) methodology to guide leaders in applying the most appropriate leadership attributes at critical moments. Emphasizing competency-based development, the study introduces a Leadership Competency Framework and a Self-Assessment Tool to support leaders in evaluating and improving their performance. These tools are tailored to the unique demands of healthcare settings, promoting both personal and organizational effectiveness. Furthermore, the adoption of strategic diffusion techniques enables healthcare systems to implement the right tools in the right contexts, thereby improving care delivery, streamlining processes, and enhancing patient outcomes. The findings presented throughout this work aim to enrich the scholarly discourse on healthcare leadership and provide policymakers and researchers with actionable strategies to address real-world challenges, improve care quality, and foster sustainable leadership capacity.

UNIQUE CONTRIBUTIONS OF THIS RESEARCH

This book's research on healthcare leadership aligns with and expands upon existing literature in the field of healthcare leadership. Several studies and frameworks have already explored leadership styles, competencies, and the impact of leadership on healthcare organizations. However, this book takes a more comprehensive approach by analyzing leadership effectiveness through a multi-dimensional lens, specifically focusing on thirty-four domain statements (attributes) of healthcare leadership, While the aforementioned leadership models and frameworks provide critical insights into healthcare leadership, this study distinguishes itself through its integrated approach to leadership effectiveness in healthcare organizations. By assessing thirty-four distinct leadership domains, this study provides a much more granular understanding of healthcare leadership, one that spans beyond traditional leadership styles. The inclusion of Systems Thinking, Population Health Assessment, and Crisis Management introduces a modern approach to leadership, emphasizing the need for healthcare leaders to understand and manage complex systems, adapt to crises, and promote public health. Furthermore, the SMART methodology for goal setting within healthcare organizations offers a structured approach that many of the existing leadership frameworks do not fully address. This methodology allows leaders to break down complex strategies into actionable, measurable steps, ensuring that leadership development and organizational improvements can be tracked and evaluated over time. The Personal Action Plan created from this study serves as a comprehensive tool for healthcare leaders to not only improve their leadership effectiveness but also to enhance the overall organizational culture and performance. By directly integrating feedback from subordinates and fostering continuous personal development, the study aligns with best practices but also goes further by ensuring that feedback loops are not just encouraged, but systematically embedded into leadership practice.

In conclusion, this research contributes significantly to the existing body of knowledge on healthcare leadership by offering a detailed, actionable framework for developing leadership competencies across various domains. Through a comparative lens, this book adds depth to existing leadership theories by incorporating strategic frameworks and self-assessment tools that are adaptable to the unique challenges faced by healthcare leaders in healthcare organizations and beyond. By emphasizing the practical application of leadership theories and focusing on actionable, data-driven strategies, this book bridges the gap between theory and practice in healthcare leadership. It equips current and future healthcare leaders with the tools to navigate complexity, drive change, and improve patient care outcomes in an evolving healthcare environment.

CONTRIBUTIONS TO EXISTING KNOWLEDGE

The research findings contribute to a broader understanding of the factors that drive successful healthcare leadership, and similar healthcare environments. These insights can aid policymakers in crafting informed strategies for improving leadership practices, ensuring that healthcare organizations are led by competent, compassionate, and effective leaders who are capable of navigating both day-to-day challenges and broader systemic shifts. This study will be of particular value to healthcare policymakers and researchers tackling the challenges faced by healthcare leaders. It provides a roadmap for addressing the leadership gaps that often hinder healthcare systems and offers practical, research-backed solutions to enhance patient care and organizational performance. By integrating these findings and recommendations, healthcare organizations can build more effective, responsive, and resilient leadership teams capable of advancing patient care, promoting organizational growth, and addressing healthcare challenges effectively.

PERSPECTIVES OF HEALTHCARE LEADERS AND EXECUTIVES

Narratives from healthcare leaders and executives reveal the profound complexities, burdens, and adaptive strategies embedded in their roles. For instance, Dr. Amaka, a public hospital director in Nigeria, described how her greatest challenge was not the lack of ideas but convincing exhausted staff that change was possible amid unreliable electricity, inconsistent drug supplies, and overcrowded wards. One night, during a blackout in the neonatal unit, she held a flashlight while nurses resuscitated a premature baby, reminding her that leadership is not merely about policies but about being present when it matters. She built trust through dawn meetings with frontline staff, forming improvement teams, negotiating with local businesses for backup generators, and engaging political officials for timely budget releases, demonstrating that leadership in such contexts is grounded in relational adaptability and community negotiation (Onwujekwe et al., 2019). Similarly, Mr. Samuel, a supply chain manager in Kenya, recounted how, during COVID-19, he spent endless nights calling private pharmacies, truck drivers, boda boda riders, and local suppliers for PPE and oxygen. His proudest moment came not from national shipments but when community health volunteers made homemade masks for villages, highlighting that leadership in crisis is often about improvisation and informal networks (Waithaka & Kimani, 2021). In Bangladesh, Dr. Laila, director of a rural health center, emphasized that her greatest challenge was not funding but cultural perceptions, as many families preferred traditional birth attendants. She spent evenings with elders, midwives, and the local imam, gradually building trust that enabled mobile antenatal care camps in mosque yards, underscoring that leadership here requires cultural humility and learning the community's language to reduce maternal mortality. Other narratives from global executives illustrate the emotional and ethical weight of healthcare leadership. One leader shared, "Every morning, I walk into the hospital knowing my decisions may alter thousands of lives. During COVID-19 surges, I spent sleepless nights recalculating ventilator allocations, knowing each policy hid a nurse about to break. Real leadership is carrying these silent burdens with humility," (Persad & Joffe, 2021). Another, a CFO, described leading with empathy amid financial pressures, stating, "Seeing budget red flags while thinking of the single mother in admissions or the veteran environmental worker with health issues forced me to listen deeper than ever before" (Frandsen & Johansen, 2010; Garman & Johnson, 2006). A hospital CEO reflected on personal burnout, recalling, "After endless 18-hour days, my 14-year-old asked why I never smiled anymore. I realised I was modelling the burnout culture I claimed to fight, so I committed to reshaping our leadership development to prioritise self-leadership" (West, Dyrbye, & Shanafelt, 2018; Schein, 2017). A Chief Medical Officer described learning to share power:

"Micromanagement suffocated our brightest clinicians. Shifting to coaching instead of commanding let initiatives flourish without my constant intervention, humbling me deeply" (Goleman, Boyatzis, & McKee, 2013; Kouzes & Posner, 2023). Another administrator recounted approving devastating home health program cuts due to state funding shortfalls, later overhearing a coordinator explain the changes to an elderly patient and feeling physically ill, stating, "Leading healthcare is rarely black and white. It is shades of impossible choices" (Dean, Talbot, & Caplan, 2020; Epstein & Delgado, 2010). Finally, a Black female executive recalled the isolation of being the only Black woman at a hospital leadership conference, where discussions of equity felt intellectual to others but were her lived reality, fuelling her resolve to build diverse leadership pipelines: "Representation is not a diversity metric – it is a lever for justice" (Marcelin et al., 2019; Nivet & Fair, 2016). These narratives collectively underscore key leadership themes: adaptive and relational leadership, use of informal networks to compensate for systemic gaps, political and community negotiation, cultural humility, trust-building, improvisation under resource constraints, confronting moral injury, and advancing representation as a vehicle for equity and justice in healthcare leadership. Another review of the success stories of four healthcare executives in the Middle East, this time focused on how they helped healthcare leadership. The examples focus on Dr. Sherif Bishara, Dr. Jamil Ahmed, Dr. Maryam Matar, and Dr. Samia al-Amoudi, and show how they are innovative, culturally competent, and in line with the concepts of Leadership and Management in Healthcare by Gopee and Galloway (2017): Dr. Sherif Bishara is the CEO of American Hospital Dubai (Egypt/UAE), where he has turned it into a top center for advanced healthcare in the Middle East. His leadership has pushed the hospital to be a leader in technological innovation, such as when it worked with Siemens Healthineers to set up the region's first Center of Excellence for AI and digital diagnostics. Bishara makes sure that patients get high-quality, patient-centered care by using the latest technology, such as robotic surgery and precision oncology. He wants to "revolutionize regional healthcare by blending accessible innovation with exceptional personal care" (Gulf News, 2025). This is in line with Gopee and Galloway's (2017) focus on transformational leadership as a strategy to bring about change and improve patient outcomes. Dr. Jamil Ahmed is the founder and managing director of Prime Healthcare Group (UAE) (Bishara, 2025). He expanded the company from a small outpatient clinic into a large healthcare network that serves thousands of people every day in the UAE. His leadership style is based on "personalized care with a personal touch," which puts a high value on trust, empathy, and digital innovation. Ahmed has created a culture of excellence by encouraging strong communication within the company and giving employees more power. He stresses that "leadership thrives when people feel trusted, valued, and inspired to excel" (Prime Healthcare Group, 2021). This method is in line with Gopee and Galloway's (2017) focus on teamwork and Asif et al.'s (2019) view of leadership's role in improving service quality. Dr. Maryam Matar is a geneticist and health executive in the UAE. She is the first Emirati woman to be Director-General of the Community Development Authority and has achieved great progress in genetic research and public health leadership. She started statewide genetic screening initiatives to promote preventive healthcare as the head of the UAE Genetic Diseases Association. Her perspective stresses getting people involved in their communities before they need treatment. She says, “True healthcare leadership begins with prevention and raising community awareness” (Johns Hopkins Aramco Healthcare, 2025). Her work exemplifies cultural competency by addressing local health issues, along with Warrick’s (2017) perspectives on culturally competent leadership. Dr. Samia al-Amoudi, an obstetrician and health advocate from Saudi Arabia, is the last person on the list. After publicly announcing her diagnosis, she became a leader in women's health activism in Saudi Arabia. Her brave leadership fought against cultural taboos about cancer, changed health policy, and raised awareness. Her attitude, which is based on being real and strong, is best summed up by her words: “My cancer journey empowered me to drive change in both medicine and society” (Al-Amoudi et al., 2016). This corresponds with Gopee and Galloway’s (2017) focus on emotional intelligence in leadership and Seljemo, Viksveen, and Ree’s (2020) results indicating that leadership enhances patient outcomes via cultural sensitivity.

REFERENCES

Al-Amoudi, S., Al-Shugtani, T., Al-Maatouq, M., Sindi, A., & Qureshi, N. (2016). Breast cancer knowledge among male high school students in Saudi Arabia. *Journal of Cancer Education, 31*(4), 784–788. pubmed.ncbi.nlm.nih.gov. DOI: 10.1007/s13187-015-0951-8 PMID: 26611278

American Hospital Dubai. (2022, January 26). American Hospital collaborates with Siemens Healthineers as key technology partner for advanced diagnostics solutions. American Hospital Dubai. Retrieved August 6, 2025, from https://www.ahdubai.com/news/american-hospital-dubai-collaborates-with-siemens-healthineers-as-key-technology-partner-for-advance khaleejtimes.com+13gulfnews.com+13ahdubai.com+

Asif, M., Jameel, A., Hussain, A., Hwang, J., & Sahito, N. (2019). Linking transformational leadership with nurse-assessed adverse patient outcomes and the quality of care: Assessing the role of job satisfaction and structural empowerment. *International Journal of Environmental Research and Public Health, 16*(13), 1–15. https://pubmed.ncbi.nlm.nih.gov/31277478/ PMID: 31277478

Bishara, S. (2025). Sherifbishara.com. https://sherifbishara.com/

Dean, W., Talbot, S. G., & Caplan, A. (2020). Clarifying the language of clinician distress. *Journal of the American Medical Association, 323*(10), 923–924. https://pubmed.ncbi.nlm.nih.gov/32003769/ PMID: 32003769

Epstein, E., & Delgado, S. (2010, September 30). *Understanding and Addressing Moral Distress | OJIN: The Online Journal of Issues in Nursing*. Ojin.nursingworld.org. https://ojin.nursingworld.org/table-of-contents/volume-15-2010/number-3-september-2010/understanding-moral-distress/

Frandsen, F., & Johansen, W. (2010). Strategy, management, leadership, and public relations. The *SAGE handbook of public relations*, 293-306.

Garman, A. N., & Johnson, M. P. (2006). Leadership Competencies: An Introduction. *Journal of Healthcare Management, 51*(1), 13. https://journals.lww.com/jhmonline/Citation/2006/01000/Leadership_Competencies__An_Introduction.4.aspx PMID: 16479746

Goleman, D., Boyatzis, R., & McKee, A. (2013). *Primal Leadership: Unleashing the Power of Emotional Intelligence*. Harvard Business Press.

Gopee, N., & Galloway, J. (2017). *Leadership and Management in Healthcare* (3rd ed.). Sage. (Original work published 2008)

Gulf News. (2025, January 27). *American Hospital Dubai unveils future health at Arab Health 2025*. Gulf News: Latest UAE News, Dubai News, Business, Travel News, Dubai Gold Rate, Prayer Time, Cinema. https://gulfnews.com/gn-focus/american-hospital-dubai-unveils-future-health-at-arab-health-2025-1.500023515

Johns Hopkins Aramco Healthcare. (2025). *Dr. Mariam Matar Bio*. Jhah.com. https://www.jhah.com/en/bios/dr-mariam-matar-bio

Kouzes, J. M., & Posner, B. Z. (2023). *The Leadership Challenge* (7th ed.). Jossey-Bass.

Marcelin, J. R., Siraj, D. S., Victor, R., Kotadia, S., & Maldonado, Y. A. (2019). The Impact of Unconscious Bias in healthcare: How to Recognize and Mitigate It. *The Journal of Infectious Diseases*, *220*(2), 62–73. DOI: 10.1093/infdis/jiz214 PMID: 31430386

Nivet, M. A., & Fair, M. (2016). Defining diversity in quality care. In *Diversity and inclusion in quality patient care* (pp. 3–9). Springer International Publishing.

Onwujekwe, O., Ezumah, N., Mbachu, C., Obi, F., Ichoku, H., Uzochukwu, B., & Wang, H. (2019). Exploring effectiveness of different health financing mechanisms in Nigeria; what needs to change and how can it happen? *BMC Health Services Research*, *19*(1). Advance online publication. DOI: 10.1186/s12913-019-4512-4 PMID: 31519181

Persad, G., & Joffe, S. (2021). Allocating scarce life-saving resources: The proper role of age. *Journal of Medical Ethics*, *47*(12), 836–838. PMID: 33753473

Prime HealthCare Group LLC. (2021). About Prime HealthCare Group. Retrieved August 6, 2025, from https://www.primehealth.ae/prime-healthcare-group/about-prime-group

Schein, E. H. (2017). *Organizational Culture and Leadership* (5th ed.). Wiley.

Seljemo, C., Viksveen, P., & Ree, E. (2020). The Role of Transformational leadership, Job Demands and Job Resources for Patient Safety Culture in Norwegian Nursing homes: A cross-sectional Study. *BMC Health Services Research*, *20*(1), 1–8. DOI: 10.1186/s12913-020-05671-y PMID: 32847598

Waithaka, R. K., & Kimani, J. G. (2021). Effect of e-procurement practices on supply chain performance. *Global Journal of Purchasing and Procurement Management*, *1*(1), 32–42.

. Warrick, D. D. (2017). What leaders need to know about organizational culture. *Business Horizons, 60*(3), 395–404. ScienceDirect. DOI: 10.1016/j.bushor.2017.01.011

West, C. P., Dyrbye, L. N., & Shanafelt, T. D. (2018). Physician burnout: Contributors, consequences and solutions. *Journal of Internal Medicine*, *283*(6), 516–529. DOI: 10.1111/joim.12752 PMID: 29505159

Chapter 12
Distinctive Strengths and Research Excellence of Healthcare Leadership

ABSTRACT

This chapter provides valued information about the new healthcare leadership studies and researches by pointing out the significant healthcare leadership skills needed to deal with these problems. The book manuscript might make its use in real-world healthcare settings even better by linking these skills to relevant case studies or well-known leadership theories. This would make the skills' real-world effects clearer. A big part of the book is how it combines theory and practice. It effectively connects basic leadership theories, such transformational, authentic, and servant leadership, with real-world examples that are specifically designed for healthcare settings. The book gives readers useful tactics that can be used in clinical, operational, and strategic settings by connecting these abstract concepts to real-life actions. This combination makes it easier for those who run complicated healthcare systems to understand and use leadership principles.

DISTINCTIVE STRENGTHS OF HEALTHCARE LEADERSHIP BOOK

The main feature of the article is that it clearly explains the problems that healthcare systems face and how important good leadership is. It provides a lot of value by pointing out the important leadership skills needed to deal with these problems. To make better use of this strength, the manuscript might make its use in real-world healthcare settings even better by linking these skills to relevant case studies or well-known leadership theories. This would make the skills' real-world effects clearer. A

DOI: 10.4018/979-8-3373-2225-4.ch012

big part of the book is how it combines theory and practice. It effectively connects basic leadership theories, such transformational, authentic, and servant leadership, with real-world examples that are specifically designed for healthcare settings. The book gives readers useful tactics that can be used in clinical, operational, and strategic settings by connecting these abstract concepts to real-life actions. This combination makes it easier for those who run complicated healthcare systems to understand and use leadership principles.

The book is even more unique because it puts things in the context of healthcare systems. It goes into great detail about variables that are peculiar to each sector, such as regulatory pressures, the dynamics of interdisciplinary teams, ethical decision-making, and patient-centered treatment. This focus on real-world healthcare organizations and policy frameworks sets this text distinct from other leadership tools that are more general. Using case studies and examples from the real world makes the content much better. First-person stories from healthcare executives, nurses, doctors, and administrators make the experience more interesting and give real-world examples of leadership achievements and problems. These real-life stories help people learn by putting theory into the context of everyday leadership situations. The book provides competency frameworks for different levels of leadership, from frontline staff to executives. These frameworks give explicit direction on the abilities and behaviors that are important. This organized method helps with focused leadership development that is in line with evidence-based practice and the goals of the company.

Change management and innovation are two very crucial parts of modern healthcare. The book uses modern theories like complexity science and relational coordination to provide strong frameworks that help executives successfully lead organizational change and quality improvement efforts. Leadership based on ethics and values is a big part of everything. Aligning leadership development with professional codes, patient safety concerns, and societal expectations builds the moral basis necessary for trustworthy and accountable healthcare leadership. The manuscript's easy-to-read language and focus on practitioners make it easy for healthcare professionals to use right away. This makes it a better resource for leadership development programs and ongoing professional improvement. The book encourages a comprehensive approach by including ideas from fields such as organizational behavior, public health, systems thinking, and clinical sciences. For healthcare leaders to deal with the many problems they encounter, they need to look at things from a wide angle.

The fact that the book is included in professional certification programs like ACHE Fellowships and nursing leadership certifications shows that it is credible and useful for training leaders to meet the changing needs of healthcare organizations. Finally, its focus on the future addresses new leadership concerns like digital health,

AI, virtual team management, and health equality, getting leaders ready to deal with changes in how healthcare is delivered. The references used in the manuscript are mostly good, relevant, and up-to-date, which makes them a great base for ideas about healthcare leadership. The choice shows a good mix of classic works and newer studies that add to the conversation on what makes a good leader and how those methods affect healthcare results. Dye's Leadership in Healthcare (2023) is one important foundational texts that explain leadership framework, cost-quality issues, and how organizations work. Wachter's The Digital Doctor (2015) is another modern work that adds to the material by looking at how technology is becoming more important in healthcare settings.

But the reference base may be better if it included more recent empirical studies and systematic reviews that looked at how well leaders work in the healthcare system after the epidemic. Adding literature that talks about transformational, servant, and collaborative leadership models in healthcare will better reflect the contemporary paradigms that are important in modern practice. To stay up to date, it is important to read studies over the last five years that include crisis leadership, innovation, and equity-focused skills. Gabel et al's (2022) review of transformational leadership in healthcare organizations, Cummings et al's (2018) systematic analysis of leadership styles and patient care quality, Kahn's (2020) look at leadership during crises and innovation, and Ospina's (2017) outline of future healthcare leadership research agendas are all good examples of what to add. These studies, along with other sources, would make sure that the book incorporates timeless leadership concepts and the most recent changes that are affecting how healthcare executives work around the world.

Overall, this book about healthcare leadership is great because it combines theory with practice in a way that is very relevant to real life, and it focuses on skills and new ideas. It is an essential resource for present and future healthcare professionals who need to understand the intricacies of today's fast-changing healthcare environment because it uses real-world examples and plain, easy-to-understand language.

EVIDENCE OF HIGH-QUALITY RESEARCH IN THE HEALTHCARE LEADERSHIP BOOK

The healthcare leadership book shows that it is well-researched by using reliable, evidence-based sources that have both solid theoretical bases and real-world applications. It uses well-known leadership theories, like transformational and servant leadership, in a variety of healthcare settings to make sure the ideas are strong. The studies that are included use strong methods including systematic reviews, meta-analyses, mixed-methods designs, and validated tools like the Multifactor

Leadership Questionnaire (MLQ). This makes the results more reliable, comparable, and credible. The book's research covers a wide range of countries and situations, looking at both global and specific leadership problems. It also stresses the need of measurable results that are related to patient safety, workforce well-being, and organizational performance. The book also takes a multidisciplinary and patient-centered approach to health fairness, diversity, and the use of new technologies like AI and telemedicine in leadership. It suggests practical changes based on real-world evidence, such as improving crisis leadership and change management and building digital skills. Clear recommendations for methodological rigor, longitudinal research, and stakeholder participation make the study even stronger. These are all excellent practices in healthcare leadership research. The book is a great example of high-quality scholarship since it uses strict methodologies, is useful in the real world, and is relevant to healthcare around the world to improve both academic knowledge and leadership in healthcare. As a last suggestion and To move healthcare leadership research and practice forward, we need to build on the strong foundation shown in this book by putting methodological rigor, contextual variety, and interdisciplinary collaboration at the top of the list. In the future, we should focus on increasing longitudinal and mixed-methods research to find out how leadership interventions affect healthcare settings around the world over time. Researchers and practitioners also need to provide standardized ways to measure digital and crisis leadership skills, with a focus on procedures that are fair, ethical, and culturally sensitive. Adding real-world case studies and getting stakeholders involved—like frontline personnel and patients—will make study findings more useful and relevant. By using these tactics, healthcare executives may adapt to the challenges of healthcare settings that are becoming more complicated, technology-driven, and diverse. This will lead to better patient outcomes, more resilient workforces, and more effective organizations.

TARGET AUDIENCE FOR HEALTHCARE LEADERSHIP BOOKS AND RESEARCH

Healthcare leadership publications and studies are useful to a wide range of people around the world, including CEOs, doctors, teachers, policymakers, consultants, and new leaders. These tools are carefully made to meet the specific demands, duties, and responsibilities of individuals who lead, manage, or have an impact on healthcare organizations and systems all over the world.

First and foremost, healthcare CEOs and senior leaders are a vital group of people to reach out to. This group includes Chief Executive Officers (CEOs), Chief Medical Officers (CMOs), Chief Nursing Officers (CNOs), Chief Financial Officers (CFOs), and other C-suite leaders including Chief Operating Officers (COOs) and

Chief Innovation Officers (CIOs). These people are in charge of making strategic decisions, creating and carrying out policies, keeping an eye on how well the organization is doing, and finding their way through complicated regulatory, financial, and operational environments. They look for leadership resources that offer strategic frameworks, case studies from similar high-stakes situations, and tools to help them lead large-scale change efforts while still providing good care for patients. This group would benefit greatly from books like The Healthcare Imperative and Management Lessons from Mayo Clinic since they focus on managing costs, improving quality, building a positive work culture, and achieving high levels of performance. Second, mid-level and frontline managers make up another important group. This group comprises people who work at the operational and tactical levels, like department heads, unit managers, clinical supervisors, practice managers, and team leaders. Their jobs include turning strategic plans into everyday tasks, managing workers, managing workflows, settling disagreements, and promoting ongoing quality improvement. Exceptional Leadership and Leadership in Healthcare are two examples of resources that provide practical skills, tools for managing performance, and frameworks for leading a team well. These managers often prefer content that balances leadership theory with actionable guidance relevant to interdisciplinary teams and patient-facing settings. Third, a key group of people to reach out to are new and aspiring leaders. This includes doctors getting ready to take on leadership responsibilities and students in healthcare management, health administration, public health, or nursing leadership programs. These future leaders learn the basics of communication, decision-making, emotional intelligence, and systems thinking. Patients Come Second and other books like it speak to this group by using simple, practitioner-friendly language and real-world examples, introspective exercises, and tactics to help them connect their clinical skills with their leadership duties.

Healthcare educators and trainers are the fourth category that depends on these texts a lot. Teachers who are in charge of designing the curriculum, developing courses, and continuing professional education use these kinds of resources to teach their students and trainees evidence-based leadership concepts, case studies, and critical thinking skills. They look for publications that have structured theoretical frameworks, competence models, and teaching aids that may be used in both undergraduate and graduate school.

Fifth, policymakers and health system planners, such as government officials, health policy analysts, and leaders in regulatory agencies, read healthcare leadership literature to learn more about how important leadership is in making changes to the system, running it, and putting policies into action. Books like The New Health Care for Profit talk about how the market works, how to keep costs down, and the effects of regulations. These books give this audience an idea of how leadership affects health equity, policy outcomes, and population health methods.

The sixth group of people who read this are researchers and professors. People who study healthcare management, leadership, organizational psychology, and public health leadership use these books because they have useful theories, thorough literature reviews, conceptual frameworks, and real-life case studies. Leading Change in Healthcare and other books like it are popular with this group because they carefully combine theory and practice and help set the agenda for future research, grant bids, and academic publications. Seventh, healthcare consultants and leadership coaches use these tools to help with change management, organizational development, and executive coaching projects. They employ the frameworks, assessments, and competency models in these books to create custom programs for clients, run leadership retreats, and carry out organizational transformation initiatives that are founded on research. Books about digital leadership, complexity science, and relationship-centered care give consultants the tools they need to help leaders deal with technological changes, cultural shifts, and system redesigns.

Finally, change agents and innovators, like Chief Innovation Officers, digital transformation leads, and telehealth program directors, read books and articles about healthcare leadership to learn more about change management, implementation science, and leadership skills that are important for innovation and disruptive change. Books like The Digital Doctor and Digital Leadership in Healthcare are especially useful since they combine ideas about leadership with ideas about digital health strategy and the future of the workforce.

REFERENCES

Cummings, G. G., Tate, K., Lee, S., Wong, C. A., Paananen, T., Micaroni, S. P. M., & Chatterjee, G. E. (2018). Leadership Styles and Outcome Patterns for the Nursing Workforce and Work environment: A Systematic Review. *International Journal of Nursing Studies*, *85*(1), 19–60. DOI: 10.1016/j.ijnurstu.2018.04.016 PMID: 29807190

Dye, C. F. (2023). *Leadership in healthcare: Essential values and skills* (4th ed.). Health Administration Press.

Gabel Shemueli, R., Tzafrir, S., Rodriguez Perez, B., Bahamonde, D., & Enosh, G. (2022). Collective compass to unit performance: Linking transformational leadership climate, trust and engagement. *Leadership and Organization Development Journal*, *43*(5), 802–813.

Kahn, L. H. (2020). *Who's in Charge?: Leadership During Epidemics, Bioterror Attacks, and Other Public Health Crises*. Bloomsbury Publishing USA.

Ospina, S. M. (2017). Collective leadership and context in public administration: Bridging public leadership research and leadership studies. *Public Administration Review*, *77*(2), 275–287.

Wachter, R. (2015). *The Digital Doctor: Hope, Hype, and Harm at the Dawn of Medicine's Computer Age*. Mcgraw-Hill Education.

Chapter 13
A Conceptual Model and Self-Assessment Framework for Healthcare Leadership

ABSTRACT

This chapter introduces a proposed Healthcare Leadership Competency Framework Self-Assessment Tool, designed to evaluate and enhance leadership capabilities across key domains such as strategic thinking, adaptability, communication, and collaboration. Complementing this tool is an Integrated Healthcare Leadership Framework that merges diverse leadership philosophies—transformational, authentic, servant, and distributed—into a cohesive model. It emphasizes leadership as a context-driven, relational process shaped by systemic dynamics, organizational culture, and external policies. This framework recognizes healthcare systems as complex adaptive environments that demand flexible, collaborative leadership strategies. It serves as a foundation for leadership development programs, empirical research, and organizational policy design. While the framework offers a structured and comprehensive approach, it also highlights the need for further theoretical refinement, empirical validation, and contextual customization.

CONCEPTUAL MODEL PROPOSAL FOR LEADERSHIP IN HEALTHCARE

By incorporating a theoretical framework, this book aims to enhance readers' comprehension of healthcare leadership, providing deeper insights into its com-

DOI: 10.4018/979-8-3373-2225-4.ch013

plexities and applications. Integrated Healthcare Leadership Framework as shown in **Table 1** below

Table 1. Proposed integrated healthcare leadership framework

Construct	Key Elements	Expected Outcomes
Leadership Philosophy	Transformational, Authentic, Servant, Distributed	Enhanced staff morale, empowerment, and motivation
Leadership Behaviors	Visioning, role modeling, ethical conduct, coaching	Improved team performance, communication, and innovation
Organizational Context	Culture, structure, resource availability	Moderates leadership impact on outcomes
Systemic Dynamics	Interprofessional collaboration, policies, external pressures	Influences leadership adaptability and strategic effectiveness
Outcomes	Patient safety, care quality, staff retention, organizational resilience	Positive organizational performance and patient-centered care

There are a few important assumptions that the suggested framework is based on that affect how it can be used and understood in healthcare settings. First, it assumes that leadership is always based on relationships and the situation, and that good leadership comes from how people connect with each other in certain situations. Second, it says that diverse leadership philosophies work together rather than against each other, which means that using more than one style makes leadership more effective. Third, the framework recognizes that healthcare systems are complex adaptive systems, which means that they need leadership styles that are spread out and based on systems thinking to deal with their built-in problems. Finally, it assumes that organizational culture and external policy and environmental issues affect how well leaders do their jobs. This shows how important it is to make sure that leadership practices are in line with both internal dynamics and larger contextual elements.

The Integrated Healthcare Leadership Framework can be a helpful tool in many areas. In empirical study, it can be used to look at how different leadership styles, organizational settings, and patient outcomes are related. This framework gives leadership development programs a starting point for creating curricula that include skills from transformational, authentic, servant, and dispersed leadership styles. In addition, it can help shape policy and structure in organizational strategy to encourage collective and adaptive leadership practices, which will ultimately improve the performance of the entire healthcare system. Figure 1 shows the proposed Integrated Healthcare Leadership Framework

Figure 1. Integrated healthcare leadership framework details

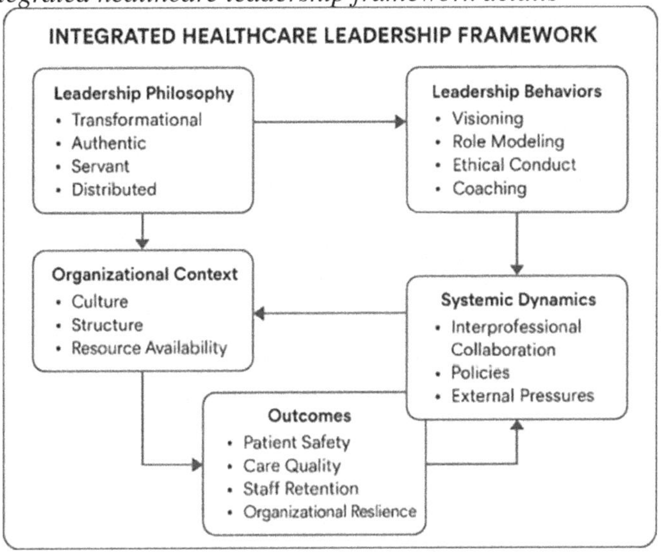

Healthcare leaders work in a complicated and ever-changing environment that is formed by teams from many fields and changing patient requirements. A proposed theoretical framework has been put forward to combine and integrate known leadership theories with the particular elements that affect healthcare. This will help leaders in this field see the whole picture and see things through a structured lens. This framework looks at leadership constructs, how they relate to each other, and how they all affect healthcare outcomes. It provides a strong basis for research, practical use, and leadership development programs that aim to improve patient outcomes and make healthcare organizations more resilient. But even if it has some good points, the framework has big holes in its theoretical scope, empirical validation, practical applicability, and contextual relevance. By filling up these gaps with more comprehensive theoretical integration, strict longitudinal and mixed-methods research designs, customized implementation plans for different roles and contexts, and a global viewpoint, it will become more useful and effective. By filling in these gaps, the framework can help healthcare administrators deal with the growing complexities, technological advances, and cultural differences of modern healthcare. This will lead to improved patient care, higher morale among staff, and better overall performance by the company.

HEALTH CARE LEADERSHIP COMPETENCY FRAMEWORK SELF-ASSESSMENT TOOL (PROPOSED TOOL)

Healthcare leadership book introduces a **Healthcare Leadership Competency Framework Self-Assessment Tool**, designed to evaluate and strengthen the competencies of healthcare leaders. This tool offers a structured approach for leaders to assess their skills and identify areas for improvement across key leadership domains. It covers critical areas such as strategic thinking, communication, crisis management, adaptability, and team collaboration. By using this self-assessment, healthcare leaders can gain valuable insights into their leadership effectiveness, track personal development, and align their practices with organizational goals. The proposed tool aims to enhance leadership capabilities, ultimately contributing to improved healthcare outcomes

HEALTHCARE LEADERSHIP ASSESSMENT CASE STUDY

This section presents a detailed case study on healthcare leadership, focusing on the real-world application of leadership principles in a healthcare setting. It examines how effective leadership shapes the culture, operations, and overall success of healthcare organizations. Through the lens of a specific case, the chapter explores various leadership styles, decision-making processes, and the challenges faced by healthcare leaders in improving patient care, managing resources, and fostering team collaboration. The case study highlights the importance of strategic thinking, emotional intelligence, communication, and crisis management in navigating complex healthcare environments. Additionally, it provides practical insights on leadership strategies that can drive innovation, enhance operational efficiency, and promote high-quality patient outcomes. By analyzing the leadership approaches employed in the case, this chapter offers valuable lessons for current and aspiring healthcare leaders, encouraging reflection on their leadership practices and the impact they have on organizational success.

Methods

This section demonstrates the study methodology developed based on the literature review, Methodology developed based on the comprehensive broad literature review (related literature periodicals, books, scientific journals), The design of this tool is descriptive in nature consist of descriptive analytical-qualitative approach and quantitative research (Rutberg & Bouikidis, 2018; Briggs, Coleman, & Morrison, n.d.), Qualitative to explore deep insights into the multifaceted nature of healthcare

Leadership and Quantitative research, uncovering the key domains (attributes), strategies, and competencies required to lead in this challenging environment effectively to explore deep insights into the multifaceted nature of healthcare leadership and uncovering the key domains (attributes), and competencies required to lead in this challenging environment by developing a customized survey questionnaire developed as the primary data collection instrument from respondents to achieve the study's objectives. Through (a collaborative process with inputs from country health systems experts from healthcare professionals, distinguished researches and word wide world health organizations societies and experts groups, The Jordanian hospitals leaders, and the Jordanian Ministry of Health, quoted from different global assessment tools (American College of Healthcare, Executives, National Health Service Leadership Academy, distributed to healthcare leaders expert and practitioner and Global Healthcare Leadership Competency Model), and review with internationally successful organizational case studies.

Additionally, the researcher sought input from expert arbitrators and specialists in the subject area (DeVellis, 2016) by performing interviews with key informants, all of whom are healthcare leaders in the field who were purposively selected for their expertise in healthcare leadership positions.

Population and Sample Size

The population refers to the entire set of values or individuals the researcher is interested in. As a result, it refers to the set or group of all the units to which the research findings are to be applied (Gupta & Singh, 2014). The formulation of the hypothesis takes the form of a phrase consisting of variables denoting the characteristics of individuals or things that make up the statistical community, which is defined as all individuals, people, or things. Therefore, the researcher must define a population study before choosing the measuring tool or gathering data after defining the research problem and its hypotheses (Gupta & Singh, 2014).

Sampling is selecting a portion of the population to estimate the characteristics of the entire population. The first benefits of sampling are cost savings and accelerated data collection. Each advertisement assesses an extra task or subject that uninfluenced people discover. Sampling is primarily used to collect data on the population in cohort studies, medical studies, and agricultural research; the people-selection approach to data-idea selection has been updated such that it is mainly based exclusively on the literature review (Gupta & Singh, 2014).

The researcher defined the population study in the Jordanian Hospital before choosing the measuring tool. The study population included the Leadership in the Jordanian Hospital (2000) employees. The estimated sample size required was 322 workers in the hospital; researchers distributed (450) questionnaires, (45) questionnaires were rejected for not completing the answer, 30 samples were rejected for lack of credibility of the answer, and (83) samples were not retrieved so that the current study received (322) responses, indicating the use of an appropriate sample as a sampling tool, in line with (Sekaran & and Bougie, 2016), sample size and other methods of sample calculations.

Table 2. Sample size table

N	S	N	S	N	S
30	28	280	162	1500	306
40	36	290	165	1600	310
50	44	300	169	1700	313
60	52	320	175	1800	317
70	59	340	181	1900	320
80	66	360	186	**2000**	**322**
90	73	400	196	2200	327
95	76	420	201	2400	331
100	80	440	205	2600	335
110	86	460	210	2800	338
120	92	480	214	3000	341
130	97	500	217	3500	346
140	103	550	226	4500	354
150	108	600	234	5000	357
160	113	650	242	6000	361
170	118	700	248	7000	364
180	123	750	254	8000	367
190	127	800	260	9000	368
200	132	850	265	10000	370
210	136	900	269	15000	375
220	140	950	274	20000	377
230	144	1000	278	30000	379
240	148	1100	285	40000	380
250	152	1200	291	50000	381
260	155	1300	297	75000	382
270	159	1400	302	1000000	384

(Sekaran & Bougie, 2016)

Data Collection Procedures

The study relied on the quantitative approach to obtain the necessary information to prepare the theoretical and practical side. However, these sources are Primary data sources: To provide data and information related to the study, the questionnaire was designed after taking the opinions of a group of researchers and professionals in the field (in this study, the The Jordanian hospital employees) the field of study to obtain primary data to complete the applied aspect of the study. The study addresses the study questions and tests its hypotheses. Secondary data sources: information related to the theoretical side of studies, research, university theses, articles, scientific books, academic journals, research, and previous articles specialized in the subject of the study.

Study Tool

To achieve the aim of the study and answer its questions, a questionnaire was prepared to evaluate the leadership effectiveness mentioned in Table 3.2 below; the questionnaire in its initial form consists of 162 items, with intended answers on a five-point Likert scale Table 3 below as follow: which ranged from (1-5) degrees where ((strongly Agree(5);Agree(4);Neutral(3); Disagree(2);Strongly Disagree(1)). The highest score (5) and the lowest score (1) for each statement.

Methodology developed based on the comprehensive broad literature review, The design of this tool is descriptive in nature consist of descriptive analytical-qualitative approach and quantitative research (Rutberg & Bouikidis, 2018; Briggs, Coleman, & Morrison, n.d.) to explore deep insights into the multifaceted nature of healthcare leadership and uncovering the key domains (attributes), and competencies required to lead in this challenging environment by developing a structured survey questionnaire customized to consists of a set of standardized questions with a predetermined framework that sets the precise language and sequence of the questions developed through (a collaborative process with inputs from country health systems experts from, the hospitals leaders, and Jordanian ministry of health, quoted from different global assessment tools (American College of Healthcare, Executives, National Health Service Leadership Academy, distributed to healthcare leaders expert and practitioner and Global Healthcare Leadership Competency Model), Additionally, the researcher sought input from expert arbitrators and specialists in the subject area (DeVellis, 2016) by performing interviews with key informants, all of whom are healthcare leaders in the field who were purposively selected for their expertise in healthcare leadership positions. The researcher defined the population study in the public The Hospital before choosing the measuring tool (Gupta & Singh, 2014). total population consisted of (2000) employees, according to (Sekaran & Bougie,

2016), and the estimated sample size required was 322 employees in the hospital; researchers distributed (450) questionnaires, (45) questionnaires were rejected for not completing the answer, 30 samples were rejected for Lack of credibility of the answer, and (83) samples were not retrieved so that the current study received (322) responses, indicating the use of an appropriate sample as a sampling tool, in line with (Sekaran & Bougie, 2016) sample size and other methods of sample calculations. The questionnaire was prepared to assess the leadership effectiveness of thirty-four domains (Attributes) in improving healthcare quality in the Hospitals. A questionnaire was developed to identify the critical quality characteristics of an effective leader. The study involved a dependent variable assessment of current Senior healthcare leadership effectiveness and an independent variable consisting of 34 domains (attributes) with 162 questions, detailed shown in Table 5 below the 34 leadership domains (attributes) characteristics consist of 162 questions chosen. The questionnaire in its initial form, with intended answers on a five-point Likert scale, ranging from (1-5) degrees where (Strongly Agree (5; Agree (4; Neutral (3; Disagree (2; Strongly Disagree (1)). The highest score (5) and the lowest score (1) for each statement. The final tool was tested and revised, clarifying the healthcare leadership effectiveness of each characteristic. This study design and format were chosen to facilitate expeditious completion of the tool. A cover memo was sent with the survey, assuring confidentiality and anonymity; potential participants were contacted and asked to participate using different platforms to obtain sample saturation. Questionnaire replies were collected. Subject individuals completed the questionnaire and met the 95% confidence interval and a maximum error of 5%; they were also considered valid (with no missing outliers). The sample size of this study is 322 valid responses, which is large enough for evaluation of the data; regular normality **testing** in this case is not highly required (Brown & Robinson, 2002).

Results and Discussion

Potential participants were contacted and asked to participate in the survey using different platforms to obtain sample saturation. Questionnaire replies were collected. Subject individuals completed the questionnaire and met the 95% confidence interval and a maximum error of 5%; they were also considered valid (with no missing outliers).

Table 3. Likert 5-point scale

Strongly agree	Agree	Neutral	Disagree	Strongly Disagree
5	4	3	2	1

(Joshi et al., 2015)

The study involved a dependent variable assessment of current Senior leadership effectiveness in improving healthcare quality and an independent variable consisting of 34 domain (attributes) items with 162 questions. The sample size of this study is 322 valid responses, which is large enough for evaluation of the data; regular normality **testing** in this case is not highly required *(Brown & Robinson, 2002).*

The questionnaire components were distributed into a set of questions and paragraphs divided into two parts:

Part One: Demographic Variables

This part of the questionnaire aims to identify the prevailing healthcare leader's personal and functional characteristics and characteristics workers in The Jordanian Hospital started with demographic questions by answering five questions represented by (1. Gender, 2. Age, 3. Educational Qualification, 4. Trade, and 5. Years of Experience), then evaluated the (34) Domains statements (attributes) with (162) different questions as shown in Table 3 above (full version) attached in Appendices.

Validity and Reliability of Study Tool

The purpose of testing the validity of the research tool is to verify the correctness of the language, clarity of its meanings, and coherence of its paragraphs and to ensure that the questionnaire can meet the objectives for which it was created and that it can be used to collect information on the subject of study (Pandey & Pandey, 2021), While The stability test of the study tool is used to ensure the degree of clarity, objectivity, accuracy, the possibility of obtaining a degree of relative stability in its answers, coherence, and interconnection between paragraphs and to verify this by calculating Cronbach's alpha coefficient, which ranges from (zero to one) and values close to 1 indicates The scores are of high stability and good consistency, (Amirrudin, Nasution, & Supahar, 2021).

Table 4. Summary of reliability coefficient

Reliability coefficient	below 0.60	0.7	0.8	0.90 and higher
Remarks	Poor reliability	Acceptable reliability	Good reliability	Excellent reliability

(Amirrudin, Nasution, & Supahar, 2021).

Research Data Analysis data using the Statistical Package for Social Science (SPSS) version 28., exclude irrelevant, missing data, and non-interacting responses, computed the relative importance through the mean and standard deviation of each item computed employing an equation that incorporates the quadrant scale for the individual item and calculates the average of the study sample's responses to each item and Table 3-6 shows the results of the study instrument's stability test.

The questionnaire components were distributed into a set of questions and paragraphs divided into two parts: Part One: Demographic Variables aims to identify the prevailing personal and functional characteristics in the Hospitals by answering five questions represented by (1. Gender, 2. Age, 3. Educational Qualification, 4. Trade, and 5. Years of Experience), then part two where the study involved a dependent variable assessment of current Senior leadership effectiveness and an independent variable consisting of 34 items with total of 162 questions as shown in Table 5 below.

Table 5. Healthcare leadership domains, number of each domain questions reliability coefficients

	Domain	Number Of Questions	Cronbach's Alpha	Reliability Remarks
1	General Parameters (Systems Perspective)	18	0.973	Excellent
2	Professional, Ethical, and Social Responsibility:	10	0.947	Excellent
3	Commitment to Advancing People-Centered Services	8	0.919	Excellent
4	Emotional Intelligence and Self-Awareness	4	0.887	Good
5	Continuous Improvement	4	0.913	Excellent
6	Translation and Implementation	3	0.923	Excellent
7	Strategic Financial Management	5	0.922	Excellent
8	Human Resource Management	7	0.934	Excellent
9	Information Management	4	0.894	Good
10	Administration and Business Development	7	0.927	Excellent
11	Quality Improvement and Patient Safety	5	0.869	Good
12	Monitoring and Evaluation	3	0.890	Good
13	Visionary Leadership	7	0.928	Excellent
14	Governance	6	0.926	Excellent
15	Preparedness and Crisis Management	6	0.945	Excellent
16	Digital Technologies in Healthcare	2	0.751	Acceptable
17	Executive Communication	3	0.808	Good
18	Employee Support and Development	2	0.810	Good
19	Compassionate Leadership	2	0.822	Good
20	Interpersonal Relationships	5	0.891	Good
21	Problem-Solving and Negotiation	2	0.797	Acceptable
22	Systems Thinking	3	0.862	Good

continued on following page

Table 5. Continued

	Domain	Number Of Questions	Cronbach's Alpha	Reliability Remarks
23	Engaging Culture and Environment	5	0.844	Good
24	Population Health Assessment and Promotion	3	0.834	Good
25	Networks and Alliances	3	0.880	Good
26	Advocacy	2	0.789	Acceptable
27	Public Relations and Marketing	3	0.816	Good
28	Regulations and Health Systems	3	0.731	Acceptable
29	Strategic Planning	7	0.891	Good
30	Sustainability Leadership	3	0.850	Good
31	Organizational Resilience	5	0.910	Excellent
32	Innovation and Entrepreneurship	3	0.865	Good
33	Change Management	3	0.918	Excellent
34	Ongoing Learning and Sharing	6	0.917	Excellent
	Total		0.984	Excellent

Between 34 domains of the respondents who took part in this survey; most of the participants are males with a percentage of (57.1%), and it revealed that there is no gender effect since they almost have the same percentage, (50.0%) of the subjects their age between(31 $\leq$ 40 years;76.7%) most of them are bachelor's degree holders and (33.6%) of the study sample,(45.0% are nurses followed by 37% doctors) and (and most of the subjects have more than 11 years' experience (50%) experience ranges from 10 20 years. The stability test of the study tool is used to ensure the degree of clarity, objectivity, accuracy, the possibility of obtaining a degree of relative stability in its answers, coherence, and interconnection between paragraphs and to verify this by calculating Cronbach's alpha(CA) coefficient, CA widely used reliability coefficient in social research to assess the internal consistency of the instrument's parts (Rezaei et al., 2021) and ranges from (zero to one) and value close to 1 indicates the scores are of high stability and good consistency and (Amirrudin, Nasution, & Supahar, 2021). where the Summary of reliability coefficient as follows Less than 0.60 (Poor), 0.7(Acceptable),0.8(Good), 0.90 and higher (Excellent). The researchers computed the reliability statistics(RS); the reliability statistics table 1 above presents a meticulous examination of the survey instrument's internal consistency and reliability of the measurement scales across various domains, as indicated by Cronbach's Alpha coefficients and for different domains within the assessed healthcare leadership context and provide a comprehensive overview of the survey's internal consistency, and dependability of the assessment tool, allowing for a robust evaluation of various dimensions within the healthcare setting while pointing to areas that could benefit from further methodological refinement. Cronbach alpha values are computed for all of the values above (0.7), which reveals that the scale is reliable (Sekkaran & Bougie, 2019; Vaske, Beaman, & Sponarski., 2017; Hair et al., 2009; Cronk & Bartram, 2018; DeVellis, 2016). The overall reliability of the entire assessment, with a Cronbach's Alpha of 0.984, is deemed excellent. Domains such as (General Parameters, Professional, Ethical, and Social Responsibility, and Commitment to Advancing People-Centered Services) demonstrate outstanding reliability, with alpha values of (0.973;0.947), and (0.919), respectively. These high coefficients underscore the robustness of the survey in capturing essential aspects of hospital leadership, providing confidence in the consistent measurement of these constructs. Notably, the survey excels in domains related to (Continuous Improvement (alpha = 0.913), Translation and Implementation (alpha = 0.923), and Governance (alpha = 0.926)), signifying strong internal coherence in evaluating hospitals' proficiency in these critical areas. However, it is crucial to acknowledge certain domains, such as Digital Technologies in Healthcare and Advocacy, which exhibit slightly lower alpha coefficients (0.751 and 0.789). These lower values suggest a potential need for refinement in the survey questions or the underlying constructs, aiming to enhance measurement reliability in these domains. To determine the Healthcare Leadership Effectiveness (The relative importance of Currant Senior Leadership parameters _in the Jordanian Hospital the following formula has been applied:

$$Period\ length = (Upper\ limit - Lower\ Limit/\ No\ of\ Level) =$$

(5- 1)/3=1.33.. (1)

The level of relative importance was determined based on the value of the arithmetic mean, standard deviation, agreement degree, and rank the weights, the answers to the paragraphs of the study tool, and its variables, according to three levels, as follows (Less than 2.33 (low) 2.34 - 3.66 (Medium)and 3.67- 5.00 (High)), computed the relative importance through each item data's mean and standard deviation using the Statistical Package for Social Science (SPSS) version 28., exclude irrelevant, missing data, and non-interacting responses, computed employing an equation that incorporates the quadrant scale for the individual item and calculates the average of the study sample's responses to each item where Leadership effectiveness represents the independent variable in the study, as this variable was measured through the mentioned (34)domains Table 5 above. The study results showed that healthcare Leadership has a significant Influence. There is a statistically significant effect at the significance level ($\alpha \geq 0.05$) for Healthcare Leadership effectiveness in the Jordanian Hospital in terms of its (34) dimensions (attributes), and this improves the Healthcare Quality in The Hospitals. For each attribute, analysis shows that the following sub-hypotheses are derived from this hypothesis: The study results showed a statistically significant effect at a significant level ($\alpha \geq 0.05$) of creative leadership in terms of its dimensions. Tables 6 to 41 below show the research results regarding The Hospital's healthcare leadership performance. The Hospital's relative importance of currant senior leadership domains (attributes) description and analysis represented in the arithmetic mean, standard deviation, rank with Detailed Domains Statistical Analysis and interpretation. The hospitals' healthcare leadership performance results narratives and divided into four quartiles according to survey mean results.

The first highest means quartile includes the dimensions of (Employee Support and Development, Organizational Resilience, Quality Improvement and Patient Safety, General Parameters (Systems Perspective), Professional, Ethical, and Social Responsibility, Preparedness and Crisis Management, Emotional Intelligence, and Self-Awareness) ranked in the first quartile of healthcare leadership). The second highest means quartile includes: (Translation and Implementation, Information Management Change Management, Problem-Solving, and Negotiation, Population Health Assessment and Promotion, Executive Communication, and Public Relations and Marketing Governance, in the second quartile of healthcare leadership). The third highest means quartile includes the: (dimensions of Visionary Leadership, Commitment to Advancing People-Centered Services, Ongoing Learning and Sharing, Innovation and Entrepreneurship, Systems Thinking Advocacy, Sustainability Leadership, and Compassionate Leadership in the third quartile of healthcare). The fourth highest means quartile includes the: (Networks and Alliances, Regulations and Health Systems Framework Digital Technologies in Healthcare, Administration and Business Development, Interpersonal Relationships, Continuous Improvement, Engaging Culture and Environment, Strategic Planning, Human Resource Management, and Monitoring and Evaluation Strategic Financial Management in the fourth quartile of healthcare), Analysis of variance, or ANOVA, is used to separate observed variance data into different components for additional tests. A one-way ANOVA was used for the groups of data (Gender, Age, Trade, Experience, and Years of experience, to gain information about the relationship between the dependent and independent variables and assess the significance of variations in study individuals' responses toward study axes across different age groups, all of them yields a non-significant p-value suggesting that the differences in responses among age groups in this domain are not statistically significant.

Also, the study **suggests a broad action plan, that** applies the most effective leadership attributes and diffusion techniques for scaling up the **right tools at the right time in the right plac**e within a health system, to help healthcare organizations and HCL **make a significant impact**. It contains a detailed **strategic framework,** takes the user through a **process that could be replicated** in the healthcare organization, has an initial series of "**next steps" in translating knowledge into a large-scale** change in the local health industry, Offered in goal setting approach (**Specific, Measurable, Achievable, Relevant, And Time-Bound (SMART**) methodology to enhance health care leadership detailed plan. The detailed Jordanian Hospital healthcare leadership Personal Action Plan was done by the following customized action plans (the Leadership Development Module used by (www.leadershipacademy.nhs.uk/leadership-development-module).

Detailed Domains Statistical Analysis

General Parameters (Systems Perspective)

Table 6 comprehensively evaluates general parameters within a systems perspective applied to a healthcare institution, presumably Public Hospitals. The mean scores indicate high perceived effectiveness and alignment with specified criteria. Notably, the Hospitals's possession of adequate assets to deliver services effectively receives a high mean score of 4.34 with a standard deviation of 0.928, underscoring a robust consensus among stakeholders on the sufficiency of resources. Similarly, the Hospitals's adeptness in addressing regional healthcare needs is reflected in a mean score of 4.24 with a standard deviation of 0.989, highlighting a strong agreement on the institution's capacity to cater to the specified healthcare demands of its region. Additionally, the Hospitals's commitment to customer-focused excellence models, as denoted by a mean score of 4.18 with a standard deviation of 1.022, further substantiates a positive evaluation of its strategic approach to enhancing service quality. Furthermore, the leadership's dedication to fostering a competitive position in Jordanian healthcare services is evidenced by a mean score of 4.17 with a standard deviation of 0.986, affirming a shared perception of the Hospitals's strategic positioning within the healthcare landscape. The overall mean of 4.06 with a standard deviation of 1.34 signifies a consistently high level of agreement across the evaluated parameters, emphasizing the institution's comprehensive excellence in health services. This nuanced analysis provides valuable insights into the multi-faceted dimensions of Hospitals management and leadership, shedding light on key strengths and areas of emphasis within the specified healthcare setting.

Table 6. General parameters (systems perspective)

Items	Mean	SD	Agreement Degree
Hospitals HAVE ENOUGH ASSETS enough resources to provide its services effectively and satisfactorily to customers	4.34	0.928	High
Hospitals approaches ADDRESS THE Hospitals AND HEALTH SERVICES need sat specified region	4.24	0.989	High
Hospitals apply the CUSTOMER-FOCUSED EXCELLENCE models.	4.18	1.022	High
Hospitals have a COMPETITIVE POSITION in healthcare services in Jordan	4.17	0.986	High
Hospitals' leaders ensure fair treatment for different CUSTOMERS, CUSTOMER groups, and market SEGMENTS.	4.00	1.037	High
Hospitals leaders INSPIRE AND MOTIVATE your team members LEADERS create an ENVIRONMENT FOR SUCCESS now and in the future.	4.00	0.989	High
Hospitals SENIOR LEADERS communicate with and engage the entire WORKFORCE, KEY PARTNERS, and KEY CUSTOMERS.effectivly	3.98	0.940	High
Hospitals capable of AGILITY AND RESILIENCE Health Services Results are excellent	3.94	0.965	High
Hospitals focus on success, INNOVATING, AND IMPROVING enough to promote higher-order health services.	3.94	1.027	High
Hospitals' leadership adheres to KEY STRATEGIC CHALLENGES and ADVANTAGES	3.93	1.071	High
Hospitals' SENIOR leader, set and deployed the Hospitals's VISION AND Articulates a vision for the future	3.93	1.021	High
Hospitals' leadership promotes patient safety and drives quality improvement initiatives.	3.92	1.043	High
Hospitals SENIOR LEADERS' actions demonstrate their commitment to legal and ETHICAL BEHAVIOR. And be role models of ETHICAL BEHAVIOR AND TRANSPARENCY	3.91	1.045	High
Hospitals leaders improve WORK PROCESSES and support PROCESSES to improve products and PROCESS PERFORMANCE, enhance your CORE COMPETENCIES, and reduce variability.	3.91	1.019	High
Hospitals leaders state the organization's KEY STRATEGIC OBJECTIVES and their most critical related GOALS.	3.87	1.036	High
Public Hospitals leaders in achieving excellent patient care and recognizing the importance of teamwork as part of the service experience?	3.87	1.086	High
Hospitals SENIOR LEADERS ensure responsible GOVERNANCE	3.87	1.067	High
Hospitals PROCESSES CONSISTENTLY EFFECTIVE and the results of health services in Public Hospitals are excellent.	3.86	0.985	High
Total	**4.06**	**1.34**	**High**

Visionary Leadership

Table 7 quantitatively assesses visionary leadership within healthcare delivery, emphasizing key dimensions such as transparency, ethical conduct, societal contributions, and workforce engagement. Notably, the mean scores reflect a high level of consensus on the upheld values and commitments. Transparency, respect, equity, and diversity in operations receive a mean score of 4.04 with a standard deviation of 1.013, indicating a strong agreement on adherence to these fundamental principles. Furthermore, the Hospitals's commitment to significant societal contributions, excellence, integrity, and altruism in healthcare delivery is underscored by a mean score of 4.00 with a standard deviation of 1.009, revealing a shared perception of the institution's dedication to societal well-being. Additionally, the mean score of 3.92 with a standard deviation of 1.41 for the overall assessment reinforces the robust consensus on visionary leadership within the healthcare setting. This nuanced analysis highlights the multifaceted dimensions of leadership excellence, providing insights into the institution's commitment to ethical, transparent, and socially responsible healthcare practices

Table 7. Visionary leadership

Items	Mean	SD	Agreement Degree
Transparency, respect, equity, and diversity are upheld in operations.	4.04	1.013	High
Hospitals make SIGNIFICANT SOCIETAL CONTRIBUTIONS aqnd demonstrates a commitment to excellence, integrity, and altruism in healthcare delivery.	4.00	1.009	High
Established ethical structures are effectively used to resolve ethical issues.	3.99	1.038	High
A balance between personal and professional accountability is maintained, focusing on patient and community needs.	3.98	1.057	High
The Hospitals commits to high ethical conduct and decision-making. in all interactions and strengthen	3.97	1.024	High
The Hospitals promotes quality and safety of care for patients.	3.95	1.029	High
Psychological safety is ensured for employees in the workplace.	3.82	1.101	High
Hospitals apply the VALUING PEOPLE POLICY.	3.79	1.065	High
The Hospitals upholds equity, social and environmental commitment in its service delivery.	3.73	1.169	High
A positive reinforcement culture engages, educates, supports, mentors, and energizes the workforce.	3.70	1.241	High
Total	**3.92**	**1.41**	**High**

Professional, Ethical, and Social Responsibility

Table 8 systematically evaluates the healthcare context's professional, ethical, and social responsibility dimensions, specifically focusing on leadership practices and institutional commitments. The mean scores signify a robust consensus on the effectiveness of the Hospitals's leaders in enabling customers to seek information and support (mean = 4.34, SD = 0.928), emphasizing a high degree of agreement on the leaders' facilitation of customer engagement. Furthermore, the commitment to patient-centred care, as reflected in the mean score of 4.20 with a standard deviation of 1.045, underscores the prioritization of patients in decision-making processes, aligning with ethical principles. The table also highlights the institution's dedication to continuous improvement based on current research and good practices (mean = 3.84, SD = 1.079) and the inclusion of diverse perspectives in decision-making (mean = 3.84, SD = 1.047), both indicative of a commitment to professional and ethical standards. The overall mean of 4.05 with a standard deviation of 1.29 underscores a pervasive high level of agreement, emphasizing the Hospitals's comprehensive commitment to professional, ethical, and socially responsible healthcare practices. This nuanced analysis provides valuable insights into the multifaceted dimensions of institutional responsibility and leadership in healthcare.

Table 8. Professional, ethical, and social responsibility

Items	Mean	SD	Agreement Degree
Hospitals' leaders enable CUSTOMERS to seek information and support.	4.34	0.928	High
Hospitals' leaders listen to, interact with, and observe CUSTOMERS to obtain actionable information and manage CUSTOMER complaints	4.24	0.989	High
Hospitals' leaders prioritize patient-centered care by putting patients at the center of decision-making processes.	4.20	1.045	High
The Hospitals commits to continuous improvement based on current research and good practices.	3.84	1.079	High
Perspectives of patients, families, and the community are included in decision-making, respecting cultural differences.	3.84	1.047	High
Patient care excellence is prioritized while recognizing workforce contribution.	3.74	1.032	High
Total	**4.05**	**1.29**	**High**

Quality Improvement and Patient Safety

Table 9 assesses quality improvement and patient safety aspects within the healthcare context, focusing on leadership qualities and institutional commitments. The mean scores suggest a high level of consensus on critical dimensions. The Hospitals demonstrates a noteworthy understanding of its role and implications, continuously leading and inspiring others, as reflected in the mean score of 4.18 with a standard deviation of 1.023. Additionally, Hospitals leaders' cultivation of a culture of empathy and compassion among healthcare professionals receives a mean score of 4.17 with a standard deviation of 0.986, indicating a robust agreement on the importance of these attributes in enhancing patient care and safety. The commitment to self-care, wellbeing, and self-resilience, with a mean score of 3.94 and a standard deviation of 0.965, underscores the institution's recognition of personal wellness's crucial role in maintaining high-quality healthcare practices. The overall mean of 4.11 with a standard deviation of 1.28 signifies a pervasive high level of agreement on the Hospitals's dedication to quality improvement and patient safety, emphasizing the significance of leadership qualities and institutional commitments in these critical healthcare domains.

Table 9. Quality improvement and patient safety

Items	**Mean**	**SD**	**Agreement Degree**
The Hospitals demonstrates an understanding of its role and related implications, continuously leading and inspiring others.	4.18	1.023	High
Hospitals leaders foster a culture of empathy and compassion among healthcare professionals	4.17	0.986	High
Public Hospitals shows commitment to self-care, wellbeing, and self-resilience, utilizing support structures when needed.	3.94	0.965	High
Hospitals' leaders demonstrate SELF-AWARENESS and manage their emotions effectively and. show EMPATHY AND UNDERSTANDING toward others	3.86	0.985	High
Total	**4.11**	**1.28**	**High**

Commitment to Advancing People-Centered Services

Table 10 evaluates the Hospitals's commitment to advancing people-centred services, emphasizing self-development, continuous improvement, and organizational learning. The mean scores reflect a high level of consensus on critical dimensions. The Hospitals's commitment to self-development, including lifelong learning, networking, and personal improvement, is underscored by a mean score of 3.94 with a standard deviation of 1.027, indicative of a robust agreement on the institution's dedication to fostering individual growth among its workforce. Moreover, the Hospitals identifies areas for improvement and its proactive efforts to address them, serving as a role model for others. This is evident in the mean score of 3.93, with a standard deviation of 1.021. The commitment to the health services organizational learning program, as reflected in the mean score of 3.87 with a standard deviation of 1.036, further emphasizes the institution's dedication to collective learning and improvement. The overall mean of 3.91 with a standard deviation of 1.34 signifies a pervasive high level of agreement, emphasizing the Hospitals's comprehensive commitment to advancing people-centred services through individual and organizational development. This nuanced analysis provides valuable insights into the multifaceted dimensions of the institution's commitment to continuous improvement and learning within the specified healthcare setting.

Table 10. Commitment to advancing people-centered services

Items	Mean	SD	Agreement Degree
The Hospitals demonstrates commitment to self-development, including lifelong learning, networking, and personal improvement.	3.94	1.027	High
The Hospitals identifies areas for improvement and works on them, serving as a role model for others.	3.93	1.021	High
Hospitals applying for the health services organizational LEARNING PROGRAM	3.87	1.036	High
Reflective leadership is evident in measuring strengths and weaknesses using self-assessment and feedback from others.	3.87	1.086	High
Total	**3.91**	**1.34**	**High**

Compassionate Leadership

Table 11 shows the assessment of compassionate leadership dimensions within the healthcare context, focusing on analytical thinking, agility, organizational systems knowledge, and effective decision-making. The mean scores suggest a high level of consensus on key leadership attributes. The Hospitals's demonstration of analytical thinking and agility in problem-solving, with a mean score of 3.93 and a standard deviation of 1.071, highlights a pervasive agreement on the institution's adeptness in addressing challenges with a thoughtful and adaptable approach. Additionally, the practical application of organizational systems theories and behaviours, as reflected in a mean score of 3.92 with a standard deviation of 1.043, underscores a shared perception of the Hospitals's proficiency in understanding and navigating complex organizational dynamics. Promoting solutions, effective delegation, and encouragement of decision-making, with a mean score of 3.91 and a standard deviation of 1.019, further signifies a consensus on the Hospitals's commitment to fostering leadership qualities that promote a compassionate and empowering work environment. The overall mean of 3.83 with a standard deviation of 1.40 emphasizes a pervasive high level of agreement, highlighting the Hospitals's comprehensive approach to compassionate leadership, incorporating analytical acumen, organizational understanding, and supportive decision-making. This nuanced analysis provides valuable insights into the multifaceted dimensions of leadership excellence within the specified healthcare setting.

Table 11. Compassionate leadership

Items	Mean	SD	Agreement Degree
The Hospitals demonstrates analytical thinking and agility when facing problems and takes appropriate action.	3.93	1.071	High
Public Hospitals effectively applies knowledge of organizational systems theories and behaviours.	3.92	1.043	High
The Hospitals promotes solutions, delegates effectively, and encourages decision-making.	3.91	1.019	High
Total	**3.83**	**1.40**	**High**

Emotional Intelligence and Self-Awareness

Table 12 systematically evaluates the dimensions of emotional intelligence and self-awareness within the healthcare context, focusing on resource management, fiscal responsibility, and strategic planning. The mean scores indicate a high level of consensus on critical attributes. The Hospitals's ability to balance short-term and long-term effects and outcomes in resource management, with a mean score of 4.00 and a standard deviation of 1.037, reflects a robust agreement on the institution's capacity to navigate the complexities of resource allocation with a forward-looking perspective. Moreover, the commitment of Hospitals leaders to ensure the availability of financial and other resources to support action plans is underscored by a mean score of 4.00 with a standard deviation of 0.989, indicative of a shared perception of effective leadership in resource mobilization. The overall mean of 4.03 with a standard deviation of 1.30 signifies a pervasive high level of agreement, emphasizing the Hospitals's comprehensive approach to emotional intelligence and self-awareness in resource management, strategic planning, and fiscal responsibility. This nuanced analysis provides valuable insights into the multifaceted dimensions of the institution's leadership acumen within the specified healthcare setting.

Table 12. Emotional intelligence and self-awareness

Items	Mean	SD	Agreement Degree
The Hospitals balances short-term and long-term effects and outcomes in resource management.	4.00	1.037	High
Hospitals' leaders ensure that financial and other resources are available to support achieving Hospitals ACTION PLANS.	4.00	0.989	High
The Hospitals can justify and solicit resources from funders or authorities.	3.99	0.941	High
Public Hospitals effectively uses key accounting principles and fiscal management tools. project Hospitals organization's future financial PERFORMANCE	3.91	1.045	High
The Hospitals guides the planning, execution, and monitoring of resources for optimal health outcomes and quality-cost controls.	3.87	1.067	High
Total	**4.03**	**1.30**	**High**

Executive Communication

Table 13 presents executive communication within the healthcare context, specifically focusing on key performance measures, leadership roles, workforce engagement, diversity, and strategic workforce management. The mean scores indicate a high level of consensus on various dimensions. Hospitals leaders' utilization of key performance measures to track the effectiveness of action plans, with a mean score of 4.04 and a standard deviation of 1.013, underscores a robust agreement on the importance of data-driven evaluation in leadership decision-making. Additionally, the clarity of defined leadership roles and responsibilities, considering equity, inclusion, and diversity, is reflected in a mean score of 4.00 with a standard deviation of 1.009, indicating a shared perception of effective and inclusive leadership structures. The overall mean of 3.96 with a standard deviation of 1.43 signifies a pervasive high level of agreement, emphasizing the Hospitals's comprehensive approach to executive communication, workforce engagement, and strategic leadership within the specified healthcare setting. This nuanced analysis provides valuable insights into the multifaceted dimensions of effective organizational communication and leadership excellence.

Table 13. Executive communication

Items	*Mean*	**SD**	**Agreement Degree**
Hospitals leaders use KEY PERFORMANCE MEASURES or INDICATORS to track the achievement and EFFECTIVENESS of Hospitals ACTION PLANS.	4.04	1.013	High
Leadership roles, responsibilities, and accountabilities are clearly defined, considering equity, inclusion, and diversity.	4.00	1.009	High
Hospitals Leaders Assess WORKFORCE ENGAGEMENT RESULTS support WORKFORCE PERFORMANCE management system support HIGH PERFORMANCE.	3.97	1.024	High
The Hospitals optimizes healthcare workforce performance, even in evolving contexts and critical issues.	3.95	1.029	High
Hospitals' leaders Ensure diversity in leadership positions, including representation from various backgrounds, cultures, and perspectives.	3.82	1.101	High
Effective strategies for workforce engagement, wellbeing, resilience, and retention are integrated and guided by the Hospitals.	3.73	1.169	High
Hospitals leaders assess Hospitals WORKFORCE CAPABILITY and CAPACITY needs. prepare Hospitals WORKFORCE for changing CAPABILITY and CAPACITY needs.	3.70	1.241	High
Total	**3.96**	**1.43**	**High**

Employee Support and Development

Table 14 assesses the dimensions of employee support and development within the healthcare context, focusing on data-driven decision-making, strategic planning, and compliance with privacy and security requirements. The mean scores indicate a high level of consensus on critical attributes. Hospitals leaders' selection of comparative data to support fact-based decision-making, with a mean score of 4.24 and a standard deviation of 0.987, underscores a robust agreement on the importance of informed decision-making supported by relevant data. Additionally, the commitment of Hospitals leaders to collecting and analyzing data for strategic planning processes, as reflected in a mean score of 4.20 with a standard deviation of 1.045, signifies a shared perception of effective leadership in utilizing data for informed strategic decision-making. The overall mean of 4.68 with a standard deviation of 1.38 signifies a pervasive high level of agreement, emphasizing the Hospitals's comprehensive approach to employee support and development, particularly in fostering data-driven decision-making and ensuring compliance with information privacy and security requirements within the specified healthcare setting. This nuanced analysis provides valuable insights into the multifaceted dimensions of effective leadership in employee support and development.

Table 14. Employee support and development

Items	Mean	SD	Agreement Degree
Hospitals' leaders select comparative data and information to support fact-based decision-making	4.24	0.987	High
Hospitals leaders collect and analyze relevant data and develop information for Hospitals strategic planning PROCESS. critically assesses, and analyses relevant data for data-driven decision-making	4.20	1.045	High
Hospitals leaders ensure the availability of organizational data and information and optimally and cost-effectively uses information and trend analysis.	3.84	1.046	High
Public Hospitals ensures compliance with privacy and security requirements for information.	3.84	1.079	High
Total	**4.68**	**1.38**	**High**

Human Resource Management

Table 15 shows human resource management within the healthcare context, focusing on learning and development, performance reviews, administrative decision-making, alignment with organizational values, and leadership skills. The mean scores indicate varying levels of consensus on different dimensions. Hospitals leaders' support for learning and development systems, with a mean score of 3.80 and a standard deviation of 1.030, suggests a high level of agreement on the importance of fostering personal and organizational growth. However, performance reviews for continuous improvement and innovation (mean = 3.74, SD = 1.072) and application of administrative matters based on facts (mean = 3.72, SD = 1.133) reflect a slightly lower, albeit still substantial, agreement. The overall mean of 3.66 with a standard deviation of 1.25 falls into the medium agreement category, indicating varying degrees of consensus across the evaluated dimensions of human resource management within Public Hospitals. This nuanced analysis provides insights into the multifaceted nature of human resource practices, highlighting areas of more substantial alignment and others with potential for further enhancement within the specified healthcare setting.

Table 15. Human resource management

Items	Mean	SD	Agreement Degree
Hospitals leaders support learning and development systems to support the personal development of members of your workforce and the needs of your organization	3.80	1.030	High
Hospitals' leaders use findings from PERFORMANCE reviews to develop priorities for continuous improvement and opportunities for INNOVATION.	3.74	1.072	High
Public Hospitals leaders apply administrative matters based on facts	3.72	1.133	High
The Hospitals demonstrates knowledge of essential business practices and evaluates alignment with organizational values and plans.	3.70	1.065	High
Public Hospitals leaders develop transformational leadership skills	3.65	1.019	Medium
Public Hospitals leaders provide opportunities for growth and development	3.60	1.055	Medium
Public Hospitals leaders have performance expectations for planning prospects in the short and long term	3.57	1.101	Medium
Total	**3.66**	**1.25**	**Medium**

Monitoring and Evaluation

Table 16 assesses monitoring and evaluation practices within the healthcare context, focusing on quality outcomes, patient satisfaction, safety programs, and leaders' adaptability to changes and technological advancements. The mean scores suggest varying levels of consensus on different dimensions. The Hospitals's guidance in the development, implementation, and tracking of quality outcomes, satisfaction, and safety programs (mean = 3.80, SD = 0.967) and leaders' adaptability to changes and new approaches for patients (mean = 3.79, SD = 1.143) indicate a high level of agreement, highlighting a commitment to quality improvement and responsiveness to evolving healthcare dynamics. However, the mean score of 3.64 with a standard deviation of 1.34 for the overall assessment falls into the medium agreement category, suggesting varied levels of consensus across the evaluated dimensions. Notably, the Hospitals's development and tracking of indicators using recognized frameworks (mean = 3.65, SD = 1.004) and leaders' determination of customer satisfaction, dissatisfaction, and engagement (mean = 3.39, SD = 1.283) exhibit lower levels of agreement. This nuanced analysis provides insights into the multifaceted nature of monitoring and evaluation practices within Public Hospitals, emphasizing areas of strength and potential for improvement within the specified healthcare setting.

Table 16. Monitoring and evaluation

Items	Mean	SD	Agreement Degree
The Hospitals guides the development, implementation, and tracking of quality outcomes, satisfaction, and safety programs.	3.80	0.967	High
Hospitals leaders ADAPT TO CHANGES and embrace new approaches for patients	3.79	1.143	High
Hospitals LEADERS stay abreast of EMERGING TECHNOLOGIES and innovative solutions that can improve patient care, operational efficiency, and overall outcomes	3.68	1.154	High
Public Hospitals develops and tracks indicators using recognized frameworks for quality outcomes, satisfaction, and safety.	3.65	1.004	Medium
Hospitals' leaders determine CUSTOMER satisfaction, dissatisfaction, and ENGAGEMENT	3.39	1.283	Medium
Total	**3.64**	**1.34**	**Medium**

Strategic Financial Management

Table 17 assesses strategic financial management within the healthcare context, focusing on leveraging data and analytics, producing relevant data sets, and informed decision-making by Hospitals leaders. The mean scores suggest a medium level of consensus on the evaluated dimensions. The encouragement of leaders to leverage data and analytics for informed decision-making (mean = 3.60, SD = 1.247) indicates a moderate level of agreement, emphasizing the importance of data-driven decision-making in strategic financial management. Similarly, the production of relevant data sets and monitoring systems to ensure standards in clinical, corporate, and administrative functions (mean = 3.43, SD = 1.201) and leaders' making informed decisions based on thorough analysis (mean = 3.33, SD = 1.286) exhibit comparable levels of agreement. The overall mean of 3.51 with a standard deviation of 1.55 falls into the medium agreement category, suggesting a moderate consensus on the effectiveness of strategic financial management practices within Public Hospitals. This nuanced analysis provides insights into the complex landscape of financial management in healthcare, highlighting areas with moderate agreement and potential for improvement within the specified setting.

Table 17. Strategic financial management

Items	Mean	SD	Agreement Degree
Encourage leaders to LEVERAGE DATA AND ANALYTICS to make informed decisions.	3.60	1.247	Medium
Relevant data sets are produced, and monitoring systems ensure standards are met in clinical, corporate, and administrative functions.	3.43	1.201	Medium
Hospitals leaders MAKE INFORMED DECISIONS based on thorough analysis	3.33	1.286	Medium
Total	**3.51**	**1.55**	**Medium**

Interpersonal Relationships

Table 18 systematically evaluates interpersonal relationships within the healthcare context, focusing on leadership practices related to patient safety, quality improvement initiatives, strategic objectives, and vision communication. The mean scores indicate a high level of consensus on key dimensions. The promotion of patient safety and driving quality improvement initiatives by Hospitals leadership, with a mean score of 4.34 and a standard deviation of 0.928, underscores a robust agreement on the pivotal role of leadership in ensuring patient welfare and continuous quality enhancement. Additionally, leadership's development and communication of a clear strategy for achieving the vision (mean = 4.24, SD = 0.987) and balancing strategic objectives to achieve an appropriate organizational balance (mean = 4.20, SD = 1.045) reflect strong agreement on effective leadership practices. The overall mean of 3.78 with a standard deviation of 1.12 signifies a pervasive high level of agreement, emphasizing the Hospitals's comprehensive approach to interpersonal relationships, leadership communication, and strategic alignment within the specified healthcare setting. This nuanced analysis provides valuable insights into the multifaceted

Table 18. Interpersonal relationships

Items	Mean	SD	Agreement Degree
Hospitals' leadership promotes patient safety and drives quality improvement initiatives.	4.34	0.928	High
Hospitals' leadership DEVELOP AND COMMUNICATE A CLEAR STRATEGY for achieving the vision.	4.24	0.987	High
Hospitals' leaders balance the STRATEGIC OBJECTIVES to achieve an appropriate balance among varying and potentially competing organizational needs	4.20	1.045	High
Hospitals' leadership DEVELOP AND COMMUNICATE A CLEAR STRATEGY for achieving the vision.	3.84	1.081	High

continued on following page

Table 18. Continued

Items	Mean	SD	Agreement Degree
Hospitals' leadership ALIGN GOALS AND OBJECTIVES with the OVERALL VISION.	3.84	1.046	High
Hospitals Leadership Articulates a vision for the future	3.79	1.064	High
Hospitals' leadership adheres to KEY STRATEGIC CHALLENGES and ADVANTAGES.	3.75	1.033	High
Total	**3.78**	**1.12**	**High**

Information Management

Table 19 shows information management within the healthcare context, focusing on the engagement of governing bodies, executive decision-making, succession planning, data tracking, and evaluation of leadership and governance performance. The mean scores indicate a high level of consensus on key dimensions. The engagement and commitment of key governing bodies to the organizational strategy and vision, with a mean score of 4.19 and a standard deviation of 1.022, underscore a robust agreement on the importance of strategic alignment at the leadership level. Similarly, the making and implementation of executive decisions according to governance structure, policies, and values (mean = 4.17, SD = 0.988) and succession planning for continuity of oversight in alignment with values and strategic direction (mean = 3.95, SD = 0.964) reflect strong consensus on effective information management practices. The overall mean of 4.00 with a standard deviation of 0.86 signifies a pervasive high level of agreement, emphasizing the Hospitals's comprehensive approach to information management, strategic governance, and performance evaluation within the specified healthcare setting. This nuanced analysis provides valuable insights into the multifaceted dimensions of effective information management and governance practices within Public Hospitals.

Table 19. Information management

Items	Mean	SD	Agreement Degree
Key governing bodies are engaged and committed to the organizational strategy and vision.	4.19	1.022	High
Executive decisions are made and implemented according to governance structure, policies, and values.	4.17	0.988	High
Succession planning is built for continuity of oversight in alignment with values and strategic direction.	3.95	0.964	High

continued on following page

Table 19. Continued

Items	Mean	SD	Agreement Degree
Hospitals leaders track data and information on daily operations and overall organizational PERFORMANCE.	3.94	1.027	High
Hospitals ADDRESS CURRENT AND ANTICIPATE FUTURE legal, regulatory, and community concerns with Hospitals HEALTH SERVICES and operations.	3.87	1.086	High
Hospitals evaluate the PERFORMANCE of SENIOR LEADERS and the GOVERNANCE board.	3.86	0.984	High
Total	**4.00**	**0.86**	**High**

Ongoing Learning and Sharing

Table 20 systematically evaluates the domain of Ongoing Learning and Sharing within the healthcare context, focusing on risk management, decision-making, diverse perspectives, and responsiveness to changing circumstances. The mean scores indicate a high level of consensus on key dimensions. Hospitals leaders' commitment to weighing risks and benefits before making decisions (mean = 3.93, SD = 1.070), understanding risk management principles and guiding relevant programs and strategies (mean = 3.93, SD = 1.023), and actively anticipating, managing, and mitigating significant risks during emergencies (mean = 3.93, SD = 1.042) all demonstrate strong agreement on the importance of risk-aware decision-making and crisis management. Furthermore, the consideration of diverse perspectives and seeking input from others (mean = 3.91, SD = 1.019), along with the ability to respond quickly to circumstances requiring a shift in action plans and rapid execution of new plans (mean = 3.90, SD = 1.050), highlights a shared recognition of the value of inclusivity and adaptability in leadership practices. Additionally, the Hospitals's planning for service continuity during potential health and other emergencies (mean = 3.87, SD = 1.036) further emphasizes a proactive approach to ensuring ongoing operations amidst challenging circumstances.

Table 20. Ongoing learning and sharing

Items	Mean	SD	Agreement Degree
Hospitals leaders WEIGH RISKS AND BENEFITS before making decisions.	3.93	1.070	High
Public Hospitals understands risk management principles and guides relevant programs and strategies.	3.93	1.023	High
The Hospitals actively anticipates, manages, and mitigates major risks during emergencies.	3.93	1.042	High

continued on following page

Table 20. Continued

Items	Mean	SD	Agreement Degree
Hospitals LEADERS CONSIDER DIVERSE PERSPECTIVES And seek input from others	3.91	1.019	High
Hospitals leaders respond quickly when circumstances require a shift in ACTION PLANS and rapid execution of new plans.	3.90	1.050	High
The Hospitals plans for service continuity during potential health and other emergencies.	3.87	1.036	High
Total	**3.91**	**0.92**	**High**

Continuous Improvement

Table 21 shows the domain of Continuous Improvement within the healthcare context, focusing on recognising the potential and limitations of health technologies and the cost-effective implementation of digital technologies aligned with organizational strategy. The mean scores indicate a high level of consensus among respondents, with scores of 3.79 and 3.76 for the respective items and an overall mean of 3.77, along with a standard deviation of 0.89, signifying a high degree of agreement. The Hospitals's acknowledgement of the potential and limitations of health technologies underscores a nuanced understanding of the evolving landscape of healthcare, with a mean score of 3.79. Additionally, the cost-effective implementation of digital technologies aligned with organizational strategy, with a mean score of 3.76, highlights a commitment to strategic and efficient utilization of technological resources. The low standard deviation affirms the uniformity of responses, indicating a robust consensus on the Hospitals's continuous improvement practices in the specified dimensions. This nuanced analysis provides valuable insights into the healthcare institution's approach to leveraging technology for ongoing enhancement within Public Hospitals.

Table 21. Continuous improvement

Items	Mean	SD	Agreement Degree
The Hospitals recognizes the potential and limitations of health technologies and digital outreach.	3.79	0.982	High
Digital technologies are implemented cost-effectively in alignment with the organizational strategy.	3.76	1.006	High
Total	**3.77**	**0.89**	**High**

Preparedness and Crisis Management

Table 22 presents the Preparedness and Crisis Management domain within the healthcare context, focusing on communication strategies and consistency in conveying organizational mission, vision, values, and priorities. The mean scores indicate a high level of consensus among respondents, with scores of 4.23, 4.11, and 3.81 for the respective items and an overall mean of 4.05. The low standard deviation of 0.84 further signifies a high degree of agreement. The Hospitals's commitment to customized messaging and communication methods tailored for different groups to optimize impact, as reflected in the mean score of 4.23, suggests a strategic and nuanced approach to crisis communication. Moreover, presenting information in a factual, credible, and understandable way to decision-makers, with a mean score of 4.11, highlights the importance of clarity and reliability in disseminating critical information during crises. While the articulation and consistent communication of the mission, vision, values, and priorities to stakeholders, with a mean score of 3.81, slightly deviate from the higher scores of the other items, it still falls within the high agreement category.

Table 22. Preparedness and crisis management

Items	Mean	SD	Agreement Degree
Messaging and means of communication are customized for separate groups to optimize impact.	4.23	0.967	High
Information is presented in a factual, credible, and understandable way to decision-makers.	4.11	0.991	High
The Hospitals articulates and communicates the mission, vision, values, and priorities consistently to stakeholders.	3.81	1.020	High
Total	**4.05**	**0.84**	**High**

Organizational Resilience

Table 23 presents the domain of Organizational Resilience within the healthcare context, focusing on leadership development through mentoring, coaching, and continuous development, as well as providing constructive feedback in a professional and respectful environment. The mean scores for both items, 4.33 and 4.17, respectively, and the overall mean of 4.25 indicate a high level of consensus among respondents. The low standard deviation of 0.81 further underscores a strong agreement among participants. Moreover, The Hospitals's commitment to developing others through mentoring, coaching, and continuous development, as reflected in the mean score of

4.33, signifies a proactive approach to leadership cultivation and constant improvement. Additionally, providing constructive feedback in a professional and respectful environment, with a mean score of 4.17, highlights a supportive and growth-oriented organizational culture.

Table 23. Organizational resilience

Items	Mean	SD	Agreement Degree
The Hospitals develops others through mentoring, coaching, and promoting continuous development.	4.33	0.859	High
Constructive feedback about performance is provided in a professional and respectful environment.	4.17	0.899	High
Total	**4.25**	**0.81**	**High**

Problem-Solving and Negotiation

Table 24 presents the domain of Problem-Solving and Negotiation within the healthcare context, focusing on leadership behaviours characterized by compassion and collaboration and the value and understanding of transparent, shared decision-making. The mean scores for both items, 3.99 and 3.98, respectively, and the overall mean of 3.99, indicate a high level of consensus among respondents. The low standard deviation of 0.91 further underscores a strong agreement among participants. Also, Adopting compassionate and collaborative leadership behaviours, as reflected in the mean score of 3.99, suggests a commitment to fostering a positive and cooperative work environment, which is crucial for effective problem-solving and negotiation. Additionally, the value placed on transparent, shared decision-making, with a mean score of 3.98, highlights the importance of open communication and inclusive decision processes within Public Hospitals

Table 24. Problem-solving and negotiation

Items	Mean	SD	Agreement Degree
Compassionate and collaborative leadership behaviours are adopted.	3.99	1.041	High
Transparent, shared decision-making is valued and understood.	3.98	0.942	High
Total	**3.99**	**0.91**	**High**

Systems Thinking

Table 25 shows the domain of Systems Thinking within the healthcare context, focusing on leadership behaviours related to transparent communication, listening skills, adaptation of communication style to different audiences, development and sustenance of positive workforce and stakeholder relationships, and ensuring clarity and understanding in Hospitals communication. The mean scores for all items range from 3.82 to 3.96, resulting in an overall mean of 3.90, indicating a high consensus level among respondents. The low standard deviation of 0.80 further emphasizes a strong agreement among participants. The Hospitals leaders' commitment to fostering an open and transparent communication culture (mean = 3.96) suggests a dedication to clarity and openness within the organizational communication framework. Demonstrating intense listening and communication skills, including non-verbal communication (mean = 3.93) and adapting communication style to different audiences (mean = 3.91), underscores the importance of effective communication tailored to diverse stakeholders.

The mean scores for developing and sustaining positive workforce and stakeholder relationships (mean = 3.89) and ensuring clarity and understanding in Hospitals communication (mean = 3.82) further highlight the Hospitals's commitment to fostering a supportive and communicative environment.

Table 25. Systems thinking

Items	Mean	SD	Agreement Degree
Hospitals Leaders Foster an open and transparent communication culture.	3.96	0.972	High
Strong listening and communication skills, including non-verbal communication, are demonstrated.	3.93	0.957	High
Hospitals leaders adapt Hospitals communication style to different audiences.	3.91	0.913	High
Positive workforce and stakeholder relationships are developed and sustained.	3.89	0.912	High
Hospitals leaders Ensure Clarity and understanding in Hospitals communication.	3.82	1.029	High
Total	**3.90**	**0.80**	**High**

Population Health Assessment and Promotion

Table 26 evaluates the domain of Population Health Assessment and Promotion within the healthcare context, focusing on collaborative discussion of conflicting perspectives and the demonstration of problem-solving skills, including conflict management through mediation and negotiation. The mean scores for both items,

4.03 and 3.95, respectively, result in an overall mean of 3.99, indicating a high level of consensus among respondents. The low standard deviation of 0.85 further underscores a strong agreement among participants. Also, the collaborative discussion of conflicting perspectives leading to mutually beneficial solutions (mean = 4.03) suggests a commitment to inclusive decision-making and resolution of differing viewpoints within Public Hospitals. Demonstrating problem-solving skills and managing conflicts through mediation and negotiation (mean = 3.95) highlights a proactive approach to addressing challenges and fostering positive outcomes.

Table 26. Population health assessment and promotion

Items	Mean	SD	Agreement Degree
Conflicting perspectives are discussed collaboratively, leading to mutually beneficial solutions.	4.03	0.930	High
Problem-solving skills are demonstrated, and conflicts are managed through mediation and negotiation.	3.95	0.928	High
Total	**3.99**	**0.85**	**High**

Networks and Alliances

Table 27 assesses the domain of Networks and Alliances within the healthcare context, focusing on Public Hospitals's systemic approach considering other sectors' priorities in the community, recognition of local implications of regional and global health events, and the balancing and connecting of inter-relationships among access, quality, safety, cost, and more. The mean scores for all items range from 3.81 to 3.91, resulting in an overall mean of 3.87, indicating a high level of consensus among respondents. The low standard deviation of 0.89 further emphasizes a strong agreement among participants. Moreover, the Hospitals's adoption of a systemic approach considering other sectors' priorities in the community (mean = 3.91) suggests a comprehensive and collaborative approach to healthcare that considers broader community needs. The recognition of local implications of regional and global health events (mean = 3.88) reflects a proactive stance in understanding and addressing the potential impact of external factors on the community served by the Hospitals. So, the mean score for balancing and connecting inter-relationships among access, quality, safety, cost, and more (mean = 3.81) highlights the Hospitals's commitment to achieving a harmonious and integrated healthcare system that considers multiple factors.

Table 27. Networks and alliances

Items	Mean	SD	Agreement Degree
Public Hospitals adopts a systemic approach considering other sectors' priorities in the community.	3.91	1.005	High
The Hospitals recognizes local implications of regional and global health events, understanding their impact on communities.	3.88	1.059	High
Public Hospitals balances and connects inter-relationships among access, quality, safety, cost, and more.	3.81	0.967	High
Total	**3.87**	**0.89**	**High**

Advocacy

Table 28 presented the domain of Advocacy within the healthcare context, focusing on leadership behaviours that encourage interdisciplinary collaboration, break down silos, create opportunities for staff collaboration, and foster a culture of collaboration and teamwork. The mean scores, ranging from 3.89 to 4.10, reflect a high level of consensus among respondents, with an overall mean of 3.98, indicating a strong agreement. Leadership's encouragement of interdisciplinary collaboration and the breakdown of silos scored exceptionally high at 4.10, suggesting a commitment to fostering a collaborative environment for addressing complex problems and delivering high-quality care. Facilitating an organizational culture built on mutual trust, inclusion, and transparency received a mean score of 4.02, emphasizing the Hospitals's dedication to creating a supportive and transparent work environment. The overall high agreement among respondents underscores the Hospitals's robust advocacy practices, particularly in promoting collaboration, creating a supportive culture, and maintaining awareness of community factors within Public Hospitals.

Table 28. Advocacy

Items	Mean	SD	Agreement Degree
Hospitals leaders encourage INTERDISCIPLINARY COLLABORATION, BREAK down silos, and create opportunities for staff to work together to solve complex problems and deliver high-quality care	4.10	0.933	High
The Hospitals facilitates development of an organizational culture built on mutual trust, inclusion, and transparency.	4.02	0.939	High
Hospitals leaders FOSTER A CULTURE of collaboration and teamwork.	3.98	1.017	High
The Hospitals maintains awareness of factors impacting the community and organization's services.	3.90	1.030	High

continued on following page

Table 28. Continued

Items	Mean	SD	Agreement Degree
Teamwork, multidisciplinary teams, and cross-boundary engagement are promoted at Public Hospitals.	3.89	0.961	High
Total	**3.98**	**0.77**	**High**

Engaging Culture and Environment

Table 29 evaluates the domain of Engaging Culture and Environment within the healthcare context, focusing on the Hospitals's utilization of vital statistics and health indicators to identify priorities, incorporation of an understanding of social and environmental determinants of health into strategies and decisions, and assessment of healthcare cost and accessibility to meet patient population needs. The mean scores for all items range from 3.73 to 3.75, resulting in an overall mean of 3.74, indicating a high level of consensus among respondents. The standard deviation of 0.99 emphasizes a strong agreement among participants. The Hospitals's use of vital statistics and health indicators (mean = 3.75) suggests a data-informed approach to prioritize areas for intervention and decision-making. Understanding social and environmental determinants of health (mean = 3.75) underscores a comprehensive strategy considering broader contextual factors. The assessment of healthcare cost and accessibility to meet patient population needs (mean = 3.73) further reflects the Hospitals's commitment to evaluating and addressing healthcare delivery's financial and logistical aspects. The table provides insights into the Hospitals's practices in engaging culture and environment, particularly in utilizing data, considering social determinants, and assessing healthcare cost and accessibility. The high agreement among respondents indicates a shared understanding of the significance of these practices within Public Hospitals.

Table 29. Engaging culture and environment

Items	Mean	SD	Agreement Degree
The Hospitals uses vital statistics and health indicators to identify priorities and guide decision-making.	3.75	1.062	High
Public Hospitals incorporates an understanding of social and environmental determinants of health into strategies and decisions.	3.75	1.164	High
Public Hospitals assesses healthcare cost and accessibility to meet patient population needs.	3.73	1.209	High
Total	**3.74**	**0.99**	**High**

Innovation and Entrepreneurship

Table 30 evaluates the domain of Innovation and Entrepreneurship within the healthcare context, focusing on the promotion of relevant partnerships and networks to advance efficient care delivery, the establishment of relationships for effective, coordinated, and integrated care with other providers, and the alignment of partnerships with corporate social responsibility and environmental sustainability practices. The mean scores for all items range from 3.88 to 3.94, resulting in an overall mean of 3.91, indicating a high level of consensus among respondents. The low standard deviation of 0.93 emphasizes a strong agreement among participants. Promoting relevant partnerships and networks (mean = 3.94) suggests a strategic approach to advancing efficient care delivery through collaborative efforts. Establishing relationships for effective, coordinated, and integrated care (mean = 3.91) reflects the Hospitals's commitment to building connections with other providers for seamless healthcare delivery. Furthermore, aligning partnerships with corporate social responsibility and environmental sustainability practices (mean = 3.88) underscores the Hospitals's emphasis on responsible and sustainable healthcare practices. In summary, the table provides insights into the Hospitals's robust practices in innovation and entrepreneurship, particularly in fostering partnerships, collaboration, and aligning efforts with social and environmental responsibility. The high agreement among respondents indicates a shared understanding of the significance of these practices within Public Hospitals.

Table 30. Innovation and entrepreneurship

Items	Mean	SD	Agreement Degree
Relevant partnerships and networks are promoted to advance efficient care delivery.	3.94	1.076	High
The Hospitals establishes relationships for effective, coordinated, and integrated care with other providers.	3.91	0.996	High
Partnerships align with corporate social responsibility and environmental sustainability practices.	3.88	1.037	High
Total	**3.91**	**0.93**	**High**

Change Management

Table 31 assesses the domain of Change Management within the healthcare context, focusing on advocating for patients' rights and their participation in designing health services and the Hospitals's advocacy for healthcare policy initiatives aligned with priorities and quality of care. Both items received a mean score of 4.00, resulting in an overall mean of 4.00, indicating a high level of consensus among respondents. The low standard deviation of 0.91 emphasizes a strong agreement among participants. The high mean scores suggest that Public Hospitals is effectively advocating for patients' rights and actively involving them in the design of health services. Furthermore, the Hospitals demonstrates a commitment to supporting healthcare policy initiatives that align with priorities and uphold the quality of care. The table provides insights into the Hospitals's effective change management practices, particularly in prioritizing patient rights, engaging them in healthcare service design, and advocating for policies aligned with quality care. The high agreement among respondents indicates a shared understanding of the importance of these practices within Public Hospitals.

Table 31. Change management

Items	Mean	SD	Agreement Degree
Patients' rights are advocated for, and their participation in designing health services is assured.	4.00	1.006	High
Public Hospitals advocates for healthcare policy initiatives aligned with priorities and quality of care.	4.00	0.987	High
Total	**4.00**	**0.91**	**High**

Strategic Planning

Table 32 shows the domain of Strategic Planning within the healthcare context, specifically focusing on applying marketing and social marketing principles for community outreach and health literacy, as well as the Hospitals's proficiency in media, public relations, and effective communication. The mean scores for the items range from 3.67 to 3.82, resulting in an overall mean of 3.73, indicating a high level of consensus among respondents. The low standard deviation of 0.81 emphasizes a strong agreement among participants. Applying marketing and social marketing principles (mean = 3.82) suggests a strategic approach to community outreach and health literacy initiatives, demonstrating the Hospitals's commitment to effective communication. The proficiency in media, public relations, and effective communication (mean = 3.67) underscores the Hospitals's capability to manage its public image and maintain effective communication channels. The table provides insights into the Hospitals's strategic planning practices, particularly in utilizing marketing principles for community outreach and emphasizing proficiency in media and public relations. The high agreement among respondents indicates a shared understanding of the importance of these practices within Public Hospitals.

Table 32. Strategic planning

Items	Mean	SD	Agreement Degree
Marketing and social marketing principles are applied for appropriate community outreach and health literacy.	3.82	0.857	High
c	3.72	0.895	High
The Hospitals demonstrates proficiency in media, public relations, and effective communication.	3.67	1.081	High
Total	**3.73**	**0.81**	**High**

Regulations and Health Systems

Table 33 provided evaluates the domain of Regulations and Health Systems within the healthcare context, focusing on the Hospitals's assurance of compliance with applicable laws and regulations in the healthcare sector, interpretation of public policy, legislative, and advocacy processes into strategic objectives, and understanding of the local and national healthcare system structure, funding mechanisms, and integrated care delivery networks. The mean scores for the items range from 3.74 to 3.94, resulting in an overall mean of 3.84, indicating a high level of consensus among respondents. The low standard deviation of 0.71 emphasizes a strong agreement among participants. The Hospitals's assurance of compliance with laws and regulations (mean = 3.94) suggests a commitment to legal and regulatory adherence in healthcare practices. The interpretation of public policy into strategic objectives (mean = 3.84) underscores the Hospitals's alignment with broader healthcare policy initiatives. Furthermore, understanding the local and national healthcare system structure (mean = 3.74) reflects the Hospitals's proficiency in navigating the complexities of healthcare networks. The table provides insights into Public Hospitals's strong adherence to regulations, strategic alignment with policy initiatives, and understanding of healthcare system structures. The high agreement among respondents indicates a shared understanding of the significance of these practices within the Hospitals.

Table 33. Regulations and health systems

Items	Mean	SD	Agreement Degree
The Hospitals ensures compliance with applicable laws and regulations in the healthcare sector.	3.94	0.857	High
Public policy, legislative, and advocacy processes are interpreted into the Hospitals's strategic objectives.	3.84	0.846	High
Public Hospitals understands the local and national healthcare system structure, funding mechanisms, and integrated care delivery networks.	3.74	0.940	High
Total	**3.84**	**0.71**	**High**

Public Relations and Marketing

Table 34 evaluates the domain of Public Relations and Marketing within the healthcare context, focusing on leadership decisions regarding key processes to be accomplished by the Hospitals workforce and external partners, the Hospitals's leadership in developing key planning processes for strategic and clinical service plans, monitoring and alignment of operating-unit strategic objectives with the Hospitals's mission and strategy, understanding and organization of patient pathways and service design for effective delivery, and the conduct of Hospitals strategic planning stating the organization's key strategic objectives and their most critical related goals. All items received mean scores ranging from 3.91 to 3.99, resulting in an overall mean of 3.95, indicating a high level of consensus among respondents. The low standard deviation of 0.73 emphasizes a strong agreement among participants. The leadership decisions on key processes (mean = 3.99) highlight effective decision-making in resource allocation and collaboration with external partners. The Hospitals's leadership in key planning processes (mean = 3.96) underscores its proactive strategic and clinical service planning approach. Additionally, the understanding and organization of patient pathways (mean = 3.93) demonstrate a focus on optimizing healthcare delivery. So, the table provides insights into Public Hospitals's strong public relations and marketing practices, emphasizing effective decision-making, strategic planning, and organizational alignment. The high agreement among respondents indicates a shared understanding of the importance of these practices within the Hospitals.

Table 34. Public relations and marketing

Items	Mean	SD	Agreement Degree
Hospitals' leaders decide which key processes will be accomplished by Hospitals workforce and external suppliers, partners, and collaborators.	3.99	0.903	High
Public Hospitals leads the development of key planning processes for strategic and clinical service plans.	3.96	0.853	High
Operating-unit strategic objectives are monitored and aligned with the Hospitals's mission and strategy.	3.95	0.869	High
Patient pathways and service design are understood and organized for effective delivery.	3.93	0.890	High
Hospitals leaders conduct Hospitals strategic planning state the organization's key strategic objectives and their most critical related goals	3.91	0.860	High
Total	**3.95**	**0.73**	**High**

Sustainability Leadership

Table 35 assesses the domain of Sustainability Leadership within the healthcare context, focusing on aspects such as short- and long-term master plans of action, the development and implementation of climate impact measures and quality standards as part of the Hospitals's strategy, understanding sustainability as a multi-dimensional concept in decision-making, balancing strategic objectives to address diverse and competing organizational needs, and the identification and oversight of priorities and actions related to climate impact reduction and sustainability. The mean scores for the items range from 3.79 to 3.98, resulting in an overall mean of 3.89, indicating a high level of consensus among respondents. The low standard deviation of 0.77 emphasizes a strong agreement among participants. The Hospitals leaders' possession of short- and long-term master plans (mean = 3.98) suggests a proactive approach to sustainability planning. The development and implementation of climate impact measures (mean = 3.97) highlight the Hospitals's commitment to environmental responsibility as part of its overall strategy. Furthermore, understanding sustainability as a multi-dimensional concept (mean = 3.86) indicates a comprehensive approach to decision-making. In summary, the table provides insights into Public Hospitals's strong practices in sustainability leadership, emphasizing strategic planning, environmental responsibility, and a holistic understanding of sustainability. The high agreement among respondents indicates a shared understanding of the importance of these practices within the Hospitals.

Table 35. Sustainability leadership

Items	Mean	SD	Agreement Degree
Public Hospitals leaders have short- and long-term master plans of action.	3.98	0.877	High
Climate impact measures and quality standards are developed and implemented as part of the Hospitals's strategy.	3.97	0.965	High
The Hospitals understands sustainability as a multi-dimensional concept in decision-making.	3.86	0.886	High
Public Hospitals leaders balance strategic objectives to strike the appropriate balance between diverse and competing organizational needs	3.84	1.067	High
Priorities and actions related to climate impact reduction and sustainability are identified and overseen.	3.79	1.038	High
Total	**3.89**	**0.77**	**High**

Digital Technologies in Healthcare

Table 36 presents the domain of Digital Technologies in Healthcare, focusing on Hospitals leaders' adaptation to changes and embracing new approaches, understanding resilience and enhancing strategies for sustainability, demonstrating resilience in difficult situations, and effectively managing the interdependency and logistics of supply chain services, including procurement and waste management. The mean scores for the items range from 3.69 to 3.97, resulting in an overall mean of 3.83, indicating a high level of consensus among respondents. The standard deviation of 0.96 suggests a relatively strong agreement among participants. The Hospitals leaders' adaptation to changes and embracing new approaches (mean = 3.97) reflects a proactive stance towards integrating digital technologies in healthcare. Understanding resilience and enhancing strategies for sustainability (mean = 3.95) underscores the Hospitals's commitment to long-term technological resilience. The effective management of supply chain services (mean = 3.73) indicates a focus on logistics and procurement, which is crucial for successful digital technology implementation. The table provides insights into Public Hospitals's practices in embracing digital technologies in healthcare, emphasizing adaptability, resilience, and effective supply chain management. The high agreement among respondents indicates a shared understanding of the importance of these practices within the Hospitals.

Table 36. Digital technologies in healthcare

Items	Mean	SD	Agreement Degree
Hospitals leaders ADAPT TO CHANGES and embrace new approaches	3.97	1.024	High
Public Hospitals understands resilience and enhances strategies for sustainability.	3.95	1.029	High
Public Hospitals leaders show resilience in difficult situations	3.82	1.099	High
Interdependency and logistics of supply chain services are effectively managed, including procurement and waste management.	3.73	1.169	High
Hospitals LEADERS MAINTAIN COMPOSURE and positivity under pressure.	3.69	1.239	High
Total	**3.83**	**0.96**	**High**

Administration and Business Development

Table 37 shows the Administration and Business Development table assesses various aspects, including incorporating innovation in the strategy development process, encouraging diversity of perspectives to support innovation and improvement, and promoting innovative cultures and methods supporting experimentation and innovation. The mean scores for the items range from 3.69 to 3.98, resulting in an overall mean of 3.83, indicating a high level of consensus among respondents. The standard deviation of 1.00 suggests a moderate level of agreement among participants. The Hospitals leaders' incorporation of innovation in the strategy development process (mean = 3.98) reflects a proactive approach to integrating innovative practices into the Hospitals's overall business strategy. The encouragement of diversity of perspectives (mean = 3.82) signifies a commitment to fostering a workplace culture that values and incorporates diverse viewpoints to drive innovation. Promoting innovative cultures and methods (mean = 3.69) indicates a proactive stance in creating an environment that supports experimentation and innovation. The table provides insights into the Hospitals's administration and business development practices, emphasizing a commitment to innovation and a culture that encourages diverse perspectives and experimentation. The high agreement among respondents indicates a shared understanding of the importance of these practices within the Hospitals.

Table 37. Administration and business development

Items	Mean	SD	Agreement Degree
Hospitals leaders incorporate INNOVATION in strategy development PROCESS.	3.98	1.026	High
Diversity of perspectives is encouraged to support innovation and improvement.	3.82	1.099	High
Innovative cultures and methods are promoted, supporting experimentation and innovation.	3.69	1.239	High
Total	**3.83**	**1.00**	**High**

Translation and Implementation

Table 38 shows the Translation and Implementation table evaluates aspects of change processes, leadership's ability to minimize resistance to change, and the Hospitals's performance measurement system's responsiveness to rapid or unexpected changes. The mean scores for the items range from 3.98 to 4.04, resulting in an overall mean of 4.01, indicating a high level of consensus among respondents. The standard deviation of 0.96 suggests a moderate level of agreement among participants. The championing and optimizing change processes (mean = 4.04) signify a commitment to driving and sustaining impactful changes within the Hospitals. Leadership's ability to minimize resistance to change (mean = 3.99) reflects a proactive approach to ensuring successful implementation by addressing potential challenges associated with organizational change. The assurance that the Hospitals's performance measurement system can respond to rapid or unexpected changes (mean = 3.98) underscores the Hospitals's commitment to adaptability and the timely availability of relevant data. Overall, the table provides insights into the Hospitals's capabilities in translating and implementing changes effectively, with a high agreement among respondents regarding the importance of these practices within the organization.

Table 38. Translation and implementation

Items	Mean	SD	Agreement Degree
Change processes are championed and optimized for sustained impact.	4.04	1.013	High
Hospitals leaders can minimize resistance to change and ensure successful implementation.	3.99	1.038	High
Hospitals' leaders ensure that the Hospitals PERFORMANCE measurement system can respond to rapid or unexpected organizational or external changes and provide timely data.	3.98	1.057	High
Total	**4.01**	**0.96**	**High**

Governance

Table 39 shows Governance assesses the Hospitals's commitment to leadership development, ongoing education, organizational learning programs, and knowledge-sharing practices. The mean scores for the items range from 3.88 to 4.00, resulting in an overall mean of 3.93, indicating a high level of consensus among respondents. The low standard deviation of 0.25 suggests a strong agreement among participants. Providing comprehensive training programs and mentorship opportunities for healthcare professionals (mean = 4.00) reflects the Hospitals's commitment to nurturing leadership skills. The emphasis on ongoing education and professional development (mean = 3.95) underscores the recognition of the importance of staying updated with healthcare advancements and industry best practices. The Hospitals's active participation in organizational learning programs (mean = 3.94) highlights its dedication to continuous improvement and knowledge enhancement. Contributing to healthcare management and leadership advancement through knowledge-sharing (mean = 3.92) signifies a commitment to the broader healthcare community. Overall, the table indicates a robust governance framework that prioritizes leadership development, education, and organizational learning, with a high level of agreement among respondents on the significance of these initiatives.

Table 39. Governance

Items	Mean	SD	Agreement Degree
Hospitals Leaders Provide comprehensive training programs, workshops, and mentorship opportunities to develop the leadership skills of healthcare professionals.	4.00	0.502	High
Hospitals leaders should PRIORITIZE ONGOING EDUCATION and professional development to stay updated with healthcare advancements, leadership techniques, and industry best practices.	3.95	0.539	High
Hospitals applying for the health services organizational LEARNING PROGRAM	3.94	0.571	High
Public Hospitals contributes to advancing healthcare management and leadership through sharing evidence, knowledge, and experience.	3.92	0.483	High
Information-seeking from various sources is promoted to support organizational performance.	3.91	0.536	High
Organizational introspection and lessons learned are valued for continuous improvement.	3.88	0.524	High
Total	**3.93**	**0.25**	**High**

ANALYSIS OF VARIANCE (ANOVA)

Age Variables

Firstly, one-way analysis of variance (ANOVA) to determine the significance of the differences in the answers of study individuals towards the study axes according to age

Table 40. ANOVA for age

domain	Contrast Source	Sum of Squares	df	Mean Square	F	Sig.
D1	Between Groups	4.5	2.0	2.3	1.27	0.283
	Within Groups	569.8	319.0	1.8		
	Total	574.3	321.0			
D2	Between Groups	0.9	2.0	0.4	0.22	0.799
	Within Groups	639.5	319.0	2.0		
	Total	640.4	321.0			
D3	Between Groups	0.0	2.0	0.0	0.01	0.991
	Within Groups	536.9	319.0	1.7		
	Total	536.9	321.0			

continued on following page

Table 40. Continued

domain	Contrast Source	Sum of Squares	df	Mean Square	F	Sig.
D4	Between Groups	1.4	2.0	0.7	0.41	0.662
	Within Groups	525.9	319.0	1.6		
	Total	527.2	321.0			
D5	Between Groups	0.2	2.0	0.1	0.05	0.950
	Within Groups	576.9	319.0	1.8		
	Total	577.1	321.0			
D6	Between Groups	1.8	2.0	0.9	0.46	0.634
	Within Groups	626.7	318.0	2.0		
	Total	628.5	320.0			
D7	Between Groups	0.2	2.0	0.1	0.06	0.942
	Within Groups	543.8	319.0	1.7		
	Total	544.0	321.0			
D8	Between Groups	0.8	2.0	0.4	0.20	0.817
	Within Groups	654.9	319.0	2.1		
	Total	655.7	321.0			
D9	Between Groups	5.6	2.0	2.8	1.46	0.233
	Within Groups	607.8	319.0	1.9		
	Total	613.4	321.0			
D10	Between Groups	4.5	2.0	2.3	1.45	0.236
	Within Groups	499.9	319.0	1.6		
	Total	504.4	321.0			
D11	Between Groups	3.8	2.0	1.9	1.08	0.342
	Within Groups	569.0	319.0	1.8		
	Total	572.8	321.0			
D12	Between Groups	7.7	2.0	3.9	1.61	0.201
	Within Groups	765.3	319.0	2.4		
	Total	773.0	321.0			
D13	Between Groups	0.6	2.0	0.3	0.23	0.797
	Within Groups	399.6	319.0	1.3		
	Total	400.2	321.0			
D14	Between Groups	0.1	2.0	0.1	0.10	0.907
	Within Groups	239.7	319.0	0.8		
	Total	239.8	321.0			

continued on following page

Table 40. Continued

domain	Contrast Source	Sum of Squares	df	Mean Square	F	Sig.
D15	Between Groups	0.3	2.0	0.1	0.15	0.857
	Within Groups	272.0	319.0	0.9		
	Total	272.2	321.0			
D16	Between Groups	3.5	2.0	1.7	2.20	0.113
	Within Groups	250.5	319.0	0.8		
	Total	253.9	321.0			
D17	Between Groups	0.2	2.0	0.1	0.14	0.866
	Within Groups	228.6	319.0	0.7		
	Total	228.8	321.0			
D18	Between Groups	0.6	2.0	0.3	0.46	0.634
	Within Groups	208.0	319.0	0.7		
	Total	208.6	321.0			
D19	Between Groups	2.1	2.0	1.1	1.27	0.282
	Within Groups	266.6	319.0	0.8		
	Total	268.7	321.0			
D20	Between Groups	0.8	2.0	0.4	0.61	0.544
	Within Groups	204.4	319.0	0.6		
	Total	205.2	321.0			
D21	Between Groups	1.5	2.0	0.7	1.01	0.364
	Within Groups	228.8	319.0	0.7		
	Total	230.2	321.0			
D22	Between Groups	1.3	2.0	0.6	0.81	0.447
	Within Groups	255.8	319.0	0.8		
	Total	257.1	321.0			
D23	Between Groups	0.8	2.0	0.4	0.66	0.515
	Within Groups	187.8	319.0	0.6		
	Total	188.6	321.0			
D24	Between Groups	1.8	2.0	0.9	0.91	0.404
	Within Groups	314.8	319.0	1.0		
	Total	316.6	321.0			
D25	Between Groups	0.2	2.0	0.1	0.13	0.879
	Within Groups	278.2	319.0	0.9		
	Total	278.4	321.0			

continued on following page

Table 40. Continued

domain	Contrast Source	Sum of Squares	df	Mean Square	F	Sig.
D26	Between Groups	4.0	2.0	2.0	2.49	0.085
	Within Groups	259.5	319.0	0.8		
	Total	263.5	321.0			
D27	Between Groups	0.6	2.0	0.3	0.44	0.645
	Within Groups	211.0	319.0	0.7		
	Total	211.6	321.0			
D28	Between Groups	0.1	2.0	0.1	0.13	0.882
	Within Groups	162.1	319.0	0.5		
	Total	162.3	321.0			
D29	Between Groups	0.8	2.0	0.4	0.78	0.461
	Within Groups	170.3	319.0	0.5		
	Total	171.1	321.0			
D30	Between Groups	2.2	2.0	1.1	1.87	0.156
	Within Groups	186.6	319.0	0.6		
	Total	188.8	321.0			
D31	Between Groups	0.2	2.0	0.1	0.11	0.893
	Within Groups	293.1	319.0	0.9		
	Total	293.3	321.0			
D32	Between Groups	0.2	2.0	0.1	0.10	0.901
	Within Groups	319.4	319.0	1.0		
	Total	319.6	321.0			
D33	Between Groups	0.2	2.0	0.1	0.10	0.901
	Within Groups	295.9	319.0	0.9		
	Total	296.1	321.0			
D34	Between Groups	0.0	2.0	0.0	0.06	0.939
	Within Groups	19.9	319.0	0.1		
	Total	19.9	321.0			

The one-way analysis of variance (ANOVA) results, presented in the table above, assesses the significance of variations in study individuals' responses towards study axes across different age groups, represented by domains D1 to D34. The table provides insights into partitioning variance into between-groups and within-groups components for each part. For instance, in domain D1, the between-groups sum of squares (SS) is 4.5, distributed across 2 degrees of freedom (df), resulting in a mean square (MS) of 2.3. The F-statistic of 1.27, however, yields a non-significant p-value of 0.283, suggesting that the differences in responses among age groups in this domain are not statistically significant. Similar patterns of non-significance are observed in several other domains (e.g., D2, D3), where F-statistics and associated p-values exceed conventional thresholds for significance, underscoring the absence of substantial age-related variations in responses.

Conversely, some domains exhibit F-statistics with p-values below the conventional threshold, indicating potential significance. For instance, in domain D26, the F-statistic is 2.49 with a p-value of 0.085, suggesting a marginal significance level. Further examination of such domains may be warranted to explore the nature of differences in individuals' responses across age groups. Overall, this ANOVA analysis contributes to our understanding of the nuanced relationship between age and study axes responses, shedding light on non-significant and potentially significant patterns within the studied domains.

Experience Variables

Secondly: one-way analysis of variance (ANOVA) was used to determine the significance of the differences in study participants' responses towards the study domains according to experience.

Table 41. ANOVA for experience variables

domain	Contrast Source	Sum of Squares	df	Mean Square	F	Sig.
D1	Between Groups	10.9	3.0	3.6	2.04	0.108
	Within Groups	563.4	318.0	1.8		
	Total	574.3	321.0			
D2	Between Groups	8.1	3.0	2.7	1.36	0.255
	Within Groups	632.3	318.0	2.0		
	Total	640.4	321.0			
D3	Between Groups	3.1	3.0	1.0	0.61	0.609
	Within Groups	533.8	318.0	1.7		
	Total	536.9	321.0			
D4	Between Groups	4.5	3.0	1.5	0.92	0.432
	Within Groups	522.7	318.0	1.6		
	Total	527.2	321.0			
D5	Between Groups	4.1	3.0	1.4	0.75	0.523
	Within Groups	573.0	318.0	1.8		
	Total	577.1	321.0			

continued on following page

Table 41. Continued

domain	Contrast Source	Sum of Squares	df	Mean Square	F	Sig.
D6	Between Groups	5.7	3.0	1.9		
	Within Groups	622.8	317.0	2.0	0.96	0.410
	Total	628.5	320.0			
D7	Between Groups	5.6	3.0	1.9		
	Within Groups	538.4	318.0	1.7	1.11	0.346
	Total	544.0	321.0			
D8	Between Groups	20.4	3.0	6.8		
	Within Groups	635.3	318.0	2.0	3.40	0.018
	Total	655.7	321.0			
D9	Between Groups	6.0	3.0	2.0		
	Within Groups	607.4	318.0	1.9	1.04	0.374
	Total	613.4	321.0			
D10	Between Groups	9.9	3.0	3.3		
	Within Groups	494.5	318.0	1.6	2.13	0.096
	Total	504.4	321.0			
D11	Between Groups	10.1	3.0	3.4		
	Within Groups	562.7	318.0	1.8	1.91	0.128
	Total	572.8	321.0			
D12	Between Groups	6.1	3.0	2.0		
	Within Groups	766.9	318.0	2.4	0.84	0.473
	Total	773.0	321.0			
D13	Between Groups	0.3	3.0	0.1		
	Within Groups	399.9	318.0	1.3	0.07	0.974
	Total	400.2	321.0			
D14	Between Groups	3.7	3.0	1.2		
	Within Groups	236.2	318.0	0.7	1.65	0.177
	Total	239.8	321.0			
D15	Between Groups	3.8	3.0	1.3		
	Within Groups	268.4	318.0	0.8	1.51	0.212
	Total	272.2	321.0			
D16	Between Groups	3.5	3.0	1.2		
	Within Groups	250.5	318.0	0.8	1.47	0.223
	Total	253.9	321.0			

continued on following page

Table 41. Continued

domain	Contrast Source	Sum of Squares	df	Mean Square	F	Sig.
D17	Between Groups	2.2	3.0	0.7	1.01	0.391
	Within Groups	226.7	318.0	0.7		
	Total	228.8	321.0			
D18	Between Groups	0.5	3.0	0.2	0.23	0.873
	Within Groups	208.2	318.0	0.7		
	Total	208.6	321.0			
D19	Between Groups	6.1	3.0	2.0	2.45	0.063
	Within Groups	262.6	318.0	0.8		
	Total	268.7	321.0			
D20	Between Groups	0.9	3.0	0.3	0.49	0.690
	Within Groups	204.3	318.0	0.6		
	Total	205.2	321.0			
D21	Between Groups	2.2	3.0	0.7	1.01	0.390
	Within Groups	228.1	318.0	0.7		
	Total	230.2	321.0			
D22	Between Groups	0.9	3.0	0.3	0.39	0.764
	Within Groups	256.1	318.0	0.8		
	Total	257.1	321.0			
D23	Between Groups	1.4	3.0	0.5	0.80	0.493
	Within Groups	187.2	318.0	0.6		
	Total	188.6	321.0			
D24	Between Groups	1.2	3.0	0.4	0.39	0.758
	Within Groups	315.4	318.0	1.0		
	Total	316.6	321.0			
D25	Between Groups	1.0	3.0	0.3	0.38	0.769
	Within Groups	277.4	318.0	0.9		
	Total	278.4	321.0			
D26	Between Groups	2.0	3.0	0.7	0.79	0.498
	Within Groups	261.5	318.0	0.8		
	Total	263.5	321.0			
D27	Between Groups	7.0	3.0	2.3	3.65	0.013
	Within Groups	204.6	318.0	0.6		
	Total	211.6	321.0			

continued on following page

Table 41. Continued

domain	Contrast Source	Sum of Squares	df	Mean Square	F	Sig.
D28	Between Groups	3.9	3.0	1.3	2.60	0.053
	Within Groups	158.4	318.0	0.5		
	Total	162.3	321.0			
D29	Between Groups	4.9	3.0	1.6	3.09	0.027
	Within Groups	166.3	318.0	0.5		
	Total	171.1	321.0			
D30	Between Groups	2.8	3.0	0.9	1.58	0.193
	Within Groups	186.0	318.0	0.6		
	Total	188.8	321.0			
D31	Between Groups	5.6	3.0	1.9	2.06	0.106
	Within Groups	287.7	318.0	0.9		
	Total	293.3	321.0			
D32	Between Groups	7.7	3.0	2.6	2.61	0.051
	Within Groups	311.9	318.0	1.0		
	Total	319.6	321.0			
D33	Between Groups	8.1	3.0	2.7	2.97	0.032
	Within Groups	288.0	318.0	0.9		
	Total	296.1	321.0			
D34	Between Groups	0.0	3.0	0.0	0.02	0.997
	Within Groups	19.9	318.0	0.1		
	Total	19.9	321.0			

The presented table encapsulates the outcomes of a one-way analysis of variance (ANOVA) aimed at discerning the statistical significance of disparities in responses among study participants concerning study axes based on their experience level. Each row corresponds to a distinct domain (D1 to D34), representing different facets of the study. At the same time, columns elucidate essential components of the ANOVA, such as Between Groups and Within Groups, sum of squares, degrees of freedom, mean square, F-statistic, and associated significance levels (p-values). An examination of the F-statistic and corresponding p-values unveils noteworthy patterns. For instance, in domain D8, the Between Groups sum of squares is 20.4 with 3 degrees of freedom, yielding a substantial F-statistic of 3.40 and a significant p-value of 0.018, indicating a likely meaningful discrepancy in responses across experience levels. In contrast, domains like D3 and D18 exhibit non-significant p-values of 0.609 and 0.873, respectively, suggesting no discernible differences in responses among participants with varying experience levels in these domains.

Additionally, some domains elicit marginal significance, exemplified by D26 with a p-value of 0.085, emphasizing the need for nuanced exploration. The outcomes contribute nuanced insights into the interplay between participants' experience levels and their responses to the study domains, offering a comprehensive understanding of the potential impact of experience on the study variables.

Level of Education Variables

Thirdly, one-way analysis of variance (ANOVA) was used to determine whether there were significant differences in study participants' responses towards the study domains, depending on their educational level.

Table 42. ANOVA for experience variables

domain	Contrast Source	Sum of Squares	df	Mean Square	F	Sig.
D1	Between Groups	6.6	2.0	3.3	1.86	0.157
	Within Groups	567.7	319.0	1.8		
	Total	574.3	321.0			
D2	Between Groups	5.9	2.0	3.0	1.49	0.227
	Within Groups	634.5	319.0	2.0		
	Total	640.4	321.0			
D3	Between Groups	6.5	2.0	3.3	1.96	0.142
	Within Groups	530.4	319.0	1.7		
	Total	536.9	321.0			
D4	Between Groups	5.0	2.0	2.5	1.54	0.217
	Within Groups	522.2	319.0	1.6		
	Total	527.2	321.0			
D5	Between Groups	3.8	2.0	1.9	1.06	0.348
	Within Groups	573.2	319.0	1.8		
	Total	577.1	321.0			
D6	Between Groups	10.6	2.0	5.3	2.73	0.066
	Within Groups	617.8	318.0	1.9		
	Total	628.5	320.0			
D7	Between Groups	1.5	2.0	0.8	0.46	0.635
	Within Groups	542.4	319.0	1.7		
	Total	544.0	321.0			

continued on following page

Table 42. Continued

domain	Contrast Source	Sum of Squares	df	Mean Square	F	Sig.
D8	Between Groups	6.4	2.0	3.2	1.56	0.211
	Within Groups	649.3	319.0	2.0		
	Total	655.7	321.0			
D9	Between Groups	4.8	2.0	2.4	1.25	0.288
	Within Groups	608.6	319.0	1.9		
	Total	613.4	321.0			
D10	Between Groups	11.2	2.0	5.6	3.62	0.028
	Within Groups	493.2	319.0	1.5		
	Total	504.4	321.0			
D11	Between Groups	5.4	2.0	2.7	1.52	0.220
	Within Groups	567.4	319.0	1.8		
	Total	572.8	321.0			
D12	Between Groups	2.1	2.0	1.1	0.44	0.645
	Within Groups	770.9	319.0	2.4		
	Total	773.0	321.0			
D13	Between Groups	0.4	2.0	0.2	0.15	0.859
	Within Groups	399.8	319.0	1.3		
	Total	400.2	321.0			
D14	Between Groups	5.7	2.0	2.8	3.85	0.022
	Within Groups	234.2	319.0	0.7		
	Total	239.8	321.0			
D15	Between Groups	5.3	2.0	2.6	3.14	0.044
	Within Groups	267.0	319.0	0.8		
	Total	272.2	321.0			
D16	Between Groups	2.7	2.0	1.3	1.70	0.185
	Within Groups	251.3	319.0	0.8		
	Total	253.9	321.0			
D17	Between Groups	1.3	2.0	0.7	0.94	0.394
	Within Groups	227.5	319.0	0.7		
	Total	228.8	321.0			
D18	Between Groups	0.3	2.0	0.1	0.20	0.820
	Within Groups	208.4	319.0	0.7		
	Total	208.6	321.0			

continued on following page

Table 42. Continued

domain	Contrast Source	Sum of Squares	df	Mean Square	F	Sig.
D19	Between Groups	2.8	2.0	1.4	1.67	0.190
	Within Groups	265.9	319.0	0.8		
	Total	268.7	321.0			
D20	Between Groups	0.7	2.0	0.4	0.56	0.572
	Within Groups	204.5	319.0	0.6		
	Total	205.2	321.0			
D21	Between Groups	1.1	2.0	0.5	0.74	0.478
	Within Groups	229.2	319.0	0.7		
	Total	230.2	321.0			
D22	Between Groups	0.7	2.0	0.4	0.45	0.636
	Within Groups	256.3	319.0	0.8		
	Total	257.1	321.0			
D23	Between Groups	0.9	2.0	0.5	0.78	0.459
	Within Groups	187.7	319.0	0.6		
	Total	188.6	321.0			
D24	Between Groups	1.6	2.0	0.8	0.81	0.444
	Within Groups	315.0	319.0	1.0		
	Total	316.6	321.0			
D25	Between Groups	0.3	2.0	0.1	0.16	0.853
	Within Groups	278.2	319.0	0.9		
	Total	278.4	321.0			
D26	Between Groups	0.1	2.0	0.0	0.05	0.953
	Within Groups	263.4	319.0	0.8		
	Total	263.5	321.0			
D27	Between Groups	0.4	2.0	0.2	0.29	0.750
	Within Groups	211.2	319.0	0.7		
	Total	211.6	321.0			
D28	Between Groups	0.5	2.0	0.2	0.49	0.614
	Within Groups	161.8	319.0	0.5		
	Total	162.3	321.0			
D29	Between Groups	3.2	2.0	1.6	3.06	0.048
	Within Groups	167.9	319.0	0.5		
	Total	171.1	321.0			

continued on following page

Table 42. Continued

domain	Contrast Source	Sum of Squares	df	Mean Square	F	Sig.
D30	Between Groups	1.5	2.0	0.8	1.28	0.280
	Within Groups	187.3	319.0	0.6		
	Total	188.8	321.0			
D31	Between Groups	3.9	2.0	1.9	2.13	0.121
	Within Groups	289.4	319.0	0.9		
	Total	293.3	321.0			
D32	Between Groups	3.8	2.0	1.9	1.94	0.145
	Within Groups	315.8	319.0	1.0		
	Total	319.6	321.0			
D33	Between Groups	3.9	2.0	1.9	2.11	0.123
	Within Groups	292.2	319.0	0.9		
	Total	296.1	321.0			
D34	Between Groups	0.0	2.0	0.0	0.11	0.898
	Within Groups	19.9	319.0	0.1		
	Total	**19.9**	**321.0**			

The provided table encapsulates the outcomes of a one-way analysis of variance (ANOVA), assessing the statistical significance of differences in responses among study participants regarding study axes within distinct domains. Each row represents a specific domain (D1 to D34), and the table delineates critical ANOVA components, including Between Groups and Within Groups, the sum of squares, degrees of freedom, mean square, F-statistic, and corresponding significance levels (p-values). Notably, in domain D10, the Between Groups sum of squares is 11.2, associated with 2 degrees of freedom, yielding a substantial F-statistic of 3.62 and a significant p-value of 0.028, implying a likely meaningful variation in responses. Conversely, domains like D3 and D18 display non-significant p-values of 0.142 and 0.820, respectively, indicating no discernible differences in responses among participants in these domains. Furthermore, domains such as D14 and D29 exhibit marginal significance with p-values of 0.022 and 0.048, respectively, warranting further exploration to unravel nuanced patterns within these domains. This ANOVA analysis contributes valuable insights into the interplay between participants' responses to study axes across different domains, elucidating instances of both significant and non-significant variations.

Notably, the F-statistics and associated p-values across various domains provide a nuanced understanding of the impact of domain-specific factors on participants' responses. For instance, in domain D8, the Between Groups sum of squares is 6.4 with 2 degrees of freedom, resulting in an F-statistic of 1.56 and a p-value of 0.211, indicating a non-significant trend. Additionally, domain D30 displays a non-significant p-value of 0.280, implying that differences in responses across the experience levels represented by this domain are not statistically significant. The ANOVA outcomes thus offer a comprehensive examination of the potential response variations among study participants within the specified domains, providing researchers with valuable insights for further investigation and interpretation.

Trade Variables

Fourthly, one-way analysis of variance (ANOVA) was used to determine whether there were significant differences in the responses of study participants towards the study axes, depending on their trade.

Table 43. ANOVA for trade

domain	Contrast Source	Sum of Squares	df	Mean Square	F	Sig.
	Between Groups	0.7	3.0	0.2		
D1	Within Groups	573.6	318.0	1.8	0.13	0.941
	Total	574.3	321.0			
	Between Groups	1.5	3.0	0.5		
D2	Within Groups	638.9	318.0	2.0	0.25	0.858
	Total	640.4	321.0			
	Between Groups	2.7	3.0	0.9		
D3	Within Groups	534.1	318.0	1.7	0.55	0.652
	Total	536.9	321.0			
	Between Groups	2.0	3.0	0.7		
D4	Within Groups	525.2	318.0	1.7	0.41	0.749
	Total	527.2	321.0			
	Between Groups	3.1	3.0	1.0		
D5	Within Groups	574.0	318.0	1.8	0.57	0.634
	Total	577.1	321.0			
	Between Groups	5.8	3.0	1.9		
D6	Within Groups	622.7	317.0	2.0	0.98	0.404
	Total	628.5	320.0			

continued on following page

Table 43. Continued

domain	Contrast Source	Sum of Squares	df	Mean Square	F	Sig.
D7	Between Groups	3.8	3.0	1.3	0.75	0.524
	Within Groups	540.2	318.0	1.7		
	Total	544.0	321.0			
D8	Between Groups	2.4	3.0	0.8	0.39	0.761
	Within Groups	653.3	318.0	2.1		
	Total	655.7	321.0			
D9	Between Groups	4.1	3.0	1.4	0.72	0.541
	Within Groups	609.2	318.0	1.9		
	Total	613.4	321.0			
D10	Between Groups	10.4	3.0	3.5	2.24	0.084
	Within Groups	494.0	318.0	1.6		
	Total	504.4	321.0			
D11	Between Groups	12.8	3.0	4.3	2.43	0.065
	Within Groups	560.0	318.0	1.8		
	Total	572.8	321.0			
D12	Between Groups	10.2	3.0	3.4	1.42	0.236
	Within Groups	762.7	318.0	2.4		
	Total	773.0	321.0			
D13	Between Groups	0.4	3.0	0.1	0.10	0.961
	Within Groups	399.8	318.0	1.3		
	Total	400.2	321.0			
D14	Between Groups	0.4	3.0	0.1	0.17	0.918
	Within Groups	239.5	318.0	0.8		
	Total	239.8	321.0			
D15	Between Groups	1.4	3.0	0.5	0.53	0.659
	Within Groups	270.9	318.0	0.9		
	Total	272.2	321.0			
D16	Between Groups	1.2	3.0	0.4	0.52	0.670
	Within Groups	252.7	318.0	0.8		
	Total	253.9	321.0			
D17	Between Groups	3.0	3.0	1.0	1.41	0.239
	Within Groups	225.8	318.0	0.7		
	Total	228.8	321.0			

continued on following page

Table 43. Continued

domain	Contrast Source	Sum of Squares	df	Mean Square	F	Sig.
D18	Between Groups	3.4	3.0	1.1	1.75	0.156
	Within Groups	205.2	318.0	0.6		
	Total	208.6	321.0			
D19	Between Groups	0.3	3.0	0.1	0.10	0.960
	Within Groups	268.5	318.0	0.8		
	Total	268.7	321.0			
D20	Between Groups	1.5	3.0	0.5	0.78	0.503
	Within Groups	203.7	318.0	0.6		
	Total	205.2	321.0			
D21	Between Groups	3.3	3.0	1.1	1.55	0.201
	Within Groups	226.9	318.0	0.7		
	Total	230.2	321.0			
D22	Between Groups	4.7	3.0	1.6	1.97	0.118
	Within Groups	252.4	318.0	0.8		
	Total	257.1	321.0			
D23	Between Groups	0.9	3.0	0.3	0.51	0.677
	Within Groups	187.7	318.0	0.6		
	Total	188.6	321.0			
D24	Between Groups	1.0	3.0	0.3	0.34	0.797
	Within Groups	315.6	318.0	1.0		
	Total	316.6	321.0			
D25	Between Groups	5.3	3.0	1.8	2.06	0.105
	Within Groups	273.1	318.0	0.9		
	Total	278.4	321.0			
D26	Between Groups	3.4	3.0	1.1	1.40	0.242
	Within Groups	260.1	318.0	0.8		
	Total	263.5	321.0			
D27	Between Groups	0.6	3.0	0.2	0.30	0.823
	Within Groups	211.0	318.0	0.7		
	Total	211.6	321.0			
D28	Between Groups	1.3	3.0	0.4	0.87	0.458
	Within Groups	160.9	318.0	0.5		
	Total	162.3	321.0			

continued on following page

Table 43. Continued

domain	Contrast Source	Sum of Squares	df	Mean Square	F	Sig.
D29	Between Groups	2.2	3.0	0.7	1.35	0.257
	Within Groups	169.0	318.0	0.5		
	Total	171.1	321.0			
D30	Between Groups	1.6	3.0	0.5	0.90	0.440
	Within Groups	187.2	318.0	0.6		
	Total	188.8	321.0			
D31	Between Groups	1.4	3.0	0.5	0.51	0.672
	Within Groups	291.9	318.0	0.9		
	Total	293.3	321.0			
D32	Between Groups	2.5	3.0	0.8	0.82	0.482
	Within Groups	317.1	318.0	1.0		
	Total	319.6	321.0			
D33	Between Groups	0.4	3.0	0.1	0.14	0.937
	Within Groups	295.7	318.0	0.9		
	Total	296.1	321.0			
D34	Between Groups	0.6	3.0	0.2	3.09	0.027
	Within Groups	19.3	318.0	0.1		
Total		**19.9**	**321.0**			

The presented table outlines the results of a one-way analysis of variance (ANOVA), examining potential differences in responses across various domains (D1 to D34) concerning specified study axes. Each domain's statistical analysis is characterized by components such as Between Groups and Within Groups, sum of squares, degrees of freedom, mean square, F-statistic, and the associated significance level (Sig.). A notable finding is observed in domain D34, where the Between Groups sum of squares is 0.6, accompanied by 3 degrees of freedom, resulting in a substantial F-statistic of 3.09 and a significant p-value of 0.027. This implies a statistically significant difference in responses within this domain, warranting further investigation into the underlying factors contributing to this variation. Conversely, several domains, such as D1, D2, D3, and D19, exhibit non-significant p-values, suggesting no discernible differences in responses among participants in these domains. Moreover, domains like D10 and D11 display marginally significant p-values of 0.084 and 0.065, respectively, indicating potential trends that warrant additional scrutiny.

Notably, the F-statistics and associated p-values in the table provide insights into the variability of responses across different domains. For example, in domain D8, the F-statistic is 0.39 with a non-significant p-value of 0.761, indicating that the observed response variation is not statistically significant. Similarly, domain D33 exhibits a non-significant p-value of 0.937, suggesting that differences in responses within this domain are not statistically meaningful. Overall, the ANOVA outcomes furnish a comprehensive overview of the significance of domain-specific factors on participants' responses, allowing researchers to identify domains with substantial variations that may warrant further exploration and interpretation

REFERENCES

Brown, C. A., & Robinson, D. M. (2002). Skewness and kurtosis implied by option prices: A correction. *Journal of Financial Research, 25*(2), 279–282.

Devellis, R. F. (2016). *Scale Development: Theory and Applications* (4th ed.). SAGE Publications.

Gupta, V., & Singh, S. (2014). Psychological capital as a mediator of the relationship between leadership and creative performance behaviors: Empirical evidence from the Indian R&D sector. *International Journal of Human Resource Management, 25*(10), 1373–1394.

Briggs, A., Coleman, M., & Morrison, M. (n.d.). *Research Methods in Educational Leadership and Management 3rd Edition Supplementary resources*. Retrieved August 8, 2025, from https://us.sagepub.com/sites/default/files/upm-assets/47320_book_item_47320.pdf

Rutberg, S., & Bouikidis, C. D. (2018). Focusing on the Fundamentals: A Simplistic Differentiation Between Qualitative and Quantitative Research. *Nephrology Nursing Journal : Journal of the American Nephrology Nurses' Association, 45*(2), 209–212.

Sekaran, U., & Bougie, R. (2016). *Research Methods for Business: A Skill-building Approach* (7th ed.). John Wiley & Sons.

Joshi, A., Kale, S., Chandel, S., & Pal, D. K. (2015). *Likert scale: Explored and explained.* ResearchGate. https://www.researchgate.net/publication/276394797_Likert_Scale_Explored_and_Explained

Rezaei, B., Mousavi, E., Heshmati, B., & Asadi, S. (2021). Low back pain and its related risk factors in health care providers at hospitals: A systematic review. *Annals of Medicine and Surgery (2012), 70*, 102903. DOI: 10.1016/j.amsu.2021.102903

Amirrudin, M., Nasution, K., & Supahar, S. (2021). Effect of Variability on Cronbach Alpha Reliability in Research Practice. *Jurnal Matematika. Statistika Dan Komputasi, 17*(2), 223–230. DOI: 10.20956/jmsk.v17i2.11655

Pandey, P., & Pandey, M. M. (2021). *Research Methodology Tools and Techniques.* Bridge Center.

Cronk, R., & Bartram, J. (2018). Environmental conditions in health care facilities in low- and middle-income countries: Coverage and inequalities. *International Journal of Hygiene and Environmental Health, 221*(3), 409–422. DOI: 10.1016/j.ijheh.2018.01.004

Hair, J. F.Jr, Black, W. C., Babin, B. J., & Anderson, R. E. (2009). *Multivariate Data Analysis* (7th ed.). Prentice Hall.

Vaske, J. J., Beaman, J., & Sponarski, C. C. (2017). Rethinking internal consistency in Cronbach's alpha. *Leisure Sciences*, *39*(2), 163–173. DOI: 10.1080/01490400.2015.1127189

Chapter 14
Hospital Healthcare Leadership Assessment Personal Action Plan

ABSTRACT

This chapter focuses on the development of a comprehensive Hospital Healthcare Leadership Assessment Personal Action Plan. This chapter provides a structured approach for healthcare leaders to assess their leadership effectiveness, identify areas for improvement, and establish targeted goals for professional growth. Through self-reflection and feedback from peers, staff, and stakeholders, leaders can evaluate their leadership competencies across key domains, including communication, decision-making, team management, and patient-centered care. The chapter emphasizes the importance of continuous learning and the need for a personalized action plan that aligns with the individual's career aspirations and the hospital's strategic objectives. It also outlines methods for tracking progress, incorporating regular feedback, and adapting the plan to evolving challenges in the healthcare sector. Ultimately, this chapter serves as a guide for healthcare leaders to take actionable steps toward improving their leadership practices, fostering a culture of excellence.

INTRODUCTION

The book suggests an action plan that helps healthcare organizations and healthcare leadership (HCL) make a significant impact. It contains a detailed strategic framework for functional action planning, guiding users through a replicable process within healthcare organizations. The plan includes an initial series of "next steps" to translate knowledge into large-scale change within the local health industry. Additionally, it applies effective diffusion techniques to scale the right tools at the right

DOI: 10.4018/979-8-3373-2225-4.ch014

time and place within the health system. The framework also employs the SMART (Specific, Measurable, Achievable, Relevant, and Time-bound) methodology to set actionable goals tailored for the local health context, aiming to enhance healthcare delivery, (Damschroder et al., 2009; Kotter, 1996; Moore et al., 2015).

Key Strengths

Public Hospitals leadership in healthcare demonstrates a multitude of noteworthy attributes, including:

Dedication to Enhancing Patient-Centered Services, Continuous Commitment to Improvement, Rigorous Focus on Quality Enhancement and Patient Safety, Proficient Executive Communication Skills, Compassionate Leadership Style, Skillful Problem-solving and Negotiation Techniques, Adherence to Regulatory Standards and Health Systems Knowledge and Ongoing Commitment to Learning and Knowledge Sharing. These strengths collectively exemplify Public Hospitals' commendable leadership in the healthcare sector.

Key Development Needs

The primary essential development keys include enhancing the following through training, updating regulations, and better financial support:

Proficiency in Managing Change, Effective Information Management, Encouragement of Innovation and Entrepreneurship, Profound Emphasis on Professionalism, Efficient Administration and Business Development, Utilization of Digital Technologies in Healthcare, Application of Systems Thinking in Decision-making, and Effective Advocacy for Healthcare Initiatives.

Development Need

The most significant development needs are *(Reason for choosing):*

1. Proficiency in managing change: effective information management, encouragement of innovation, and entrepreneurship is crucial (Kotter, 1996; Armenakis & Harris, 2009).
2. Adaptability to Evolving Healthcare Landscape: The healthcare industry is constantly evolving due to advancements in technology, changes in regulations, and shifts in patient needs. Proficiency in managing change ensures that Public Hospitals can effectively navigate these shifts and continue to provide high-quality care (D'Aunno, Succi, & Alexander, 2000; Ferlie & Shortell, 2001).

3. Optimized Resource Allocation: Effective information management allows for the efficient use of resources. This includes patient data, staff schedules, and inventory. When information is organized and accessible, the Hospitals can make informed decisions about resource allocation, leading to better patient outcomes (Kaplan & Norton, 2004; McNabb, 2016).
4. Staying Competitive and Relevant: In a rapidly changing healthcare environment, innovation is essential for staying competitive. Encouraging innovation and entrepreneurship fosters a culture of creativity and problem-solving. This can lead to development of new treatments, processes, or technologies that can set Public Hospitals apart from others in the field (Christensen. Grossman, & Hwang, 2017; West & Anderson, 1996).
5. Improved Patient Care and Experience: Managing change effectively ensures that any improvements or updates in healthcare practices are seamlessly integrated. This can lead to better patient care and a more positive patient and family experience (Institute of Medicine, 2001; Berwick, 2003).
6. Enhanced Operational Efficiency: Proficiency in managing change and effective information management streamlines processes and workflows. This leads to improved operational efficiency, reducing bottlenecks and delays in patient care (Hammer & Champy, 1993; Womack & Jones, 2003).
7. Anticipation of Future Trends: By encouraging innovation and entrepreneurship, Public Hospitals can proactively identify and address emerging trends in healthcare. This positions them at the forefront of developments in the field, providing the best possible care for patients (Rogers, 2003; Greenhalgh et al., 2004).
8. Risk Mitigation: Effectively managing change includes anticipating and mitigating potential risks associated with new initiatives or processes. This helps to prevent costly errors or disruptions in patient care (Hillson, 2003; Reason, 2016).
9. Fostering a Culture of Continuous Improvement: These practices create an environment where continuous learning and improvement are valued. This benefits not only patient care but also the professional development and satisfaction of the Hospitals staff (Deming, 1986; Senge, 1990).
10. Financial Sustainability: Innovation and effective change management can lead to cost savings and revenue generation opportunities. This contributes to the financial sustainability of Public Hospitals, allowing them to invest in further improvements and expansion of services (Porter & Teisberg, 2006; Kaplan & Porter, 2011).

In summary, these three strengths work in synergy to ensure that Public Hospitals remain adaptable, efficient, and innovative in an ever-changing healthcare landscape, ultimately leading to improved patient care and sustained success in the industry.

Goal (Desired New Behavior in Specific, Measurable, Achievable, Relevant, and Time-Bound (SMART) Terms

Specific, measurable, achievable, relevant, and time-bound (SMART) goals allow leaders to focus on strategies to improve their leadership skills (Doran, 1981; Locke & Latham, 2002). Healthcare administrators can use the SMART method to set themselves up for success in the ever-changing industry (Moran & Brightman, 2000). By breaking down and defining goals into more manageable ones, administrators can make complex tasks easier to tackle (Bovend'Eerdt, Botell, & Wade, 2009). By setting SMART goals for leadership development, individuals and organizations can create a clear roadmap for achieving their desired outcomes and drive continuous improvement in their leadership practices (Rubin, 2002). Here are the proposed SMART goals for healthcare leadership at Public Hospitals. The right SMART goals have the power to help you reach new heights within Public Hospitals —and they can also do wonders when it comes to staff morale as everyone works together towards a common goal (Locke & Latham, 2002).

Develop a Leadership Skill Set

"I aim to develop a leadership skill set to motivate better, communicate, and engage with the staff. Within eight months, I will complete a training course to teach me the necessary skills to lead my team effectively."

Specific: The aim is explicit because it identifies what skills must be developed.
Measurable: This can be measured by completing the training course in 8 months.
Attainable: The statement is possible by enrolling in the specified training course.
Relevant: Developing a leadership skill set applies to communicating and engaging with the staff.
Time-based: Goal attainment is expected within eight months.

Be More Adaptable to Change

By developing the ability to adapt to change, leaders can inspire confidence and trust in their team members. As a goal example, you can complete a change management training course and apply what you have learned in the following six months. In this period, track instances where you swiftly adapted to unexpected changes.

Here is why this is a SMART goal:

Specific: Complete a change management course and apply what you learn during workdays.
Measurable: After completing the course, track instances where you successfully dealt with unexpected changes in the workplace.
Achievable: Achieve this goal by investing in a practical course that provides guidelines or resources to execute the content. The course should have a timeline of completion.
Relevant: Adaptability can help leaders stay agile and resilient in unexpected challenges.
Time-bound: Achieve this goal in six months while continuously seeking ways to increase adaptability in different settings.

Increase the Efficiency of Staff

"I will strive to ensure staff has the tools and resources to perform their jobs efficiently. I will use benchmarking, process improvement, and decision-making to increase staff efficiency by 20% in the next eight months."

Specific: You will assess and enhance the tools, resources, and processes available to staff.
Measurable: You will ideally track success by a 20% increase in staff efficiency.
Attainable: It is realistic to expect process improvement within eight months.
Relevant: Improving staff efficiency contributes directly to organizational success.
Time-based: You should anticipate reaching success in 8 months.

Improve Patient Satisfaction

"I want to increase our patient satisfaction scores by 10% within six months. I will survey patients' experiences and use the feedback to create an improvement plan. I will also meet with staff to discuss potential changes and ensure high quality of care."

Specific: The goal states what will be done and the time frame.
Measurable: You can measure patient satisfaction scores to track progress.

Attainable: This is achievable because it is realistic to increase patient satisfaction scores by 10% in 6 months.
Relevant: Improving patient satisfaction is essential for providing better care.
Time-based: There is a 6-month deadline for completing this goal.

Develop Training Programs

"I will create and implement training programs that help our existing staff to improve their skills by the end of 5 months. These programs will be based on our team members' feedback and include shadowing and seminars."

Specific: The goal outlines the type of training programs that will be created and a timeline for completion.
Measurable: Track the development of training programs by giving updates at team meetings and tracking feedback from staff.
Attainable: Given the right resources and planning, this is achievable within five months.
Relevant: The training programs will help existing staff improve their skills, making them suitable for organizational growth.
Time-based: Completion of this SMART goal is expected after five months.

Implement Safety Measures

"I will introduce a set of safety measures to help protect healthcare workers and patients in the Hospitals over the six months ahead. The measures will include protocols for PPE, hygiene, patient/staff interaction, and other relevant areas."

Specific: This goal is explicit because the person will introduce safety measures in all relevant areas.
Measurable: Ensure the safety measures are implemented correctly to minimize risk.
Attainable: The goal can be met if you take the time to assess the Hospitals's needs and create an effective plan.
Relevant: This is relevant for any healthcare administrator, as safety is paramount in the industry.
Time-based: Six months are required to achieve success.

Leverage Data Analytics

"As a healthcare administrator, I will leverage data analytics to improve patient outcomes and ensure efficiency in administrative processes within ten months. I need to be able to identify where improvements can be made and have the ability to make those changes quickly."

Specific: The goal states the objective and timeline for leveraging data analytics.
Measurable: Track the improvements in patient outcomes and administrative processes over time.
Attainable: By focusing on understanding and utilizing data, this goal is achievable within ten months.
Relevant: Data analytics can be used to gain insights into patient outcomes and administrative processes, making it an appropriate goal.
Time-based: The statement has an end date of 10 months.

Improve Communication Skills

Communication is one of the most important skills one can learn in the workplace to cultivate a culture of transparency. For example, you might complete a short communication course every six months. After six months, ask for feedback from team members and management, choosing new course topics based on their feedback.

Here is a breakdown of this SMART goal:

Specific: Complete a specific communication course based on feedback every month.
Measurable: The measurable part is completing a monthly course for six months.
Achievable: Schedule a date and time to complete each course.
Relevant: Effective communication can help leaders build strong team relationships and reduce misunderstandings.
Time-bound: The goal will end in six months.

Promote Knowledge-Sharing Systems

You must have systems for sharing knowledge and resources to ensure your team works effectively and efficiently. For instance, you can build a hub of standard operating procedures (SOPs) regarding your team's processes. After three months, note how often team members require direct assistance and adjust SOPs as needed.

We can see this goal's SMART criteria below:

Specific: Build a shareable hub of your team's SOPs.
Measurable: Once the hub is available, note how often team members require direct assistance and adjust SOPs as needed.
Achievable: This can be achieved by listing the processes and building a shareable SOP hub in a specific timeframe, such as one quarter.
Relevant: A leader can develop a more skilled team by supporting their professional growth and providing opportunities for skill-building.
Time-bound: Launch this project over the next three months, training everyone on the SOPs.

Learn to Give Constructive Feedback

Now that you feel more confident about receiving constructive criticism, you can learn to give constructive feedback to your team. To give an example, aim to provide constructive feedback respectfully. For the next quarter, track occasions where you provided high-quality, helpful feedback. Each month, ask for your team's feedback on your efforts and re-evaluate if necessary.

Here is how this example meets the SMART goal criteria:

Specific: Provide constructive feedback to your team members in a respective manner.
Measurable: Track occasions where you gave constructive feedback to team members, what you said, and how you felt. Ask for feedback on your efforts each month.
Achievable: Achieve this goal by taking time to prepare for each session.
Relevant: Giving constructive feedback can help team members identify areas for improvement and foster a culture of accountability and continuous learning and improvement.
Time-bound: Practice this skill for the next three months.

Foster Interdisciplinary Communication

"I want to introduce weekly interdisciplinary meetings by the end of three months. These meetings will be attended by members of management and other professionals involved in patient care to foster coordination between departments."

Specific: The individual wants to establish weekly interdisciplinary meetings involving all healthcare administrators.
Measurable: Success can be measured by the number of attendees at the meetings.

Attainable: It is feasible to establish the meetings within three months.
Relevant: This goal is relevant to fostering communication between departments and improving patient care.
Time-based: You have a concrete timeline of three months to be completed.

Build Internal Talent

A leader who aims to build internal talent can create a culture of learning and development within the company. For example, you can implement talent development workshops or mentorship programs every three months for one year and track how many team members participate.

Build internal talent with this SMART goal example:

Specific: Implement talent development workshops or mentorship programs for your team.
Measurable: Track how many team members participate in each of these sessions.
Achievable: Search for relevant workshops and make them accessible to your team.
Relevant: Developing internal talent helps retain top-performing staff while enhancing the company's talent pool.
Time-bound: Achieve this goal within the following year, looking for tools and opportunities for professional development.

Show Appreciation and Recognition

Showing appreciation and recognition involves acknowledging team members' hard work and accomplishments with positive feedback. To plan monthly events exclusively for your team. Aft to show appreciation for your team members for six months, ask for feedback, and readjust if needed.

Here is the SMART goal example broken down:

Specific: Plan fun events for your team to show your appreciation.
Measurable: The measurable part is having monthly events for six months and asking for feedback from your members about the experience.
Achievable: It is achievable by setting aside a company budget and scheduling a monthly fun event.
Relevant: Showing appreciation and recognition can empower team members and improve morale and motivation.
Time-bound: Complete this goal over six months.

Improve Financial Performance

"I want to identify ways to reduce operating costs while maximizing revenue for this year. I will analyze our healthcare administration's financial performance and look for improvement areas."

Specific: The goal is clear and focused on enhancing financial performance.
Measurable: By looking at the healthcare administration's finances, there are ways to measure progress.
Attainable: LoThis goal is feasible as the individual can access financial data for this
Relevant: The goal is appropriate for improving the administration's financial performance.
Time-based: Realize that success will be reached within this year.

Reduce Administrative Costs

"To cut administrative costs, I will reduce paperwork and manual processes by 20% by the end of 7 months. I aim to automate processes, introduce digital tools, and leverage technology to save time and money."

Specific: This goal includes what needs to be done (reduce paperwork and manual processes) and how much you need to reduce it (20%).
Measurable: You can measure the reduction of administrative costs with financial records.
Attainable: With proper planning and implementation, this SMART goal is feasible.
Relevant: Reducing administrative costs can have a positive financial impact and increase efficiency.
Time-based: Goal achievement will be expected after seven months.

Build Relationships within your Team

Building relationships with team members can create a supportive and engaging environment. For example, you can schedule monthly check-ins with each employee to touch base about projects and general career topics. After three months, ask for feedback about the check-ins and readjust the approach as necessary.

Here is a breakdown of this SMART goal example:

Specific: The goal is to meet with each team member in a monthly relaxed setting months to know them.
Measurable: The measurable part is having monthly check-ins for three months.
Achievable: It is achievable by setting aside 30 minutes a few times each month.
Relevant: Creating a positive work environment and boosting productivity requires building solid relationships with your team members.
Time-bound: The goal will end in three months.

Run Effective Meetings

Sometimes, a simple email suffices over a meeting, but meetings remain crucial to the workplace. One way to achieve this is to improve your meeting and presentation skills by using a meeting schedule for the next two months. Have team members provide feedback and iterate as needed.

Here is how this example meets the SMART goal criteria:

Specific: Improve your meeting and presentation skills.
Measurable: The measurable action is keeping meetings within your team's schedule and keeping track of everything that goes over or under the time estimate.
Achievable: Plan to keep team members informed and share the meeting schedule and agenda
Relevant. Conducting efficient meetings saves time and keeps everyone focused on their tasks, allowing you to communicate efficiently.
Time-bound: Work on this goal for two months.

Benefits Max Describe the Benefits of Reaching this Goal

Many benefits include increasing the trust in leadership since it is the single most significant contributor to employee satisfaction (which drives retention) and, ultimately, the success of an organization, besides increasing the Organizational Performance and effectiveness in meeting its goals.

Increase the efficiency of business functions, areas, and processes. Increase customer satisfaction and supplier relationships (Happier employees will lead to happier customers), improve brand image and recognition; brand image is a leading indicator of success regarding how people feel about the organization, helps motivate employees, and increases employer competence. Researchers have found that setting and meeting goals can help employees feel more connected to their organization. Not only does this contribute to increased optimism in the office, but it also encourages better employee performance. Ensures employees are working toward a shared vision where everyone is aligned and helps you understand when it may be necessary to give feedback to get workers back on track. Help keep everyone accountable and ensure that they are working and moving toward a specific outcome. Quantify success, where we can use goals that clearly define success and indicate how far you have come and how far you must go to achieve them. Moreover, it can help employees feel more fulfilled and valued. That could mean you will experience fewer hiring-related costs in the future.

RISKS INVOLVED IN REACHING THIS GOAL

Development Need

Risks Involved in Reaching this Goal

The state of the overall economy, government rules and regulations, lack of financial support, Human resources, credentialing, staffing, Medication management, emergency Preparedness, Patient Safety, and Environmental safety. While companies may not be able to avoid business risk altogether, they can take steps to mitigate its impact, including developing a strategic risk plan.

Potential Obstacles

Barriers and Obstacles that Keep Organizations from Reaching Their Goals

No buy-in from employees

Lack of a streamlined process & tool and heavily invested in the process improvement

Lack of focus and goals are not discussed frequently

Poor response to change

Poor planning and line of sight

Lack of measurement standards

Poor communication

Poor alignment of goals

Inconsistent policies

Lack of clear strategy, processes, infrastructure, human capability, and culture.

How are you Going to Overcome Them?

Simplify interventions; train "scale-up leaders" and health workers dedicated to scale-up; reach and engage communities; match the best delivery strategy to the specific health problem and context; and raise the low profile of implementation science, (Yamey, 2012).

Resources/Support

From the Ministry of Health and The Health Care Accreditation Council ("HCAC").

Where Available?

Ministry of Health, the health care accreditation council ("HCAC"), and academic institutions, like industrial engineering departments.

Table 1. Action plan - part two

Action Steps	Target Date
Professionals from the Ministry of Health, the health care accreditation council ("HCAC"), and academic institutions, like industrial engineering departments. Meetings to discuss the research and start an action plan.	To be assigned by HCAC and healthcare profisionals

Review

When will you review your progress towards your goals?
The review will be aperiodic every three months after agreeing on the goals.

REFERENCES

Armenakis, A. A., & Harris, S. G. (2009). Reflections: Our Journey in Organizational Change Research and Practice. *Journal of Change Management, 9*(2), 127–142. DOI: 10.1080/14697010902879079

Berwick, D. M. (2003). Disseminating Innovations in Health Care. *Journal of the American Medical Association, 289*(15), 1969. DOI: 10.1001/jama.289.15.1969 PMID: 12697800

Bovend'Eerdt, T. J., Botell, R. E., & Wade, D. T. (2009). Writing SMART Rehabilitation Goals and Achieving Goal Attainment scaling: a Practical Guide. *Clinical Rehabilitation, 23*(4), 352–361. *Sage Journals*. DOI: 10.1177/0269215508101741

Christensen, C. M., Grossman, J. H., & Hwang, J. (2017). *The innovator's prescription: a disruptive solution for health care*. Mcgraw-Hill Education.

D'aunno, T., Succi, M., & Alexander, J. A. (2000). The role of institutional and market forces in divergent organizational change. *Administrative Science Quarterly, 45*(4), 679–703.

Damschroder, L. J., Aron, D. C., Keith, R. E., Kirsh, S. R., Alexander, J. A., & Lowery, J. C. (2009). Fostering implementation of health services research findings into practice: A consolidated framework for advancing implementation science. *Implementation Science : IS, 4*(1), 50. DOI: 10.1186/1748-5908-4-50 PMID: 19664226

Deming, W. E. (1986). *Out of the crisis*. The Mit Press.

Doran, G. T. (1981). There's a S.M.A.R.T. way to write management's goals and objectives. *Management Review, 70*(11), 35–36. https://community.mis.temple.edu/mis0855002fall2015/files/2015/10/S.M.A.R.T-Way-Management-Review.pdf

Ferlie, E. B., & Shortell, S. M. (2001). Improving the Quality of Health Care in the United Kingdom and the United States: A Framework for Change. *The Milbank Quarterly, 79*(2), 281–315. https://www.commonwealthfund.org/publications/journal-article/2002/feb/improving-quality-health-care-united-kingdom-and-united#:~:text=In%20%22Improving%20the%20Quality%20of%20Health%20Care%20in,improving%20quality%20in%20each%20nation%27s%20health%20care%20system PMID: 11439467

Greenhalgh, T., Robert, G., Macfarlane, F., Bate, P., & Kyriakidou, O. (2004). Diffusion of Innovations in Service Organizations: Systematic Review and Recommendations. *The Milbank Quarterly, 82*(4), 581–629. DOI: 10.1111/j.0887-378x.2004.00325.x PMID: 15595944

Hammer, M., & Champy, J. (1993). *Reengineering the Corporation: A Manifesto for Business Revolution*. Collins Business Essentials.

Hillson, D. (2003). *Effective Opportunity Management for Projects*. CRC Press., DOI: 10.1201/9780203913246

Institute of Medicine. (2001). *Crossing the Quality Chasm: A New Health System for the 21st Century*. PubMed. https://pubmed.ncbi.nlm.nih.gov/25057539/

Kaplan, R. S., & Norton, D. P. (2004). *Strategy Maps: Converting Intangible Assets into Tangible Outcomes*. Harvard Business School Press.

Kaplan, R. S., & Porter, M. E. (2011). How to solve the cost crisis in health care. *Harvard Business Review*, *89*(9), 46–52, 54, 56–61 passim. https://pubmed.ncbi.nlm.nih.gov/21939127/ PMID: 21939127

Kotter, J. P. (1996). *Leading Change*. Harvard Business School Press.

Locke, E., & Latham, G. (2002). *Building a practically useful theory of goal setting and task motivation: A 35-year odyssey.* Psycnet.apa.org. https://psycnet.apa.org/record/2002-15790-003

Mcnabb, D. E. (2016). *Research methods for political science: quantitative and qualitative approaches*. Routledge, Taylor Et Francis Group.

Moore, G. F., Audrey, S., Barker, M., Bond, L., Bonell, C., Hardeman, W., Moore, L., O'Cathain, A., Tinati, T., Wight, D., & Baird, J. (2015). Process evaluation of complex interventions: Medical Research Council guidance. *BMJ (Clinical Research Ed.)*, *350*(350), h1258–h1258. DOI: 10.1136/bmj.h1258 PMID: 25791983

Moran, J. W., & Brightman, B. K. (2000). Leading organizational change. *Journal of Workplace Learning*, *12*(2), 66–74. DOI: 10.1108/13665620010316226

Porter, M. E., & Teisberg, E. O. (2006). *Redefining health care: creating value-based competition on results*. Harvard Business School Press.

Reason, J. T. (2016). *Managing the risks of organizational accidents*. Routledge Taylor & Francis Group.

Rogers, E. M. (2003). *Diffusion of Innovations* (5th ed.). Free Press., https://books.google.jo/books?id=9U1K5LjUOwEC&printsec=frontcover&redir_esc=y#v=onepage&q&f=false

Rubin, R. S. (2002). Will the real SMART goals please stand up? *The Industrial-Organizational Psychologist*, *39*(4), 26–27. https://www.researchgate.net/publication/255601388_Will_the_real_SMART_goals_please_stand_up

Senge, P. M. (1990). *The Fifth Discipline: the Art and Practice of the Learning Organization*. Doubleday.

West, M. A., & Anderson, N. R. (1996). Innovation in Top Management Teams. *The Journal of Applied Psychology*, *81*(6), 680–693. DOI: 10.1037/0021-9010.81.6.680

Appendix

QUESTIONNAIRE

Health Care Leadership Competency Framework Self-Assessment tool

Part I: Demographic Data (information about groups of people according to specific attributes such as age, sex, and place of residence)

Personal Information

1. Gender:
   - Male
   - Female
2. Age:
   - 25 ≤ 30 years
   - 31 ≤ 40 years
   - 41 ≤ 50 years
   - More than 51 years
3. Years of Experience:
   - less than 5 years
   - 5 ≤ 10 years
   - 11 ≤ 20years
   - More than 20 years
4. Academic Qualification
   - Diploma
   - Bachelor's
   - Postgraduate
5. **Trade**
   - Medical professions Doctors
   - Medical professions Nurses

- Technical Affairs
- Administrative Affairs

Part II:

Table 1. Evaluation of Domain Statements (Attributes) Survey

#	Evaluation Domain Statements (Attributes;Assessment of Currant Senior Healthcare Leadership)	Strongly Disagree (1)	Disagree (2)	Neutral (3)	Agree (4)	Strongly Agree (5)
General Parameters (Systems Perspective)						
1	The Jordanian Hospitals approaches ADDRESS THE HOSPITALS AND HEALTH SERVICES need a specified region.					
2	The Jordanian Hospitals has enough resources to provide its services effectively and satisfactorily to customers.					
3	The Jordanian Hospitals have a COMPETITIVE POSITION in healthcare services in Jordan.					
4	The Jordanian Hospitals applies the CUSTOMER-FOCUSED EXCELLENCE models.					
5	The Jordanian Hospitals is capable of AGILITY AND RESILIENCE Health Services. The results are excellent.					
6	The Jordanian Hospital processes are consistently effective, and the health services results in Hospitals are excellent.					
7	The Jordanian Hospitals focus on success, INNOVATING, AND IMPROVING enough to promote higher-order health services.					
8	Hospital leaders in achieving excellent patient care and recognizing the importance of teamwork as part of the service experience.					
9	The Jordanian Hospital's senior leader set and deployed the hospital's VISION AND Articulated a vision for the future.					
10	The Jordanian Hospital leaders state the organization's KEY STRATEGIC OBJECTIVES and their most critical related GOALS.					
11	The Jordanian Hospitals' leadership promotes patient safety and drives quality improvement initiatives.					
12	The Jordanian Hospitals' leadership adheres to KEY STRATEGIC CHALLENGES and ADVANTAGES.					
13	The Jordanian Hospitals leaders improve WORK PROCESSES and support PROCESSES to improve products and PROCESS PERFORMANCE, enhance your CORE COMPETENCIES, and reduce variability.					
14	The Jordanian Hospital's SENIOR LEADERS' actions demonstrate their commitment to legal and ETHICAL BEHAVIOR. Moreover, they are role models of ethical behavior and transformation.					
15	The Jordanian Hospitals SENIOR LEADERS ensure responsible GOVERNANCE					
16	The Jordanian Hospitals' leaders ensure fair treatment for different CUSTOMERS, CUSTOMER groups, and market SEGMENTS.					

continued on following page

Table 1. Continued

#	Evaluation Domain Statements (Attributes;Assessment of Currant Senior Healthcare Leadership)	Strongly Disagree (1)	Disagree (2)	Neutral (3)	Agree (4)	Strongly Agree (5)
17	The Jordanian Hospital senior LEADERS effectively communicate with and engage the entire WORKFORCE, KEY PARTNERS, and KEY.					
18	The Jordanian Hospitals leaders, INSPIRE AND MOTIVATE your team members. LEADERS create an ENVIRONMENT FOR SUCCESS now and in the future.					
Professional, Ethical, and Social Responsibility						
1	The Jordanian Hospitals makes SIGNIFICANT SOCIETAL CONTRIBUTIONS and demonstrates a commitment to excellence, integrity, and altruism in healthcare delivery.					
2	The hospital promotes quality and safety of care for patients.					
3	The hospital upholds equity, social, and environmental commitment in its service delivery.					
4	Psychological safety is ensured for employees in the workplace.					
5	A positive reinforcement culture engages, educates, supports, mentors, and energizes the workforce.					
6	The hospital commits to high ethical conduct and decision-making. In all interactions and strengthen.					
7	Transparency, respect, equity, and diversity are upheld in operations.					
8	Established ethical structures are effectively used to resolve ethical issues.					
9	A balance between personal and professional accountability is maintained, focusing on patient and community needs.					
10	The Jordanian Hospitals apply the VALUING PEOPLE POLICY.					
Commitment to Advancing People-Centred Services						
1	Patient care excellence is prioritized while recognizing workforce contribution.					
2	Perspectives of patients, families, and the community are included in decision making, respecting cultural differences.					
3	The hospital commits to continuous improvement based on current research and good practices.					
4	The Jordanian Hospitals' leaders prioritize patient-centered care by putting patients at the center of decision-making processes.					
5	The Jordanian Hospitals' leaders listen to, interact with, and observe CUSTOMERS to obtain actionable information and manage CUSTOMER complaints.					
6	The Jordanian Hospitals' leaders enable CUSTOMERS to seek information and support.					
Emotional Intelligence and Self-Awareness						
1	The Jordanian Hospital leaders foster a culture of empathy and compassion among healthcare professionals.					
2	The hospital demonstrates an understanding of its role and related implications, continuously leading and inspiring others.					
3	Hospital shows commitment to self-care, well-being, and self-resilience, utilizing support structures when needed.					

continued on following page

Table 1. Continued

#	Evaluation Domain Statements (Attributes;Assessment of Currant Senior Healthcare Leadership)	Strongly Disagree (1)	Disagree (2)	Neutral (3)	Agree (4)	Strongly Agree (5)
4	The Jordanian Hospitals' leaders demonstrate SELF-AWARENESS and manage their emotions effectively. Show EMPATHY AND UNDERSTANDING toward others					
Continuous improvement						
1	The hospital is committed to self-development, including lifelong learning, networking, and personal improvement.					
2	Reflective leadership is evident in measuring strengths and weaknesses using self-assessment and feedback from others.					
3	The hospital identifies areas for improvement and works on them, serving as a role model for others.					
4	The Jordanian Hospitals applying for the health services organizational LEARNING PROGRAM					
Translation and Implementation						
1	Hospital effectively applies knowledge of organizational systems theories and behaviors.					
2	The hospital demonstrates analytical thinking and agility when facing problems and takes appropriate action.					
3	The hospital promotes solutions, delegates effectively, and encourages decision-making.					
Strategic financial management						
1	Hospital effectively uses vital accounting principles and fiscal management tools. Project hospital organization's future financial PERFORMANCE					
2	The hospital guides the planning, execution, and monitoring of resources for optimal health outcomes and quality-cost controls.					
3	The hospital balances short-term and long-term effects and outcomes in resource management.					
4	The hospital can justify and solicit resources from funders or authorities.					
5	The Jordanian Hospitals' leaders ensure that financial and other resources are available to support achieving hospital ACTION PLANS.					
Human resource management						
1	Leadership roles, responsibilities, and accountabilities are clearly defined, considering equity, inclusion, and diversity.					
2	The hospital optimizes healthcare workforce performance, even in evolving contexts and critical issues.					
3	The hospital integrates and guides practical strategies for workforce engagement, well-being, resilience, and retention.					
4	The Jordanian Hospitals' leaders Ensure diversity in leadership positions, including representation from various backgrounds, cultures, and perspectives.					
5	The Jordanian Hospital leaders assess hospital WORKFORCE CAPABILITY and CAPACITY needs. Prepare hospital WORKFORCE for changing CAPABILITY and CAPACITY needs.					

continued on following page

Table 1. Continued

#	Evaluation Domain Statements (Attributes;Assessment of Currant Senior Healthcare Leadership)	Strongly Disagree (1)	Disagree (2)	Neutral (3)	Agree (4)	Strongly Agree (5)
6	The Jordanian Hospitals Leaders Assess WORKFORCE ENGAGEMENT RESULTS support WORKFORCE PERFORMANCE management system support HIGH PERFORMANCE.					
7	The Jordanian Hospital leaders use KEY PERFORMANCE MEASURES or INDICATORS to track the achievement and EFFECTIVENESS of hospital ACTION PLANS.					
Information management						
1	The Jordanian Hospital's leaders ensure the availability of organizational data and information and optimally and cost-effectively use information and trend analysis.					
2	Hospital ensures compliance with privacy and security requirements for information.					
3	The Jordanian Hospital leaders COLLECT AND ANALYZE relevant data and develop information for hospital strategic planning PROCESS. Critically assesses and analyses relevant data for data-driven decision-making.					
4	The Jordanian Hospitals' leaders select comparative data and information to support fact-based decision-making.					
Administration and Business Development						
1	The hospital demonstrates knowledge of essential business practices and evaluates Alignment with organizational values and plans.					
2	The Jordanian Hospitals' leaders use findings from PERFORMANCE reviews to develop priorities for continuous improvement and opportunities for INNOVATION.					
3	The Jordanian Hospital leaders support learning and development systems to support the personal development of members of your workforce and the needs of your organization.					
4	Hospital leaders provide opportunities for growth and development.					
5	Hospital leaders develop transformational leadership skills.					
6	Hospital leaders have performance expectations for planning prospects in the short and long term.					
7	Hospital leaders apply administrative matters based on facts.					
Quality Improvement and Patient Safety						
1	The hospital guides the development, implementation, and tracking of quality outcomes, satisfaction, and safety programs.					
2	Hospital develops and tracks indicators using recognized frameworks for quality outcomes, satisfaction, and safety.					
3	The Jordanian Hospital's LEADERS stay abreast of EMERGING TECHNOLOGIES and innovative solutions that can improve patient care, operational efficiency, and overall outcomes.					
4	The Jordanian Hospital leaders ADAPT TO CHANGES and embrace new approaches for patients.					
5	The Jordanian Hospitals' leaders determine CUSTOMER satisfaction, dissatisfaction, and ENGAGEMENT.					

continued on following page

Table 1. Continued

#	Evaluation Domain Statements (Attributes;Assessment of Currant Senior Healthcare Leadership)	Strongly Disagree (1)	Disagree (2)	Neutral (3)	Agree (4)	Strongly Agree (5)
Monitoring and Evaluation						
1	Relevant data sets are produced, and monitoring systems ensure standards are met in clinical, corporate, and administrative functions.					
2	The Jordanian Hospital leaders MAKE INFORMED DECISIONS based on thorough analysis.					
3	Encourage leaders to LEVERAGE DATA AND ANALYTICS to make informed decisions.					
Visionary leadership						
1	The Jordanian Hospital's Leadership Articulates a vision for the future.					
2	The Jordanian Hospitals' leadership adheres to KEY STRATEGIC CHALLENGES and ADVANTAGES.					
3	The Jordanian Hospitals' leadership ALIGN GOALS AND OBJECTIVES with the OVERALL VISION.					
4	The Jordanian Hospitals' leadership DEVELOP AND COMMUNICATE A CLEAR STRATEGY for achieving the vision.					
5	The Jordanian Hospitals' leaders balance the STRATEGIC OBJECTIVES to achieve an appropriate balance among varying and potentially competing organizational needs.					
6	. The Jordanian Hospitals' leadership DEVELOP AND COMMUNICATE A CLEAR STRATEGY for achieving the vision.					
7	The Jordanian Hospitals' leadership promotes patient safety and drives quality improvement initiatives.					
Governance						
1	Executive decisions are made and implemented according to governance structure, policies, and values.					
2	Key governing bodies are engaged and committed to the organizational strategy and vision.					
3	Succession planning is built for continuity of oversight in Alignment with values and strategic direction.					
4	The Jordanian Hospitals evaluates the PERFORMANCE of SENIOR LEADERS and the GOVERNANCE board.					
5	The Jordanian Hospital's leaders track data and information on daily operations and overall organizational PERFORMANCE.					
6	The Jordanian Hospitals ADDRESS CURRENT AND ANTICIPATE FUTURE legal, regulatory, and community concerns with hospital HEALTH SERVICES and operations.					
Preparedness and Crisis Management						
1	Hospital understands risk management principles and guides relevant programs and strategies.					
2	The hospital plans for service continuity during potential health and other emergencies.					
3	The hospital actively anticipates, manages, and mitigates significant risks during emergencies.					

continued on following page

Table 1. Continued

#	Evaluation Domain Statements (Attributes;Assessment of Currant Senior Healthcare Leadership)	Strongly Disagree (1)	Disagree (2)	Neutral (3)	Agree (4)	Strongly Agree (5)
4	The Jordanian Hospital leaders WEIGH RISKS AND BENEFITS before making decisions.					
5	The Jordanian Hospital leaders CONSIDER DIVERSE PERSPECTIVES And seek input from others.					
6	The Jordanian Hospital leaders respond quickly when circumstances require a shift in ACTION PLANS and rapid execution of new plans.					
Digital Technologies in Healthcare						
1	Digital technologies are implemented cost-effectively in Alignment with the organizational strategy.					
2	The hospital recognizes the potential and limitations of health technologies and digital outreach.					
Executive communication						
1	The hospital articulates and communicates its mission, vision, values, and priorities consistently to stakeholders.					
2	Information is presented in a factual, credible, and understandable way to decision-makers.					
3	Messaging and means of communication are customized for separate groups to optimize impact.					
Employee Support and Development						
1	The hospital develops others through mentoring, coaching, and promoting continuous development.					
2	Constructive feedback about performance is provided in a professional and respectful environment.					
Compassionate leadership						
1	Compassionate and collaborative leadership behaviors are adopted.					
2	Transparent, shared decision-making is valued and understood.					
Interpersonal relationships						
1	Positive workforce and stakeholder relationships are developed and sustained.					
2	Strong listening and communication skills, including non-verbal communication, are demonstrated.					
3	The Jordanian Hospital leaders ENSURE CLARITY and understanding in HOSPITAL communication.					
4	The Jordanian Hospital leaders adapt the HOSPITAL communication style to different audiences.					
5	The Jordanian Hospital leaders Foster an open and TRANSPARENT COMMUNICATION culture.					
Problem-Solving and Negotiation						
1	Problem-solving skills are demonstrated, and conflicts are managed through mediation and negotiation.					
2	Conflicting perspectives are discussed collaboratively, leading to mutually beneficial solutions.					

continued on following page

Table 1. Continued

#	Evaluation Domain Statements (Attributes;Assessment of Currant Senior Healthcare Leadership)	Strongly Disagree (1)	Disagree (2)	Neutral (3)	Agree (4)	Strongly Agree (5)
Systems thinking						
1	Hospital balances and connects inter-relationships among access, quality, safety, cost, etc.					
2	The hospital recognizes the local implications of regional and global health events, understanding their impact on communities.					
3	Hospital adopts a systemic approach, considering other sectors' priorities in the community.					
Engaging Culture and Environment						
1	The hospital facilitates the development of an organizational culture built on mutual trust, inclusion, and transparency.					
2	Teamwork, multidisciplinary teams, and cross-boundary engagement are promoted at Hospital.					
3	The hospital maintains awareness of factors impacting the community and organization's services.					
4	The Jordanian Hospitals leaders encourage INTERDISCIPLINARY COLLABORATION, BREAK down silos, and create opportunities for staff to work together to solve complex problems and deliver high-quality care.					
5	The Jordanian Hospitals leaders FOSTER A CULTURE of collaboration and teamwork.					
Population Health Assessment and Promotion						
1	Hospital incorporates an understanding of social and environmental determinants of health into strategies and decisions.					
2	The hospital uses vital statistics and health indicators to identify priorities and guide decision-making.					
3	Hospital assesses healthcare costs and accessibility to meet patient population needs.					
Networks and Alliances						
1	The hospital establishes relationships for effective, coordinated, and integrated care with other providers.					
2	Relevant partnerships and networks are promoted to advance efficient care delivery.					
3	Partnerships align with corporate social responsibility and environmental sustainability practices.					
Advocacy						
1	Hospital advocates for healthcare policy initiatives aligned with priorities and quality of care.					
2	Patients' rights are advocated for, and their participation in designing health services is assured.					
Public Relations and Marketing						
1	The hospital demonstrates proficiency in media, public relations, and effective communication.					

continued on following page

Table 1. Continued

#	Evaluation Domain Statements (Attributes;Assessment of Currant Senior Healthcare Leadership)	Strongly Disagree (1)	Disagree (2)	Neutral (3)	Agree (4)	Strongly Agree (5)
2	Marketing and social marketing principles are applied for appropriate community outreach and health literacy.					
3	The Jordanian Hospital leaders determine hospital CUSTOMER groups and market SEGMENTS.					
Regulations and Health Systems						
1	Public policy, legislative, and advocacy processes are interpreted into the hospital's strategic objectives.					
2	Hospital understands the local and national healthcare system structure, funding mechanisms, and integrated care delivery networks.					
3	The hospital ensures compliance with applicable laws and regulations in the healthcare sector.					
Strategic planning						
1	Hospital leads the development of key planning processes for strategic and clinical service plans.					
2	Operating-unit strategic objectives are monitored and aligned with the hospital's mission and strategy.					
3	Patient pathways and service design are understood and organized for effective delivery.					
4	The Jordanian Hospital leaders CONDUCT HOSPITAL STRATEGIC PLANNING, state the organization's KEY STRATEGIC OBJECTIVES and their most critical related GOALS.					
5	The Jordanian Hospitals' leaders decide which KEY PROCESSES will be accomplished by hospital WORKFORCE and external suppliers, PARTNERS, and COLLABORATORS.					
6	Hospital leaders have short- and long-term master plans of action.					
7	Hospital leaders balance strategic objectives to strike the appropriate balance between diverse and competing organizational needs.					
Sustainability leadership						
1	The hospital understands sustainability as a multi-dimensional concept in decision-making.					
2	Priorities and actions concerning climate impact reduction and sustainability are identified and overseen.					
3	Climate impact measures and quality standards are developed and implemented in the hospital's strategy.					
Organizational resilience						
1	Hospital understands resilience and enhances strategies for sustainability.					
2	Interdependency and logistics of supply chain services are effectively managed, including procurement and waste management.					
3	Hospital leaders show resilience in difficult situations.					
4	The Jordanian Hospitals LEADERS MAINTAIN COMPOSURE and positivity under pressure.					

continued on following page

Table 1. Continued

#	Evaluation Domain Statements (Attributes;Assessment of Currant Senior Healthcare Leadership)	Strongly Disagree (1)	Disagree (2)	Neutral (3)	Agree (4)	Strongly Agree (5)
5	The Jordanian Hospital leaders ADAPT TO CHANGES and embrace new approaches					
Innovation and Entrepreneurship						
1	Diversity of perspectives is encouraged to support innovation and improvement.					
2	Innovative cultures and methods are promoted, supporting experimentation and innovation.					
3	The Jordanian Hospital leaders incorporate INNOVATION in strategy development PROCESS.					
Change management						
1	Change processes are championed and optimized for sustained impact.					
2	The Jordanian Hospital leaders can minimize resistance to change and ensure successful implementation.					
3	The Jordanian Hospitals' leaders ensure that the hospital PERFORMANCE measurement system can respond to rapid or unexpected organizational or external changes and provide timely data.					
Ongoing Learning and Sharing						
1	Information-seeking from various sources is promoted to support organizational performance.					
2	Organizational introspection and lessons learned are valued for continuous improvement.					
3	Hospital contributes to advancing healthcare management and leadership through sharing evidence, knowledge, and experience.					
4	The Jordanian Hospital leaders should PRIORITIZE ONGOING EDUCATION and professional development to stay updated with healthcare advancements, leadership techniques, and industry best practices.					
5	The Jordanian Hospitals Leaders Provide comprehensive training programs, workshops, and mentorship opportunities to develop the leadership skills of healthcare professionals.					
6	The Jordanian Hospitals applying for the health services organizational LEARNING PROGRAM					

Compilation of References

Abdulaziz-al-Humaidan, A. (2025). The effect of innovation and sustainability ethics on reputation: A moderating role of social media. *Social Responsibility Journal*, *21*(6), 1205–1223. https://www.emerald.com/insight/content/doi/10.1108/srj-09-2024-0634/full/html

Abdullah, K. H., & Abd Aziz, F. S. (2021). Mapping of laboratory safety research: A bibliometric review. *Malaysian Journal of Public Health Medicine*, *21*(1), 303–310. DOI: 10.37268/mjphm/vol.21/no.1/art.864

ACHE. (2015). *Leadership competencies for health services managers leadership competencies for healthcare services managers*. https://www.ache.org/-/media/ache/about-ache/leadership_competencies_healthcare_services_managers.pdf

ACHE. (2024). ACHE [*Competencies Assessment Tool*. https://www.ache.org/-/media/ache/career-resource-center/cat-competencies-assessment-tool.pdf]. *Healthcare Executive, 2024*.

Achua, C. F., & Lussier, R. N. (2010). *Effective Leadership* (4th ed.). South-Western.

Adair, K. C., Levoy, E., Tawfik, D. S., Palassof, S., Profit, J., Frankel, A., Leonard, M., & Sexton, J. B. (2022). Assessing leadership behavior in health care: Introducing the Local Leadership Scale of the SCORE Survey. [PMC]. *Joint Commission Journal on Quality and Patient Safety*, *49*(3), 166–173. DOI: 10.1016/j.jcjq.2022.12.007 PMID: 36717344

Adhanom Ghebreyesus, T. (2020). Addressing mental health needs: An integral part of COVID-19 response. *World Psychiatry; Official Journal of the World Psychiatric Association (WPA)*, *19*(2), 129–130. DOI: 10.1002/wps.20768 PMID: 32394569

Ahsan, M. J. (2023). The role of emotional intelligence in effective corporate social responsibility leadership. *The International Journal of Organizational Analysis*, *31*(8), 75–91.

Ajanaku, O. J., Lubbe, W., & Adufe, I. (2022). Transformational Leadership Style and Work Outcomes of Healthcare Professionals: A Review of Literature. *African Renaissance (1744-2532), 19*(3).

Al Issa, H. E., & Omar, M. M. S. (2024). Digital innovation drivers in retail banking: The role of leadership, culture, and technostress inhibitors. *The International Journal of Organizational Analysis*, *32*(11), 19–43.

Al Kuwaiti, A., & Al Muhanna, F. A. (2019). Challenges facing healthcare leadership in attaining accreditation of teaching hospitals. *Leadership in Health Services*, *32*(2), 170–181. PMID: 30945601

Al Masaeid, T. & Upadhyay, D. (2023). *Shared Leadership Practices on the Role of the Employees' Effectiveness*. DOI: 10.1109/icbats57792.2023.10111379

Al Zoubi, F., Khalaf, G., Beaulé, P. E., & Fallavollita, P. (2023). Leveraging machine learning and prescriptive analytics to improve operating room throughput. *Frontiers in Digital Health*, *5*. Advance online publication. DOI: 10.3389/fdgth.2023.1242214 PMID: 37808917

Al-Abri, R., & Al-Balushi, A. (2014). Patient satisfaction survey as a tool towards quality improvement. *Oman Medical Journal*, 29(1), 3–7. 22

Al-Ahmadi, H. (2009). Factors affecting performance of hospital nurses in Riyadh Region, Saudi Arabia. *International Journal of Health Care Quality Assurance*, *22*(1), 40–54. DOI: 10.1108/09526860910927943 PMID: 19284170

Al-Amoudi, S., Al-Shugtani, T., Al-Maatouq, M., Sindi, A., & Qureshi, N. (2016). Breast cancer knowledge among male high school students in Saudi Arabia. *Journal of Cancer Education*, *31*(4), 784–788. pubmed.ncbi.nlm.nih.gov. DOI: 10.1007/s13187-015-0951-8 PMID: 26611278

Al-Fadhalah, T., & Elamir, H. (2021). Organizational culture, quality of care and leadership style in government general hospitals in Kuwait: A multimethod study. *Journal of Healthcare Leadership*, 243–254. PMID: 34703349

Algahtani, A. (2014). Are leadership and management different? A review. *Journal of management policies and practices*, 2(3), 71-82.

Alghamdi, S., Tajaldeen, A., Alghamdi, A., Aljondi, R., Alghamdi, A., Alqahtani, M., Habbosh, T., & Alzahrani, W. (2024). *Investigation of utilising electronic medical records on the quality of healthcare services at hospitals in Saudi Arabia.* https://isisn.org/BR-21-4-2024/750-759-21(4)2024BR24-93.pdf

Al-Ghamdi, A. O., Al-Mtairi, K. Q., Bin Gadeeb, F. A., Ali, I., Al-Mutairi, A. O., & Al-Resheedi, F. S. (2022). Evaluating the Performance of the Health Staff and its Role in Improving the Efficiency of Services. *International Journal (Toronto, Ont.), 10*(6).

Al-Ghamdi, H. S. H., & Alshammari, S. W., sultan Alowayqil, A., Alawthah, S. H., Alyami, F. M., Almansour, M. M., ... & Alneami, S. Y. (2024). Assessment of Determinants of Managerial Competencies among Healthcare Managers in Healthcare Hospitals from their Perspectives at KSA. *Journal of International Crisis and Risk Communication Research*, *7*(S5), 819.

Al-Habib, N. M. I. (2020). Leadership and organizational performance: Is it essential in healthcare systems improvement? A review of literature. *Saudi Journal of Anaesthesia*, *14*(1), 69–76. PMID: 31998023

Al-Haddad, M., & Psych, F. R. C. (2003). Leadership in healthcare management. *Bahrain Medical Bulletin*, *25*(1), 1.

Al-Issa, H. E., & Abdelsalam, M. K. (2021). Antecedents to Leadership: A CB-SEM and PLS-SEM Validation. *International Journal of Sustainable Development and Planning*, *16*(8).

Allen, J. (2022). *The Effects of a Formal Organizational Program on Nursing Supervisor Self-Perception of Leadership*. UNM Digital Repository. https://digitalrepository.unm.edu/dnp/24/

Almalki, M. J., Fitzgerald, G., & Clark, M. (2012). Quality of work life and turnover intention of primary health care nurses in Saudi Arabia: A cross-sectional study. *BMC Health Services Research*, *12*, 314. Advance online publication. DOI: 10.1186/1472-6963-12-314 PMID: 22970764

Almomani, E., Sullivan, J., Hajjieh, M., & Leighton, K. (2020). Simulation-based education programme for upskilling non-critical care nurses for COVID-19 deployment. *BMJ Simulation and Technology Enhanced Learning*, *7*(5), bmjstel-2020-000711. DOI: 10.1136/bmjstel-2020-000711

Alqahtani, A. A., & Al-Enezi, Mutlaq M. (2025). Mastering Leadership Concepts through Utilizing Critical Thinking Strategies within Educational Administration Courses at Kuwait University. *College Student Journal*, *46*(3), 508–525. https://eric.ed.gov/?id=EJ996950

Al-Saheb, A. (2022). Effective leadership in healthcare: Essential traits for every leader. *Health Quality Magazine*. https://m-quality.net/?p=45447&utm_source=chatgpt.com

Al-Sawai, A. (2013). Leadership of Healthcare Professionals: Where Do We Stand? *Oman Medical Journal, 28*, 285. DOI: 10.5001/omj.2013.79 PMID: 23904925

Alsharari, A. F., Salihu, D., & Alshammari, F. F. (2025). Effectiveness of virtual clinical learning in nursing education: A systematic review. *BMC Nursing, 24*(1). Advance online publication. DOI: 10.1186/s12912-025-03076- PMID: 40241119

Al-Thawabiya, A., Singh, K., Al-Lenjawi, B. A., & Alomari, A. (2023). Leadership styles and transformational leadership skills among nurse leaders in qatar, a cross-sectional study. *Nursing Open, 10*(6), 3440–3446. Wiley. https://www.ncbi.nlm.nih.gov/pmc/articles/PMC10170951/

Al-Thawabiya, A., Singh, K., Al-Lenjawi, B. A., & Alomari, A. (2023). Leadership styles and transformational leadership skills among nurse leaders in Qatar, a cross-sectional study. *Nursing Open, 10*(6), 3440–3446. PMID: 36760040

Al-Touby, S. S. (2012). Functional results-oriented healthcare leadership: A novel leadership model. *Oman Medical Journal, 27*(2), 104. PMID: 22496933

Al-Zahrani, I. A., & Brek, T. M. (2024). Comprehensive Genome Analysis of Colistin-Only–Sensitive KPC-2 and NDM1-1-Coproducing *Klebsiella pneumoniae* ST11 and *Acinetobacter baumannii* ST2 From a Critically Ill Patient With COVID-19 in Saudi Arabia. *International Journal of Microbiology, 2024*(1). DOI: 10.1155/2024/9233075

Al-Zahrani, E. (2024). The Role of Healthcare Leaders in Promoting Vaccine Acceptance in Saudi Arabia. *Journal of Healthcare Leadership, 16*, 279–286. DOI: 10.2147/jhl.s470522 PMID: 39072262

Al-Zahrani, J. M., Aldossari, K. K., Abdulmajeed, I., Al-Ghamdi, S. H., Al-Shamrani, A. M., & Al-Qahtani, N. S. (2016). Daytime sleepiness and academic performance among Arab medical students. *Journal of Thoracic Disease, 8*(2). Advance online publication. DOI: 10.3978/j.issn.2072-1439.2016.AB006

Al-Zu'Bi. Ahmad (2021). *Asymmetric information, fraud, and switching costs in healthcare insurance markets.* PhD Thesis, UQ Business School, The University of Queensland. DOI: 10.14264/653d111

Amabile, T. M., & Khaire, M. (2008). Creativity and the role of the leader. *Harvard Business Review, 86*(10), 100–109, 142. https://pubmed.ncbi.nlm.nih.gov/18822674/ PMID: 18822674

Amabile, T. M., & Khaire, M. (2008). Creativity and the role of the leader. *Journal of the Management Training Institute. SAIL, Ranchi, 36*(3), 48–51.

American Hospital Dubai. (2022, January 26). American Hospital collaborates with Siemens Healthineers as key technology partner for advanced diagnostics solutions. American Hospital Dubai. Retrieved August 6, 2025, from https://www.ahdubai.com/news/american-hospital-dubai-collaborates-with-siemens-healthineers-as-key-technology-partner-for-advance khaleejtimes.com+13gulfnews.com+13ahdubai.com+

Amirrudin, M., Nasution, K., & Supahar, S. (2021). Effect of Variability on Cronbach Alpha Reliability in Research Practice. *Jurnal Matematika. Statistika Dan Komputasi*, *17*(2), 223–230. DOI: 10.20956/jmsk.v17i2.11655

Anderson, D. (2024). *From trait to transformation- The evolution of leadership theories.* Scribd. https://www.scribd.com/documcnt/687075302/from-trait-to-transformation-the-evolution-of-leadership-theories

Anderson, D. (2024). *FROM TRAIT TO TRANSFORMATION- THE EVOLUTION OF LEADERSHIP THEORIES.* Scribd. https://www.scribd.com/document/687075302/FROM-TRAIT-TO-TRANSFORMATION-THE-EVOLUTION-OF-LEADERSHIP-THEORIES

Antonakis, J., & House, R. J. (2014). Instrumental leadership: Measurement and extension of transformational–transactiona3l leadership theory. *The Leadership Quarterly*, *25*(4), 746–771. https://www.sciencedirect.com/science/article/abs/pii/S1048984314000290

Armenakis, A. A., & Harris, S. G. (2009). Reflections: Our Journey in Organizational Change Research and Practice. *Journal of Change Management*, *9*(2), 127–142. DOI: 10.1080/14697010902879079

Asegu, D. A., & Gedifew, M. T. (2022). Lived experiences of secondary school principals in practicing teacher leadership. *Global Journal of Education and Training*, *5*(8), 1–12.

Ashade, O. A. (2020). *Community Involvement in the Implementation of the National Policy on Public-private Partnership: A Study of Infrastructural Development in Lagos State, Nigeria* (Doctoral dissertation, University of KwaZulu-Natal, Howard College).

Asif, M., Jameel, A., Hussain, A., Hwang, J., & Sahito, N. (2019). Linking transformational leadership with nurse-assessed adverse patient outcomes and the quality of care: Assessing the role of job satisfaction and structural empowerment. *International Journal of Environmental Research and Public Health*, *16*(13), 1–15. https://pubmed.ncbi.nlm.nih.gov/31277478/ PMID: 31277478

Asif, M., Jameel, A., Hussain, A., Hwang, J., & Sahito, N. (2019). Linking Transformational Leadership with Nurse-Assessed Adverse Patient Outcomes and the Quality of Care: Assessing the Role of Job Satisfaction and Structural Empowerment. *International Journal of Environmental Research and Public Health, 16*(13), 2381. DOI: 10.3390/ijerph16132381 PMID: 31277478

Asif, M., Jameel, A., Sahito, N., Hwang, J., Hussain, A., & Manzoor, F. (2019). Can leadership enhance patient satisfaction? Assessing the role of administrative and medical quality. *International Journal of Environmental Research and Public Health, 16*(17), 3212. PMID: 31484308

Asmri, M. A., Almalki, M. J., Fitzgerald, G., & Clark, M. (2020). The public health care system and primary care services in Saudi Arabia: A system in transition. *Eastern Mediterranean Health Journal, 26*(4), 468–476. PMID: 32338366

Avolio, B. J. (2007). Promoting more integrative strategies for leadership theory-building. *The American Psychologist, 62*(1), 25–33. DOI: 10.1037/0003-066x.62.1.25 PMID: 17209677

Avolio, B. J., Sosik, J. J., Kahai, S. S., & Baker, B. (2014). E-leadership: Re-examining transformations in leadership source and transmission. *The Leadership Quarterly, 25*(1), 105–131. DOI: 10.1016/j.leaqua.2013.11.003

Avolio, B. J., Walumbwa, F. O., & Weber, T. J. (2009). Leadership: Current theories, research, and future directions. *Annual Review of Psychology, 60*(1), 421–449. DOI: 10.1146/annurev.psych.60.110707.163621 PMID: 18651820

Avolio, B. J., & Yammarino, F. J. (2013). *Transformational And Charismatic Leadership: The Road Ahead.* Emerald Group Publishing.

Baker, M. A., Sands, K. E., Huang, S. S., Kleinman, K., Septimus, E. J., Varma, N., Blanchard, J., Poland, R. E., Coady, M. H., Yokoe, D. S., Fraker, S., Froman, A., Moody, J., Goldin, L., Isaacs, A., Kleja, K., Korwek, K. M., Stelling, J., Clark, A., & Platt, R. (2021). The Impact of COVID-19 on Healthcare-Associated Infections. *Clinical Infectious Diseases, 74*(10). Advance online publication. DOI: 10.1093/cid/ciab688 PMID: 34370014

Barbuto, J. E.Jr, & Wheeler, D. W. (2006). Scale development and construct clarification of servant leadership. *Group & Organization Management, 31*(3), 300–326.

Basadur, M. (2004). Leading others to think innovatively together: Creative leadership. *The Leadership Quarterly, 15*(1), 103–121. DOI: 10.1016/j.leaqua.2003.12.007

Bass, B. M. (1985). *Leadership and Performance beyond Expectations.* Free Press.

Bass, B. M. (1990). *Bass & Stogdill's Handbook of Leadership: theory, research, and Managerial Applications* (3rd ed.). Free Press.

Bass, B. M., & Avolio, B. J. (1990). *Transformational leadership development: manual for the multifactor leadership questionnaire.* Consulting Psychologists Press.

Bass, B. M., & Avolio, B. J. (1994). *Improving Organizational Effectiveness Through Transformational leadership.* Sage Publications.

Bass, B. M., & Riggio, R. E. (2006). *Transformational Leadership* (2nd ed.). Routledge.

Batliwala, S. (2011). Feminist leadership for social transformation: Clearing the conceptual cloud. CREA. https://creaworld.org/resource/feminist-leadership-for-social-transformation/

Batliwala, S. (2011). *Feminist Leadership for Social Transformation.* CREA India.

Batool, I. (2025). *RealTime Health Monitoring Using 5G Networks: A Deep Learning-Based Architecture for Remote Patient Care.* ArXiv.org. https://arxiv.org/abs/2501.01027

Bauer, T., Erdogan, B., Caughlin, D., & Truxillo, D. (2023). *Human resource management: People, data, and analytics.* Sage Publications.

Beach, M. C., Price, E. G., Gary, T. L., Robinson, K. A., Gozu, A., Palacio, A., Smarth, C., Jenckes, M., Feuerstein, C., Bass, E. B., Powe, N. R., & Cooper, L. A. (2005). Cultural competence: A systematic review of health care provider educational interventions. *Medical Care, 43*(4), 356–373. DOI: 10.1097/01.mlr.0000156861.58905.96 PMID: 15778639

Beauvais, A. M. (2019). *Leadership and management competence in nursing practice: competencies, skills, decision making.* Springer Publishing Company.

Beauvais, A. M. (Ed.). (2018). *Leadership and management competence in nursing practice: Competencies, skills, decision-making.* Springer Publishing Company.

Begun, J. W., Zimmerman, B., & Dooley, K. (2003). *Health care organizations as complex adaptive systems. 253,* 253–288. https://www.researchgate.net/publication/228384399_Health_care_organizations_as_complex_adaptive_systems

Behrens, J. E. (2014). *Leadership in collaborative governance: Understanding the relationship of leadership and collaborative performance of Local Departments of Social Services executives.* Virginia Commonwealth University.

Belrhiti, Z., Giralt, A. N., & Marchal, B. (2018). Complex leadership in healthcare: A scoping review. *International Journal of Health Policy and Management, 7*(12), 1073. PMID: 30709082

Bender, M. (2016). Conceptualizing Clinical Nurse Leader practice: An Interpretive Synthesis. *Journal of Nursing Management, 24*(1), E23–E31. DOI: 10.1111/jonm.12285 PMID: 25655928

Bender, M. (2016). Conceptualizing clinical nurse leader practice: An interpretive synthesis. *Journal of Nursing Management, 24*(1), E23–E31. PMID: 25655928

Benmira, S., & Agboola, M. (2021). Evolution of Leadership Theory. *BMJ Leader, 5*(1), 3–5. DOI: 10.1136/leader-2020-000296

Bennis, W. G. (1974). Learning to lead: A workbook on becoming a leader. Addison Wesley. Retrieved from https://archive.org/details/learningtoleadwo0000benn

Bennis, W. G., & Goldsmith, J. (2010). *Learning to lead: a workbook on becoming a leader*. Basic Books.

Bensimon, E. M. (1989). The Meaning of "Good Presidential Leadership": A Frame Analysis. *Review of Higher Education, 12*(2), 107–123. DOI: 10.1353/rhe.1989.0024

Berkes, F. Colding, J., & Folke, C. (2008). *Navigating social-ecological systems: building resilience for complexity and change*. Cambridge University Press.

Berniak-Woźny, J., & Rataj, M. (2023). Towards green and sustainable healthcare: A literature review and research agenda for green leadership in the healthcare sector. *International Journal of Environmental Research and Public Health, 20*(2), 908. PMID: 36673663

Berwick, D. M. (2003). Disseminating Innovations in Health Care. *Journal of the American Medical Association, 289*(15), 1969. DOI: 10.1001/jama.289.15.1969 PMID: 12697800

Betancourt, J., Green, A., & Carrillo, J. (2002). Cultural competence in health care: Emerging frameworks and practical approaches. In *The Commonwealth Fund*. https://www.commonwealthfund.org/sites/default/files/documents/___media_files_publications_fund_report_2002_oct_cultural_com

Bishara, S. (2025). Sherifbishara.com. https://sherifbishara.com/

Bjegovic-Mikanovic, V. (2016). Governance and management of health care institutions in Serbia: An overview of recent developments. *South Eastern European Journal of Public Health, 5*(1). Advance online publication. DOI: 10.4119/UNIBI/SEEJPH-2016-94

Boal, K. B., & Hooijberg, R. (2000). Strategic leadership research: Moving on. *The Leadership Quarterly, 11*(4), 515–549. DOI: 10.1016/s1048-9843(00)00057-6

Boamah, S. (2018). Linking nurses' clinical leadership to patient care quality: The role of transformational leadership and workplace empowerment. *Canadian Journal of Nursing Research, 50*(1), 9–19. PMID: 29108423

Boamah, S. A., Laschinger, H. K. S., Wong, C., & Clarke, S. (2018). Effect of transformational leadership on job satisfaction and patient safety outcomes. *Nursing Outlook, 66*(2), 180–189. DOI: 10.1016/j.outlook.2017.10.004 PMID: 29174629

Bodenheimer, T., & Grumbach, K. (2020). *Understanding Health Policy: A Clinical Approach* (8th ed.). Mcgraw-Hill Education.

Bolton, P., Brunnermeier, M. K., & Veldkamp, L. (2013). Leadership, coordination, and corporate culture. *The Review of Economic Studies, 80*(2), 512–537.

Boonstra, A., & Broekhuis, M. (2010). Barriers to the acceptance of electronic medical records by physicians from systematic review to taxonomy and interventions. *BMC Health Services Research, 10*(1), 231. DOI: 10.1186/1472-6963-10-231 PMID: 20691097

Bourbonnais, R., Brisson, C., & Vezina, M. (2010). Long-term effects of an intervention on psychosocial work factors among healthcare professionals in a hospital setting. *Occupational and Environmental Medicine, 68*(7), 479–486. DOI: 10.1136/oem.2010.055202 PMID: 21098832

Bovend'Eerdt, T. J., Botell, R. E., & Wade, D. T. (2009). Writing SMART Rehabilitation Goals and Achieving Goal Attainment scaling: a Practical Guide. *Clinical Rehabilitation, 23*(4), 352–361. *Sage Journals*. DOI: 10.1177/0269215508101741

Bowman, R. F. (2025). Examining Six Different Leadership Styles in Relation to Constrained Change at Winona State University. *Education*, •••, 3–13. https://www.semanticscholar.org/paper/Examining-Six-Different-Leadership-Styles-in-to-at-Bowman/2699050d89d20dece685325b98e67feb6d4d146d

Braveman, P., Egerter, S., & Williams, D. R. (2011). The Social Determinants of Health: Coming of Age. *Annual Review of Public Health, 32*(1), 381–398. DOI: 10.1146/annurev-publhealth-031210-101218 PMID: 21091195

Brazier, D. K. (2005). Influence of contextual factors on health-care leadership. *Leadership and Organization Development Journal, 26*(2), 128–140. DOI: 10.1108/01437730510582563

Briggs, A., Coleman, M., & Morrison, M. (n.d.). *Research Methods in Educational Leadership and Management 3rd Edition Supplementary resources*. Retrieved August 8, 2025, from https://us.sagepub.com/sites/default/files/upm-assets/47320_book_item_47320.pdf

Brown, C. A., & Robinson, D. M. (2002). Skewness and kurtosis implied by option prices: A correction. *Journal of Financial Research*, *25*(2), 279–282.

Brown, N. O. (2021). *The Lived and Perceived Experiences of Healthcare Leaders Deploying Lean Six Sigma Methods: A Phenomenological Study*. Baker College.

Bruce, I. N., Golam, S., Steenkamp, J., Wang, P., Worthington, E., Desta, B., Psachoulia, K., Erhardt, W., & Tummala, R. (2022). Indirect treatment comparison of anifrolumab efficacy versus belimumab in adults with systemic lupus erythematosus. *Journal of Comparative Effectiveness Research*, *11*(10), 765–777. DOI: 10.2217/cer-2022-0040 PMID: 35546484

Bruning, P., & Baghurst, T. (2013). Improving ethical decision making in health care leadership. *Business and Economics Journal*, *4*(2), 1–5.

Budak, N. H., Aykin, E., Seydim, A. C., Greene, A. K., & Guzel-Seydim, Z. B. (2014). Functional Properties of Vinegar. *Journal of Food Science*, *79*(5), R757–R764. DOI: 10.1111/1750-3841.12434 PMID: 24811350

Burgess, A. (2025). *Becoming a Bridge of Collaboration: How Being Supports Doing Within the HELP Model of Leadership*. University of Massachuesetts Boston.

Burns, J. M. (2017). Leadership: A higher view. HarperCollins Publishers. https://www.harpercollins.com/products/leadership-james-m-burns

Burns, J. M. (1978). *Leadership*. Harper & Row.

Calhoun, J. G., Ramiah, K., Weist, E. M., & Shortell, S. M. (2008). Development of a Core Competency Model for the Master of Public Health Degree. *American Journal of Public Health*, *98*(9), 1598–1607. DOI: 10.2105/ajph.2007.117978 PMID: 18633093

Cannavacciuolo, L., Capaldo, G., & Ponsiglione, C. (2023). Digital innovation and organizational changes in the healthcare sector: Multiple case studies of telemedicine project implementation. *Technovation*, *120*, 102550.

Carayon, P., Karsh, B.-T., Gurses, A. P., Holden, R. J., Hoonakker, P., Schoofs Hundt, A., Montague, E., Rodriguez, A. J., & Wetterneck, T. B. (2013). Macroergonomics in Health Care Quality and Patient Safety. *Review of Human Factors and Ergonomics*, *8*(1), 4–54. DOI: 10.1177/1557234x13492976 PMID: 24729777

Carayon, P., Schoofs Hundt, A., Karsh, B.-T., Gurses, A. P., Alvarado, C. J., Smith, M., & Flatley Brennan, P. (2006). Work system design for patient safety: The SEIPS model. *Quality & Safety in Health Care, 15*(suppl_1), i50–i58. https://www.ncbi.nlm.nih.gov/pmc/articles/PMC2464868/ PMID: 17142610

Carmeli, A., Gelbard, R., & Gefen, D. (2010). The importance of innovation leadership in cultivating strategic fit and enhancing firm performance. *The Leadership Quarterly, 21*(3), 339–349.

Carragher, J., & Gormley, K. (2017). Leadership and Emotional Intelligence in Nursing and Midwifery Education and Practice: A Discussion Paper. *Journal of Advanced Nursing, 73*(1), 85–96.

Carter, M. Z., Armenakis, A. A., Feild, H. S., & Mossholder, K. W. (2013). Transformational leadership, relationship quality, and employee performance during continuous incremental organizational change. *Journal of Organizational Behavior, 34*(7), 942–958. DOI: 10.1002/job.1824

Carvajal, A. L. P., & Sanchez, R. D. (2023). Strategic considerations, challenges, and opportunities in establishing the International Journal of Open-access, Interdisciplinary, and New Educational Discoveries (iJOINED). *International Journal of Open-access* [iJOINED ETCOR]. *Interdisciplinary and New Educational Discoveries of ETCOR Educational Research Center*, 2(2), 539–546.

Catinella, A. P., & Esparza, M. J. A. (2021). Leading virtual teams: A review of best practices. *Donald School Journal of Ultrasound in Obstetrics and Gynecology, 15*(4), 371–376.

Cawthorn, D. (2017). *Philosophical foundations of leadership*. Routledge.

Chatterjee, R., Suy, R., Yen, Y., & Chhay, L. (2018). Literature review on leadership in healthcare management. *J Soc Sci Stud, 5*(1), 38–47.

Chemers, M. M. (2000). Leadership research and theory: A functional integration. *Group Dynamics, 4*(1), 27–43. DOI: 10.1037/1089-2699.4.1.27

Chen, J. K., & Sriphon, T. (2022). Authentic leadership, trust, and social exchange relationships under the influence of leader behavior. *Sustainability, 14*(10), 5883.

Chen, L. J. (2025). Health Policy Challenges for 2025 and Beyond. *JAMA Health Forum, 6*(1), e250184. DOI: 10.1001/jamahealthforum.2025.0184 PMID: 39883473

Chen, L., Evans, T., Anand, S., Boufford, J. I., Brown, H., Chowdhury, M., Cueto, M., Dare, L., Dussault, G., Elzinga, G., Fee, E., Habte, D., Hanvoravongchai, P., Jacobs, M., Kurowski, C., Michael, S., Pablos-Mendez, A., Sewankambo, N., Solimano, G., & Stilwell, B. (2004). Human resources for health: Overcoming the crisis. *Lancet*, *364*(9449), 1984–1990. DOI: 10.1016/s0140-6736(04)17482-5 PMID: 15567015

Choucair, I. (2023). *Perceptions of Business Leaders on Achieving Organizational Alignment: A Qualitative Exploratory Case Study* (Doctoral dissertation, University of Phoenix).

Christensen, C. M., Grossman, J. H., & Hwang, J. (2017). *The innovator's prescription: a disruptive solution for health care*. Mcgraw-Hill Education.

Claramita, M., & Susilo, A. P. (2024). *The Hierarchical Culture and Communication in Health Care*. 1–17. DOI: 10.1007/978-981-97-4320-9_1

Clark, C. R., Wilkins, C. H., Rodriguez, J. A., Preininger, A. M., Harris, J., DesAutels, S., Karunakaram, H., Rhee, K., Bates, D. W., & Dankwa-Mullan, I. (2021). Health Care Equity in the Use of Advanced Analytics and Artificial Intelligence Technologies in Primary Care. *Journal of General Internal Medicine*, *36*(10), 3188–3193. DOI: 10.1007/s11606-021-06846-x PMID: 34027610

Cleary, S., Toit, A. D., Scott, V., & Gilson, L. (2018). Enabling relational leadership in primary healthcare settings: Lessons from the DIALHS collaboration. *Health Policy and Planning*, *33*(suppl_2), ii65–ii74. PMID: 30053037

Cleveland Clinic. (2018). *Financial Information & Annual Reports*. Cleveland Clinic. https://my.clevelandclinic.org/about/overview/financial-information

Cloud, A. (2023). *Understanding the Role of an Advisory Board at a Privately Held Professional Company*. Advisorycloud.com. https://advisorycloud.com/blog/understanding-the-role-of-an-advisory-board-at-a-privately-held-professional-company

Conger, J. A., & Kanungo, R. N. (1987). Toward a behavioral theory of charismatic leadership in organizational settings. *Academy of Management Review*, *12*(4), 637–647. DOI: 10.2307/258069

Connor, M., & Pokora, J. (2017). *Coaching and mentoring at work: Developing effective practice* (3rd ed.). Open University Press.

Contreras, C. M., Metzger, G. A., Beane, J. D., Dedhia, P. H., Ejaz, A., & Pawlik, T. M. (2020). Telemedicine: Patient-provider clinical engagement during the COVID-19 pandemic and beyond. *Journal of Gastrointestinal Surgery*, *24*(7), 1692–1697. DOI: 10.1007/s11605-020-04623-5 PMID: 32385614

Cronk, R., & Bartram, J. (2018). Environmental conditions in health care facilities in low- and middle-income countries: Coverage and inequalities. *International Journal of Hygiene and Environmental Health, 221*(3), 409–422. DOI: 10.1016/j.ijheh.2018.01.004

Culp, C. A. (1992). *Leadership styles in organizations committed to continuous quality improvement and those not committed to continuous improvement.* United States International University.

Cummings, G. G., Tate, K., Lee, S., Wong, C. A., Paananen, T., Micaroni, S. P. M., & Chatterjee, G. E. (2018). Leadership Styles and Outcome Patterns for the Nursing Workforce and Work environment: A Systematic Review. *International Journal of Nursing Studies, 85*(1), 19–60. DOI: 10.1016/j.ijnurstu.2018.04.016 PMID: 29807190

D'aunno, T., Succi, M., & Alexander, J. A. (2000). The role of institutional and market forces in divergent organizational change. *Administrative Science Quarterly, 45*(4), 679–703.

Dakhilallah, K., & Jahdali Bsc, A. (2021). *Towards an Intelligent Holy City: Assessing the Current Training Needs for the Ministry of Hajj and Umrah.* https://irep.ntu.ac.uk/id/eprint/46404/1/Khalid%20Aljahdali%202022.pdf

Daly, J., Jackson, D., Mannix, J., Davidson, P. M., & Hutchinson, M. (2014). The importance of clinical leadership in the hospital setting. *Journal of Healthcare Leadership, 6*, 75–83. DOI: 10.2147/jhl.s46161

Damschroder, L. J., Aron, D. C., Keith, R. E., Kirsh, S. R., Alexander, J. A., & Lowery, J. C. (2009). Fostering implementation of health services research findings into practice: A consolidated framework for advancing implementation science. *Implementation Science : IS, 4*(1), 50. DOI: 10.1186/1748-5908-4-50 PMID: 19664226

Davies, B. J., & Davies, B. (2004). Strategic leadership. *School Leadership & Management, 24*(1), 29–38.

Day, D. V., Fleenor, J. W., Atwater, L. E., Sturm, R. E., & McKee, R. A. (2014). Advances in Leader and Leadership development: A Review of 25 Years of Research and Theory. *The Leadership Quarterly, 25*(1), 63–82.

De Brún, A., O'Donovan, R., & McAuliffe, E. (2019). Interventions to Develop Collectivistic Leadership in Healthcare settings: A Systematic Review. *BMC Health Services Research, 19*(1), 1–22. DOI: 10.1186/s12913-019-3883-x PMID: 30683089

De Brún, A., O'Donovan, R., & McAuliffe, E. (2019). Interventions to develop collectivistic leadership in healthcare settings: A systematic review. *BMC Health Services Research, 19*(1), 72. PMID: 30683089 de Kok, E. Schoonhoven, L., Pieterbas Lalleman, & Anne Marie Weggelaar-Jansen. (2023). Understanding rebel nurse leadership-as-practice: Challenging and changing the status quo in hospitals. *Nursing Inquiry*, *30*(4). Advance online publication. DOI: 10.1111/nin.12577 PMID: 37408336

de la Cruz, L. F., Llorens, M., Jassi, A., Krebs, G., Vidal-Ribas, P., Radua, J., Hatch, S. L., Bhugra, D., Heyman, I., Clark, B., & Mataix-Cols, D. (2015). Ethnic inequalities in the use of secondary and tertiary mental health services among patients with obsessive–compulsive disorder. *The British Journal of Psychiatry*, *207*(6), 530–535. DOI: 10.1192/bjp.bp.114.154062 PMID: 26206866

Dean, W., Talbot, S. G., & Caplan, A. (2020). Clarifying the language of clinician distress. *Journal of the American Medical Association*, *323*(10), 923–924. https://pubmed.ncbi.nlm.nih.gov/32003769/ PMID: 32003769

Deming, W. E. (1986). *Out of the crisis*. The Mit Press.

Denis, J. L., & Van Gestel, N. (2016). Medical doctors in healthcare leadership: Theoretical and practical challenges. *BMC Health Services Research*, *16*(Suppl 2), 158. PMID: 27230551

Denis, J.-L., Langley, A., & Rouleau, L. (2010). The Practice of Leadership in the Messy World of Organizations. *Leadership*, *6*(1), 67–88. DOI: 10.1177/1742715009354233

Denis, J.-L., Langley, A., & Sergi, V. (2012). Leadership in the Plural. *The Academy of Management Annals*, *6*(1), 211–283.

Denison, D. R., & Mishra, A. K. (1995). Toward a Theory of Organizational Culture and Effectiveness. *Organization Science*, *6*(2), 204–223. https://www.jstor.org/stable/2635122

DeRue, D. S. (2011). Adaptive leadership theory: Leading and following as a complex adaptive process. *Research in Organizational Behavior*, *31*, 125–150.

Devellis, R. F. (2016). *Scale Development: Theory and Applications* (4th ed.). SAGE Publications.

Dogan, A., & Schroevers, S. (2018). *Linking leadership: to cross-cultural expectations across nations*. Amsterdam University Of Applied Sciences.

Doran, G. T. (1981). There's a S.M.A.R.T. way to write management's goals and objectives. *Management Review*, *70*(11), 35–36. https://community.mis.temple.edu/mis0855002fall2015/files/2015/10/S.M.A.R.T-Way-Management-Review.pdf

Durrah, S. K. (2023). *Strategies for Improving Performance Through Diversity and Inclusion in the Workplace.* Walden University ScholarWorks. https://scholarworks.waldenu.edu/cgi/viewcontent.cgi?article=15955&context=dissertations

Durrah, O., & Kahwaji, A. (2023). Chameleon leadership and innovative behavior in the health sector: The mediation role of job security. *Employee Responsibilities and Rights Journal, 35*(2), 247–265. PMID: 40477989

Dwyer, J., Paskavitz, M., Vriesendorp, S., & Johnson, S. (2006). *An urgent call to professionalize leadership and management in health care worldwide.* Management Sciences for Health.

Dye, C. F. (2023). *Leadership in healthcare: Essential values and skills* (4th ed.). Health Administration Press.

Dziak, M. (2019). *Great man theory.* Salem Press Encyclopedia, 2024.

Eagly, A. H., & Johannesen-Schmidt, M. C. (2001). The Leadership Styles of Women and Men. *The Journal of Social Issues, 57*(4), 781–797. DOI: 10.1111/0022-4537.00241

Economou, C. Kaitelidou, D., Kentikelenis, A., Maresso, A., & Aris Sissouras. (2015). *The impact of the crisis on the health system and health in Greece.* Nih.gov; European Observatory on Health Systems and Policies. https://www.ncbi.nlm.nih.gov/books/NBK447857/

Edmondson, A. (1999). Psychological Safety and Learning Behavior in Work Teams. *Administrative Science Quarterly, 44*(2), 350–383. DOI: 10.2307/2666999

El-Jardali, F., & Fadlallah, R. (2017). Approaches to quality improvement in healthcare. *International Journal for Quality in Health Care : Journal of the International Society for Quality in Health Care, 29*(7), 882–887.

Ellis, P. (2021). Leadership Approaches for Modern Nursing Practice. *British Journal of Cardiac Nursing, 16*(2), 1–5. DOI: 10.12968/bjca.2020.0091

Ellis, P. (2025). *Leadership, management and team working in nursing.* Learning Matters Limited.

Epstein, E., & Delgado, S. (2010, September 30). *Understanding and Addressing Moral Distress | OJIN: The Online Journal of Issues in Nursing.* Ojin.nursingworld.org. https://ojin.nursingworld.org/table-of-contents/volume-15-2010/number-3-september-2010/understanding-moral-distress/

Eva, N., Robin, M., Sendjaya, S., van Dierendonck, D., & Liden, R. C. (2019). Servant leadership: A systematic review and call for future research. *The Leadership Quarterly*, *30*(1), 111–132. DOI: 10.1016/j.leaqua.2018.07.004

FasterCapital. (2025). *Healthcare leadership: The power of leadership in transforming healthcare organizations*. Retrieved from https://www.fastercapital.com/content/Healthcare-leadership--The-Power-of-Leadership-in-Transforming-Healthcare-Organizations.html fastercapital.co.

Ferlie, E. B., & Shortell, S. M. (2001). Improving the Quality of Health Care in the United Kingdom and the United States: A Framework for Change. *The Milbank Quarterly*, *79*(2), 281–315. https://www.commonwealthfund.org/publications/journal-article/2002/feb/improving-quality-health-care-united-kingdom-and-united#:~:text=In%20%22Improving%20the%20Quality%20of%20Health%20Care%20in,improving%20quality%20in%20each%20nation%27s%20health%20care%20system PMID: 11439467

Ferlie, E., & Shortell, S. M. (2001). Improving the quality of healthcare in the United Kingdom and the United States: A framework for change. *The Milbank Quarterly*, *79*(2), 281–315. DOI: 10.1111/1468-0009.00206 PMID: 11439467

Fernandez, C. S. P., Noble, C. C., Jensen, E. T., & Chapin, J. (2016). Improving Leadership Skills in Physicians: A 6-Month Retrospective Study. *Journal of Leadership Studies*, *9*(4), 6–19. DOI: 10.1002/jls.21420

Fiedler, F. E. (1967). *A theory of leadership effectiveness*. Mcgraw-Hill.

Figueroa, C. A., Harrison, R., Chauhan, A., & Meyer, L. (2019). Priorities and challenges for health leadership and workforce management globally: A rapid review. *BMC Health Services Research*, *19*(1), 239. PMID: 31014349

Finzel, H. (2007). *The top ten mistakes leaders make*. Colorado Springs, Col. Cook.

Foronda, C., MacWilliams, B., & McArthur, E. (2016). Interprofessional communication in healthcare: An integrative review. *Nurse Education in Practice*, *19*(1), 36–40. DOI: 10.1016/j.nepr.2016.04.005 PMID: 27428690

Frandsen, F., & Johansen, W. (2010). Strategy, management, leadership, and public relations. The *SAGE handbook of public relations*, 293-306.

Frenk, J., Chen, L., & Bhutta, Z. A. (2010). Health Professionals for a New century: Transforming Education to Strengthen Health Systems in an Interdependent World. *Lancet*, *376*(9756), 1923–1958. PMID: 21112623

Frich, J. C., Brewster, A. L., Cherlin, E. J., & Bradley, E. H. (2015). Leadership development programs for physicians: A systematic review. *Journal of General Internal Medicine*, *30*(5), 656–674. PMID: 25527339

Frumence, G., Nyamhanga, T., & Anaeli, A. (2017). Facilitators and barriers to health care access among the elderly in Tanzania: A health system perspective from managers and service providers. *Journal of Ageing Research and Healthcare*, *2*(1), 20–31. DOI: 10.14302/issn.2474-7785.jarh-16-1354

Fullan, M. (2016). *The New Meaning of Educational Change* (4th ed.). Teachers College Press.

Gabel Shemueli, R., Tzafrir, S., Rodriguez Perez, B., Bahamonde, D., & Enosh, G. (2022). Collective compass to unit performance: Linking transformational leadership climate, trust and engagement. *Leadership and Organization Development Journal*, *43*(5), 802–813.

Garman, A. N., Tyler, J. L., & Darnall, J. S. (2004). Development and validation of a 360-degree-feedback instrument for healthcare administrators. *Journal of Healthcare Management / American College of Healthcare Executives, 49*(5), 307–321; discussion 321-2. https://pubmed.ncbi.nlm.nih.gov/15499805/

Garman, A. N., & Johnson, M. P. (2006). Leadership Competencies: An Introduction. *Journal of Healthcare Management*, *51*(1), 13. https://journals.lww.com/jhmonline/Citation/2006/01000/Leadership_Competencies__An_Introduction.4.aspx PMID: 16479746

Garman, A. N., & Johnson, M. P. (2006). Leadership competencies: An introduction. *Journal of Healthcare Management*, *51*(1), 13–17. PMID: 16479746

Garrido, T., Jamieson, L., Zhou, Y., Wiesenthal, A., & Liang, L. (2005). Effect of electronic health records in ambulatory care: Retrospective, serial, cross sectional study. *BMJ (Clinical Research Ed.)*, *330*(7491), 581. PMID: 15760999

Geerts, J. M. (2018). *Optimal leadership development for professionals* (Doctoral dissertation).

Giallonardo, L. M., Wong, C. A., & Iwasiw, C. L. (2010). Authentic leadership of preceptors: Predictor of new graduate nurses' work engagement and job satisfaction. *Journal of Nursing Management*, *18*(8), 993–1003. DOI: 10.1111/j.1365-2834.2010.01126.x PMID: 21073571

Gifford, R., van de Baan, F., Westra, D., Ruwaard, D., & Fleuren, B. (2023). Through the looking glass: Confronting health care management's biggest challenges in the wake of a crisis. *Health Care Management Review*, *48*(2), 185–196. PMID: 36792956

Gilmartin, M. J., & D'Aunno, T. A. (2007). Leadership Research in Healthcare. *The Academy of Management Annals, 1*(1), 387–438. DOI: 10.5465/078559813

Gini, A. (1997). Moral leadership and business ethics. *The Journal of Leadership Studies, 4*(4), 64–81.

Gini, A. (2020). Moral Leadership and Business Ethics. *Journal of Leadership Studies, 4*(4), 64–81. DOI: 10.1177/107179199700400406

Goleman, D., Boyatzis, R., & McKee, A. (2013). *Primal Leadership: Unleashing the Power of Emotional Intelligence*. Harvard Business Press.

Golinelli, D., Boetto, E., Carullo, G., Nuzzolese, A. G., Landini, M. P., & Fantini, M. P. (2020). How the COVID-19 pandemic favored the adoption of digital technologies in healthcare: A systematic review of early scientific literature (Preprint). *Journal of Medical Internet Research, 22*(11). https://www.ncbi.nlm.nih.gov/pmc/articles/PMC7652596/ PMID: 33079693

Gopee, N., & Galloway, J. (2017). *Leadership and Management in Healthcare* (3rd ed.). Sage. (Original work published 2008)

Gosbee, J. (2002). Human factors engineering and patient safety. *Quality & Safety in Health Care, 11*(4), 352–354. PMID: 12468696

Green, J. P. (2020). *A taxonomy of leadership situations: Development, validation, and implications for the science and practice of leadership* (Doctoral dissertation, George Mason University).

Greenhalgh, T., Robert, G., Macfarlane, F., Bate, P., & Kyriakidou, O. (2004). Diffusion of Innovations in Service Organizations: Systematic Review and Recommendations. *The Milbank Quarterly, 82*(4), 581–629. DOI: 10.1111/j.0887-378x.2004.00325.x PMID: 15595944

Greenleaf, R. K. (1970). *The Servant as Leader*. Greenleaf Center for Servant Leadership.

Greenleaf, R. K. (1977). *Servant leadership: A Journey into the Nature of Legitimate Power and Greatness*. Paulist Press.

Griffith, A. (2023). The creativity lab: Interdisciplinary creativity in higher education. *Journal of Interdisciplinary Studies in Education, 12*(1), 85–108.

Guglielmin, M., Shankardass, K., Bayoumi, A., O'Campo, P., Kokkinen, L., & Muntaner, C. (2022). A Realist Explanatory Case Study Investigating How Common Goals, Leadership, and Committed Staff Facilitate Health in All Policies Implementation in the Municipality of Kuopio, Finland. *International Journal of Health Policy and Management*. Advance online publication. DOI: 10.34172/ijhpm.2022.6355 PMID: 35247936

Gulf News. (2025, January 27). *American Hospital Dubai unveils future health at Arab Health 2025*. Gulf News: Latest UAE News, Dubai News, Business, Travel News, Dubai Gold Rate, Prayer Time, Cinema. https://gulfnews.com/gn-focus/american-hospital-dubai-unveils-future-health-at-arab-health-2025-1.500023515

Guo, W. (2023). Exploring the value of AI technology in optimizing and implementing supply chain data for pharmaceutical companies. *Innovation in Science and Technology*, *2*(3), 1–6.

Gupta, V., & Singh, S. (2014). Psychological capital as a mediator of the relationship between leadership and creative performance behaviors: Empirical evidence from the Indian R&D sector. *International Journal of Human Resource Management*, *25*(10), 1373–1394.

Hair, J. F.Jr, Black, W. C., Babin, B. J., & Anderson, R. E. (2009). *Multivariate Data Analysis* (7th ed.). Prentice Hall.

Halili, E. (2022). *The gender gap in technical maritime industry leadership in Lithuania: why women are not progressing as fast in leadership positions as men in this industry* (Doctoral dissertation, LCC tarptautinis universitetas).

Hammer, M., & Champy, J. (1993). *Reengineering the Corporation: A Manifesto for Business Revolution*. Collins Business Essentials.

Hantula, D. A. (2018). Job satisfaction: The management tool and leadership responsibility. In *Leadership and Cultural Change* (pp. 123–136). Routledge.

Hargadon, A. B., & Bechky, B. A. (2006). When collections of creatives become creative collectives: A field study of problem solving at work. *Organization Science*, *17*(4), 484–500.

Hargett, C., Doty, J., Hauck, J., Webb, A., Cook, S., Tsipis, N., Neumann, J., Andolsek, K., & Taylor, D. (2017). Developing a Model for Effective Leadership in healthcare: A Concept Mapping Approach. *Journal of Healthcare Leadership*, *9*(9), 69–78. DOI: 10.2147/JHL.S141664 PMID: 29355249

Hartley, J., & Benington, J. (2010). *Leadership for healthcare*. Policy Press.

Hasan, A. A., Ahmad, S. Z., & Osman, A. (2023). Transformational leadership and work engagement as mediators on nurses' job performance in healthcare clinics: Work environment as a moderator. *Leadership in Health Services*, *36*(4), 537–561. PMID: 37093237

Hashimy, S., Jahromi, A., Hamza, M., Naaz, I., & Nyamwero, N., Sayed, & Hashimy, Q. (2023). Nurturing Leadership and Capacity Building for Success: Empowering Growth International Journal of Rehabilitation and Special Education. *International Journal of Rehabilitation and Special Education*, *3*(3). Advance online publication. DOI: 10.48165/ijrse.2023.3.2.5

Health Metric Network. (2023) *Assessing the National Health Information System An Assessment Tool*. Iris.who.int. Retrieved May 13, 2025, from https://iris.who.int/bitstream/handle/10665/43932/9789241547512_eng.pdf?sequence=1

Heifetz, R., & Linsky, M. (2002, June). *A survival guide for leaders*. Harvard Business Review. https://hbr.org/2002/06/a-survival-guide-for-leaders

Heifetz, R. A., & Linsky, M. (2002). *Leadership on the line: Staying alive through the dangers of change*. Harvard Business Review Press.

Heinen, M., van Oostveen, C., Peters, J., Vermeulen, H., & Huis, A. (2019). An integrative review of leadership competencies and attributes in advanced nursing practice. *Journal of Advanced Nursing*, *75*(11), 2378–2392. PMID: 31162695

Helbling, N. (2023). *Rural Healthcare Finance: An Examination of Challenges and Opportunities* (Master's thesis, The College of St. Scholastica).

Hillson, D. (2003). *Effective Opportunity Management for Projects*. CRC Press., DOI: 10.1201/9780203913246

Hipp, F. (2023). *The Effect of a Leadership Development Program on Healthcare Leaders* (Doctoral dissertation, The University of North Carolina at Charlotte).

Hirst, G., Van Knippenberg, D., Chen, C. H., & Sacramento, C. A. (2018). How does bureaucracy impact individual creativity? A cross-level investigation of team contextual influences on goal orientation–creativity relationships. *Academy of Management Journal*, *54*(3), 624–641. https://www.jstor.org/stable/23045099

Hoffmeister, K., Gibbons, A., Schwatka, N., & Rosecrance, J. (2015). Ergonomics Climate Assessment: A measure of operational performance and employee well-being. *Applied Ergonomics*, *50*(1), 160–169. DOI: 10.1016/j.apergo.2015.03.011 PMID: 25959331

Hofstede, G. (1984). *Culture's consequences: International Differences in Work-related Values.* Sage Publications.

Hofstede, G. (2001). *Culture's Consequences: Comparing values, behaviors, institutions, and Organizations across Nations* (2nd ed.). Sage.

House, R. J. (1976, October). *A 1976 Theory of Charismatic Leadership. Working Paper Series 76-06.* Ed.gov. https://eric.ed.gov/?id=ED133827

Hsieh, C.-C., Huang, H.-P., & Tung, T.-H., Chen, I-Chien., Beaton, R. D., & Jane, S.-W. (2019). The exploration of the knowledge, attitudes and practice behaviors of advanced care planning and its related predictors among Taiwanese nurses. *BMC Palliative Care, 18*(1). Advance online publication. DOI: 10.1186/s12904-019-0483-9 PMID: 31711482

Hutchinson, M., & Jackson, D. (2013). Transformational Leadership in nursing: Towards a More Critical Interpretation. *Nursing Inquiry, 20*(1), 11–22. PMID: 23033817

Institute of Medicine. (2001). *Crossing the Quality Chasm: A New Health System for the 21st Century.* PubMed. https://pubmed.ncbi.nlm.nih.gov/25057539/

International Hospital Federation. (2023). *Competencies for future-focused leadership Global Healthcare Leadership Competency Model 2023.* https://ihf-fih.org/wp-content/uploads/2023/06/IHF-Global-Healthcare-Leadership-Competency-Model-2023.pdf

Intuitive Surgical. (2020). *Da Vinci surgical system: Clinical evidence and outcomes.* Intuitive. https://www.intuitive.com/en-us/about-us/company/clinical-evidence

Ireland, R. D., & Hitt, M. A. (1999). Achieving and Maintaining Strategic Competitiveness in the 21st Century: The Role of Strategic Leadership. *The Academy of Management Perspectives, 13*(1), 43–57.

Ismayilova, K., & Bolander Laksov, K. (2023). Teaching creatively in higher education: The roles of personal attributes and environment. *Scandinavian Journal of Educational Research, 67*(4), 536–548.

Issa, W. B., & Shorbagi, A., Alham Al-Sharman, Rababa, M., Khalid Al-Majeed, Radwan, H., Ahmed, F. R., Nabeel Al-Yateem, Mottershead, R., Abdelrahim, D. N., Hijazi, H., Wafa Khasawneh, Ali, I., Abbas, N., & Fakhry, R. (2024). Shaping the future: perspectives on the Integration of Artificial Intelligence in health profession education: a multi-country survey. *BMC Medical Education, 24*(1). Advance online publication. DOI: 10.1186/s12909-024-06076-9 PMID: 39425151

Iwuoha, V. C., Aniche, E. T., Obiora, C. A., & Umeifekwem, U. T. (2021). Citizens lack access to healthcare facilities: How COVID-19 lockdown and social distancing policies boost roadside chemist businesses in South-Eastern Nigeria. *The International Journal of Health Planning and Management*, *36*(6), 2411–2423. DOI: 10.1002/hpm.3316 PMID: 34476845

Izadi, A., Jahani, Y., Rafiei, S., Masoud, A., & Vali, L. (2017). Evaluating health service quality: Using importance performance analysis. *International Journal of Health Care Quality Assurance*, *30*(7), 656–663. DOI: 10.1108/ijhcqa-02-2017-0030 PMID: 28809594

Javidan, M. Dorfman, P. W., Howell, J. P., & Hanges, P. (2010). Leadership and cultural context: A theoretical and empirical examination based on Project GLOBE. *ResearchGate*, 335–376. https://www.researchgate.net/publication/288927197_Leadership_and_cultural_context_A_theoretical_and_empirical_examination_ba

Javidan, M., Dorfman, P. W., Howell, J. P., & Hanges, P. J. (2010). Leadership and cultural context. *Handbook of leadership theory and practice*, 346-372.

Johns Hopkins Aramco Healthcare. (2025). *Dr. Mariam Matar Bio*. Jhah.com. https://www.jhah.com/en/bios/dr-mariam-matar-bio

Joshi, A., Kale, S., Chandel, S., & Pal, D. K. (2015). *Likert scale: Explored and explained*. ResearchGate. https://www.researchgate.net/publication/276394797_Likert_Scale_Explored_and_Explained

Junaid, M., Zhang, Q., Cao, M., & Luqman, A. (2023). Nexus between technology enabled supply chain dynamic capabilities, integration, resilience, and sustainable performance: An empirical examination of healthcare organizations. *Technological Forecasting and Social Change*, *196*, 122828.

Kahn, L. H. (2020). *Who's in Charge?: Leadership During Epidemics, Bioterror Attacks, and Other Public Health Crises*. Bloomsbury Publishing USA.

Kakemam, E., Albelbeisi, A. H., Rouzbahani, M., Gharakhani, M., Zahedi, H., & Taheri, R. (2024). Nurses' perceptions of patient safety competency: a cross-sectional study of relationships with occurrence and reporting of adverse events. Plos one, 19(1), e0297185.

Kakemam, E., Ahmed Hassan Albelbeisi, Mahtab Rouzbahani, Mehdi Gharakhani, Zahedi, H., & Taheri, R. (2024). Nurses' perceptions of patient safety competency: A cross-sectional study of relationships with occurrence and reporting of adverse events. *PLoS One*, *19*(1), e0297185–e0297185. DOI: 10.1371/journal.pone.0297185 PMID: 38271447

Kakemam, E., Liang, Z., Janati, A., Arab-Zozani, M., Mohaghegh, B., & Gholizadeh, M. (2020). Leadership and Management Competencies for Hospital Managers: A Systematic Review and Best-Fit Framework Synthesis. *Journal of Healthcare Leadership*, *12*(2), 59–68. DOI: 10.2147/jhl.s265825 PMID: 32801985

Kakemam, E., Liang, Z., Janati, A., Arab-Zozani, M., Mohaghegh, B., & Gholizadeh, M. (2020). Leadership and management competencies for hospital managers: A systematic review and best-fit framework synthesis. *Journal of Healthcare Leadership*, 59–68. PMID: 32801985

Kalaitzi, S., Cheung, K. L., Hiligsmann, M., Babich, S., & Czabanowska, K. (2019). Exploring women healthcare leaders' perceptions on barriers to leadership in Greek context. *Frontiers in Public Health*, *7*, 68. PMID: 31024874

Kalaitzi, S., Czabanowska, K., Azzopardi-Muscat, N., Cuschieri, L., Petelos, E., Papadakaki, M., & Babich, S. (2019). Women, healthcare leadership and societal culture: A qualitative study. *Journal of Healthcare Leadership*, *11*, 43–59. DOI: 10.2147/jhl.s194733 PMID: 31043802

Kaplan, R. S., & Norton, D. P. (2004). *Strategy Maps: Converting Intangible Assets into Tangible Outcomes*. Harvard Business School Press.

Kaplan, R. S., & Porter, M. E. (2011). How to solve the cost crisis in health care. *Harvard Business Review*, *89*(9), 46–52, 54, 56–61 passim. https://pubmed.ncbi.nlm.nih.gov/21939127/ PMID: 21939127

Karmysov, S. (2023). LEADERSHIP FOR EVERYONE: EMPOWERING LEADING FEMALES. In *EDULEARN23 Proceedings* (pp. 6593-6599). IATED.

Karneli, O. (2023). The role of adhocratic leadership in facing the changing business environment. [ADMAN]. *Journal of Contemporary Administration and Management*, *1*(2), 77–83.

Karsh, W. T. B., Lapin, J. A., Karsh, B. T., & Beasley, J. W. (2012). Human factors and ergonomics in primary care. *Handbook of Human Factors and Ergonomics in Health Care and Patient Safety. Boca Raton, FL: Taylor and& Francis Group*, 763-74.

Kellerman, B. (2012). *The end of leadership*. Harper Business.

Kellermann, A. L., & Jones, S. S. (2013). *What It Will Take to Achieve the As-Yet-Unfulfilled Promises of Health Information Technology*. Rand.org; Project HOPE. https://www.rand.org/pubs/external_publications/EP51265.html

Kelly, L. (2023). The contextual dynamics of mindfulness for authentic leadership: industry and work influences. In *Mindfulness for Authentic Leadership: Theory and Cases* (pp. 193–214). Springer International Publishing.

Keshtiban, A. E., Callahan, J. L., & Harris, M. (2023). Leaderlessness in social movements: Advancing space, symbols, and spectacle as modes of "Leadership". *Human Resource Development Quarterly, 34*(1), 19–43.

Khaled, S. M. (2020). STRATEGIC LEADERSHIP THROUGH CRISIS. *Ndc E-Journal, 1*(1), 1–16.

Khalifa, D. (2023). *AN EXAMINATION OF THE INTEGRATION OF SUSTAINABLE DEVELOPMENT PRINCIPLES IN GOVERNMENTAL PROJECT MANAGEMENT IN THE GOVERNMENT OF THE KINGDOM OF BAHRAIN*. PEARL. https://pearl.plymouth.ac.uk/pbs-theses/2/

Khalili, A. (2017). Creative and innovative leadership: Measurement development and validation. *Management Research Review, 40*(10), 1117–1138.

Khan, S., Vandermorris, A., Shepherd, J., Begun, J. W., Lanham, H. J., Uhl-Bien, M., & Berta, W. (2018). Embracing uncertainty, managing complexity: Applying complexity thinking principles to transformation efforts in healthcare systems. *BMC Health Services Research, 18*(1). Advance online publication. DOI: 10.1186/s12913-018-2994-0 PMID: 29562898

Khrais, H., & Nashwan, A. J. (2023). Leadership practices as perceived by emergency nurses during the COVID-19 pandemic: The role of structural and psychological empowerment. *Journal of Emergency Nursing: JEN, 49*(1), 140–147. PMID: 36369071

Khudyakov, A., Jean, C., Jankovic, M., Cardinal, J. S. L., & Bocquet, J. C. (2014). Simulation methods in the healthcare systems. In *Complex Systems Design & Management: Proceedings of the Fourth International Conference on Complex Systems Design & Management CSD&M 2013* (pp. 141-149). Cham: Springer International Publishing.

Kilic, B. E. (2023). Program development for leaders in the post-truth era: Arts-based creative leadership communication program. *Evaluation and Program Planning, 98*, 102295. PMID: 37148650

Kim, J. S. (2008). Examining the effectiveness of solution-focused brief therapy: A meta-analysis. *Research on Social Work Practice, 18*(2), 107–116. DOI: 10.1177/1049731507307807

Kim, J. Y., Farmer, P., & Porter, M. E. (2017). Redefining global healthcare delivery. *Lancet*, *382*(9897), 1060–1069. DOI: 10.1016/s0140-6736(13)61047-8 PMID: 23697823

King's Fund. (2021). "Developing leadership in healthcare: Evidence-based approaches." King's Fund Reports. https://www.kingsfund.org.uk/insight-and-analysis/reports/leadership-development-health-care

Kotter, J. (1995). *Leading change: Why transformation efforts fail*. Harvard Business Review. https://hbr.org/1995/05/leading-change-why-transformation-efforts-fail-2

Kotter, J. P. (1988). *The leadership factor*. Free Press.

Kotter, J. P. (1996). *Leading Change*. Harvard Business School Press.

Kotter, J. P. (1996). Leading change. In *Internet Archive*. Harvard Business School Press., https://archive.org/details/leadingchange0000kott

Kouzes, J. M., & Posner, B. Z. (2023). *The Leadership Challenge* (4th ed.). Jossey-Bass.

Kraus, S., Niemand, T., Besler, M., Stieg, P., & Martinez-Ciment, C. (2018). The influence of leadership styles on the internationalisation of'born-global'firms and traditionally global-expanding firms. *European Journal of International Management*, *12*(5-6), 554–575.

Kruk, M. E., Gage, A. D., Arsenault, C., Jordan, K., Leslie, H. H., Roder-DeWan, S., Adeyi, O., Barker, P., Daelmans, B., Doubova, S. V., English, M., Elorrio, E. G., Guanais, F., Gureje, O., Hirschhorn, L. R., Jiang, L., Kelley, E., Lemango, E. T., Liljestrand, J., & Malata, A. (2018). High-quality health systems in the Sustainable Development Goals era: Time for a revolution. *The Lancet. Global Health*, *6*(11), e1196–e1252. https://www.thelancet.com/journals/langlo/article/PIIS2214-109X(18)30386-3/fulltext PMID: 30196093

Kruse, C. S., Krowski, N., Rodriguez, B., Tran, L., Vela, J., & Brooks, M. (2018). Telehealth and patient satisfaction: A systematic review and narrative analysis. *BMJ Open*, *7*(8), e016242. DOI: 10.1136/bmjopen-2017-016242 PMID: 28775188

Kumar, R. D., & Khiljee, N. (2016). Leadership in healthcare. *Anaesthesia and Intensive Care Medicine*, *17*(1), 63–65.

Kutney-Lee, A., Lake, E. T., & Aiken, L. H. (2009). Development of the hospital nurse surveillance capacity profile. *Research in Nursing & Health*, *32*(2), 217–228. DOI: 10.1002/nur.20316 PMID: 19161172

Kutney-Lee, A., McHugh, M. D., Sloane, D. M., Cimiotti, J. P., Flynn, L., Neff, D. F., & Aiken, L. H. (2009). Nursing: A Key To Patient Satisfaction. *Health Affairs, 28*(Supplement 3), w669–w677. DOI: 10.1377/hlthaff.28.4.w669 PMID: 19525287

Kuwait Times. (2024). *Concrete action needed to prevent mental health risks at work: Doctor | Kuwait Times Newspaper*. Kuwait Times. https://kuwaittimes.com/article/19929/kuwait/other-news/concrete-action-needed-to-prevent-mental-health-risks-at-work-doctor/

Kwamie, A., Dijk, H. V., & Agyepong, I. A. (2014). Advancing the application of systems thinking in health: Realist evaluation of the Leadership Development Programme for district manager decision-making in Ghana. *Health Research Policy and Systems, 12*(1), 29. PMID: 24935521

Labrague, L. J. (2024). Relationship between transformational leadership, adverse patient events, and nurse-assessed quality of care in emergency units: The mediating role of work satisfaction. *Australasian Emergency Care (Online), 27*(1), 49–56. DOI: 10.1016/j.auec.2023.08.001 PMID: 37598031

Lantz, P. M. (2008). Gender and leadership in healthcare administration: 21st century progress and challenges. *Journal of Healthcare Management, 53*(5). PMID: 18856135

Lappalainen, P. (2020). Walking and talking sensors: Conceptualising restorative leadership to enhance people management education in engineering. *European Journal of Engineering Education, 45*(3), 473–490.

Lasrado, F., & Kassem, R. (2021). Let's get everyone involved! The effects of transformational leadership and organizational culture on organizational excellence. *International Journal of Quality & Reliability Management, 38*(1), 169–194.

LaVeist, T. A., & Pierre, G. (2014). Integrating the 3Ds—Social Determinants, Health Disparities, and Health-Care Workforce Diversity. *Public Health Reports, 129*(1, suppl2), 9–14. DOI: 10.1177/00333549141291s204 PMID: 24385659

Layne, D., Nemeth, L., Mueller, M., & Martin, M. (2019). Negative Behaviors among Healthcare Professionals: Relationship with Patient Safety Culture. *Health Care, 7*(1), 23. DOI: 10.3390/healthcare7010023 PMID: 30717313

Lee, T. H., Volpp, K. G., Cheung, V. G., & Dzau, V. J. (2021). Diversity and inclusiveness in health care leadership: Three key steps. *NEJM Catalyst Innovations in Care Delivery, 2*(3).

Leonard, K. L., & Masatu, M. C. (2005). The use of direct clinician observation and vignettes for health services quality evaluation in developing countries. *Social Science & Medicine, 61*(9), 1944–1951. DOI: 10.1016/j.socscimed.2005.03.043 PMID: 15936863

Leonard, M., Graham, S., & Bonacum, D. (2004). The human factor: The critical importance of effective teamwork and communication in providing safe care. *BMJ Quality & Safety, 13*(suppl 1), i85–i90. PMID: 15465961

Like, R. C. (2011). Educating Clinicians About Cultural Competence and Disparities in Health and Health Care. *The Journal of Continuing Education in the Health Professions, 31*(3), 196–206. DOI: 10.1002/chp.20127 PMID: 21953661

Liker, J. K. (2004). *The Toyota Way: 14 Management Principles from the World's Greatest Manufacturer*. McGraw-Hill.

Lipman-Blumen, J. (2005). Toxic leadership: When grand illusions masquerade as noble visions. *Leader to Leader, 2005*(36), 29–36. DOI: 10.1002/ltl.125

Lisá, E., Sousa, J., Morais, C., & Gomes, A. R. (2023). Leadership cycles, styles, and antecedent factors: The perspective of coaches and young soccer athletes from national Slovak leagues. *Frontiers in Psychology, 14*, 1218290. PMID: 37609500

Lobdell, J. (2019) Leadership—A new view. *The Actuary Magazine*. https://www.theactuarymagazine.org/wp-content/uploads/2019/09/act-2019-vol16-iss5.pdf#page=34

Lobdell, K. W., Hariharan, S., Smith, W., Rose, G. A., Ferguson, B., & Fussell, C. (2020). Improving health care leadership in the COVID-19 era. *NEJM Catalyst Innovations in Care Delivery, 1*(3).

Locke, E., & Latham, G. (2002). *Building a practically useful theory of goal setting and task motivation: A 35-year odyssey*. Psycnet.apa.org. https://psycnet.apa.org/record/2002-15790-003

Loureiro, R., Ferreira, J. J., & Simões, J. (2021). Understanding healthcare sector organizations from a dynamic capabilities perspective. *European Journal of Innovation Management, ahead-of-print*(ahead-of-print). DOI: 10.1108/ejim-02-2021-0085

Lowe, M. E. (2025). *Breaking the Stained Glass Ceiling: Collaborative Leadership Theory as a Model for Women in Theological Higher Education*. DigitalCommons@University of Nebraska - Lincoln. https://digitalcommons.unl.edu/jwel/12/

Macintosh, T., Hernandez, M., & Mehta, A. S. (2022). Identifying, Addressing, and Eliminating Microaggressions in Healthcare. *HCA Healthcare Journal of Medicine*, *3*(3). Advance online publication. DOI: 10.36518/2689-0216.1418 PMID: 37424615

Mahsud, R., Yukl, G., & Prussia, G. (2010). Leader empathy, ethical leadership, and relations-oriented behaviors as antecedents of leader-member exchange quality. *Journal of Managerial Psychology*, *25*(6), 561–577.

Mainemelis, C., Kark, R., & Epitropaki, O. (2015). Creative leadership: A multi-context conceptualization. *The Academy of Management Annals*, *9*(1), 393–482.

Marcelin, J. R., Siraj, D. S., Victor, R., Kotadia, S., & Maldonado, Y. A. (2019). The Impact of Unconscious Bias in healthcare: How to Recognize and Mitigate It. *The Journal of Infectious Diseases*, *220*(2), 62–73. DOI: 10.1093/infdis/jiz214 PMID: 31430386

Martinez, F. J., Han, M. K., Allinson, J. P., Barr, R. G., Boucher, R. C., Calverley, P. M. A., Celli, B. R., Christenson, S. A., Crystal, R. G., Fagerås, M., Freeman, C. M., Groenke, L., Hoffman, E. A., Kesimer, M., Kostikas, K., Paine, R., Rafii, S., Rennard, S. I., Segal, L. N., & Shaykhiev, R. (2018). At the Root: Defining and Halting Progression of Early Chronic Obstructive Pulmonary Disease. *American Journal of Respiratory and Critical Care Medicine*, *197*(12), 1540–1551. DOI: 10.1164/rccm.201710-2028pp PMID: 29406779

Martin, G. P., Currie, G., & Finn, R. (2009). Leadership, service reform, and public-service networks: The case of cancer-genetics pilots in the English NHS. *Journal of Public Administration: Research and Theory*, *19*(4), 769–794.

Mass General Brigham. (2019, December 12). *Partners HealthCare launches digital health initiative*. Mass General Brigham Newsroom. Retrieved August 6, 2025, from https://www.massgeneralbrigham.org/en/about/newsroom/press-releases/partners-healthcare-launches-digital-health-initiative en.wikipedia.org+15massgeneral-brigham.org+15massgeneralbrigham.org+

Massaro, M. (2023). Digital transformation in the healthcare sector through blockchain technology. Insights from academic research and business developments. *Technovation*, *120*, 102386.

Mayo Clinic. (n.d.). *Artificial intelligence (AI) in cardiovascular medicine overview*. Mayo Clinic. Retrieved August 6, 2025, from https://www.mayoclinic.org/departments-centers/ai-cardiology/overview/ovc-20486648mayoclinic.org+2news-network.mayoclinic.org+2

McAlearney, A. S. (2006). Leadership development in healthcare: A qualitative study. *Journal of Organizational Behavior*, *27*(7), 967–982. DOI: 10.1002/job.417

Mcnabb, D. E. (2016). *Research methods for political science: quantitative and qualitative approaches*. Routledge, Taylor Et Francis Group.

Mekonnin, L. (2014). *Females Participation in Educational Leadership in Secondary Schools of Ilu Aba Bora Zone* (Doctoral dissertation, The Institute of Development Studies and Partner Organisations).

Mhlanga, D. (2023). Digital transformation in the healthcare sector: The role of artificial intelligence for inclusive long-term care around the world, lessons for Africa. In *Economic inclusion in post-independence africa: An inclusive approach to economic development* (pp. 347–362). Springer Nature Switzerland.

Miller, K. A., Nagler, J., Wolff, M., Schumacher, D. J., & Pusic, M. V. (2023). It takes a village: Optimal graduate medical education requires a deliberately developmental organization. *Perspectives on Medical Education*, *12*(1), 282. PMID: 37520509

Mittal, E. V., & Sindhu, E. (2012). Emotional intelligence and leadership. *Global Journal of Management and Business Research*, *12*(16), 35–37.

Mohammed, N. (2014). Theories of Leadership: A Comprehensive Review. *Journal of Management*, *28*(2), 57–78.

Moore, G. F., Audrey, S., Barker, M., Bond, L., Bonell, C., Hardeman, W., Moore, L., O'Cathain, A., Tinati, T., Wight, D., & Baird, J. (2015). Process evaluation of complex interventions: Medical Research Council guidance. *BMJ (Clinical Research Ed.)*, *350*(350), h1258–h1258. DOI: 10.1136/bmj.h1258 PMID: 25791983

Moradi-Moghadam, M., Safari, H., Moghadam, M. R. S., & Fathi, M. R. (2023). Re-creation fundamental concepts on the culture of excellence to achieve maturity of organisational excellence. *International Journal of Business Excellence*, *30*(2), 234–256.

Moran, J. W., & Brightman, B. K. (2000). Leading organizational change. *Journal of Workplace Learning*, *12*(2), 66–74. DOI: 10.1108/13665620010316226

Morrison, K., Hughes, T., & Doi, L. (2022). Understanding the use of telehealth in the context of the Family Nurse Partnership and other early years home visiting programmes: A rapid review. *Digital Health*, *8*, 20552076221123711. PMID: 36406154

Mount Sinai Health System. (2020, May 19). *Mount Sinai first in U.S. to use artificial intelligence to analyze COVID-19 patients*. Mount Sinai Newsroom. Retrieved August 6, 2025, from https://www.mountsinai.org/about/newsroom/2020/mount-sinai-first-in-us-to-use-artificial-intelligence-to-analyze-coronavirus-covid19-patients-pr mountsinai.org+9mountsinai.org+9mountsinai.org+9)

Muhammad Ahmed Al-Maliki, Y. (2020). The reality of activating work teams in public schools within the Al-Dayer Education Office from the perspective of school leadership. *Journal of Faculty of Education-Assiut University*, *36*(4), 465–495.

Mumford, M. D., & Licuanan, B. (2004). Leading for innovation: Conclusions, issues, and directions. *The Leadership Quarterly*, *15*(1), 163–171. DOI: 10.1016/j.leaqua.2003.12.010

Mumford, M. D., & Todd, E. M. (2019). Creativity and innovation at work. In *Creativity and innovation in organizations* (pp. 1–16). Routledge.

Murray, T. A., Benz, M. R., Cole, B., Jackson, J., Llamas, D., Marquard, S., & Taylor, C. L. (2023). The journey toward inclusive excellence. *The Journal of Nursing Education*, *62*(4), 225–232. PMID: 37021946

Mutale, W., Mwanamwenge, M. T., Balabanova, D., Spicer, N., & Ayles, H. (2013). Measuring governance at health facility level: Developing and validation of simple governance tool in Zambia. *BMC International Health and Human Rights*, *13*(1). Advance online publication. DOI: 10.1186/1472-698x-13-34 PMID: 23927531

Mutonyi, B. R., González-Piñero, M., Slåtten, T., & Lien, G. (2024). Driving innovation in health care: Exploring the impact of ambidextrous leadership on creative performance among frontline health professionals in Norway. *BMC Health Services Research*, *24*(1), 268. DOI: 10.1186/s12913-024-10641-9 PMID: 38431584

Nanjundeswaraswamy, T. S., & Swamy, D. R. (2014). Leadership styles. *Advances in management,* 7(2), 57.

Newman, N., & Newman, D. (2021). Leadership behind masked faces: From uncertainty to resilience at a Jamaican academic library. *Journal of Academic Librarianship*, *47*(5), 102377.

Ng'ambi, D., & Bozalek, V. (2013). Editorial: Emerging technologies and changing learning/teaching practices. *British Journal of Educational Technology*, *44*(4), 531–535. DOI: 10.1111/bjet.12061

Ni ă, M. A. (2015). The new intelligence, the new leader and the organizational stress. *Revista de Management Comparat Interna ional*, *16*(3), 335–342.

Nivet, M. A., & Fair, M. (2016). Defining diversity in quality care. In *Diversity and inclusion in quality patient care* (pp. 3–9). Springer International Publishing.

Northouse, P. G. (2018). *Leadership: Theory and Practice* (8th ed.). Sage Publications.

Nzinga, J., McGivern, G., & English, M. (2018). Examining clinical leadership in Kenyan public hospitals through the distributed leadership lens. *Health Policy and Planning*, *33*(suppl_2), ii27–ii34. PMID: 30053035

O'Connor, S. (2014). Leadership for future libraries. *Library Management*, *35*(1/2), 78–87. https://www.emerald.com/lm/article/35/1-2/78/267697/Leadership-for-future-libraries

Omar, N. (2018). Influence of strategic leadership on performance of manufacturing companies in Kenya: A case study of Zenko Kenya Limited. *Core.ac.uk*. oai:repository.mua.ac.ke:2631

Onwujekwe, O., Ezumah, N., Mbachu, C., Obi, F., Ichoku, H., Uzochukwu, B., & Wang, H. (2019). Exploring effectiveness of different health financing mechanisms in Nigeria; what needs to change and how can it happen? *BMC Health Services Research*, *19*(1). Advance online publication. DOI: 10.1186/s12913-019-4512-4 PMID: 31519181

Osmani, S. S. N. (2013). Effective leadership – The way to excellence in health professions education. *Medical Teacher*, *35*(11), 956–958. DOI: 10.3109/0142159x.2013.818629 PMID: 23924363

Ospina, S. M. (2017). Collective leadership and context in public administration: Bridging public leadership research and leadership studies. *Public Administration Review*, *77*(2), 275–287.

Oti-Boadi, M., Oppong Asante, K., & Malm, E. K. (2019). The Experiences of Ageing Parents of Young Adults with Autism Spectrum Disorders (ASD). *Journal of Adult Development*. Advance online publication. DOI: 10.1007/s10804-018-09325-6

Padilla, A., Hogan, R., & Kaiser, R. B. (2007). The Toxic triangle: Destructive leaders, Susceptible followers, and Conducive Environments. *The Leadership Quarterly*, *18*(3), 176–194. DOI: 10.1016/j.leaqua.2007.03.001

Palmer, B., Walls, M., Burgess, Z., & Stough, C. (2001). Emotional intelligence and effective leadership. *Leadership and Organization Development Journal*, *22*(1), 5–10.

Pandey, P., & Pandey, M. M. (2021). *Research Methodology Tools and Techniques*. Bridge Center.

Paulson, M. R., Torres-Guzman, R. A., Avila, F. R., Maita, K. C., Forte, A. J., Butera, J. E., & Maniaci, M. J. (2022). Telemedicine allows for effective communication between a medically complex cancer patient and his virtual hospital medical team. *Clinical Case Reports*, *10*(10), e6456. PMID: 36245470

Perez, J. (2021). Leadership in healthcare: Transitioning from clinical professional to healthcare leader. *Journal of Healthcare Management*, *66*(4), 280–302. PMID: 33929398

Persad, G., & Joffe, S. (2021). Allocating scarce life-saving resources: The proper role of age. *Journal of Medical Ethics*, *47*(12), 836–838. PMID: 33753473

Piotrowski, C. C. (2020, January 1). *Chapter 15 - ACEs and trauma-informed care* (G. J. G. Asmundson & T. O. Afifi, Eds.). ScienceDirect; Academic Press. https://www.sciencedirect.com/science/article/abs/pii/B978012816065700015X

Piotrowski, M. (2020). Relationship of self-directed learning and resilience in healthcare middle managers. *International Journal of Self-Directed Learning*, *17*(1), 19–38.

Plowman, D. A., Baker, L. T., Beck, T. E., Kulkarni, M., Solansky, S. T., & Travis, D. V. (2007). Radical Change Accidentally: The Emergence and Amplification of Small Change. *Academy of Management Journal*, *50*(3), 515–543. DOI: 10.5465/amj.2007.25525647

Poels, J., Verschueren, M., Milisen, K., & Vlaeyen, E. (2020). Leadership styles and leadership outcomes in nursing homes: A cross-sectional analysis. *BMC Health Services Research*, *20*(1), 1009. PMID: 33148249

Polden, D. J. (2019). Army leadership and the profession. *ADP*, *6*(22), i.

Porter, M., & Lee, T. (2013). *The strategy that will fix health care*. Harvard Business Review. https://hbr.org/2013/10/the-strategy-that-will-fix-health-care

Porter, M. E., & Teisberg, E. O. (2006). *Redefining health care: creating value-based competition on results*. Harvard Business School Press.

Price, L., MacDonald, J., Gozdzielewska, L., Howe, T., Flowers, P., Shepherd, L., Watt, Y., & Reilly, J. (2018). Interventions to improve healthcare workers' hand hygiene compliance: A systematic review of systematic reviews. *Infection Control and Hospital Epidemiology*, *39*(12), 1449–1456. DOI: 10.1017/ice.2018.262 PMID: 30526716

Prime HealthCare Group LLC. (2021). About Prime HealthCare Group. Retrieved August 6, 2025, from https://www.primehealth.ae/prime-healthcare-group/about-prime-group

Professional Leadership Coaching | Coaching with CT. (2023). *Healthcare leadership development programs*. https://www.coachingwithct.com

Pyzdek, T., & Keller, P. A. (2018). *The Six Sigma Handbook* (5th ed.). Mcgraw-Hill Education.

Quinn, R. E., & Spreitzer, G. M. (1997). The road to empowerment: Seven questions every leader should consider. *Organizational Dynamics*, *26*(2), 37–49. DOI: 10.1016/s0090-2616(97)90004-8

Qureshi, J. S., Young, S., Muyco, A. P., Borgstein, E., Charles, A. G., Mulwafu, W., & Mkandawire, N. (2013). Addressing Malawi's surgical workforce crisis: A sustainable paradigm for training and collaboration in Africa. *Surgery*, *153*(2), 272–281. PMID: 23063312

Raelin, J. A. (2005). We the Leaders: In Order to Form a Leaderful Organization. *Journal of Leadership & Organizational Studies*, *12*(2), 18–30. DOI: 10.1177/107179190501200202

Raghupathi, V., & Raghupathi, W. (2020). Healthcare Expenditure and Economic Performance: Insights from the United States Data. *Frontiers in Public Health*, *8*(156). NCBI. DOI: 10.3389/fpubh.2020.00156

Ranmuthugala, G., Plumb, J. J., Cunningham, F. C., Georgiou, A., Westbrook, J. I., & Braithwaite, J. (2011). How and Why Are Communities of Practice Established in the Healthcare sector? a Systematic Review of the Literature. *BMC Health Services Research*, *11*(1). Advance online publication. DOI: 10.1186/1472-6963-11-273 PMID: 21999305

Raza, M. H., Rind, Y. M., Javed, I., Zubair, M., Mehmood, M. Q., & Massoud, Y. (2023). Smart meters for smart energy: A review of business intelligence applications. *IEEE Access : Practical Innovations, Open Solutions*, *11*, 120001–120022.

Reason, J. T. (2016). *Managing the risks of organizational accidents*. Routledge Taylor & Francis Group.

Ree, E., Ellis, L. A., & Wiig, S. (2021). Managers' role in supporting resilience in healthcare: a proposed model of how managers contribute to a healthcare system's overall resilience. *International Journal of Health Governance*, *ahead-of-print*(ahead-of-print). DOI: 10.1108/ijhg-11-2020-0129

Rezaei, B., Mousavi, E., Heshmati, B., & Asadi, S. (2021). Low back pain and its related risk factors in health care providers at hospitals: A systematic review. *Annals of Medicine and Surgery (2012)*, *70*, 102903. DOI: 10.1016/j.amsu.2021.102903

Richards, A. (2020). Exploring the Benefits and Limitations of Transactional Leadership in Healthcare. *Nursing Standard, 35*(12), 46–50. https://insight.cumbria.ac.uk/id/eprint/5755/ PMID: 33089675

Richards, A. (2020). Exploring the benefits and limitations of transactional leadership in healthcare. *Nursing Standard, 35*(12), 46–50. PMID: 33089675

Rizzo, A., & Bouchard, S. (2019). *Virtual reality for psychological and neurocognitive interventions.* Springer.

Robbins, S. P. Judge, Timothy, A. (2023). *Organizational Behavior* (19th ed.). Pearson.

Robbins, B., & Davidhizar, R. (2020). Transformational leadership in health care today. *The Health Care Manager, 39*(3), 117–121. PMID: 32701607

Rogers, E. M. (2003). *Diffusion of Innovations* (5th ed.). Free Press., https://books.google.jo/books?id=9U1K5LjUOwEC&printsec=frontcover&redir_esc=y#v=onepage&q&f=false

Rost, J. C. (1991). *Leadership for the twenty-first century.* Praeger.

Royal College of Nursing. (2023). *RCN Clinical Leadership Programme.* Retrieved August 6, 2025, from https://www.rcn.org.uk/Professional-Development/Educational-programmes-and-services/Supporting-you-to-lead/Clinical-Leadership-Programme reddit.com+15rcn.org.uk+15youtube.com+15

Rubin, R. S. (2002). Will the real SMART goals please stand up? *The Industrial-Organizational Psychologist, 39*(4), 26–27. https://www.researchgate.net/publication/255601388_Will_the_real_SMART_goals_please_stand_up

Rundall, T. G., Wu, F. M., Lewis, V. A., Schoenherr, K. E., & Shortell, S. M. (2016). Contributions of relational coordination to care management in accountable care organizations: Views of managerial and clinical leaders. *Health Care Management Review, 41*(2), 88–100. PMID: 25978003

Rutberg, S., & Bouikidis, C. D. (2018). Focusing on the Fundamentals: A Simplistic Differentiation Between Qualitative and Quantitative Research. *Nephrology Nursing Journal : Journal of the American Nephrology Nurses' Association, 45*(2), 209–212.

Safonov, Y., Maslennikov, Y., & Lenska, N. (2018). EVOLUTION AND MODERN TENDENCIES IN THE THEORY OF LEADERSHIP. *Baltic Journal of Economic Studies, 4*(1), 304–310.

Saha, S., Beach, M. C., & Cooper, L. A. (2008). Patient Centeredness, Cultural Competence and Healthcare Quality. *Journal of the National Medical Association, 100*(11), 1275–1285. DOI: 10.1016/s0027-9684(15)31505-4 PMID: 19024223

Sahertian, P., & Graha, A. N. (2016). Exploring leadership dimension among organizations (the analysis against leadership excellence based on cultural and ethnical backgrounds in Indonesia). *Indian Journal of Commerce and Management Studies, 7*(1), 01-07.

Sahertian, P., & Jawas, U. (2021). Cultural Values and Leadership Excellence. In *2nd Annual Conference on Social Science and Humanities (ANCOSH 2020)* (pp. 310-313). Atlantis Press.

Saifman, R., Patel, S., & Williams, K. (2023). Resistance to competency-based leadership development in healthcare. *Journal of Organizational Change Management, 36*(1), 55–72.

Salman, D. A., & Auso, K. A. (2022). [Retracted] The Sequential Influence of Creative Leadership and Organizational Environment on Strategic Performance. *Journal of Environmental and Public Health, 2022*(1), 5948806. PMID: 38288294

Sarihasan, I., Dajnoki, K., Oláh, J., & Al-Dalahmeh, M. (2022). The importance of the leadership functions of a high-reliability health care organization in managing the COVID-19 pandemic in Turkey. *Economia e Sociologia, 15*(1), 78–93. DOI: 10.14254/2071-789x.2022/15-1/5

Schein, E. H. (2017). *Organizational Culture and Leadership* (5th ed.). Wiley.

Sekaran, U., & Bougie, R. (2016). *Research Methods for Business: A Skill-building Approach* (7th ed.). John Wiley & Sons.

Seljemo, C., Viksveen, P., & Ree, E. (2020). The Role of Transformational leadership, Job Demands and Job Resources for Patient Safety Culture in Norwegian Nursing homes: A cross-sectional Study. *BMC Health Services Research, 20*(1), 1–8. DOI: 10.1186/s12913-020-05671-y PMID: 32847598

Sendjaya, S., Sarros, J. C., & Santora, J. C. (2008). Defining and measuring servant leadership behaviour in organizations. *Journal of Management Studies, 45*(2), 402–424. DOI: 10.1111/j.1467-6486.2007.00761.x

Senge, P. (2006). *The Fifth Discipline: The Art and Practice of the Learning Organization* (2nd ed.). Doubleday/Currency.

Senge, P. M. (1990). *The Fifth Discipline: the Art and Practice of the Learning Organization*. Doubleday.

erban, R.-A., & Herciu, M. (2019). Performance Management Systems – Proposing and Testing a Conceptual Model. *Studies in Business and Economics, 14*(1), 231–244. DOI: 10.2478/sbe-2019-0018

Sfantou, D. F., Laliotis, A., Patelarou, A. E., Sifaki-Pistolla, D., Matalliotakis, M., & Patelarou, E. (2017). Importance of leadership style towards quality of care measures in healthcare settings: A systematic review. *Health Care*, *5*(4), 73. DOI: 10.3390/healthcare5040073 PMID: 29036901

Shalley, C. E., & Lemoine, G. J. (2018). Leader behaviors and employee creativity: Taking stock of the current state of research. *Creative leadership*, 79-94.

Shamir, B., & Eilam, G. (2005). "What's Your Story?" A Life-stories Approach to Authentic Leadership Development. *The Leadership Quarterly*, *16*(3), 395–417. DOI: 10.1016/j.leaqua.2005.03.005

Shamir, B., House, R. J., & Arthur, M. B. (1993). The motivational effects of charismatic leadership: A self-concept based theory. *Organization Science*, *4*(4), 577–594. DOI: 10.1287/orsc.4.4.577

Shanafelt, T. D., & Noseworthy, J. H. (2019). Executive Leadership and Physician Well-being. *Mayo Clinic Proceedings*, *92*(1), 129–146. https://pubmed.ncbi.nlm.nih.gov/27871627/ PMID: 27871627

Shanafelt, T., Ripp, J., & Trockel, M. (2020). Understanding and Addressing Sources of Anxiety Among Health Care Professionals During the COVID-19 Pandemic. *Journal of the American Medical Association*, *323*(21). PMID: 32259193

Shigekawa, E., Fix, M., Corbett, G., Roby, D. H., & Coffman, J. (2018). The Current State Of Telehealth Evidence: A Rapid Review. *Health Affairs*, *37*(12), 1975–1982. DOI: 10.1377/hlthaff.2018.05132 PMID: 30633674

Shingler-Nace, A. (2020). COVID-19: When Leadership Calls. *Nurse Leader*, *18*(4), 326–329. DOI: 10.1016/j.mnl.2020.03.017 PMID: 32346358

Shipton, H., Armstrong, C., West, M., & Dawson, J. (2008). The impact of leadership and quality climate on hospital performance. *International Journal for Quality in Health Care : Journal of the International Society for Quality in Health Care*, *20*(6), 439–445. DOI: 10.1093/intqhc/mzn037 PMID: 18786932

Shoukat, M. H., Shah, S. A., & Muneeb, D. (2023). Shared leadership and team performance in health care: How intellectual capital and team learning intervene in this relationship. *The Learning OrganizationL: An International Journal.* https://www.emerald.com/tlo/article/30/4/426/456261/Shared-leadership-and-team-performance-in-health

Siangchokyoo, N., & Klinger, R. L. (2021). Shared Leadership and Team Performance: The Joint Effect of Team Dispositional Composition and Collective Identification. *Group & Organization Management*, *47*(1), 105960112110199. DOI: 10.1177/10596011211019928

Siangchokyoo, N., Klinger, R. L., & Campion, E. D. (2020). Follower Transformation as the Linchpin of Transformational Leadership theory: A Systematic Review and Future Research Agenda. *The Leadership Quarterly*, *31*(1), 101341.

Sias, P. M., & Cahill, D. J. (1998). From coworkers to friends: The development of peer friendships in the workplace. *Western Journal of Communication*, *62*(3), 273–299. DOI: 10.1080/10570319809374611

Silva, A. (2016). What is Leadership? *ProQuest, 8*(1), 1–5. https://www.proquest.com/docview/1831706711?fromopenview=true&pq-origsite=gscholar

Silva, A. (2016). What is leadership?. *Journal of business studies quarterly, 8*(1), 1.

Simonsen, K. A., & Shim, R. S. (2019). Embracing diversity and inclusion in psychiatry leadership. *The Psychiatric Clinics of North America*, *42*(3), 463–471. PMID: 31358125

Simsek, Z. (2007). CEO tenure and organizational performance: An intervening model. *Strategic Management Journal*, *28*(6), 653–662.

SINGH, L., RAI, R. K., & SINGH, P. K. (2011). Assessing the utilization of maternal and child health care among married adolescent women: evidence from India. *Journal of Biosocial Science*, *44*(1), 1–26. DOI: 10.1017/s0021932011000472 PMID: 21933465

Sinsky, C., Colligan, L., Li, L., Prgomet, M., Reynolds, S., Goeders, L., Westbrook, J., Tutty, M., & Blike, G. (2016). Allocation of Physician Time in Ambulatory Practice: A Time and Motion Study in 4 Specialties. *Annals of Internal Medicine*, *165*(11), 753. DOI: 10.7326/m16-0961 PMID: 27595430

Siraj-Blatchford, I., Siraj, I., & Manni, L. (2007). *Effective leadership in the early years sector: The ELEYS study*. Institute of Education Press.

Skar, A.-M. S., Braathu, N., Peters, N., Bækkelund, H., Endsjø, M., Babaii, A., Borge, R. H., Wentzel-Larsen, T., Ehrhart, M. G., Sklar, M., Brown, C. H., Aarons, G. A., & Egeland, K. M. (2022). A stepped-wedge randomized trial investigating the effect of the Leadership and Organizational Change for Implementation (LOCI) intervention on implementation and transformational leadership, and implementation climate. *BMC Health Services Research*, *22*(1). Advance online publication. DOI: 10.1186/s12913-022-07539 PMID: 35246135

Smith, A. M., Prom, M. C., & Ng, L. C. (2024). A Qualitative Investigation of Characteristics Impacting Clinical Decision-Making in Integrated Behavioral Health Care. *The Journal of Behavioral Health Services & Research, 51*(4), 561–587. DOI: 10.1007/s11414-024-09891-6 PMID: 38982024

Smith, K., & Bhavsar, M. (2021, November). A new era of health leadership. [). Sage CA: Los Angeles, CA: SAGE Publications]. *Healthcare Management Forum, 34*(6), 332–335. PMID: 34592860

Sonnino, R. E. (2016). Health care leadership development and training: Progress and pitfalls. *Journal of Healthcare Leadership*, 19–29. PMID: 29355187

Sørensen, K., Van den Broucke, S., Fullam, J., Doyle, G., Pelikan, J., Slonska, Z., & Brand, H. (2012). Health Literacy and Public health: A Systematic Review and Integration of Definitions and Models. *BMC Public Health, 12*(1). Advance online publication. DOI: 10.1186/1471-2458-12-80 PMID: 22276600

Soriano, M. A., & Lagman, R. (2011). When the Patient Says No. *The American Journal of Hospice & Palliative Care, 29*(5), 401–404. DOI: 10.1177/1049909111421163 PMID: 21998441

Spears, L. (2010). *Character and servant leadership: Ten characteristics of effective, caring leaders* (pp. 25–30). https://www.regent.edu/wp-content/uploads/2020/12/Spears_Final.pdf

Specchia, M. L., Cozzolino, M. R., Carini, E., Di Pilla, A., Galletti, C., Ricciardi, W., & Damiani, G. (2021). Leadership styles and nurses' job satisfaction. Results of a systematic review. *International Journal of Environmental Research and Public Health, 18*(4), 1552. PMID: 33562016

Spillane, J. P. (2006). *Distributed Leadership*. ResearchGate. https://www.researchgate.net/publication/233061505_Distributed_Leadership

Spinelli, R. J. (2006). The Applicability of Bass's Model of Transformational, Transactional, and Laissez-Faire Leadership in the Hospital Administrative Environment. *Hospital Topics, 84*(2), 11–19. DOI: 10.3200/htps.84.2.11-19 PMID: 16708688

Spreier, S. W., Fontaine, M. H., & Malloy, R. L. (2006). Leadership run amok. *Harvard Business Review, 84*(6), 72–82. PMID: 16770895

St. Pierre, M., Hofinger, G., & Buerschaper, C. (Eds.). (2008). *Crisis Management in Acute Care Settings*. Springer Berlin Heidelberg., DOI: 10.1007/978-3-540-71062-2

Stanley, D. (2017). *Clinical leadership in nursing and healthcare: Values into action* (2nd ed.). John Wiley & Sons.

Stogdill, R. M. (1950). Leadership, membership and organization. *Psychological Bulletin*, *47*(1), 1–14. DOI: 10.1037/h0053857

Stone, G. & Patterson, K. (2005). *The History of Leadership Focus Servant Leadership Research Roundtable – August 2005.* https://www.regent.edu/acad/global/publications/sl_proceedings/2005/stone_history.pdf

Strack, G., & Fottler, M. D. (2002). Spirituality and effective leadership in healthcare: Is there a connection? *Frontiers of Health Services Management*, *18*(4), 3–18. PMID: 12087690

Straus, S. E., Soobiah, C., & Levinson, W. (2013). The impact of leadership training programs on physicians in academic medical centers: A systematic review. *Academic Medicine*, *88*(5), 710–723. PMID: 23524921

Strong, E. A., De Castro, R., Sambuco, D., Stewart, A., Ubel, P. A., Griffith, K. A., & Jagsi, R. (2013). Work–life balance in academic medicine: Narratives of physician-researchers and their mentors. *Journal of General Internal Medicine*, *28*(12), 1596–1603. PMID: 23765289

Sujith, A. V. L. N., Sajja, G. S., Mahalakshmi, V., Nuhmani, S., & Prasanalakshmi, B. (2022). Systematic review of smart health monitoring using deep learning and Artificial intelligence. *Neuroscience Informatics*, *2*(3), 100028. DOI: 10.1016/j.neuri.2021.100028

Sukha, N. (2019). *Influence of leadership style on organisational citizenship behaviours (OCB's) in achieving innovation.* University of Pretoria. https://core.ac.uk/download/528258795.pdf

Tabibzadeh, M., & Tran, H. (2022). Telehealth leadership competencies for digital healthcare transformation. *Journal of Telemedicine and Telecare*, 28(10), 725–732. DOI: 10.1177/1357633X221094887

Talias, M., & Pikoulis, E. (2024). A Short Assessment Tool for Management of Knowledge and Alertness in Greek Hospitals. *International Journal of Caring Sciences*, *17*(1), 1433.

Talwar, S., Talwar, M., Kaur, P., & Dhir, A. (2020). Consumers' resistance to digital innovations: A systematic review and framework development. *Australasian Marketing Journal*, *28*(4), 286–299.

Tan, K. L. (2023). Responsible leadership-a brief review of literature. *Journal of Responsible Tourism Management*, *3*, 44–55.

Tannenbaum, R., Weschler, I. R., & Massarik, F. (2015). *Leadership and organization: a behavioural science approach*. Routledge.

Terry, L. D. (1998). Administrative leadership, neo-managerialism, and the public management movement. *Public Administration Review*, 194–200.

Theaker, A., & Curran, J. (2025). The Public Relations Handbook. In *Routledge eBooks*. Informa., DOI: 10.4324/9781003517375

Thomas, A., & Suresh, M. (2023). Readiness for agility adaptability and alignment in healthcare organizations. *IISE Transactions on Healthcare Systems Engineering*, *13*(2), 161–174.

Thomas, S., Keegan, C., Barry, S., Layte, R., Jowett, M., & Normand, C. (2013). A framework for assessing health system resilience in an economic crisis: Ireland as a test case. *BMC Health Services Research*, *13*(1). Advance online publication. DOI: 10.1186/1472-6963-13-450 PMID: 24171814

Tierney, P., Farmer, S. M., & Graen, G. B. (2019). An examination of leadership and employee creativity: The relevance of traits and relationships. *Personnel Psychology*, *52*(3), 591–620. DOI: 10.1111/j.1744-6570.1999.tb00173.x

Turner, P. (2018). *Leadership in healthcare: delivering organisational transformation and operational excellence*. Springer.

Turner, P. (2018). *Leadership in healthcare: delivering organizational transformation and operational excellence*. Springer.

Turyadi, I., Zulkifli, Z., Tawil, M. R., Ali, H., & Sadikin, A. (2023). The role of digital leadership in organizations to improve employee performance and business success. *Jurnal Ekonomi*, *12*(02), 1671–1677.

Uhl-Bien, M. (2006). Relational Leadership Theory: Exploring the Social Processes of Leadership and Organizing. *The Leadership Quarterly*, *17*(6), 654–676. DOI: 10.1016/j.leaqua.2006.10.007

Uhl-Bien, M., Marion, R., & McKelvey, B. (2007). Complexity leadership theory: Shifting leadership from the industrial age to the knowledge era. *The Leadership Quarterly*, *18*(4), 298–318. DOI: 10.1016/j.leaqua.2007.04.002

Ullas, S., Pradeep, M., Surendran, S., Ravikumar, A., Bastine, A. M., Prasad, A., & Mohan, A. (2021). Telemedicine during the COVID-19 pandemic: A paradigm shift in non-communicable disease management?–a cross-sectional survey from a quaternary-care center in South India. *Patient Preference and Adherence*, 2715–2723. PMID: 34916781

Upshaw, T. L., Craig-Neil, A., Macklin, J., Gray, C. S., Chan, T. C., Gibson, J., & Pinto, A. D. (2023). Priorities for artificial intelligence applications in primary care: A Canadian deliberative dialogue with patients, providers, and health system leaders. *Journal of the American Board of Family Medicine : JABFM*, *36*(2), 210–220. PMID: 36948537

Vaccaro, I. G., Jansen, J. J. P., Van Den Bosch, F. A. J., & Volberda, H. W. (2010). Management Innovation and Leadership: The Moderating Role of Organizational Size. *Journal of Management Studies*, *49*(1), 28–51. DOI: 10.1111/j.1467-6486.2010.00976.x

van Diggele, C., Burgess, A., Roberts, C., & Mellis, C. (2020). Leadership in healthcare education. *BMC Medical Education*, *20*, 1–6. PMID: 33272264

Van Seters, D., & Field, R. (1990). The Evolution of Leadership Theory. *Journal of Organizational Change Management*, *3*, 29–45. DOI: 10.1108/09534819010142139

Van Wart, M. & Suino, P. (2017). *Leadership in Public Organizations*. Taylor & Francis Group. DOI: 10.4324/9781315268699

Van, D. (2020). Creativity stimulation in healthcare leadership. *Journal of Healthcare Innovation*, *7*(3), 26–37.

Vaske, J. J., Beaman, J., & Sponarski, C. C. (2017). Rethinking internal consistency in Cronbach's alpha. *Leisure Sciences*, *39*(2), 163–173. DOI: 10.1080/01490400.2015.1127189

Ved, R., Gupta, G., & Singh, S. (2019). India's health and wellness centres: Realizing universal health coverage through comprehensive primary health care. *WHO South-East Asia Journal of Public Health*, *8*(1), 18. DOI: 10.4103/2224-3151.255344 PMID: 30950425

Volckmann, R. (2012). Leadership in the Modern Organization: A Framework for the 21st Century. *Journal of Business Leadership*, *17*(2), 35–45.

Von Bertalanffy, L. (1968). *General system theory*. New York, 41973(1968), 40.

Vroom, V. H., & Yetton, P. W. (1973). *Leadership and decision-making*. University of Pittsburgh Press.

Wachter, R. (2015). *The Digital Doctor: Hope, Hype, and Harm at the Dawn of Medicine's Computer Age*. Mcgraw-Hill Education.

Wahlstrom, G. (2024, December). *Healthcare Leadership 2024: A Year in Review*. The Healthcare Executive. https://www.thehealthcareexecutive.net/newsletter/healthcare-leadership-2024/

Waithaka, R. K., & Kimani, J. G. (2021). Effect of e-procurement practices on supply chain performance. *Global Journal of Purchasing and Procurement Management*, *1*(1), 32–42.

Walumbwa, F. O., Avolio, B. J., Gardner, W. L., Wernsing, T. S., & Peterson, S. J. (2008). Authentic leadership: Development and validation of a theory-based measure. *Journal of Management*, *34*(1), 89–126. DOI: 10.1177/0149206307308913

Wang, Y., & Wang, Y. (2022). Developing creative leadership in the use of digital communication tools: A psychological perspective. *Sustainability*, *14*(19), 11796.

Warrick, D. D. (2017). What leaders need to know about organizational culture. *Business Horizons*, *60*(3), 395–404.

Weaver, S. J., Lubomksi, L. H., Wilson, R. F., Pfoh, E. R., Martinez, K. A., & Dy, S. M. (2013). Promoting a culture of safety as a patient safety strategy: A systematic review. *Promoting a Culture of Safety as a Patient Safety Strategy. Systematic Reviews*, *158*(5 Pt 2). https://psnet.ahrq.gov/issue/promoting-culture-safety-patient-safety-strategy-systematic-review PMID: 23460092

Weberg, D. (2010). Transformational leadership and innovation in healthcare. *Journal of Healthcare Leadership*, *2*, 35–41. https://journals.lww.com/naqjournal/fulltext/2010/07000/Transformational_Leadership_and_Staff_Retention_.8.aspx

Weberg, D. (2012, October). Complexity leadership: A healthcare imperative. *Nursing Forum*, *47*(4), •••. PMID: 23127241

Weberg, D. (2020). Transformational Leadership and Staff Retention. *Nursing Administration Quarterly*, *34*(3), 246–258. DOI: 10.1097/naq.0b013e3181e70298 PMID: 20562573

Weinger, M. B. (2012). *Human factors in anesthesiology. Handbook of Human Factors and Ergonomics in Health Care and Patient Safety* (2nd ed.). Taylor & Francis.

West, M., Armit, K., Loewenthal, L., Eckert, R., West, T., & Lee, A. (2015). *Leadership and Leadership Development in Health Care*. https://www.kingsfund.org.uk/insight-and-analysis/reports/leadership-development-health-care

West, M., Armit, K., Loewenthal, L., Eckert, R., West, T., & Lee, A. (2015, February 25). *Leadership and Leadership Development in Health Care*. https://www.kingsfund.org.uk/insight-and-analysis/reports/leadership-development-health-care

West, M., Armit, K., Loewenthal, L., Eckert, R., West, T., & Lee, A. (2015, February 25). *Leadership and Leadership Development in Health Care*. The King's Fund. https://www.kingsfund.org.uk/insight-and-analysis/reports/leadership-development-health-care

West, M., Armit, K., Loewenthal, L., Eckert, R., West, T., & Lee, A. (2015, February 25). *Leadership and Leadership Development in Health Care*. The Kings Fund; The King's Fund. https://www.kingsfund.org.uk/insight-and-analysis/reports/leadership-development-health-care

West, M., Eckert, R., & Pasmore, B. (2014). *Developing collective leadership for health care*. The King's Fund. https://www.kingsfund.org.uk/insight-and-analysis/reports/developing-collective-leadership-for-health-care

West, M., Eckert, R., & Pasmore, B. (2014, May 21). *Developing collective leadership for health care*. The King's Fund. https://www.kingsfund.org.uk/insight-and-analysis/reports/developing-collective-leadership-for-health-care

West, C. P., Dyrbye, L. N., & Shanafelt, T. D. (2018). Physician burnout: Contributors, consequences and solutions. *Journal of Internal Medicine*, *283*(6), 516–529. DOI: 10.1111/joim.12752 PMID: 29505159

West, M. A., & Anderson, N. R. (1996). Innovation in Top Management Teams. *The Journal of Applied Psychology*, *81*(6), 680–693. DOI: 10.1037/0021-9010.81.6.680

Wetterneck, T. B., Lapin, J. A., Karsh, B. T., & Beasley, J. W. (2012). *Human factors and ergonomics in primary care. Handbook of Human Factors and Ergonomics in Health Care and Patient Safety*. Taylor and& Francis Group.

White, A. N., Mische, S., & Winn, M. (2019). Leadership in Science. *Journal of Biomolecular Techniques : JBT*, *30*(Suppl), S54. https://pmc.ncbi.nlm.nih.gov/articles/PMC6938080/

WHO. (2008). *Assessing the national health information system: An assessment tool* (Version 4.00) [PDF]. Health Metrics Network. https://www.afro.who.int/sites/default/files/2017-06/AHO_HealthMetricsNetwork_Assessment_Tool_version4.00.pdf

WHO. 2010 - World Health Organization (WHO). (2010). *Leadership and Governance 85*. Geneva: WHO Press. https://cdn.who.int/media/docs/default-source/service-availability-and-readinessassessment(sara)/related-links-(sara)/who_mbhss_2010_section6_web.pdf?sfvrsn=71928980_3

Wiley (2013). *Wiley Pfeiffer learning and development resources*. Wiley Workplace Learning Solutions.http://www.pfeiffer.com/WileyCDA/Section/id-811878.html

Willie, M. M. (2023). Defining the Population and Target Population in Clinical Studies: Clarifying Terminology and Enhancing Study Validity. *Journal of Medical and Clinical Nursing Studies, 1*(1), 1–3. DOI: 10.61440/jmcns.2023.v1.03

Wiseman, L., Mckeown, G., & Covey, S. R. (2017). *Multipliers: how the best leaders make everyone smarter*. Harper Business.

Wolfson, M., & Rowe, G. (2001) . On measuring inequalities in health. Bulletin of the World Health Organization, *79* (6) , 553 - 560. World Health Organization. https://iris.who.int/handle/10665/268350

Womack, J. P., & Jones, D. T. (2003). *Lean Thinking: Banish Waste and Create Wealth in Your Corporation*. Free Press.

Wong, C. A., Cummings, G. G., & Ducharme, L. (2013). The Relationship between Nursing Leadership and Patient outcomes: A Systematic Review Update. *Journal of Nursing Management, 21*(5), 709–724. https://pubmed.ncbi.nlm.nih.gov/23865924/ PMID: 23865924

Wong, C. A., Cummings, G. G., & Ducharme, L. (2013). The relationship between nursing leadership and patient outcomes: A systematic review. *Journal of Nursing Management, 21*(5), 709–724. DOI: 10.1111/jonm.12116 PMID: 23865924

Wong, C. A., & Laschinger, H. K. S. (2019). Authentic leadership, performance, and job satisfaction: The mediating role of empowerment. *Journal of Advanced Nursing, 69*(4), 947–959. DOI: 10.1111/j.1365-2648.2012.06089.x PMID: 22764828

World Health Organization. (2010). *Framework for action on interprofessional education & collaborative practice*. World Health Organization. https://www.who.int/publications/i/item/framework-for-action-on-interprofessional-education-collaborative-practice

World Health Organization. (2010). *Monitoring the building blocks of health systems: A handbook of indicators and their measurement strategies*. https://iris.who.int/bitstream/handle/10665/258734/9789241564052-eng.pdf

World Health Organization. (2010).. . *World Health Report, 2010*, •••. Www.who.int and https://www.who.int/publications/i/item/9789241564021

World Health Organization. (2020). Global strategy on human resources for health: Workforce 2030 (ISBN 978-92-4-151113-1). https://apps.who.int/iris/bitstream/handle/10665/250368/9789241511131-eng.pdf?sequence=1 frontlinehealthworkers.org+8apps.who.int+8iris.who.int

Wosik, J., Fudim, M., Cameron, B., Gellad, Z. F., Cho, A., Phinney, D., Curtis, S., Roman, M., Poon, E. G., Ferranti, J., Katz, J. N., & Tcheng, J. (2020). Telehealth transformation: COVID-19 and the rise of virtual care. *Journal of the American Medical Informatics Association : JAMIA*, *27*(6), 957–962. DOI: 10.1093/jamia/ocaa067 PMID: 32311034

Wosny, M., Strasser, L. M., & Hastings, J. (2023). Experience of health care professionals using digital tools in the hospital: Qualitative systematic review. *JMIR Human Factors*, *10*(1), e50357. PMID: 37847535

Wu, C. H., Weisman, H., Sung, L. K., Erdogan, B., & Bauer, T. N. (2022). Perceived overqualification, felt organizational obligation, and extra-role behavior during the COVID-19 crisis: The moderating role of self-sacrificial leadership. *Applied Psychology*, *71*(3), 983–1013. PMID: 36433921

Yamey, G. (2012). What are the barriers to scaling up health interventions in low and middle income countries? A qualitative study of academic leaders in implementation science. *Globalization and Health*, *8*(1), 11. DOI: 10.1186/1744-8603-8-11 PMID: 22643120

Yorges, S. L., Weiss, H. M., & Strickland, O. J. (1999). The effect of leader outcomes on influence, attributions, and perceptions of charisma. *The Journal of Applied Psychology*, *84*(3), 428. PMID: 10380422

Yousef, H. (2023). Strategic Healthcare Leadership Assessment for Global Health Systems. *Global Health Journal (Amsterdam, Netherlands)*, *28*(1), 77 92.

Yousef, R., & Zubi, K. A. (2023). Providing Home Healthcare Services for Patients during Pandemics: Applicability in Developing Countries. *Journal of Health Management*, *25*(4), 772–778. DOI: 10.1177/09720634231215162

Yuguda, A. Abdulrazak Yuguda MADU, Abbo, U., & Shehu Jafaru Salisu. (2023, October 20). *Strategic leadership: A key to organisational effectiveness and improvement*. ResearchGate; unknown. https://www.researchgate.net/publication/374867917_strategic_leadership_a_key_t

Yukl, G. (2012). Effective Leadership Behavior: What We Know and What Questions Need More Attention. *The Academy of Management Perspectives*, *26*(4), 66–85. https://www.jstor.org/stable/23412661

Yukl, G. A. (2020). *Leadership in organizations* (8th ed.). Pearson Education, Inc.

Zaccaro, S. J., LaPort, K., & Jose, I. (2013, January 1). *Attributes of successful leaders: A performance requirements approach*. https://www.researchgate.net/publication/287105619_Attributes_of_successful_leaders_

Zaccaro, S. J., LaPort, K., & Jose, I. (2013, January 1). *Attributes of successful leaders: A performance requirements approach*. https://www.researchgate.net/publication/287105619_Attributes_of_successful_leaders_A_performance_requirements_approach

Zank, S., de Araujo, L. G., & Hanazaki, N. (2019). Resilience and adaptability of traditional healthcare systems. *Ecology and Society*, *24*(1).

Zayas-Cabán, T., & Valdez, R. S. (2012). Human factors and ergonomics in home care. *Handbook of human factors and ergonomics in health care and patient safety*, 2, 743-762.

Zenger, J., & Folkman, J. (2018). Women score higher than men in most leadership skills. *Leadership & Leaders*. https://leadershipandleaders.com/knowledge-skills-attributes-behaviours/women-score-higher-than-men-in-most-leadership-skills-jack-zenger-joseph-folkman-harvard-business-review/

Zhou, J., & George, J. M. (2003). Awakening employee creativity: The role of leader emotional intelligence. *The Leadership Quarterly*, *14*(4-5), 545–568. DOI: 10.1016/S1048-9843(03)00051-1

Zuber-Skerritt, O. (2011). *Action Leadership*. Springer Netherlands., DOI: 10.1007/978-90-481-3935-4

About the Author

Hesham Al-Momani, PhD, is an Associate Professor and chairman, of the Industrial Engineering Department, The Hashemite University, a retired Brigadier General from the Royal Jordanian Air Force with extensive academic qualifications and professional experience. He holds a Ph.D. in system science and Industrial Engineering with distinction from Binghamton University, New York (USA) in 2015, as well as Master's degrees in Management Sciences and Business Administration from Central Michigan University (USA), and a Master's degree in Aeronautics (focusing on Human Factors in Aviation) from Embry-Riddle Aeronautical University (USA) in 2006 and 2007, respectively. Additionally, he earned a Bachelor's degree in Mechanical and Aeronautical Engineering from the Jordan University of Science and Technology)1988), and leadership/Staff diploma certifications from the Joint Services Command and Staff College (UK)(1998) and the Jordan Command and Staff diploma from Command and Staff School Jordan (1996). Dr. Al Momani has a wealth of technical expertise and rare certifications, including Black and Green Belt certifications in Six Sigma from General Electric (Cincinnati, USA)(2006), and qualifications in Project Management, Quality Management, and various global aviation licenses, including from the FAA (USA) and CAA (Jordan)(2008). Dr. Hesham Al-Momani, PhD, is a distinguished academic and researcher in healthcare systems engineering. With extensive experience in industrial engineering education, he has integrated healthcare-focused courses into the 2021 bachelor's degree plan for Industrial Engineering. His commitment to advancing healthcare education further exemplifies his ongoing efforts to establish a master's degree program in Healthcare Systems Engineering. Dr. Al-Momani has a robust research portfolio and serves as a supervisor for numerous theses in healthcare systems engineering, contributing to the development of innovative solutions and methodologies in the field. His experience spans over 35 years in senior managerial and leadership roles, with expertise in technical and engineering organizations, communications, higher education, project management, dispute resolution, finance, budgeting, and time management. Since 2016, Dr. Al Momani has served as an Associate Professor in the Department of Industrial Engineering at Hashemite University, where he has been instrumental in establishing and coordinating the Master's Program in Crisis and Disaster Management, the only program of its kind in the Middle East. He also teaches in the Master's Program in Maintenance Management and supervises the ABET of the accreditation program and processes (Council of ABET Accreditation Board for Engineering and Technology Engineering and Technology in the Department of Industrial Engineering. Before his academic career, Dr. Al Momani worked as a faculty member, research assistant, and teaching associate at Binghamton University (USA), and held various senior roles in the Royal Jordanian Air Force, including Liaison Officer and Supervisor of the U.S. Military Assistance Program for Jordan at the Air Force Security Assistance Center Security Assistance and Cooperation (AFSAC) OH/USA. His teaching experience includes a wide range of courses in industrial engineering, systems engineering, crisis and disaster management, project management, and maintenance management. He has developed and taught 27 courses related to these fields, including specialized topics like risk management, Six Sigma, quality control, human factor engineering, and supply chain management. Dr. Al Momani's key achievements include: 1. Coordination of postgraduate programs, including the Master's programs in Crisis Management, Disaster Management, and Maintenance Management. 2. Strong analytical skills in systems engineering, statistical analysis, and industrial intelligence. 3. Extensive expertise in industrial engineering, particularly in quality, manufacturing, and production processes. 4. Leadership in obtaining ABET accreditation for the Department of Industrial Engineering. 5. Experience as Associate Dean and Head of the Engineering Department at Prince Faisal Technical College, part of Balqa Applied University. 6. Expertise in human factors and safety management. 7. Certification in Six Sigma Black and Green Belts from General Electric, USA. 8. Specialized knowledge in business management, project management, procurement, supply chain management, and financial cost analysis. 9. Extensive experience in aviation systems, including aircraft assembly, maintenance management, and engineering analysis, supported by global aviation licenses. 10. Leadership in high-tech projects, including assembling the Hughes MD500 helicopter for the first time in Jordan. 11. Expertise in U.S. and Foreign Military Security Assistance Programs. 12. Research in human factors and systems engineering, developing models and standards to improve quality and reliability in various professional fields. 13. Experience in financial and operational management, including budgeting, project management, and community engagement. 14. Research activities at the doctoral level focused on advancing comprehensive models in project management and quality assurance. Dr. Al Momani's professional career has been marked by a deep understanding of both technical and managerial domains, along with leadership that has significantly contributed to both academic and practical advancements in crisis management, industrial engineering, and aviation systems. His comprehensive skill set, leadership abilities, and long-standing. Full details of the biography are attached to the book.

Index

A

action plan 5, 129, 130, 152, 153, 154, 181, 182, 233, 245
administrative process 75, 76
Artificial Intelligence (AI) 11, 21, 32, 81, 93, 115, 117, 118, 122, 125, 128, 132, 133, 138

B

best practices 5, 129, 131, 151, 154, 212, 213

C

clinical decision 35, 122, 128
continuous improvement 2, 5, 7, 14, 25, 26, 27, 28, 46, 76, 83, 87, 89, 92, 99, 103, 107, 178, 180, 181, 185, 186, 187, 191, 192, 197, 198, 212, 213, 235, 236

D

domain statements 129, 152, 153

E

Electronic Health Records (EHRs) 4, 81, 117, 118, 121, 122, 124, 125, 126, 132, 136
emotional intelligence 7, 15, 16, 23, 32, 42, 50, 52, 56, 75, 78, 79, 83, 87, 91, 92, 95, 98, 101, 103, 104, 108, 111, 112, 116, 137, 157, 158, 165, 172, 178, 181, 188, 189

F

financial constraints 2, 4, 98

H

HealthCare Leadership (HCL) 1, 2, 3, 4, 5, 6, 7, 8, 11, 15, 19, 25, 28, 29, 33, 39, 40, 49, 50, 63, 67, 68, 69, 70, 73, 75, 76, 77, 78, 79, 80, 81, 83, 84, 87, 88, 89, 90, 91, 92, 93, 94, 95, 96, 97, 98, 99, 100, 101, 102, 103, 104, 107, 109, 112, 114, 115, 117, 118, 121, 122, 123, 124, 125, 128, 129, 130, 135, 136, 137, 141, 143, 144, 145, 148, 151, 152, 153, 154, 155, 156, 157, 161, 162, 163, 164, 165, 166, 169, 170, 172, 173, 175, 176, 178, 179, 180, 181, 182, 233, 236
healthcare organizations 2, 5, 6, 12, 13, 17, 28, 29, 43, 48, 49, 53, 65, 68, 75, 83, 87, 88, 94, 100, 101, 109, 114, 120, 129, 130, 136, 152, 153, 154, 162, 163, 164, 171, 172, 181, 233

I

ICU mortality 119, 121, 124, 127
inspirational motivation 41, 50, 54
intellectual stimulation 41, 50, 54
interactive influence 26, 27

J

job satisfaction 8, 17, 35, 37, 39, 40, 41, 42, 44, 46, 54, 55, 58, 59, 64, 108, 146, 149, 158

L

long-term success 14, 18, 88

O

one-way interaction 26, 27
organizational culture 14, 15, 17, 20, 30, 40, 46, 52, 84, 89, 102, 104, 110, 115, 154, 159, 169, 170, 199, 202
organizational performance 5, 18, 39, 42, 44, 49, 78, 80, 96, 114, 124, 129, 138, 152, 154, 164, 170, 196, 213, 243

organizational success 4, 13, 16, 28, 46, 67, 68, 69, 75, 78, 93, 95, 103, 172, 237

P

patient care 2, 3, 5, 14, 16, 17, 28, 30, 39, 42, 44, 47, 48, 49, 52, 54, 55, 70, 77, 78, 79, 80, 81, 88, 94, 103, 106, 123, 129, 137, 138, 147, 151, 152, 154, 159, 163, 171, 172, 183, 185, 186, 193, 235, 236, 240, 241
patient-centered care 3, 30, 43, 46, 50, 51, 88, 89, 94, 98, 117, 119, 123, 129, 137, 143, 144, 156, 170, 185, 233
patient outcomes 1, 2, 3, 4, 5, 8, 15, 17, 25, 28, 29, 30, 36, 40, 41, 42, 44, 46, 47, 49, 51, 52, 54, 58, 64, 69, 78, 89, 96, 100, 101, 103, 121, 126, 128, 135, 136, 139, 141, 145, 146, 152, 153, 156, 157, 158, 164, 170, 171, 172, 235, 239
predictive analytics 121, 122, 124, 127, 128, 135, 136, 137
psychological safety 41, 46, 52, 59, 142, 184
public health 2, 5, 8, 10, 23, 30, 31, 35, 37, 58, 68, 69, 70, 83, 104, 105, 110, 113, 126, 131, 138, 143, 146, 147, 148, 154, 157, 158, 162, 165, 166, 167

S

servant leadership 16, 22, 39, 40, 44, 52, 53, 54, 58, 59, 60, 62, 105, 113, 142, 161, 162, 163
service delivery 1, 2, 3, 5, 14, 47, 52, 55, 69, 77, 99, 102, 136, 184
strategic thinking 18, 75, 78, 79, 87, 88, 94, 95, 103, 169, 172
systems theory 48, 49, 51, 53, 55

T

technological curiosity 122, 123
Technology-Organization-Environment (TOE) 117, 118, 129
traditional management 5, 75, 76, 80
training programs 2, 6, 16, 69, 123, 127, 130, 139, 152, 153, 212, 213, 238

W

workforce morale 42, 47, 49, 123, 136, 137

www.ingramcontent.com/pod-product-compliance
Lightning Source LLC
LaVergne TN
LVHW081526300926
849161LV00006B/1322